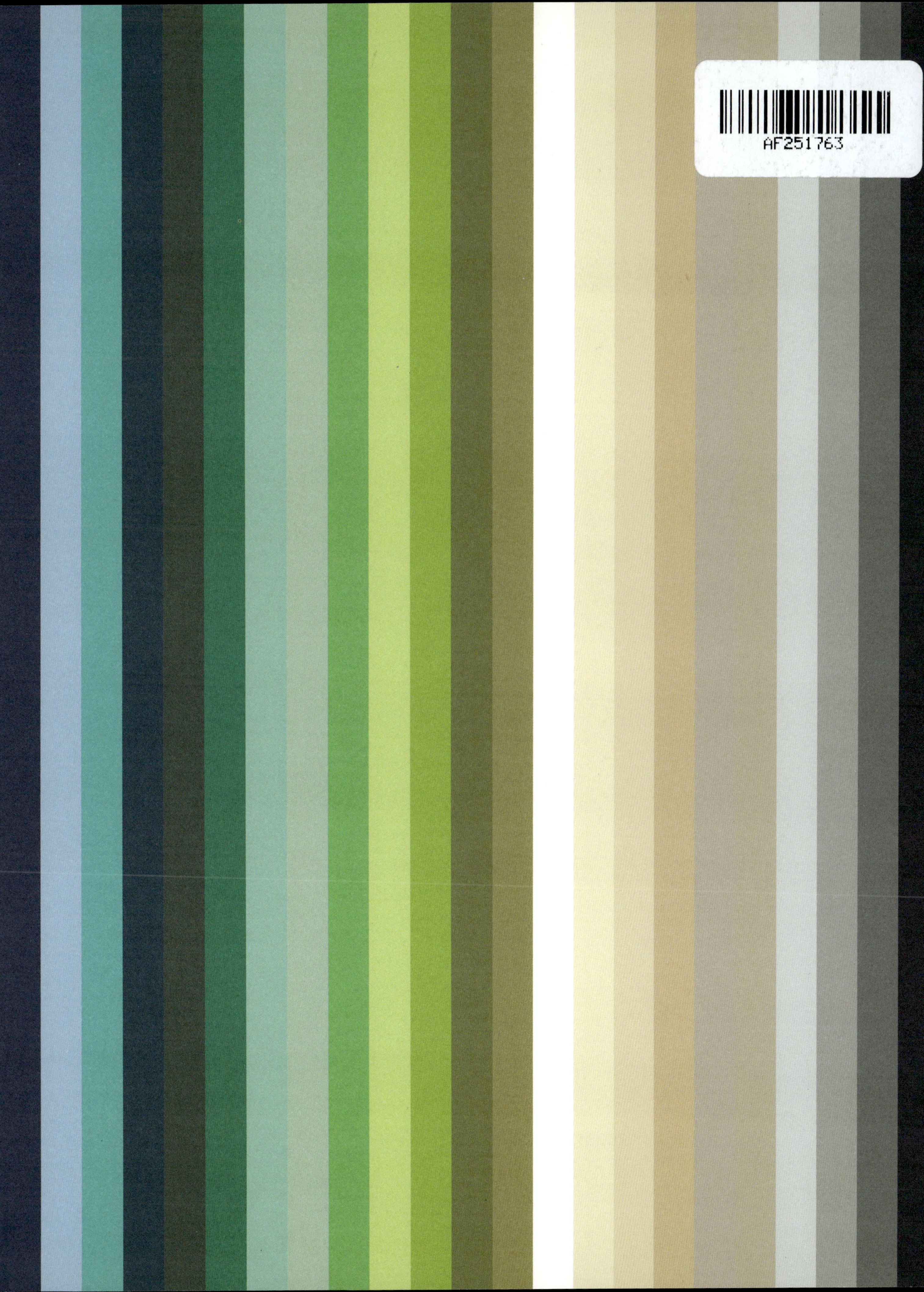
AF251763

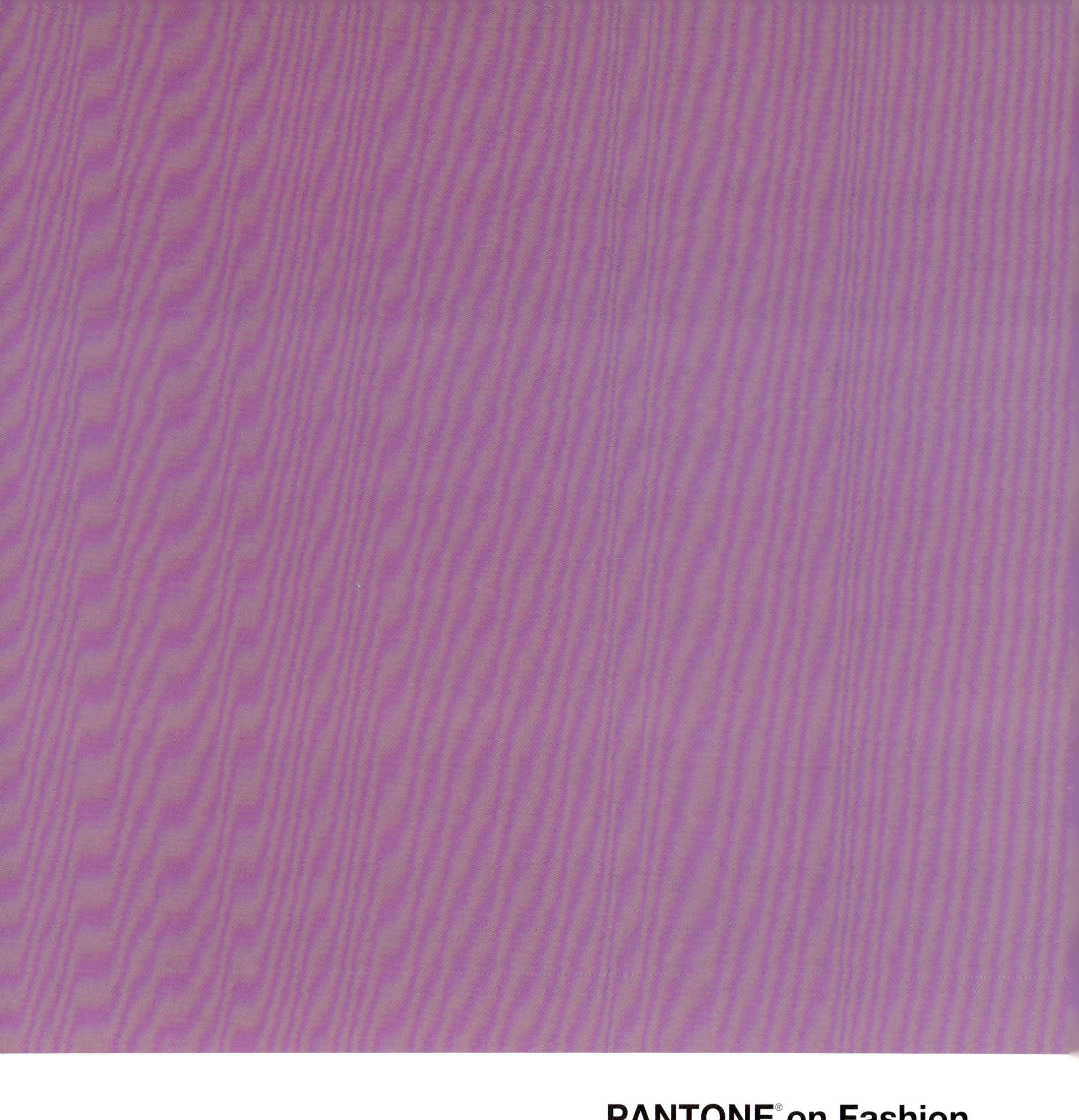

PANTONE® on Fashion

PANTONE® on Fashion
A Century of Color in Design

by Leatrice Eiseman and E. P. Cutler

Julien Tomasello, Picture Editor

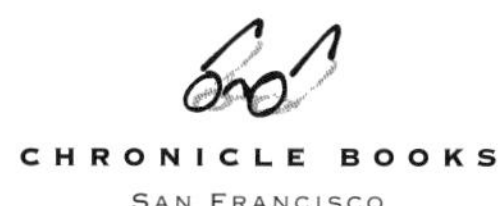

CHRONICLE BOOKS
SAN FRANCISCO

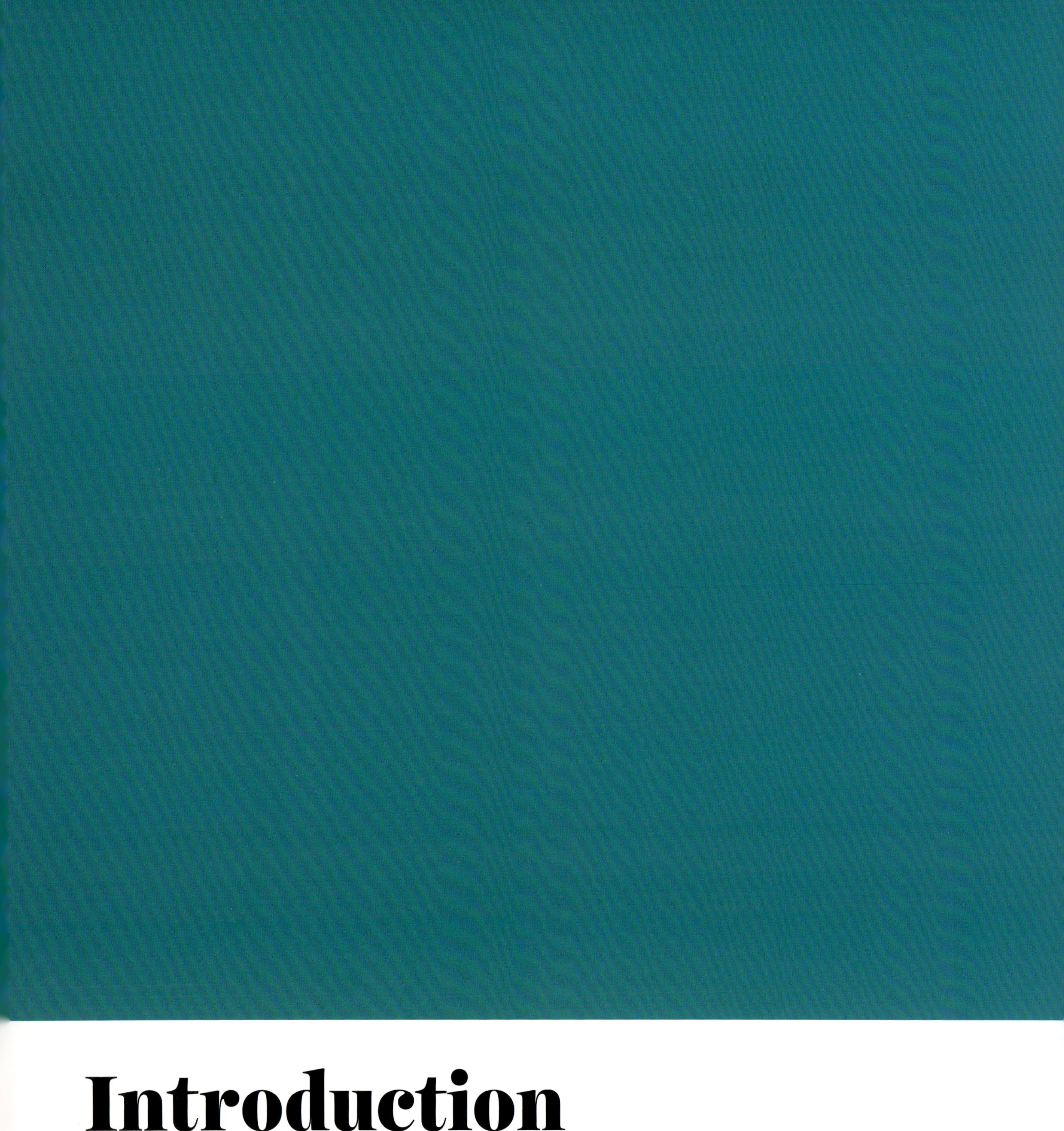

Introduction

The story of fashion is the story of color. More than any other single factor, color gives a garment (and the person who wears it) impact—both visual and emotional. A woman walking toward you in a red dress tells a very different story than the same woman in blue. Yet, the twin stories of fashion and color are rarely woven together. Everyone knows that color trends are a large part of fashion, but their importance goes far beyond the season's "must-have" color. Charted and studied over chunks of time, fascinating patterns and repetitions emerge. The fugitive nature of color speaks to the ephemerality of existence. Bold Fuchsia pops up only to hibernate for prolonged periods of time, whereas classic Navy is ever present. This book is an attempt to track and illuminate these historical color stories in the world of fashion.

Though we look here primarily at fashion and color in the 20th and early 21st centuries, the further past— even as far back as ancient history—still echoes today.

Cochineal red, historically associated with "blood, fire, fertility, and life force," still exudes sexuality and danger.[1] The alchemy of indigo, a green plant that produces a blue dye, is still revered. Purpuridae, a purple dye, which took hundreds of thousands of mollusks to produce one ounce of, still conveys wealth and drama. Our deep-seated associations with colors linger, even when technological innovations render obsolete the original artisanal processes by which clothing was dyed these shades. Our era is unique in that the emergence of synthetic dyes in the mid-1850s has since allowed for a previously unseen democratization of color; the veritable rainbow now available for all.

When delving into the history of fashion and its relationship to color, it becomes apparent that its history is inherently intertwined with history at large. Why people wear what they wear is influenced by events, local and global, political and cultural. The wars of the 20th century and beyond—from World War I, World War II, and the Vietnam War to the Gulf War and the wars in Iraq and Afghanistan—all affected the use of color in fashion. The eras of jazz, glamorous Hollywood, the nifty '50s, the youthquake, the hippie movement, the opulent '80s, the grunge '90s, and the new millennium were all also visually represented by colors in fashion.

The "meaning" of certain colors changes over time. White, traditionally associated in the West with virginity, took on a different type of "purity" during the mid-20th century when it became the modernists' color of choice. Once funereal, black became known in succession as chic, classic, sexy, and then existential, in the hands of Gabrielle "Coco" Chanel, Hubert de Givenchy, Azzedine Alaïa, and Yohji Yamamoto, respectively. One color could possess a singular meaning at the turn of the 20th century, only to twist and turn through numerous, disparate meanings by the dawn of the 21st.

Impermanent fads sped up in the modern era as fashion became increasingly available, affordable, and fast. Fashion was one of the first global industries (as antiquated trading routes prove), but the phenomenon of "globalization" nevertheless altered it. As production shifted to developing countries with lax labor laws and no minimum wage, both fashion's ethics and its pace changed radically.

But although these rapid shifts did occur in fashion and color during the 20th century, it behooves us to bear in mind, as Colin McDowell argues in his book *Fashion Today*, that the basic premises of fashion actually change quite slowly. McDowell asserts: "It is possible to say of twentieth-century fashion that there have been only two serious permanent changes: the move from long skirts to short and the adoption of trousers by women."[2] McDowell's point should be noted, and fashion considered within a vast historical context, akin to Charles and Ray Eames's film *Powers of Ten.* In the grand scheme of history, fashion does move more slowly than the public believes.

In looking at what colors were worn when and attempting to determine why, we examine historical context and explore the designers who chose them. While many of the designers' names will be familiar—like Ralph Lauren, Donna Karan, and Calvin Klein—we've blown off the dust of forgotten names—like Augusta Bernard, Sydney Wragge, and Gnyuki Torimaru—as well, bringing the garments they designed out of the archives, as it were, and re-examining their significance. History, which continues to edit itself, highlights some and ignores others. To combat this, some of the big-name designers may not be covered, and some of the lesser known illuminated. We let the colors lead the way and be our guide, and that means that this book is by no means exhaustive. Perhaps future works can include, in no particular order, Nicolas Ghesquière, Hussein Chalayan, Veronique Branquinho, Olivier Theyskens, Arnold Scaasi, Erdem Moralıoğlu, Haider Ackermann, Damir Doma, the Callot Soeurs sisters, Cédric Charlier, Phillip Lim, Karen Walker, et al.

But don't fret! Some designers have become nearly synonymous with specific colors and they, of course, are included. A work on fashion and color would be incomplete without sections on Elsa Schiaparelli and her Shocking Pink, Valentino and his signature red, and the use of black by Yohji Yamamoto and Comme des Garçons' Rei Kawakubo (whose predilections for it earned them the respective nicknames "The Monk" and "The Nun").

Many myths exist about fashion and its relationship with color. Unfortunately for the more sensationally minded among us, there is no color conspiracy. There is no secret cabal comprising the likes of Anna Wintour, Pantone executives, and Bernard Arnault who pick the "it" hues out of a hat, recline, and watch the sheeplike masses flock to their fashion whims. There is no designer phone tree, where Marc Jacobs speed-dials Anna Sui, Michael Kors, Raf Simons, and Alber Elbaz to collude on the season's tone.

In fact, two of fashion's biggest disasters came from attempts to brainwash consumers into purchasing items not in style. In 1950, Carmel Snow, the editor-in-chief at *Harper's Bazaar*, was pressured by an important advertiser to push Sunset Pink for "bags, gloves, coats, fabrics—everything," in order to promote their new train (yes, an actual train, with wheels and cars and tracks), the *Sunset Limited*.[3] Snow admitted in retrospect that dedicating pages and pages to this manufactured trend was "the height of absurdity."[4] Fashion consumers rejected or ignored this blatant ploy. This failed experiment cost Snow not only her "editorial mainstay," but also one of her best staffers, Frances McFadden, who left the magazine because of it.[5] Five years later, Edens and Gershe wrote the song "Think Pink!" as a "wicked opening anthem," for the film *Funny Face*

(1957), turning the event into a fashion joke that has run for so long now that most people no longer get the punch line.[6]

Another large fashion fiasco occurred in the 1970s when industry insiders, from *Women's Wear Daily*[7] to retailer Bergdorf Goodman,[8] insisted the "midi-skirt" (a below-the-knee length) was the height of fashion when the miniskirt rage was far from over. But the vogue for short skirts, made of less material as they were, had taken its toll on fabric producers, who wanted to drop hemlines and restore their sales. But instead, this aggressive endorsement for a zeitgeist-denying fashion simply shook the credibility of its advocates and ultimately resulted in millions of dollars lost.

As these examples clearly illustrate, fashion cannot be bridled. Rather, fashion is a dialogue between designers and consumers, with gatekeepers (like fashion journalists and editors) as intermediaries, not dictators. Designers propose their vision of the future through the medium of their collections, gatekeepers champion their favorites, and consumers either embrace or shun them. This essentially capitalist exchange is what creates fashion movements that are clearly evident in hindsight.

Like any overarching survey, this book is guilty of cementing historic myths; historians are storytellers after all, and epochs are convenient stories, easy to digest. It is important to note, though, that reality is much messier than that: older women did not throw out their corsets on January 1, 1920; not every person in the 1970s wore bell-bottoms. History, much like fashion, is enamored with the new and the outstanding. This is the arc of history often found in this book—the leaps from one innovation to the next—but we have also tried to reference nuanced reality as much as possible.

In tackling the subject matter of the history of color in fashion, numerous challenges arise. Firstly, discussing color itself is surprisingly difficult. Unlike other topics, when color is discussed in the history books, it is rarely noted. One cannot easily flip to a book's index to find if or where red is addressed in a text, though it might be extensively. Also, the English vocabulary is shockingly limited when it comes to color. The reason the services of a company like

Pantone are so essential is that not everyone means the same thing when they use color words like "light blue" or "dark green." Additionally, more subtle color terms, such as Cerulean (a misted, grayed blue) or Cerise (a purplish red), may not even be in most people's vocabulary.

Another pitfall in the discussion of color is that because it is seemingly "obvious" it is rarely expounded on. Starting in 1963, artist Dan Flavin used fluorescent lights in his installations in order to expose onlookers to the haptic and psychological effects of color, properties that fashion designers had been utilizing for far longer. However, it is only recently that scientists have begun to study our psychological and emotional reactions to certain shades. A 2009 study confirmed that red engages the "flight" reaction of the human's "lizard brain," stimulating a danger response.[9] Blue, on the other hand, is calming. Yet, this research only reinforces what we as humans have long understood intuitively. The shared human experience of color as a species-wide, wordless vocabulary means that capturing it in language is complicated, to say the least. Add to that the fact that different colors have different cultural associations depending on where you are on the globe, and the whole subject can seem downright bewildering. All the more reason for a shared vocabulary—and, even more technically precise, a numbering system—for color, such as the one Pantone provides, to exist.

This book is for the fashion-obsessed, the design-loving, the color-hungry. It is for historians and sociologists, students, and people who never want to stop learning. It is for young and old, but firmly cemented as a work of the now. Those voracious for lost anecdotes and tidbits, usually found in silent libraries and archives that smell of parchment and cedar, will, we hope, be pleased. We have used original source material whenever possible, as well as information from rare, out-of-print books. *The New York Times* and *The New Yorker* were invaluable resources, both because of their ease of accessibility and their early adoption of fashion journalism. But we all know that the nature of how information is communicated today is rapidly changing, and so blogs were utilized as well (after being fact-checked, of course).

In keeping with fashion writing and as an ode to bygone fashion journalists, French and Italian pepper these pages, and lingo of the then-and-now is prevalent. Just as science has its own language, so does fashion. To those outside the fashion community, it may seem (and literally be) foreign. This speaks to fashion's wide reach, though it is centered on the given fashion capitals: Paris, Milan, London, and New York.

In producing its *Fashion Color Report* over the past fifteen years, Pantone has forged relationships with many important designers. Much of that dialogue has occurred around New York Fashion Week, and as a result of simple geography (Pantone being a U.S. company), we realize that U.S. designers may be slightly favored herein. But fashion is nothing if not an international pursuit, and we've done our best to present a well-rounded league of nations in the designers covered.

While it is jam-packed with research, we urge readers to use this book as a road map. It is important to remember that each designer's name represents a life, full of drama, hardship, and passion, and his or her unique history (not to mention the thousands of sketches and garments they likely made over the course of their careers). But often, a single garment by a particular designer must be the part that stands in for the whole. Sporadically throughout we also name models, whether "super" or up-and-coming. This is an attempt to recognize the contribution to the industry, and indeed the personhood, of these important collaborators in the story of fashion. Their contribution deserves to be more thoroughly explored in future works.

By tracing the past ebb and flow of color, its future can be anticipated. Correlations can be drawn, as history repeats itself, mimicking Ouroboros, the mythical serpent that eats its own tail. Once this text has been consumed and considered, it is our hope that fashion, its designers, and most of all its colors take on a new significance, causing your eye to linger a little longer throughout the day on the sartorial choices of the people around you, as history unfolds from moment to moment.

Cyber Yellow

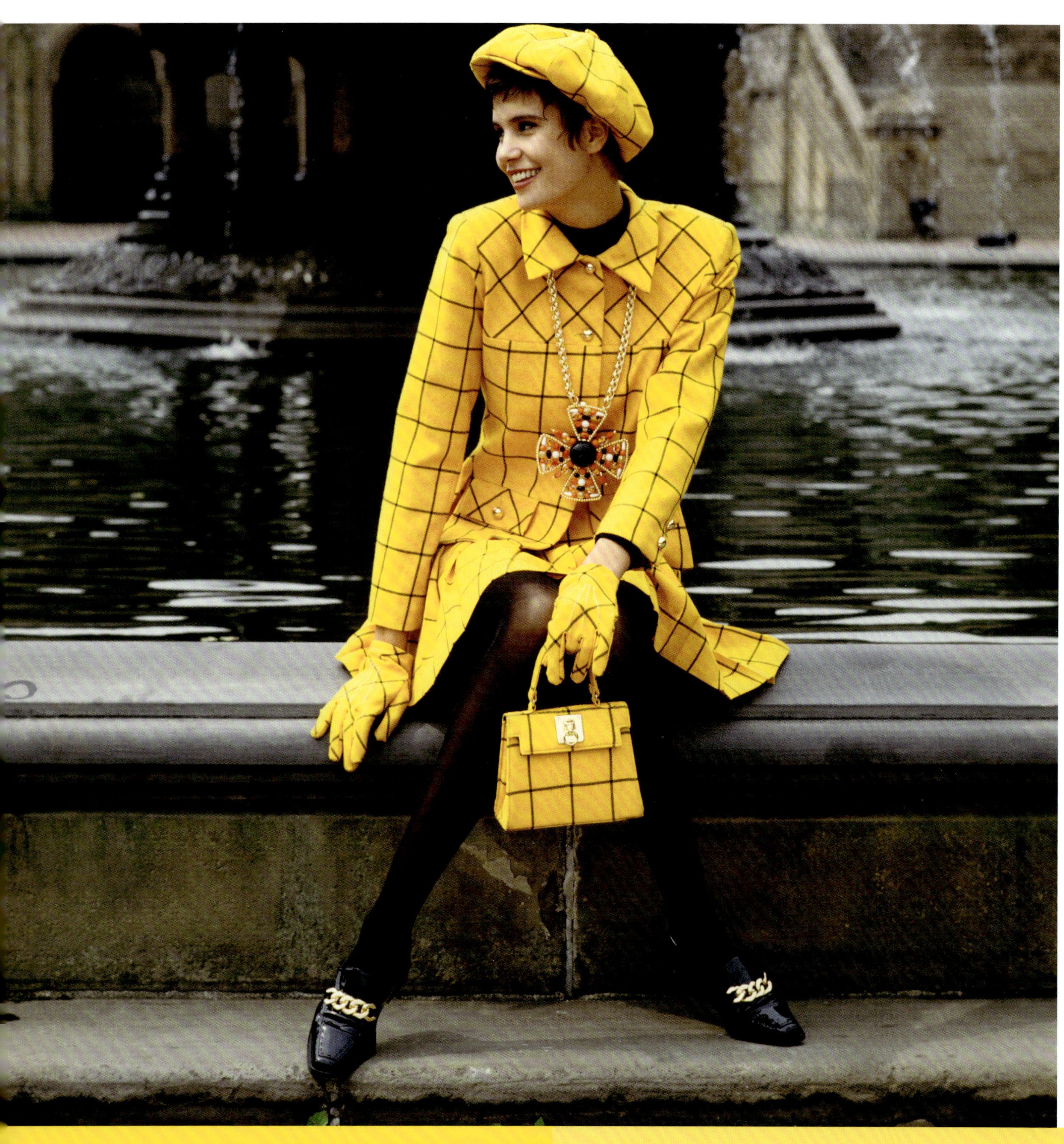

Cyber Yellow
PANTONE® 14-0760

Aspen Gold
PANTONE 13-0850

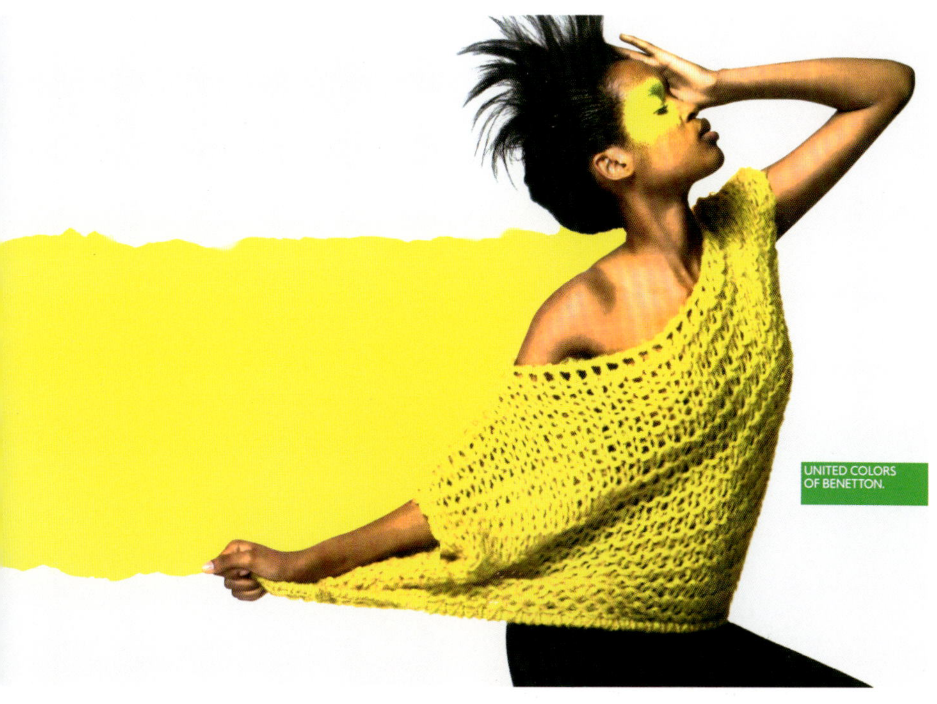

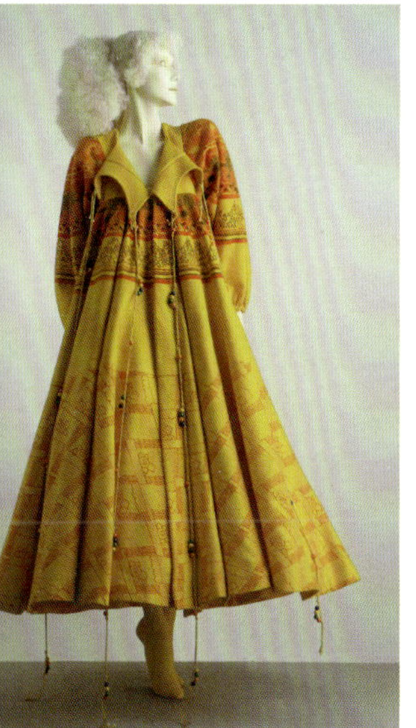

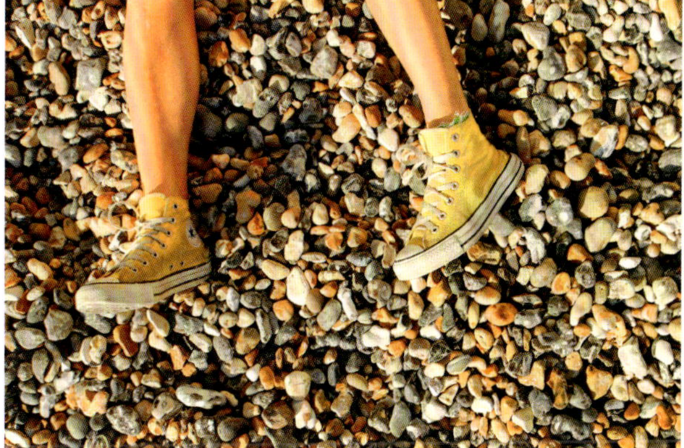

There's nothing mellow about this yellow. It's kinetic and optimistic, perfectly complementing what former model and *Vogue* creative director Grace Coddington called the "snap, crackle, and Mod of the Sixties youthquake."[10] The color not only adorned Harvey Ball's 1963 Smiley Face logo, but also garments galore. In 1969, eccentric British designer Zandra Rhodes silk-screened her "Button Flower" print onto Vibrant Yellow fabric, producing her first piece of outerwear. Introduced to "two wonderful, mad Ukrainian-American models"[11] by David Bailey, Rhodes followed their advice and headed to New York. *Vogue* editrice Diana Vreeland went wild for Rhodes's wacky work and pushed Henri Bendel to peruse it. Bendel purchased the entire collection for his high-end department store and suddenly society ladies on Fifth Avenue were looking groovy.

The unfettered joy of Vibrant Yellow is inherently confrontational, making it the perfect pigment for United Colors of Benetton. The company, originally founded by siblings Luciano and Giuliana Benetton, desired not only to promote color, but also erase society's color barriers. Oliviero Toscani's advertisements, which ignored Benetton's basic knitwear, focused instead on decidedly un-sunshiny global problems.

For Anna Sui's first runway show, she reinterpreted 1960s Carnaby Street with a punk-meets-grunge twist. Her head-to-toe Cyber Yellow look for Fall 1991 was visually affronting, perfect for Generation Xers looking to shock.

While Converse sneakers have barely changed over the last century, the demographic wearing them continues to shift. Worn first by basketball players, like Charles "Chuck" Taylor in 1918, Converse All Stars were later embraced by musicians like the Ramones and Kurt Cobain. The "alternative" crowd from Hunter S. Thompson-reading-high-schoolers to Bushwick hipsters continues to clamor for the affordable, durable footwear that singer Karen O of the Yeah Yeah Yeahs considers a "no-bullshit shoe."[12] But the bright and buttery Dandelion Converse seems to complement daylight better than nightlife.

Super Lemon

This tart lemon color varies from other yellows, possessing greenish undertones from lime to olive, which deepens its complexity. In 1947, British designer Victor Stiebel opted to use Super Lemon for his silk grosgrain day dress, which drastically departs from the rationed clothing of WWII. The pièce de résistance is the grand bow on the back, which is so large that horsehair frill has to support it underneath the skirt. The dress, gifted to the Victoria & Albert Museum by Lady Cornwallis, betrays Stiebel's clientele: English aristocracy. However, the oft-overlooked designer also catered to Hollywood royalty like Katharine Hepburn and Vivienne Leigh.

A half century later, the Bamboo color became wildly relevant again. Reality television stars vied with celebrities for the spotlight and everything (when well-edited) held the possibility of entertainment. In 2004, *Project Runway* began, a show that offered designer hopefuls the opportunity to vie for visibility and the funds to start their own fashion line. The pint-sized Christian Siriano, who interned at both Vivienne Westwood and Alexander McQueen, won over American audiences with his quirky personality and Hollywood A-listers with his notoriously big gowns.

Albert Kriemler of Akris, for Spring/Summer 2012, outfitted model Roberta Narciso in a matching sporty Ceylon Yellow top (somewhere between a crocheted cardigan and a varsity jacket) and trousers with leather tuxedo stripes down the outer seams. The only yellow look of the line was a punchy addition to the collection. The outfit's mixture of textiles is characteristic of Kriemler, who values the haptic experience of clothing. The ensemble illustrates Kriemler's perfectionistic attention to detail, uncompromising quality, and unwavering commitment to fabrics. All of which are true to the ethos of his grandmother, the founder of the label, Alice Kriemler-Schoch, for which Akris is an acronym.

For the last one hundred and fifty years, women have had a greater ability to shine than men. After the alleged Great Masculine Renunciation (when men stopped wearing vibrant hues in the late 1700s), menswear became somber and monochromatic, which did not begin to change until *le sport* and *le weekend* began to brighten up menswear between 1943 and 1953. Despite this, vibrantly colored menswear is still the exception rather than the rule. Christopher Bailey, however, takes pleasure in breaking those rules, rocking and rolling the established parameters of acceptable male attire. Bailey's metallic Sulphur trousers for Burberry Prorsum Spring/Summer 2013 are suited to both urban peacocking and beach frolicking.

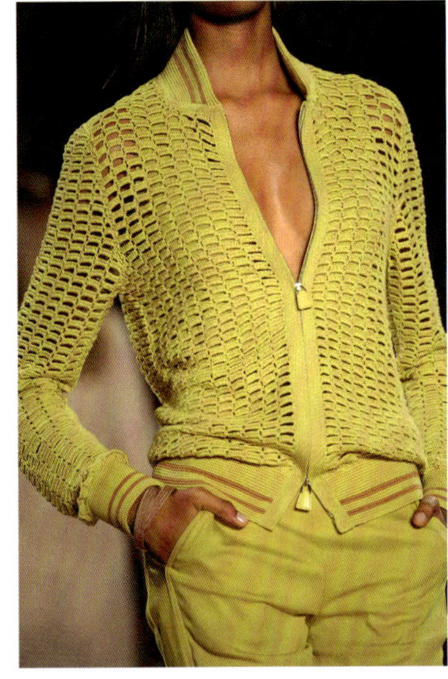

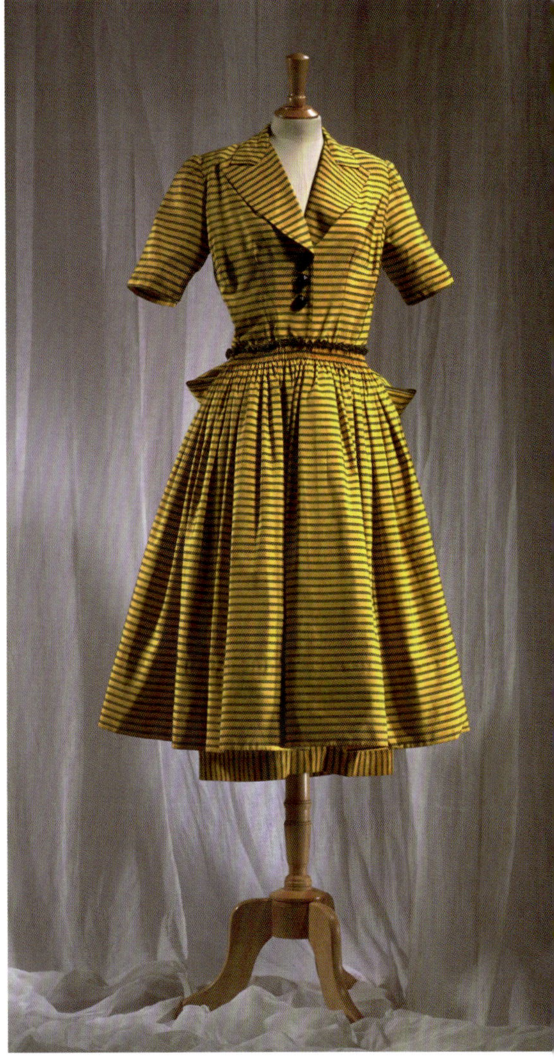

opposite, left
Sweater and pant set
Albert Kriemler for Akris
Spring/Summer 2012

opposite, right
Striped silk day dress
Victor Stiebel
1947

left
Layered chiffon dress
Christian Siriano
Spring/Summer 2009

right
Trench coat over a long printed shirt
with metallic silk pants
Christopher Bailey for Burberry
Spring/Summer 2013

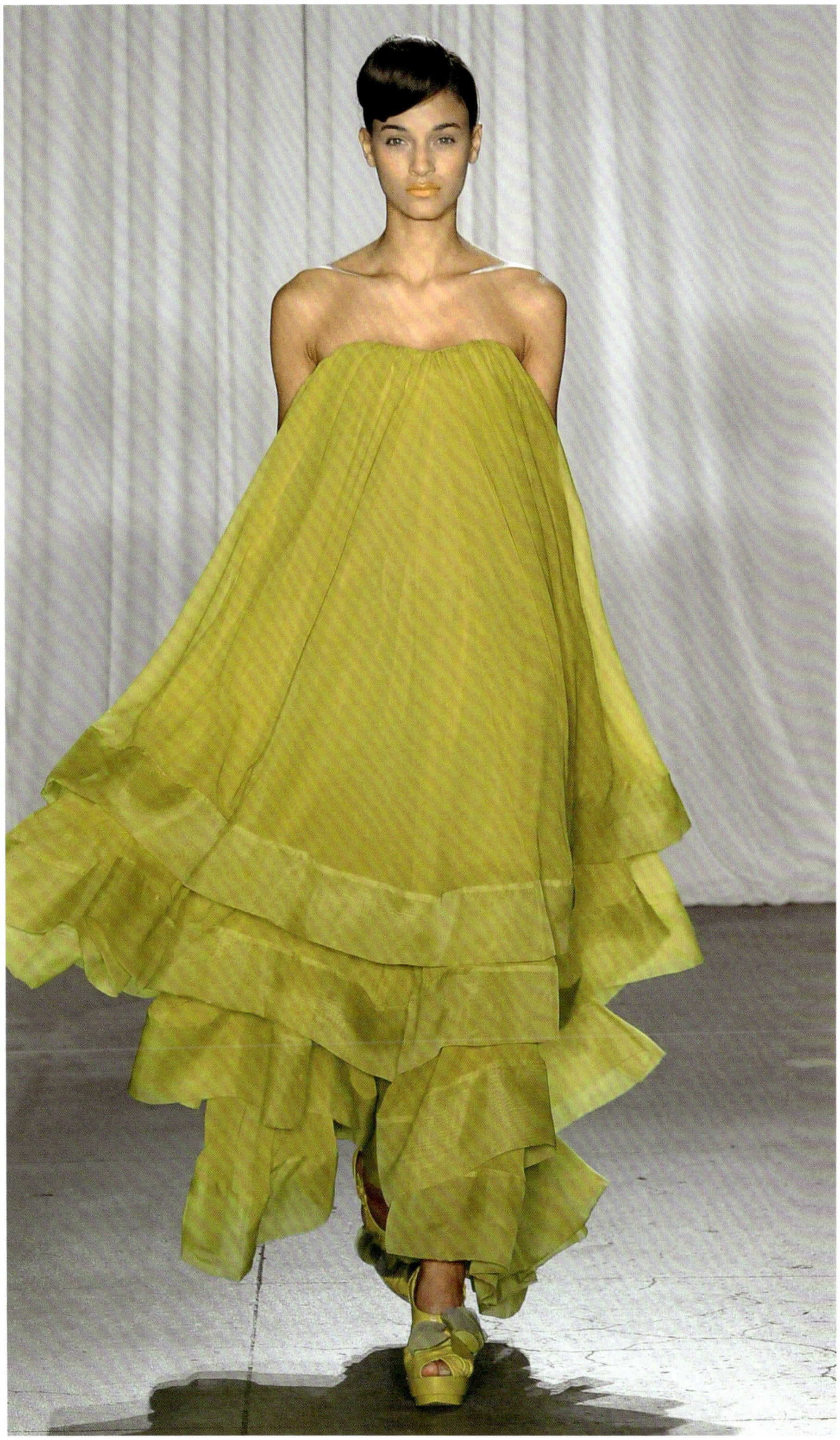

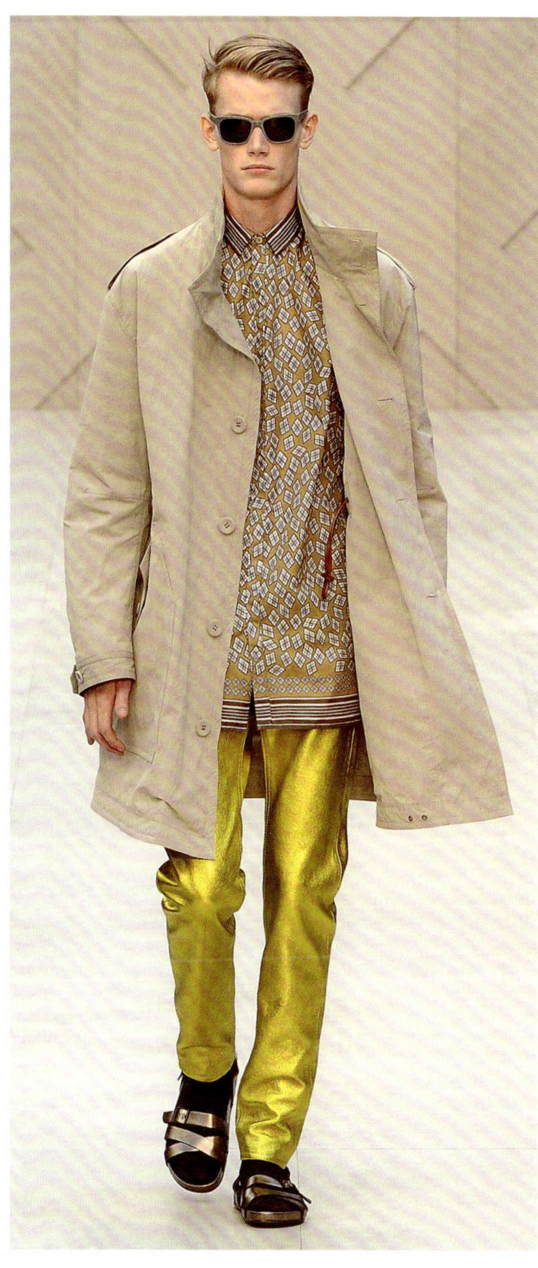

Bamboo
PANTONE 14-0740

Ceylon Yellow
PANTONE 15-0850

Golden Cream

If bright yellow got a tan, it would become the color of Golden Cream. Though the color did not make its way into menswear until later, high-end purveyor Austin Reed chose it for a 1935 advertisement illustrated by renowned poster artist Tom Purvis. The gilded color conveys the status of the London store that created bespoke suits for English gentlemen, and also Winston Churchill. Women donned the hue during 1940, as evidenced by Pierre Mourgue's illustration for *Harper's Bazaar*, which features a lithe woman in an Edward Molyneux gown the color of a sunset. The swaths of fabric and cascading pleats crafted by the London-born Molyneux mesmerized Paris. While history has not remembered him with the same gusto as others, couturiers like Balmain and Dior never forgot his "subdued elegance"[13] or "influence."[14]

Free of barbed wire and U-boats, people migrated back to the beaches after the Allied victory. Princess Irene Galitzine, an exiled Russian who called Italy home, captured the luxury of leisure with her Samoan Sun "palazzo pajamas," worn by friends Jacqueline Kennedy and Elizabeth Taylor, as well as herself. Galitzine's own social standing, after all, contributed to their fashionability.

Oscar de la Renta, like Molyneux before him, harnessed the energy of Solar Power. Forty years after starting his label, de la Renta's ability to translate sophistication and suavity into garments had not waned. The designer offset the blinding shade of his Spring/Summer 2007 gown with bold black-and-white embroidered flowers. By teasing model Natasha Poly's mane into a messy Marie Antoinette–esque bouffant, de la Renta simultaneously toned down the opulence of the dress and made it accessible for a younger demographic, like social media maven "Oscar PR Girl" Erika Bearman. Equally youthful and wry was a Sunset Gold raincoat from Stella McCartney in 2011 that would undoubtedly shine on an overcast day. McCartney's clean and strong lines were exacerbated by the primary color, especially when shown atop pristinely white trousers. The three-quarter-sleeved poncho-cum-minidress is not fully functional (Martin Margiela would approve) but does imply a level of Adidas-like athleticism when paired with aviator goggles.

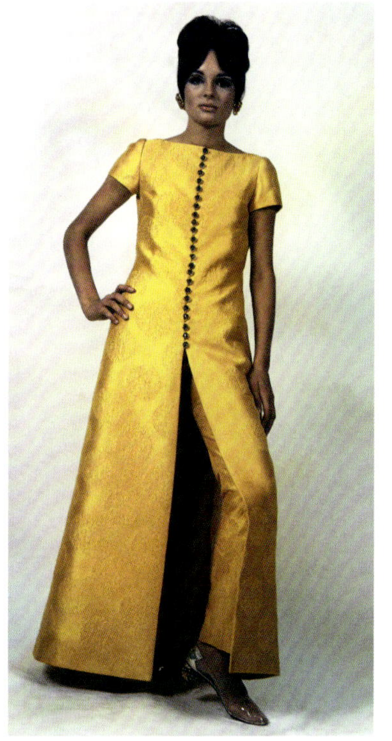

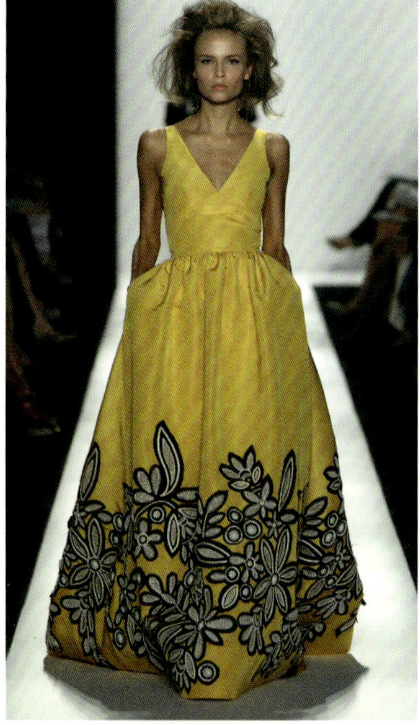

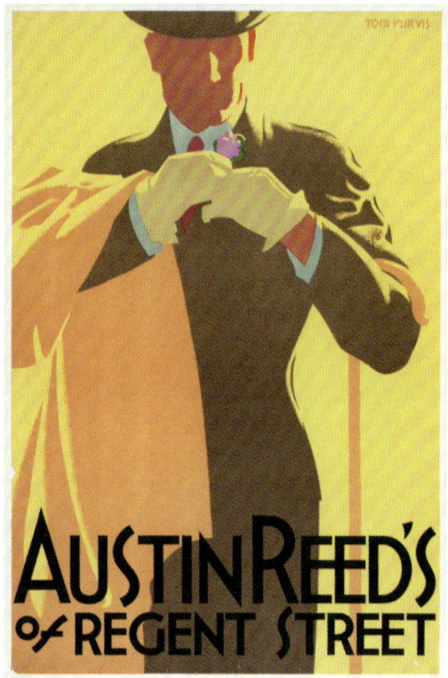

Yellow is starred by Molyneux
throughout his collection.   A lovely clear
yellow that needs the fresh
bright makeup of Elizabeth
Arden called Primula.

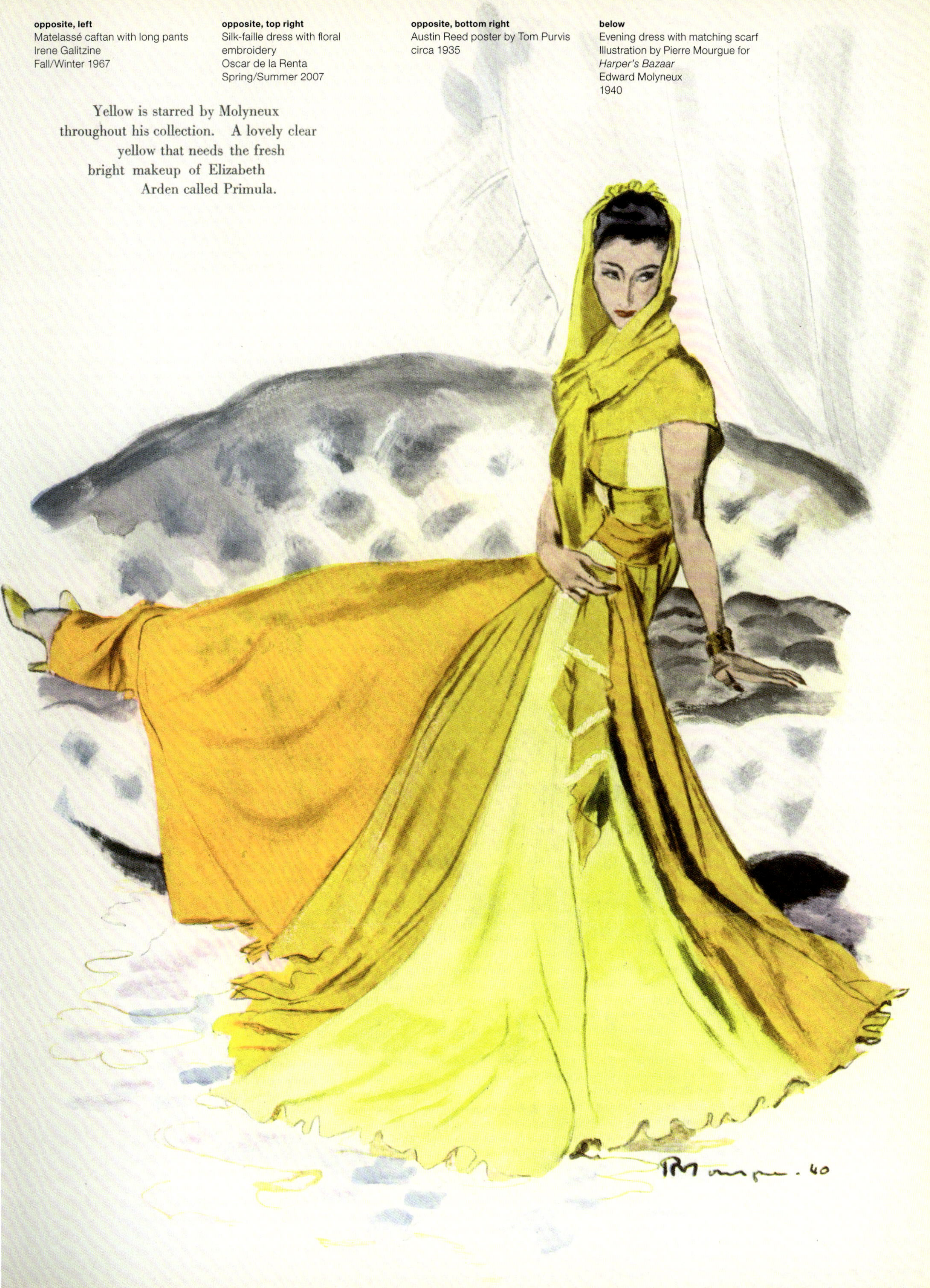

Bright Marigold

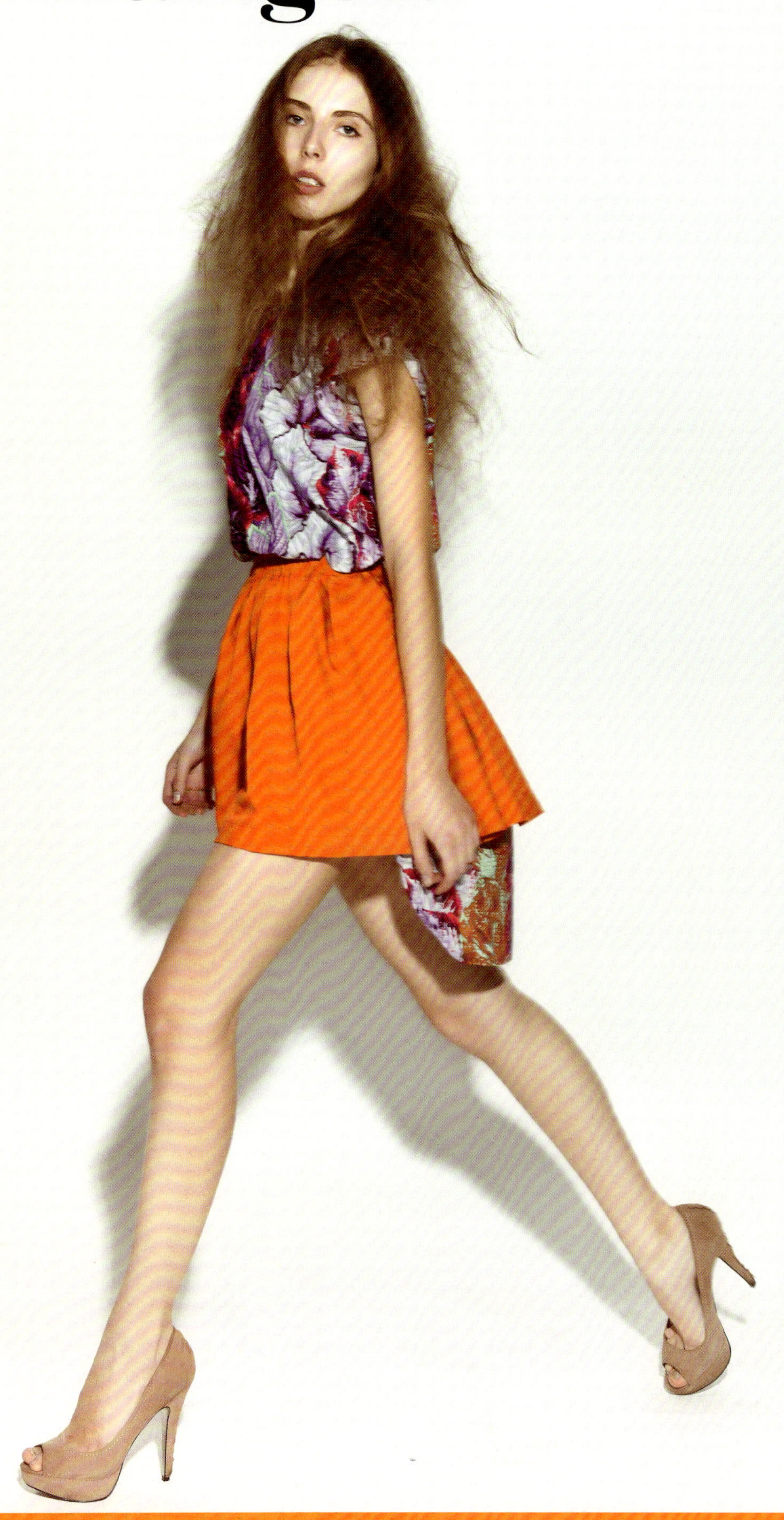

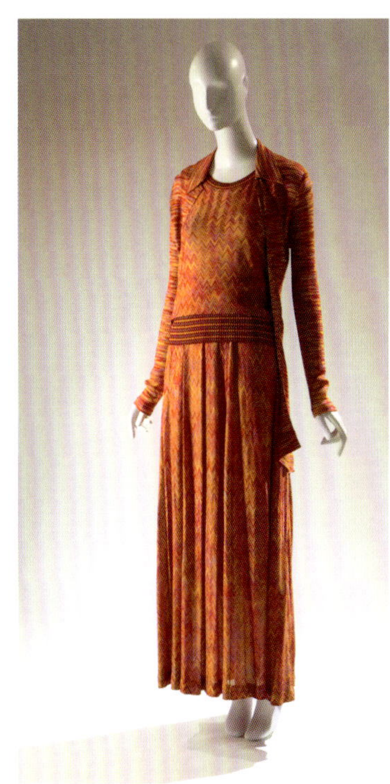

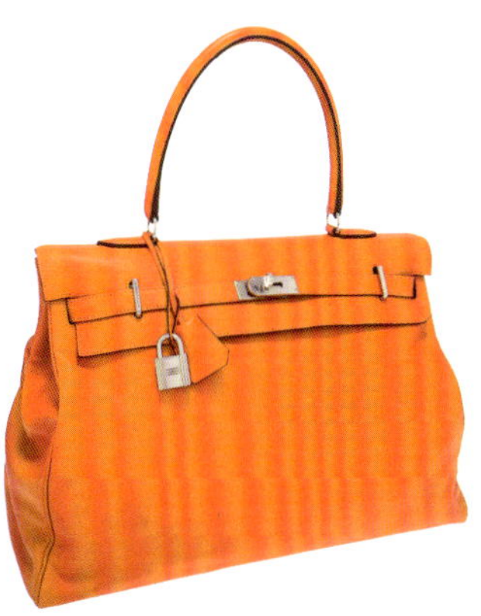

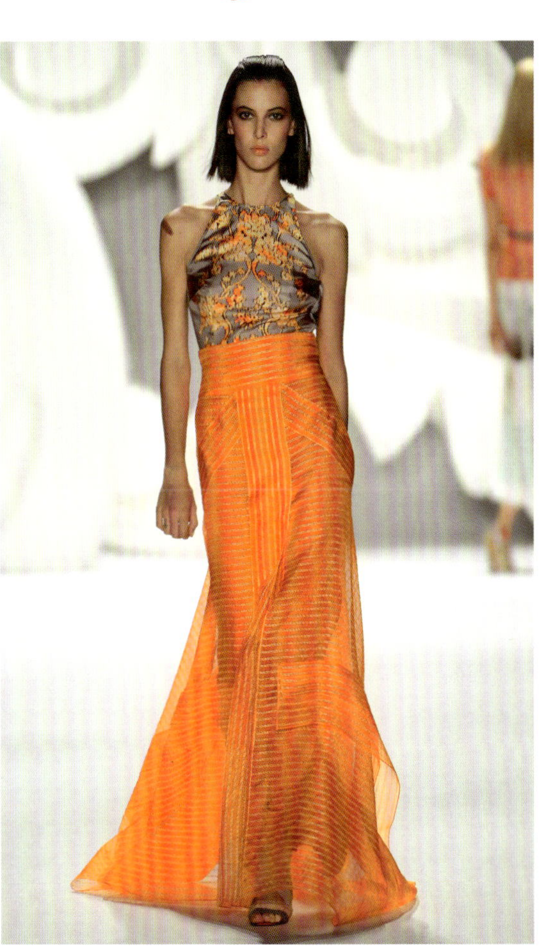

"Orange is the new red." —Carolina Herrera[15]

This color immediately sets one's heart aflutter!

The strength of Hermès lies in its ability to transition seamlessly. The house shifted its original 1837 purpose of selling luxury bridles for horse-drawn carriages to producing high-end leather accessories when automobiles began taking over the roads. Prior to WWII, Hermès used cream-colored boxes, then mustard, until paper shortages forced them to scramble and use the last paperboard available: their unmistakable orange, now synonymous with opulence. The bright orange of Hermès boxes, bags, and other packaging is now considered "the most distinctive color in retail."[16] Following the war, their "Sac à dépêches" gathered a new moniker, after Grace Kelly maneuvered the handbag to hide her pregnancy from the paparazzi. The iconic Kelly bag, which takes one craftsman two weeks to make and can run over six figures, always comes in clementine packaging.

Competing in the 1948 London Olympics, Ottavio "Tai" Missoni jumped hurdles for Italy but ended up running away with onlooker Rosita Jelmini's heart. When they were first introduced at a dinner party following the games, Octavio's interest in knitwear, which had led him to design the team's woolen tracksuits, complemented Rosita's knowledge of shawls and embroidered fabric, courtesy of her upbringing. In 1953, they were wed and began working together. Twenty years later, Missoni had their first full-scale show in America, taking over Bloomingdale's. Their space-dyed textiles, in "arresting orange to red sunset shades,"[17] were a hit and are still stealing the show today.

Born into an illustrious Venezuelan lineage, María Carolina Josefina Pacanins y Niño was always well-dressed. In 1968, after marrying her soul mate and childhood friend, jet-setter Reinaldo Herrera, Carolina Herrera quickly became known for her incomparable style that consisted of pairing Parisian couture with her own designs. Lauded by fashion critic Eleanor Lambert, Herrera debuted her first collection in 1981 for an audience that included Nan Kempner and Pat Buckley.[18] Since then, Herrera has been known for pared-down elegance. "[T]he intricacy must appear as simplicity."[19] While the orange organza used in Spring/Summer 2013 is tropical, Herrera has distanced herself from stereotypically "exotic, native fabrics."[20]

Swedish-born, Barcelona-based fashion and textile designer Ida Johansson wanted her orange-heavy Spring/Summer 2012 "Reflecting Roots" line to "light up the Swedish mind and share the spontaneous, creative energy [of] Barcelona."[21] Her primary inspiration stemmed from Bright Marigold flowers bursting through wintered soil.

Vibrant Orange

When vivid oranges (the color and the fruit) were imported
to the West, the Renaissance elite clamored to obtain these
novelties. By the 20th century, orange still captured the
exuberance of well-to-do artists and fashion designers, like
Leon Bakst of the Ballets Russes and Paul Poiret. In 1921,
a Mandarin Orange frock and matching headscarf graced
the cover of *Vogue*. Drawn by Helen Dryden, the flamboy-
ant and fantastical illustration is characteristic of the deco
period, which rebuked the reticent pastel coloring of the earlier part of the century. The youthful woman pictured appears
to be uncorseted, fun-loving, and free, in step with the times.

In the 1960s, orange could once again kick up its
energetic heels, and who better to show the rambunctious
side of orange than Jacques Tiffeau? After studying under
Dior, Tiffeau moved to New York City, where he cooked up
designs that blended French subtlety with American energy.
Almost instantaneously, he became known for "creating
clothing that grabbed attention because of its cut, shape,
and color, not because of frills or fancy design tricks."[22] In
1969, Jacques Tiffeau's Orange Peel ensemble made the
September cover of *Harper's Bazaar*.

French designer Jean Paul Gaultier, a rascal and a
provocateur, introduced the mainstream market to a queer
aesthetic with his orange conical-breasted corset dress
that was so highly *femme* and overtly sexual that it bordered
on camp. Pluckily, Gaultier began his career by sending
sketches to Pierre Cardin, despite having no fashion training.
Cardin hired and nurtured him until 1976, when Gaultier
entered the fashion world on his own. In 1983, Gaultier made
his first corset dress, which he presented to the world in his
famous "Barbès" collection. Gaultier saw corsets in the same
light as artist Richard Lindner, who used them to represent
"mixed female emotions of aggression and restraint."[23] The
blonde and ambitious Madonna, who was also fascinated
by underground gay subculture, chose to don and inhabit
Gaultier's garments during her 1990 tour, rocketing the
designer to stardom alongside her.

Born in Casablanca and raised in Israel, Alber Elbaz
received seven years of training at Geoffrey Beene, worked
at Guy Laroche, Yves Saint Laurent, and Krizia, and then
became creative director at Lanvin. In designing his first
collection for the House, Elbaz said, "I want to dress women
I know, women I want to know—and to make them look
beautiful."[24] Fall/Winter 2012–2013 marked his 10th anniversary at the brand, and the collection was electric. His
large ruffle dresses, like the one in Golden Poppy, were fun
and fresh, all the while introducing new silhouettes, a nearly
impossible feat and a testament to the genius of Alber Elbaz.

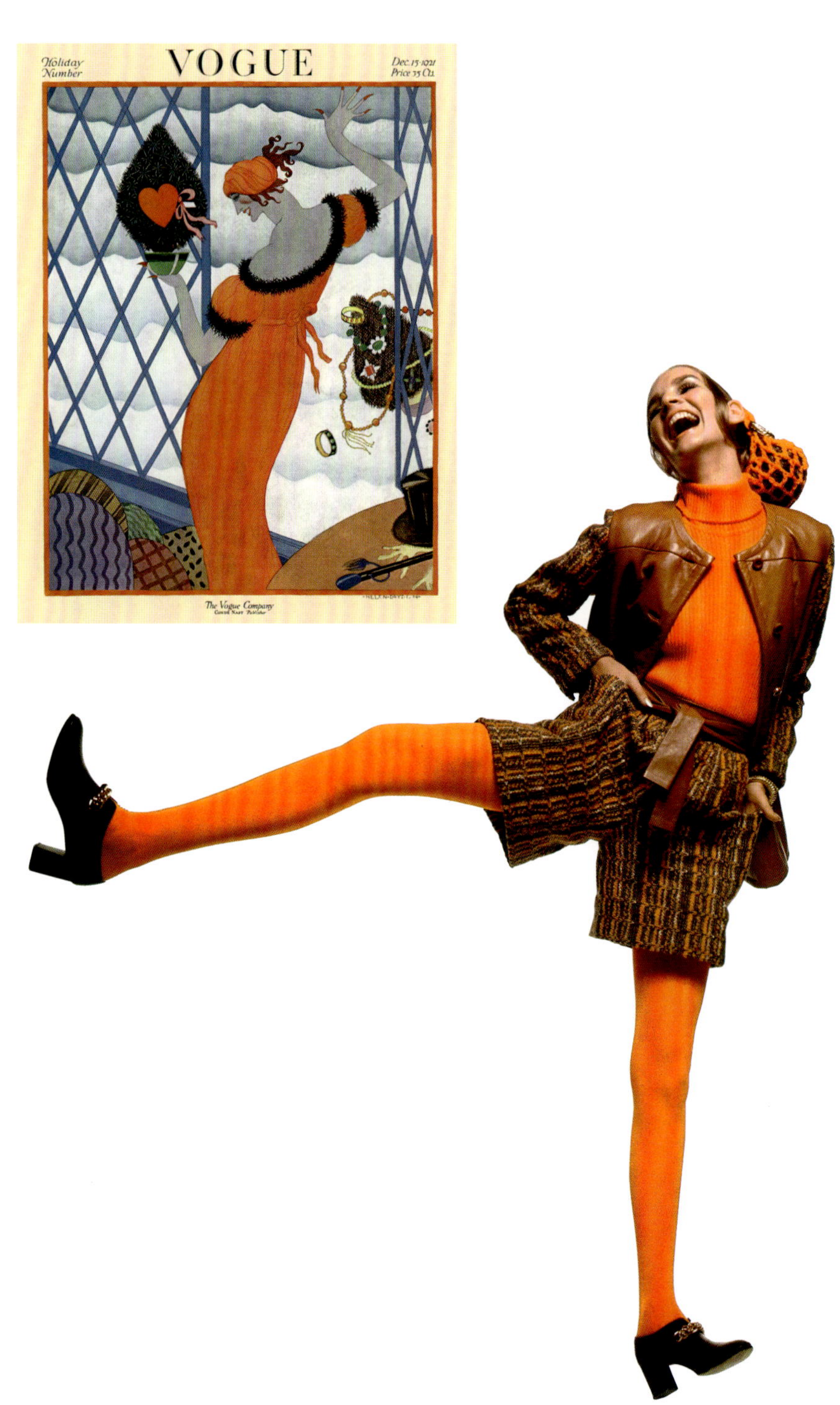

opposite, left
Cover illustration by Helen Dryden
for *Vogue*
1921

opposite, right
Tweed, leather, and wool shorts suit
with turtleneck and tights
Jacques Tiffeau
Outtake from a *Harper's Bazaar*
cover shoot photographed by
Neal Barr
1969

left
Dress with large ruffled collar
Alber Elbaz for Lanvin
Fall/Winter 2012

right
Corset dress with exaggerated
cone bust
Jean Paul Gaultier
1984

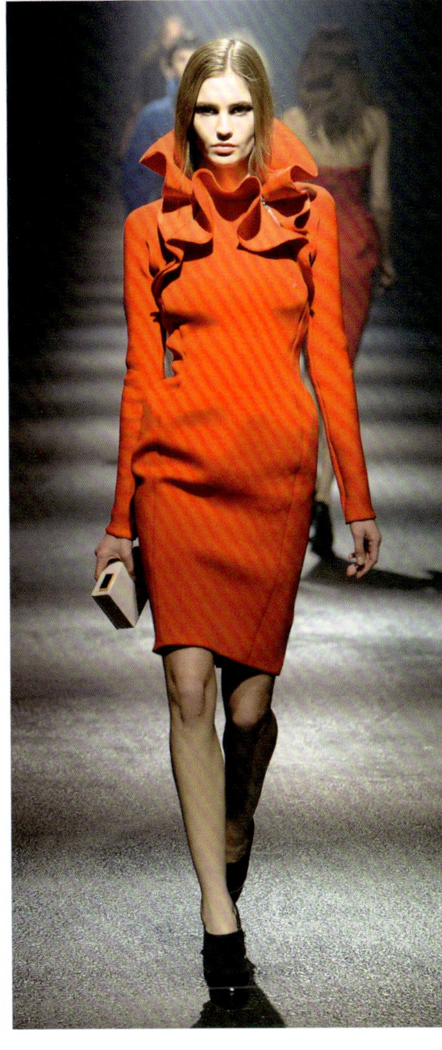

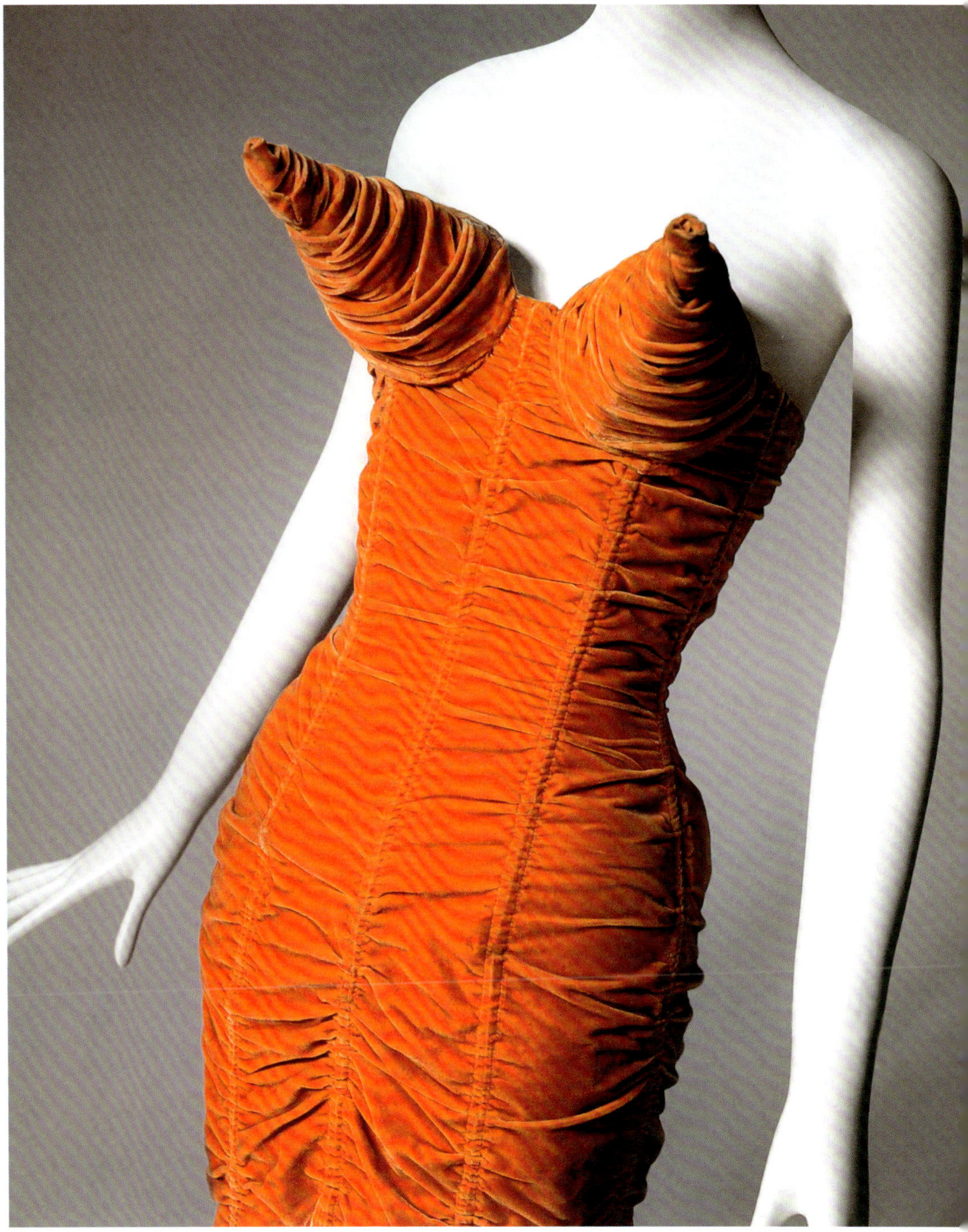

Peach

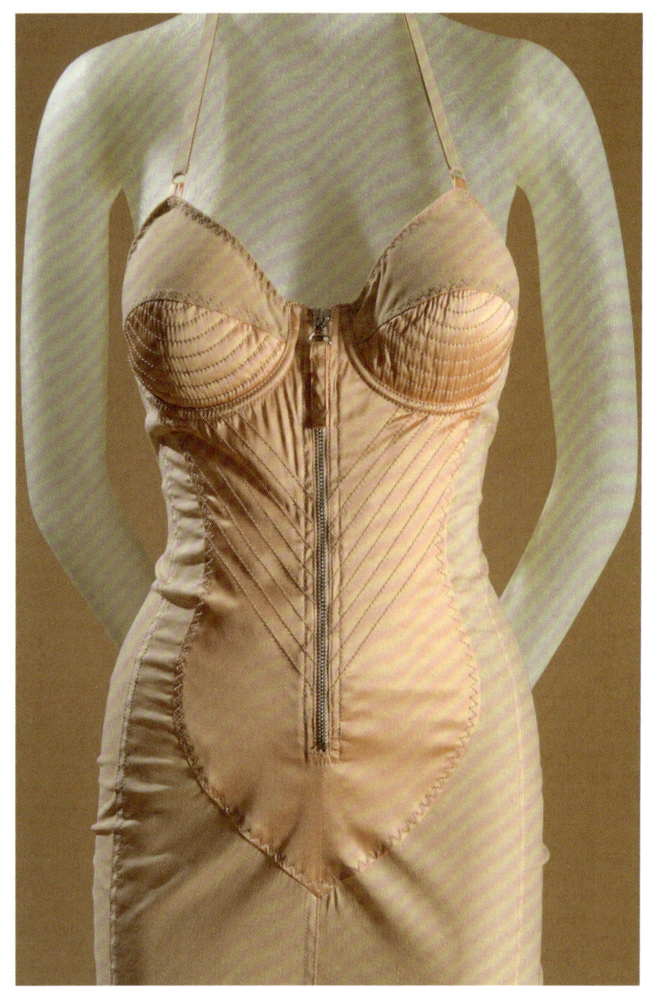

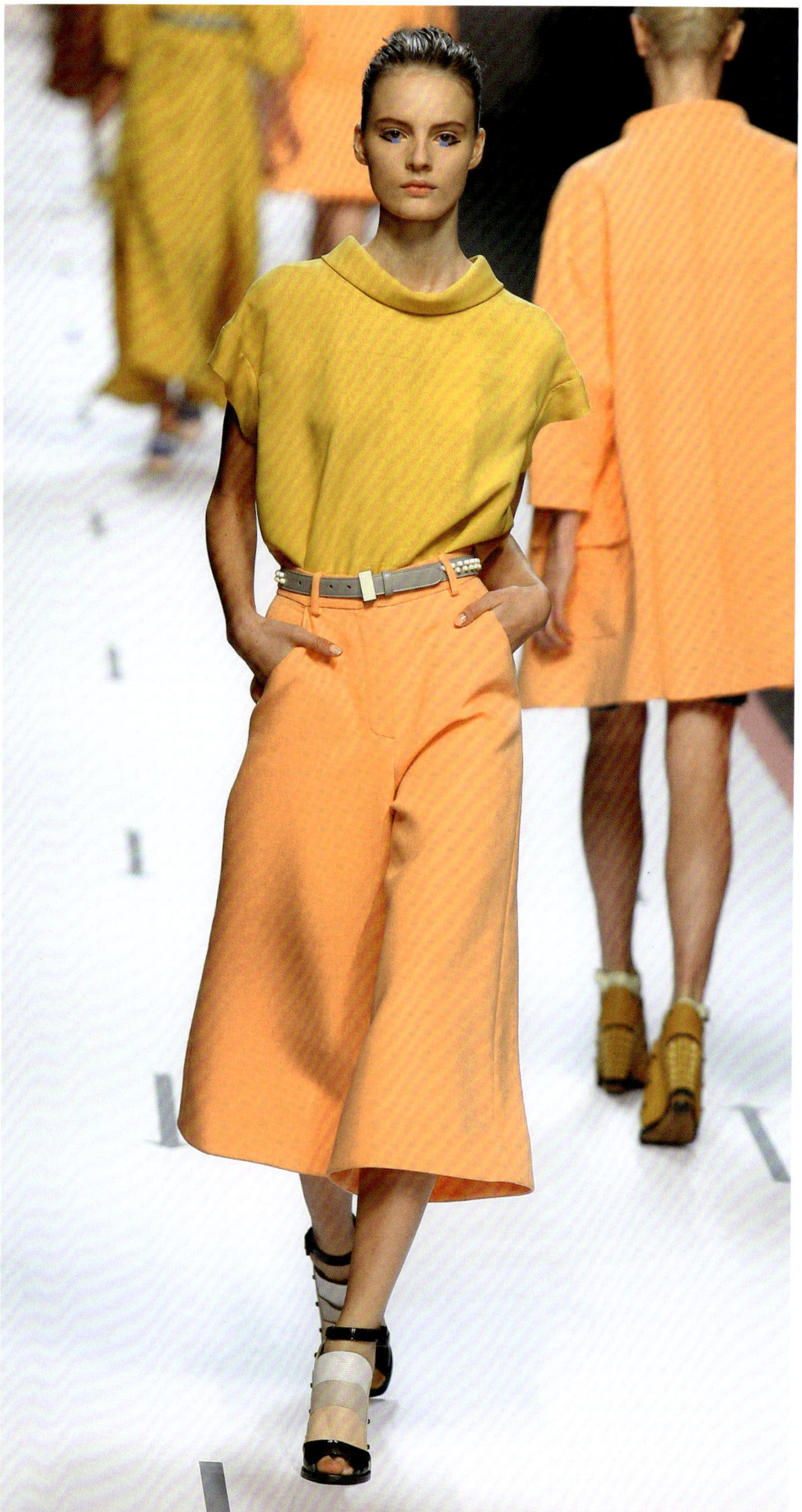

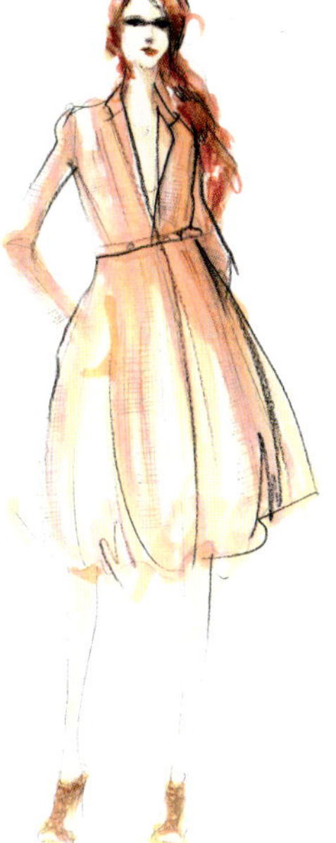

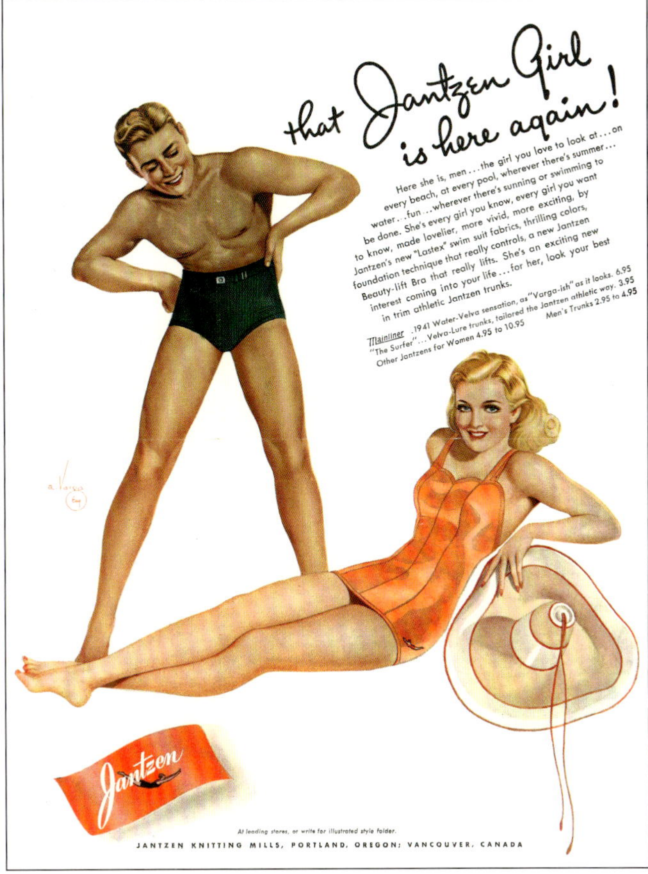

The Jantzen Girl sure is a peach. Her clingy, coral-colored swimsuit makes her even "lovelier, more vivid, [and] more exciting."[25] The head-turning beauty, illustrated in 1941 by *Esquire* artist Alberto Vargas, is flushed—either from sun or the attention! Jantzen Knitting Mills, originally christened the Portland Knitting Company, came to prominence in 1915 after knitwear designer Carl C. Jantzen perfected a rib-stitched woolen swimming suit, which ruled the waves until the early 1930s, when Lastex hit the market. Though first used for girdles, Jantzen was quick to use the hybrid textile in swimwear. The flattering fabric snuggly fit the pinup curves of Vargas Girls. While Vargas's beach babe helped to hawk Jantzen swimwear, the idealized American woman also aided the morale of troops storming other beaches.

"Gaultier, being Gaultier, turned all notions of propriety on its head" by designing underwear to be worn as outerwear.[26] Jean Paul Gaultier's lingerie-turned-couture gathered exponential momentum due to the AIDS crisis that raged during the era of his most provocative designs. The health epidemic required from society a newfound sexual honesty—in all its scientific specificity. The Sexual Revolution of the 60s had nothing on the 1980s and 1990s, when to *not* talk about sex could cost one one's life. In 1992, five years after JPG showed his Shell Coral corset dress, *Newsweek* named the late 1980s and early 1990s a period of "new voyeurism." And no one did voyeuristic wardrobes better than Mr. Gaultier.

Rather than pinup girls, Pennsylvania-born designer Shelly Steffee based her Spring/Summer 2005 line around Belgian portrait artist Fernand Khnopff's fin-de-siècle women. Steffee mused, "[Khnopff] captures a woman that directly spoke to me and that I was trying to speak to . . . very modern, very deep women."[27] Steffee's color philosophy was then influenced by Khnopff's "subtle changes of color with accents of depth."[28]

Since 1965, German-born Karl Lagerfeld has been part of the Fendi family fold. While most known for his work at Chanel, Lagerfeld has long been artistic director for the Italian house, increasingly renowned for its exceptional furs to ready-to-wear and accessories galore. For Spring/Summer 2013, Lagerfeld reinterpreted mod with an updated color scheme, like a streetlight yellow top with peachy Coral Reef culottes. Always one to look to the future, this collection boasted a new technique: "*saldatura*," an electrical welding that makes literally seamless fashion.

Nude

In a global world, it is problematic to consider Caucasian skin color "nude." But for now the word remains in the language as a name for the soft pinkish (with a beige undertone) color also known as Pale Peach. The sweet color has sensational qualities, conjuring the naked body of certain women. For this reason, it was popular in the 1920s and 1930s for undergarments, and in the late 1990s and 2000s for exterior garments.

As a United States Tariff Commission's survey proves, corsets did not suddenly disappear in 1920, though they did change to accommodate current fashions. The Metropolitan Museum of Art's Costume Institute has two corsets made in France for Saks Fifth Avenue: one by Bienjay (1920–1925) and the other by Facon (1930–1935). While both are Pale Peach, the Bienjay corset has nearly no support, hanging loosely on the bust, waist, and hips (Paul Poiret would be proud); the Facon corset is more conservative, with a supportive seamed brassiere, elastic constricting the waist and hips, and measuring six inches longer. Both eschew the earlier use of boning and are reflective of the new century's fluctuating attitudes toward fashion and bodies.

For Spring/Summer 2002, Donna Karan went uncharacteristically soft and hyperfeminine, dressing Liya Kebede in parachute silk. During WWII, women often collected parachute silk to make clothing, sometimes even running with scissors to downed planes. Though Karan didn't comment on the reasons for her specific choice of fabric, merely saying that the collection was inspired by her late husband, his art, and everything he loved—the juxtaposition of history and beauty is nevertheless a fascinating one.

Alongside Azzedine Alaïa's curve-hugging creations, Hervé Léger's body-con bandage dresses defined the late '80s and early '90s love of Lycra, an aesthetic also seen in George Michael's supermodel-filled "Freedom" music video. Yet the enchantment with the look diminished toward the end of the decade, and Max Azria of BCBG bought the brand in 1998, being the first American designer to acquire a French couture House. As Léger's original frocks used fabric typically found in undergarments and swimwear, it seems apropos that Max Azria for Hervé Léger would feature an Alesan-hued asymmetrical bathing suit on his Spring/Summer 2009 catwalk. While sexy, the suit is far from practical—who wants bondage tan lines?

Returning to neutrals, Giorgio Armani showed the other, more sedate, side of Nude, toning down "feminine exhibitionism" by creating protective, imperfection-hiding garments like a long suit jacket and knee-length flouncy skirt in Tender Peach for his 2013 "Privé" collection. Armani, awarded the Legion of Honor for his contribution to fashion, explained that he likes "women who have elegance, who have allure, who use fashion, rather than the other way around."[29]

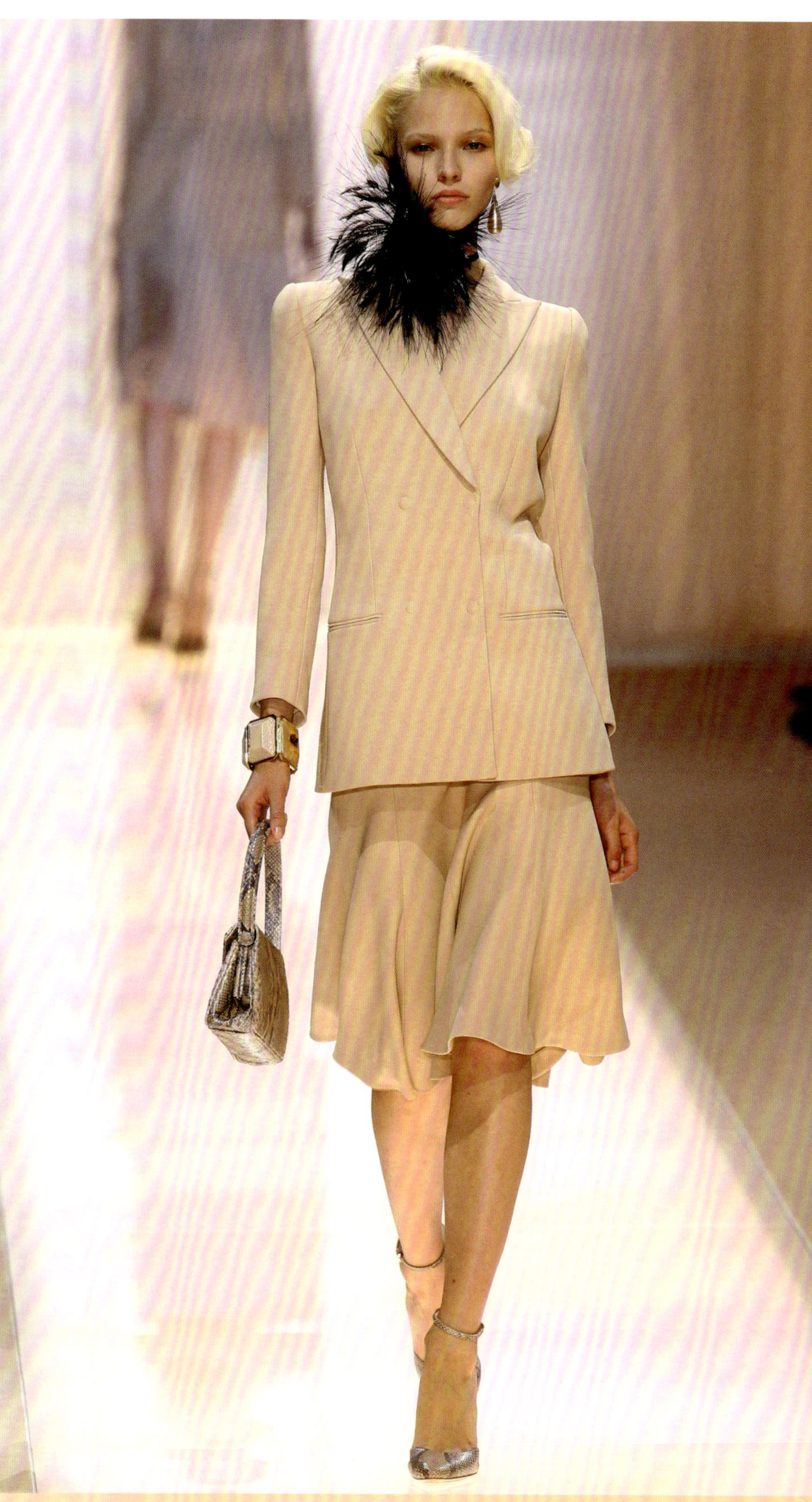

opposite
Dress suit
Giorgio Armani
Fall/Winter 2013

top left
Banded "one-piece" bathing suit
Max Azria for Hervé Léger
Spring/Summer 2009

bottom left
Strapless dress with
asymmetrical seaming
Donna Karan
Spring/Summer 2002

right
Corset in silk, elastic, and metal
Facon for Saks Fifth Avenue
circa 1930–35

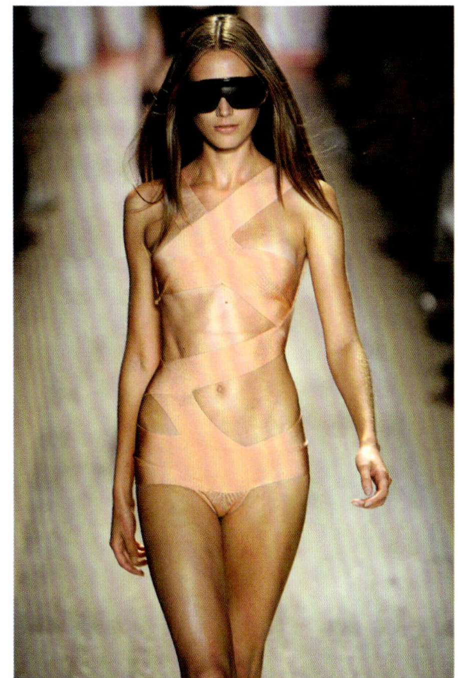

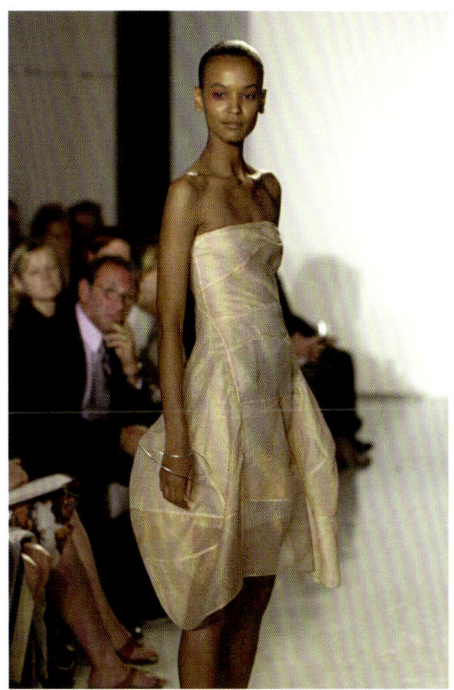

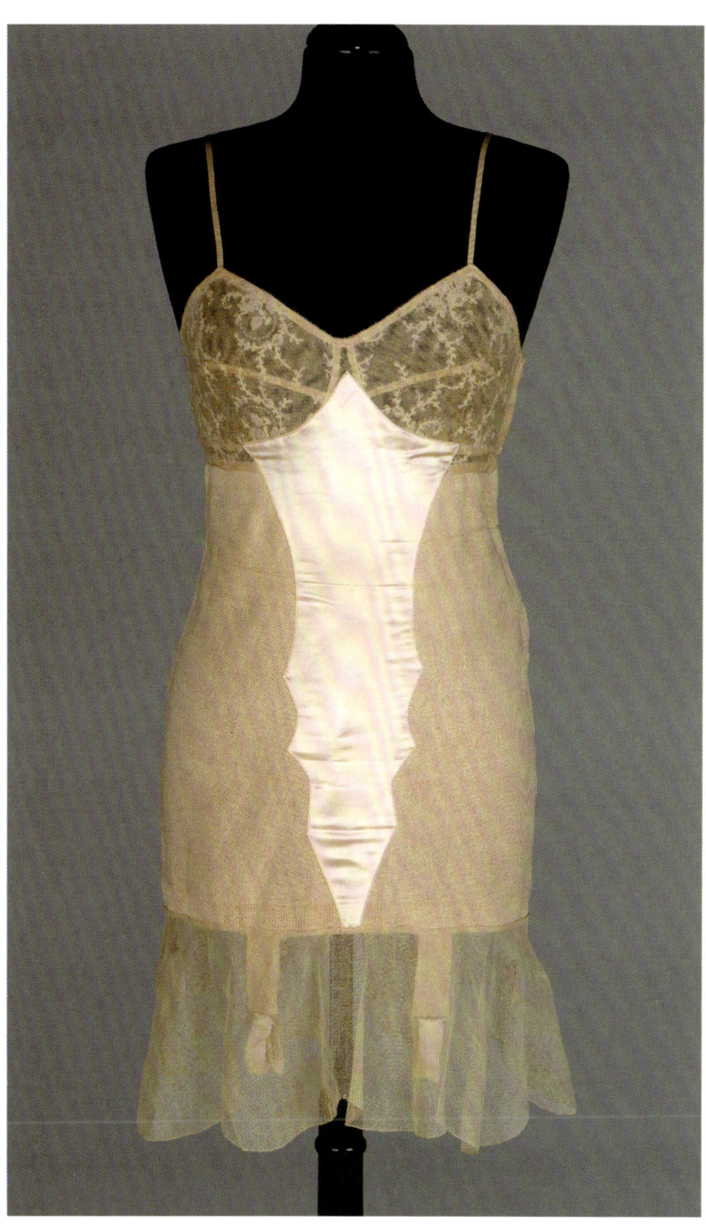

Rust

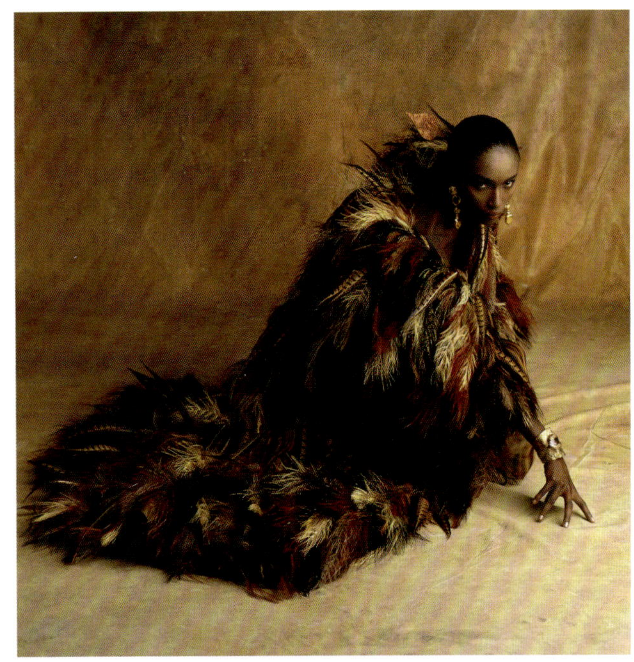

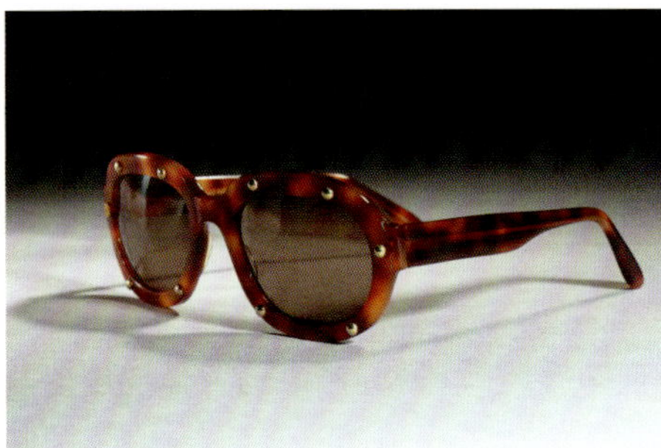

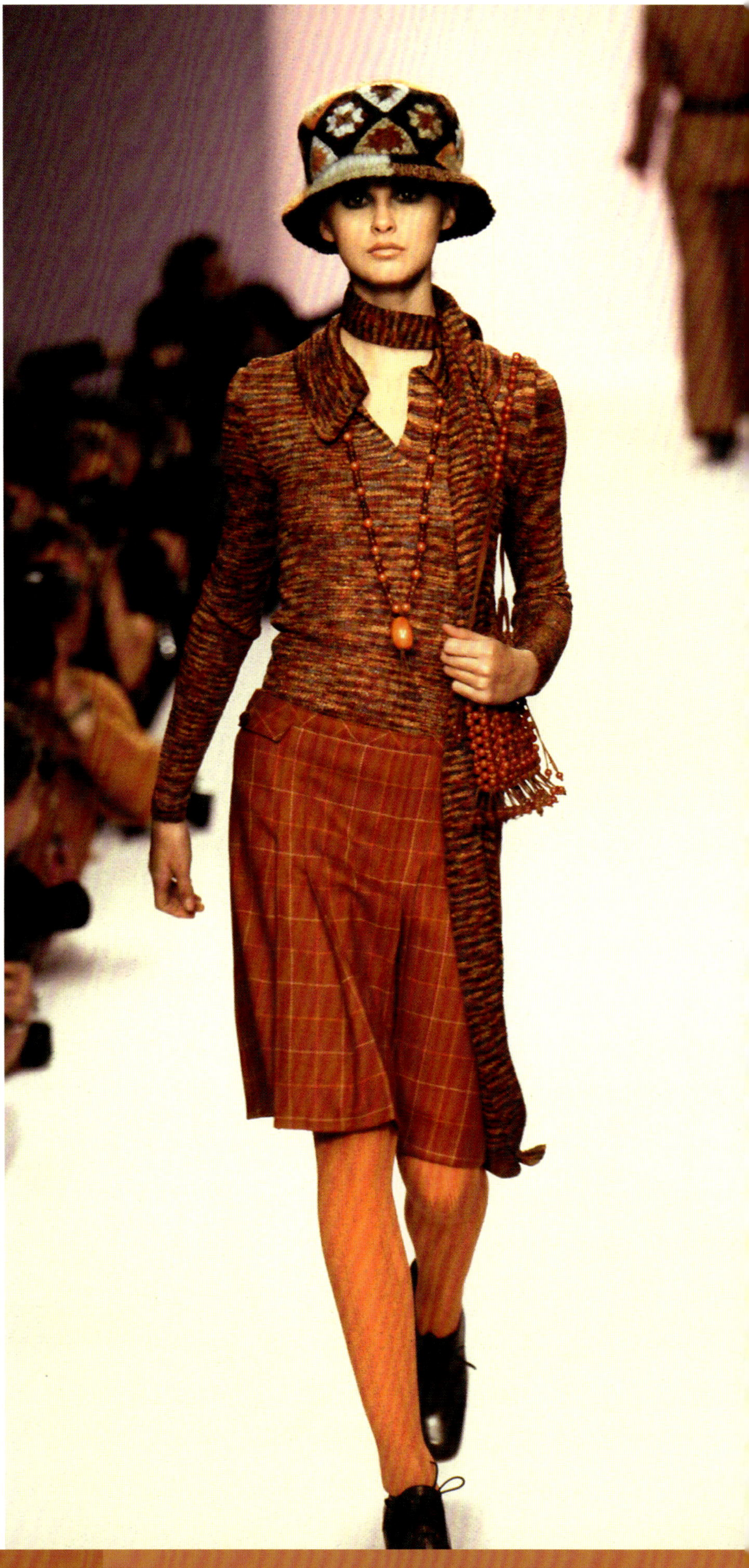

Rust gained ascendency in the practical 1930s, the earthy 1970s, and the retro 1990s.

In the first half of the 20th century, Americans unable to shop at big city department stores relied on mail-order catalogs to purchase their wardrobes. While history has remembered Sears-Roebuck and Montgomery Ward catalogs best, Aldens, Spiegel, and Bellas Hess were also widely distributed. Unlike others, Bellas Hess was illustrated in color, allowing customers to view popular color options, such as the 1936 penchant for Rust shades. The fashion journalism–inspired text welcomes housewives to indulge in a rendezvous with a tunic—for $2.98 plus 13 cents for postage.

While an integral part of the fashion world, Alexandre de Paris is best known as a designer of hair, producing *hauts coiffeurs* for the Duchess of Windsor, Elizabeth Taylor, and Sophia Loren. His accessories were designed for the purpose of adorning his hairstyles. The Victoria & Albert Museum flaunts a rare pair of Alexandre de Paris brass-studded Raw Sienna sunglasses from the 1970s, which likely looked equally fabulous when perched on top of a fabulous blowout . . . by him, of course.

Despite being hospitalized between shows, Yves Saint Laurent designed and finished his 1990 couture show in twenty days. The show, an homage to his different muses throughout the years, "covered every aspect of rich contemporary living without ever touching on the absurd."[30] One of its finest pieces was a magnificent feather gown in Rust shades. The collection, considered "the best he had ever done," received a thirteen-minute standing ovation and brought socialite Nan Kempner to tears.[31] Appropriate considering, as Loulou de la Falaise said, "One of Yves' big talents [is] making people cry, because I think when you hit moments of perfection . . . every sensitive person will be moved to tears."[32]

Anna Sui's Fall/Winter 1996–1997 collection was a historical mash-up: one part Vita Sackville-West and the Bloomsbury Group of Dorothy Todd's 1920s British *Vogue,* and one part filmmaker Ken Russell's 1970s interpretation of the post-WWI era from the Twiggy vehicle *The Boy Friend*. So, how does Anna Sui meld the 1920s and a 1970s interpretation of the 1920s for a 1990s audience? With a mix of Autumn Leaf hues including a wide-collared knit top, matching scarf, and a slightly clashing knee-length plaid skirt on model Trish Goff.

Coffee Liqueúr

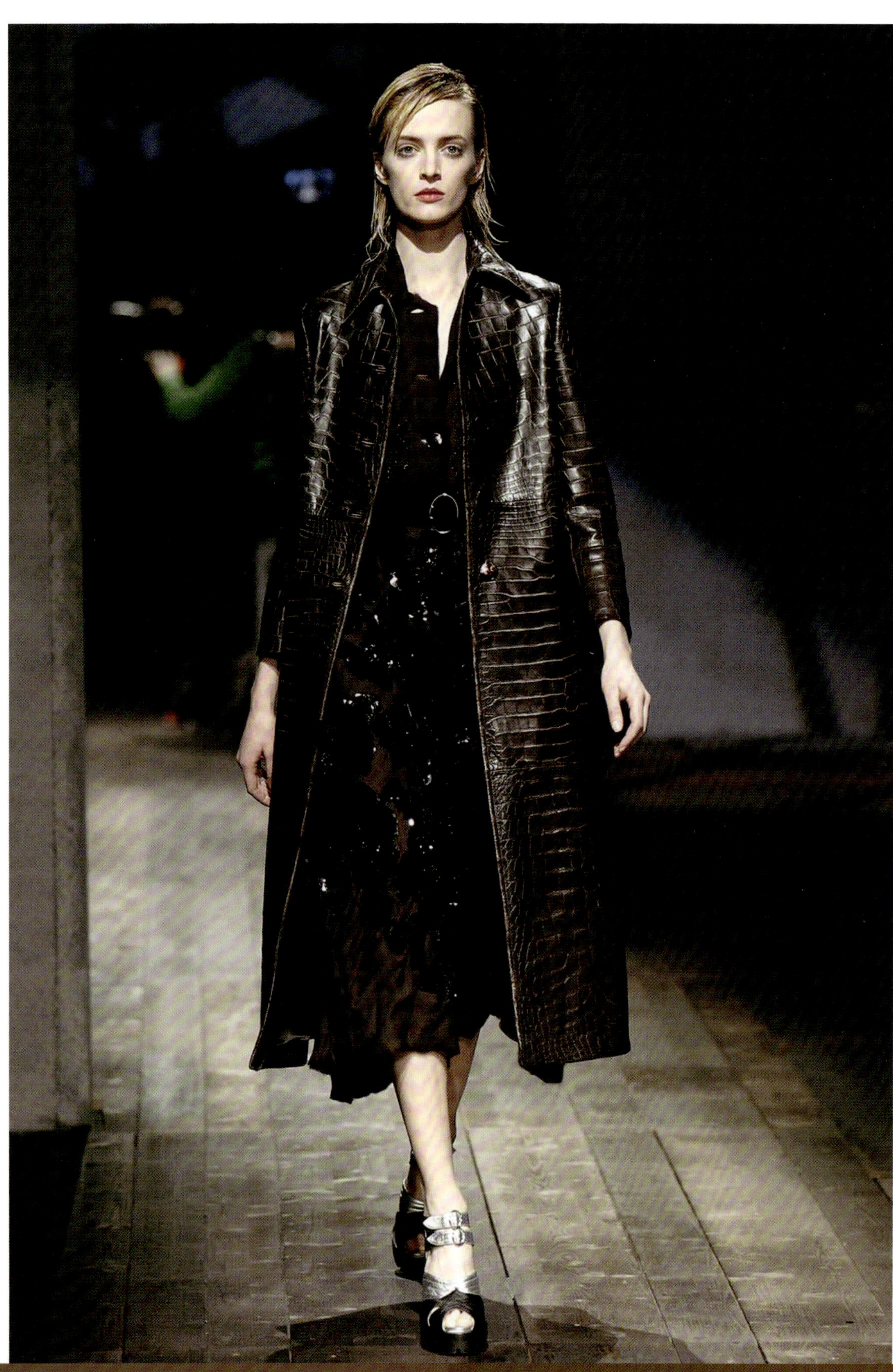

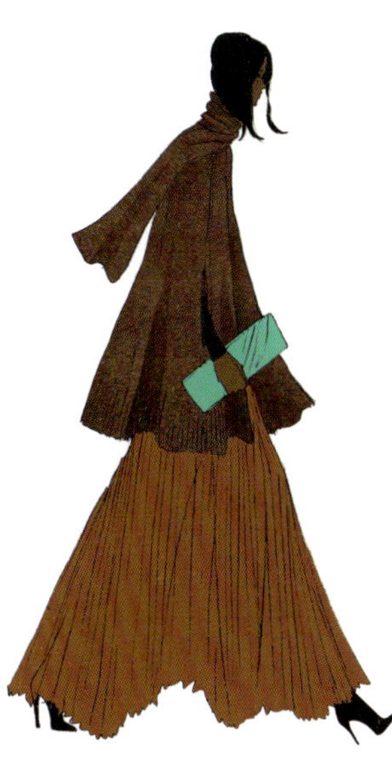

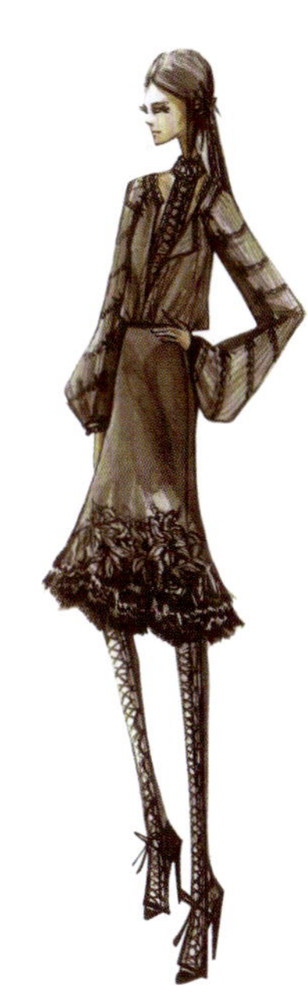

After the blinding psychedelics of the 1960s, grounding taci-turn browns entered the 1970s fashion world, symbolizing the earthiness of environmental awareness. In the 1980s, brown became more polished as the fierce "leopard look" raged. In the 1990s, the "Starbucks phenomenon" caused sumptuous coffee tones to move "into a position of promi-nence richly deserved," which still continues.[33]

Brooklyn-born designer Anne Klein, who brought sports-wear into the galaxy of high style, competed in the French fundraiser-cum-couture-battle held at Versailles in 1973, where "*les Américains*" stole the show. Despite beginning her fashion career at fifteen, she didn't develop her own manufacturing company until 1968 at age forty-five. In 1974, Klein died at fifty, but her aesthetic lived on in pieces like the brand's brown-spotted-leopard heels in Desert Palm, ideal for the urban jungle.

Elie Tahari conquered the cold, concrete city, literally going from a park bench to Park Avenue. After moving to New York from Israel with $300 in his pocket, Tahari experienced bouts of homelessness before starting his own company in 1973, which today has annual revenue of over $500 million. His success comes from not being "too fashion forward and not too conservative."[34] It's a fine line, but his Fall/Winter 2011 Coffee Liqueúr dress shows that he walks it with ease.

Educated at Parsons, Detroit-born Tracy Reese honed her trade working at Martine Sitbon, Perry Ellis, and Magaschoni before launching her own line. The internation-ally successful African-American designer was particularly excited for Fall 2011, her creativity sparked by a visit to a prestigious French fabric fair. Reese turned the knit fabric she discovered there into a cascading Teak sweater-cape worn over an accordion-pleated ankle-length skirt.

If the devil wears Prada, send us to hell! From 1913 until his death in 1958, Mario Prada sold luxury leather goods. The House then languished until his granddaughter Miuccia took over in 1977. With a doctorate in political science and five years as a professional mime, she seemed an unlikely candidate to revitalize the House. Yet, with the help of "business-shark-brained" Patrizio Bertelli, who later became her husband and company CEO, Prada became one of the world's most recognized luxury labels.[35] For Fall/Winter 2013, Prada crafted a Desert Palm brown crocodile coat (very *Super Fly*) with a similarly hued button-up and mid-calf-length skirt. Skirts have long been one of Prada's favorite garments, a "feminine symbol [that] you wear every day."[36]

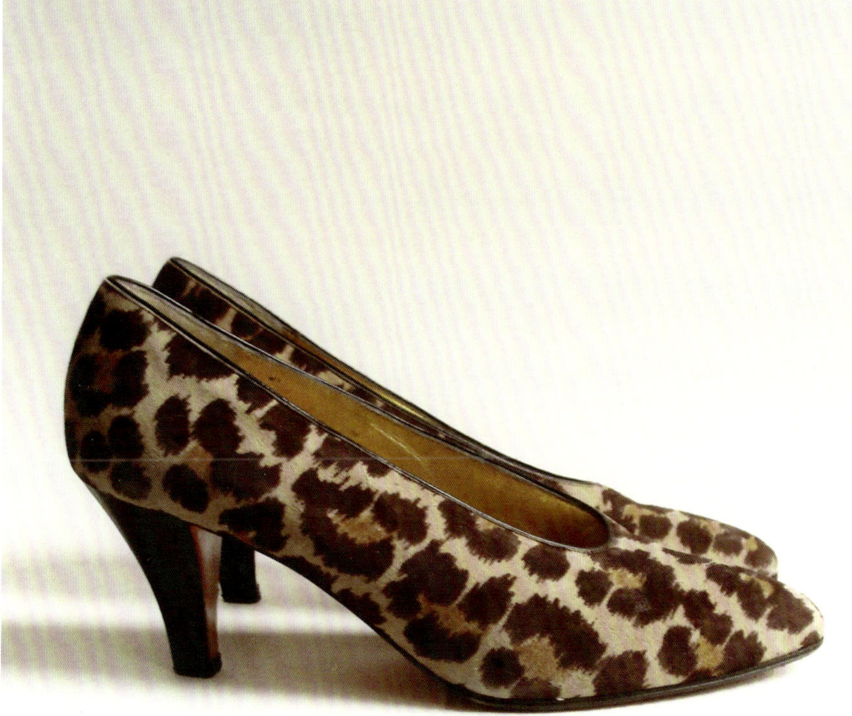

Camel

Warm, neutral brown tones are wardrobe essentials. In the late 1940s through the 1960s, high-end labels like Burberry, Traina-Norell, and Geoffrey Beene all adopted the toasty hue, as did MaxMara, Bill Blass, and Calvin Klein decades later.

Parsons not only boasts some of the best designers, but also the best dropouts. Norman Norell rarely attended his classes, instead designing for silent films in Long Island City, where he dressed Rudolph Valentino and Gloria Swanson. He later finished his education at Pratt and went on to be tutored by Hattie Carnegie for eleven years. Norell began working for Anthony Traina in 1941, accepting a lesser salary in exchange for being named on the label. In 1958, Norell designed a Toast-colored cashmere coat unexpectedly lined with sequins (to match those of the dress). Gifted to the Museum at FIT by Lauren Bacall, it is unlikely the Traina-Norell "subway" coat was ever worn underground.

In the 1990s, all hip teenagers knew the name "Todd Oldham" from supermodel Cindy Crawford's MTV show, *House of Style*. Crawford walked in the Texan-cum-New-Yorker's shows, along with "supers" Linda Evangelista and Kate Moss. Eschewing modesty, Oldham boasts, "We killed it every time. Our shows were really, really good."[37] Not one to follow fashion or trends, Oldham's 1997 Toasted Nut tweed suit and Camel-colored hat are still relevant and wearable fifteen years later.

For Spring/Summer 2000, Douglas Hannant ruminated, "At the end of the millennium, I'm feeling . . . bareness—a rebirth that begins with what is natural," hence his choice of the sunbaked tone.[38] Hannant, who anticipates the "clothing needs [of his customer] for every hour of the day," grasped that shades of Tawny Brown work for all of them.[39]

In 1981, thirty years after Achille Maramotti established Italian company MaxMara, Anna Marie Beretta designed 101801, the "codename" for their iconic Camel coat. The "under-the-radar" piece has been featured nearly every winter since.[40] For Fall/Winter 2012, the sixty-year-old label reinterpreted the piece by transforming it into a feminine belted jumpsuit *cucita a mano* (created by hand).[41]

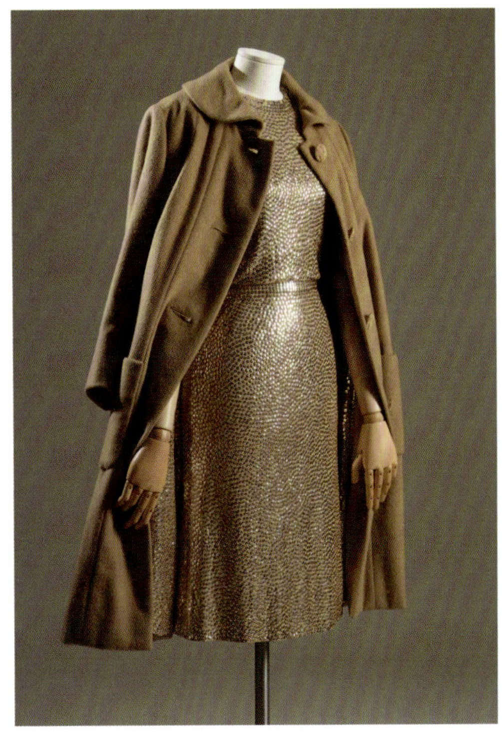

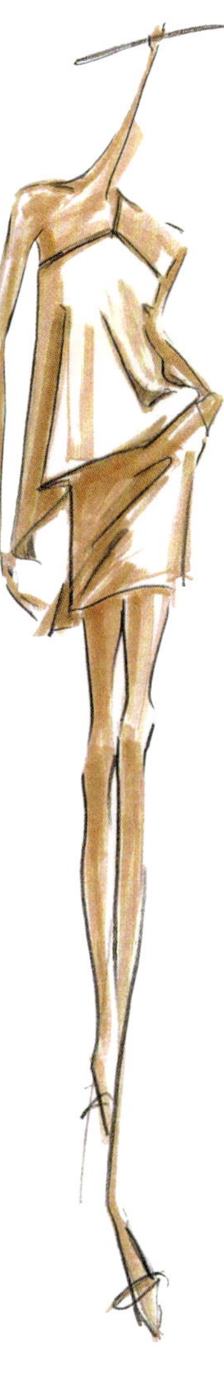

opposite, left
Cashmere coat over a silk
jersey dress with gold sequins
Norman Norell for Traina-Norell
circa 1958

opposite, right
Dress by Douglas Hannant
*Pantone 7th on Sixth Fashion
Color Report*
Spring 2000

left
Jumpsuit in double-faced cashmere
MaxMara
Fall/Winter 2012

right
Patterned tweed dress suit
with camel hat
Todd Oldham
Fall/Winter 1997

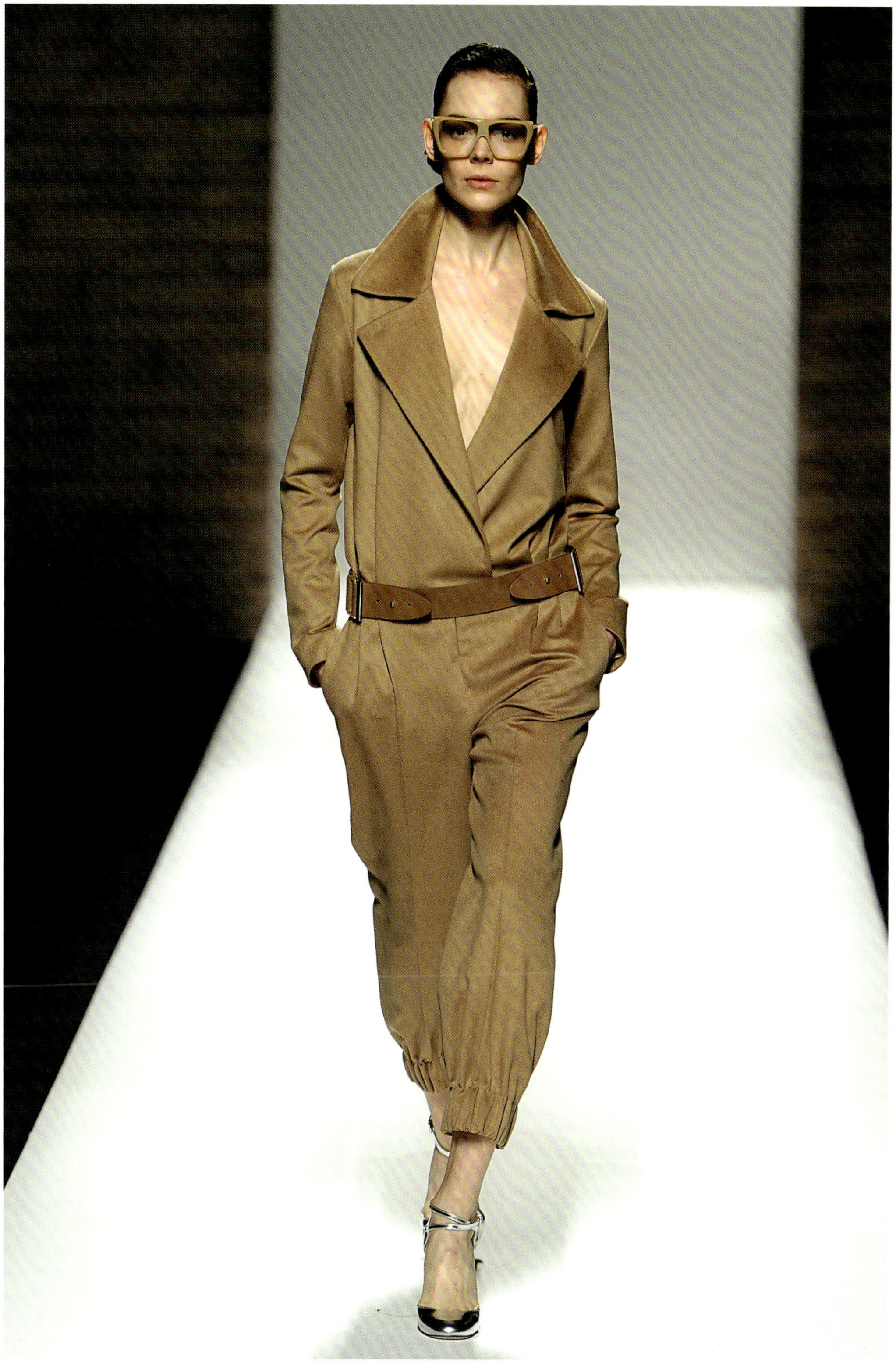

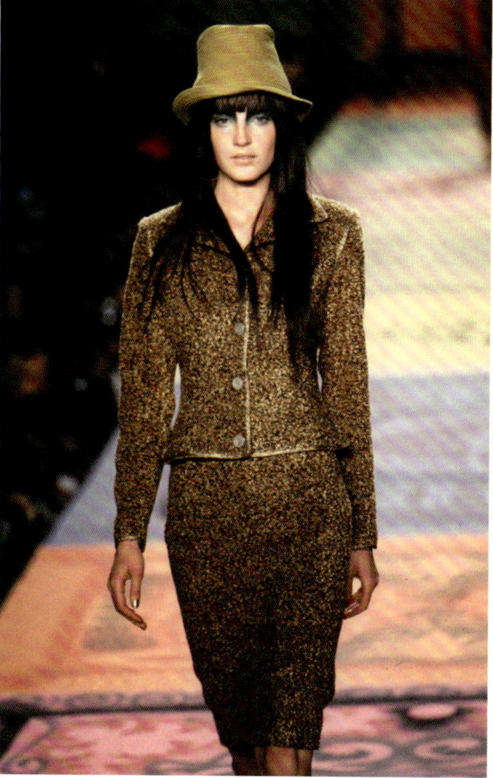

Heavenly Pink

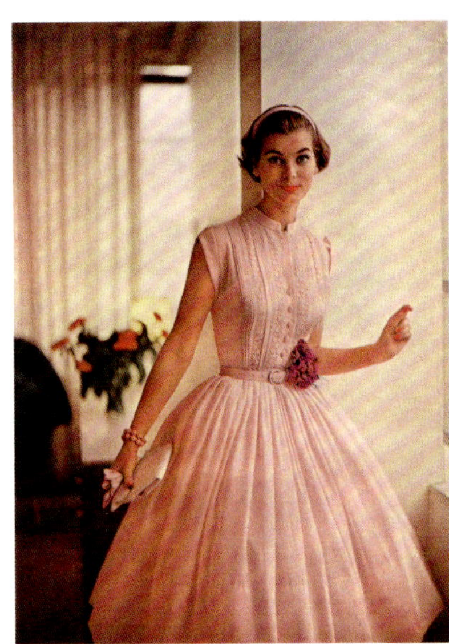

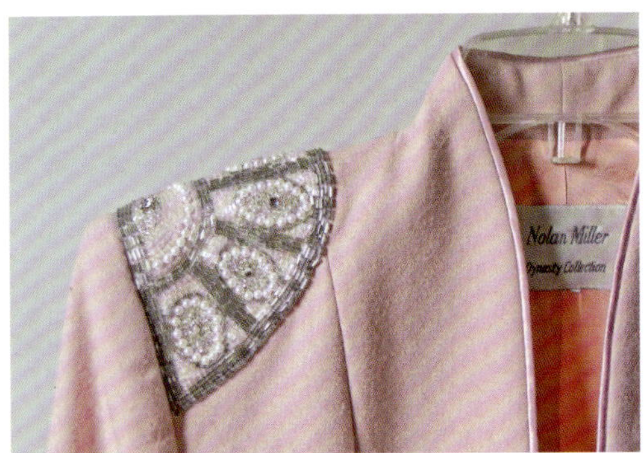

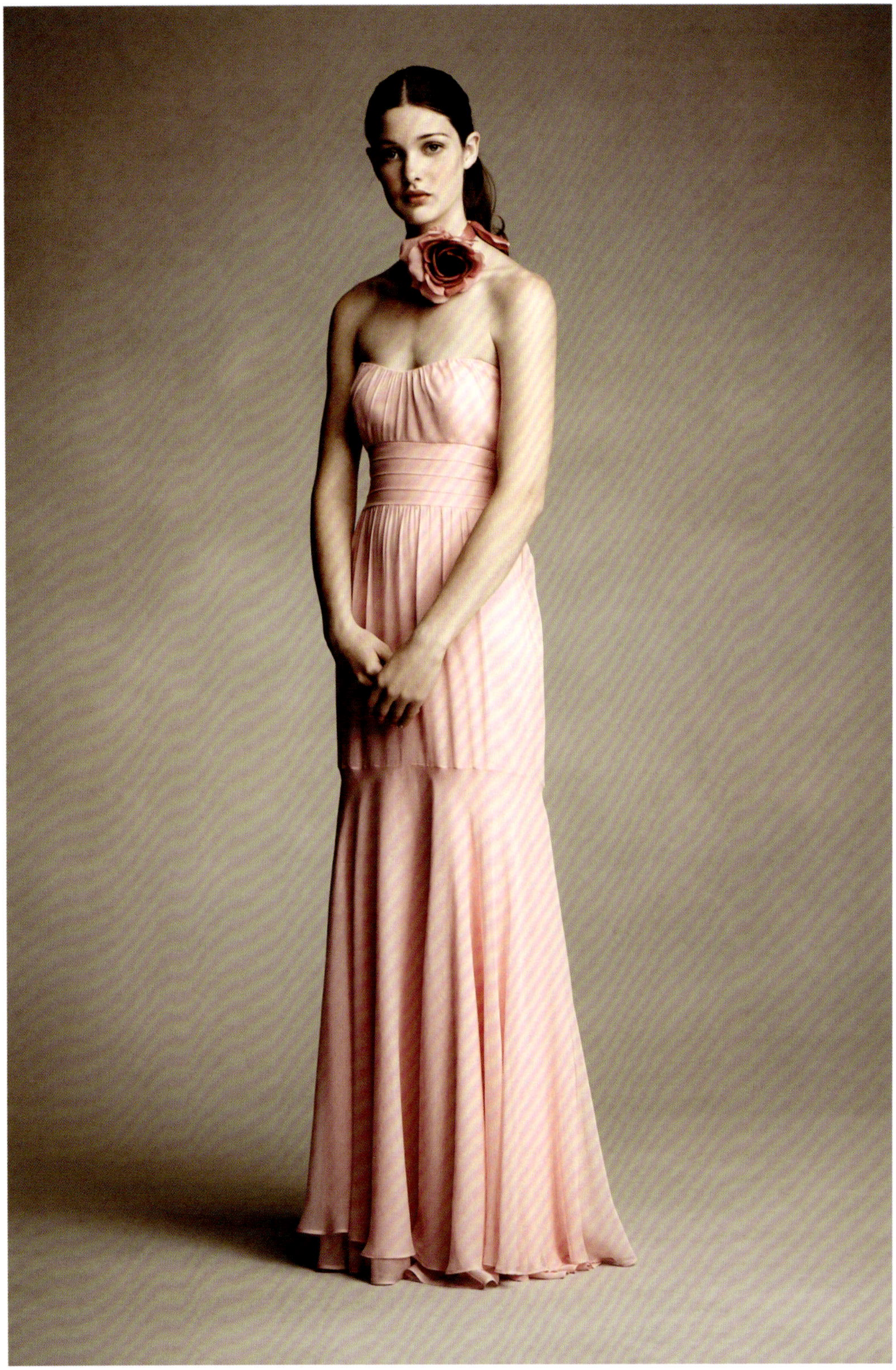

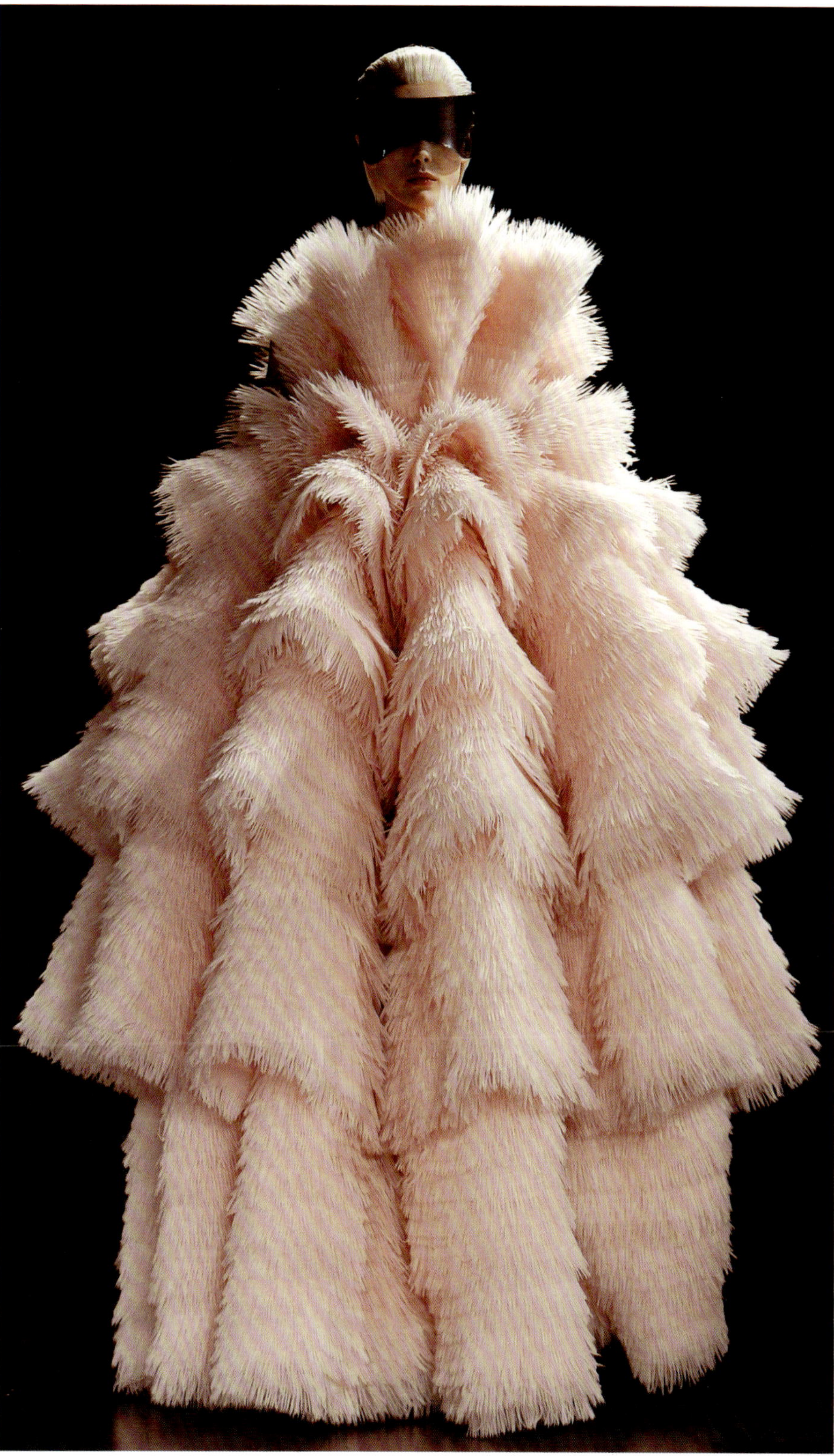

"I believe in pink. I believe in kissing, kissing a lot. I believe tomorrow is another day, and I believe in miracles."
—*Audrey Hepburn* [42]

In the 20th century, pink became the signature color of femininity: of little girls, baby dolls, ballerina slippers, and bridesmaid gowns. Over the years, Heavenly Pink has gone through a metamorphosis. In 1929, Madeleine Vionnet concocted a floaty chiffon confectionary, which would almost border on saccharine if it wasn't for its risqué neckline.

After WWII, a desperate race occurred to "normalize" gender roles. Hyper-femininity flourished. One must "Think Pink!" after all. R&K Originals' 1956 outfit perfectly encapsulates a look that was fashionable, feminine, and relatively affordable. The Manhattan-based company's slogan, "For the girl who knows clothes," reflects the pre-feminist era, when regardless of age, women were referred to as "girls."

The acid-fueled '60s didn't lend itself to the sweetness of Heavenly Pink, nor did the naturalistic '70s. But, by the '80s, powder pink was back with a punch. The female power suits of the '80s, often dazzled with sequins, were the armor of working women. Even women outside the corporate world began to adopt the clothing style. Designer Nolan Miller's *Dynasty* costumes communicated a uniquely American female power: "When she walks down the hall, you may not know who she is, but you know she's rich and you know you better get out of the way." [43]

Like Miller, Alexander McQueen also designed for ferocious women, but following his suicide, the future of his label was uncertain. Humble and hardworking, Sarah Burton had been at McQueen's side since 1997 and continues to translate his vision to the world today. Burton's "Pink Fluff" gown honors McQueen's fascination with nature as well as the surreal, while simultaneously allowing Burton's own female voice to be heard. Burton's "soft futurism" turned model Frida Gustavsson into a sci-fi heroine clad in "a huge, pastel-pink dress undulating into eight tiers of hundreds of minute chiffon tucks." [44]

Bridesmaid dresses are usually tragic, worn and then ideally burned. Seeing the low bar and wide-open market, Pennsylvania-born Jenny Yoo felt called to create flattering attire for those walking down the aisle but not headed to the altar. The Parsons graduate's empire-waist crinkle-chiffon "Hannah" gown in Pink Dogwood features a bias flounce that shapes and softens the silhouette.

Shocking Pink

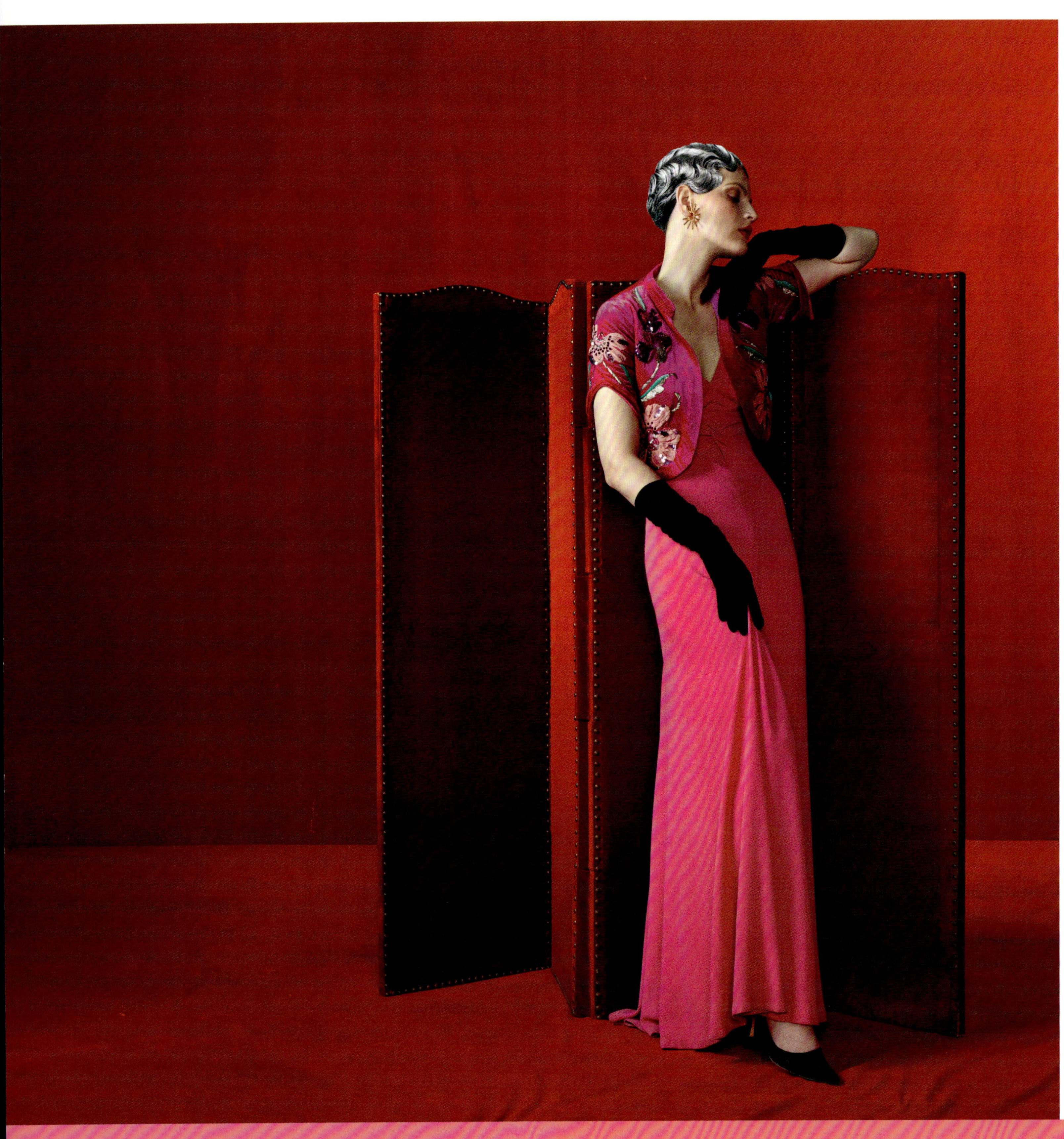

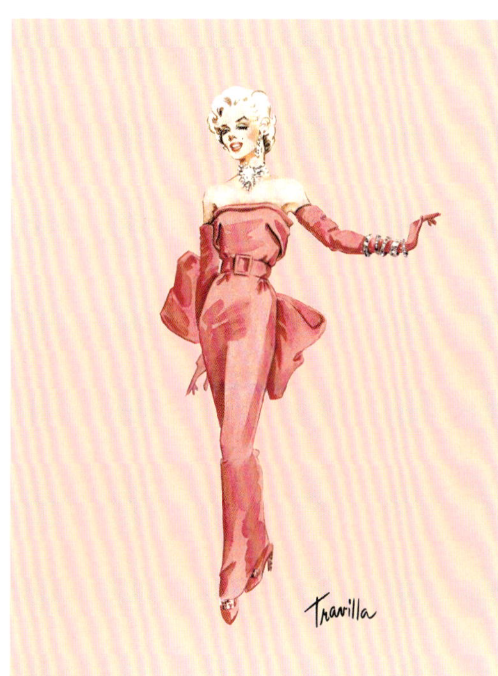

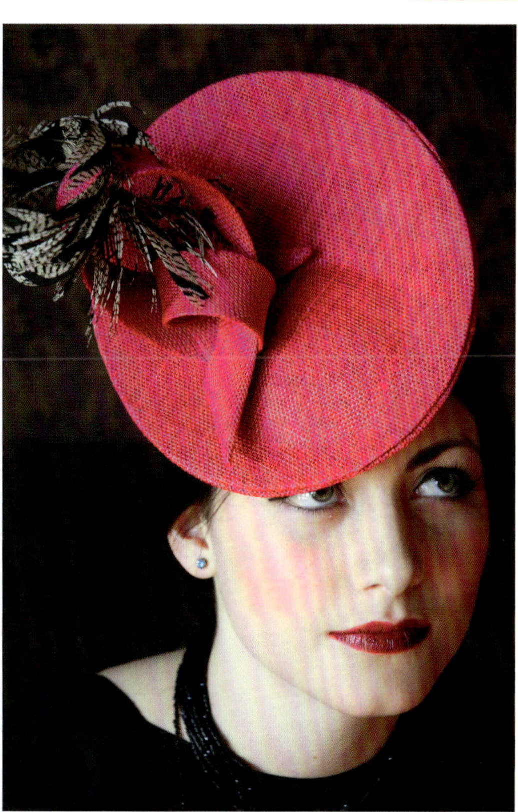

It all started with a 17.47-carat Cartier diamond. The Shocking Pink hue of heiress Daisy Fellowes's famous rock, the *Tête de Bélier*, inspired designer Elsa Schiaparelli's 1937 collection. Fashion journalist Betty Wilson may have been the first person to be shocked by the color. After seeing the vibrant hue on the catwalk, she wrote, "Schiaparelli is 'mad, and bad, and wild,'" though that "arresting pink . . . can be tremendously good."[45] Schiap considered the tint "bright, impossible, life-giving, like all the light and the birds and the fish in the world put together."[46] Legendary fashion taste-maker Diana Vreeland loved "Schiaparelli's pink, the pink of the Incas."[47] It became Schiaparelli's signature color, adorning her Shocking perfume, for which Leonor Fini designed a bottle in the buxom shape of Mae West. While the mythic diamond is long lost, the color lives on.

Shocking Pink flew from 1930s Paris to 1950s Hollywood, and once again diamonds were involved. Just before she was due to film her iconic number in *Gentlemen Prefer Blondes*, "Diamonds Are a Girl's Best Friend," Marilyn Monroe's nude calendar was exposed to the press. In a panic, the studio frantically called costume designer William Travilla. "We've got to [actually] *dress* her!" Travilla remembers them saying. "So, I made a *very covered* dress, a very famous pink dress, with a big bow in the back."[48] Monroe adored the dress and subsequently wrote him, "Billy Dear, Please dress me forever. I love you, Marilyn."[49]

Always moving in and out of favor, Hot Pink enjoyed a stint on Rudi Gernreich's mod pantyhose in 1971 and a DayGlo shout-out in the high-end, graffiti-inspired collections of Stephen Sprouse from 1983 to 1985. In 2011, the already scandalous color was taken to new heights of eroticism when Christian Louboutin featured it on a pair of stilettos with a six-and-a-half-inch heel and a two-and-a-half-inch platform. Negatively referred to as *stripper heels*, their unapologetic sexuality was nonetheless embraced, even during daylight hours, by women who didn't want to wait until nightfall to be shocking.

For those looking to be wacky and not salacious, Fandango Pink does the trick, especially in the form of outlandish millinery. Yorkshire hat-maker Justine Bradley-Hill keeps the Anglo tradition for wild headpieces alive with her "Sinamay Disk" adorned with a twisted knot and pheasant feather, an ode to the English countryside.

Poppy Red

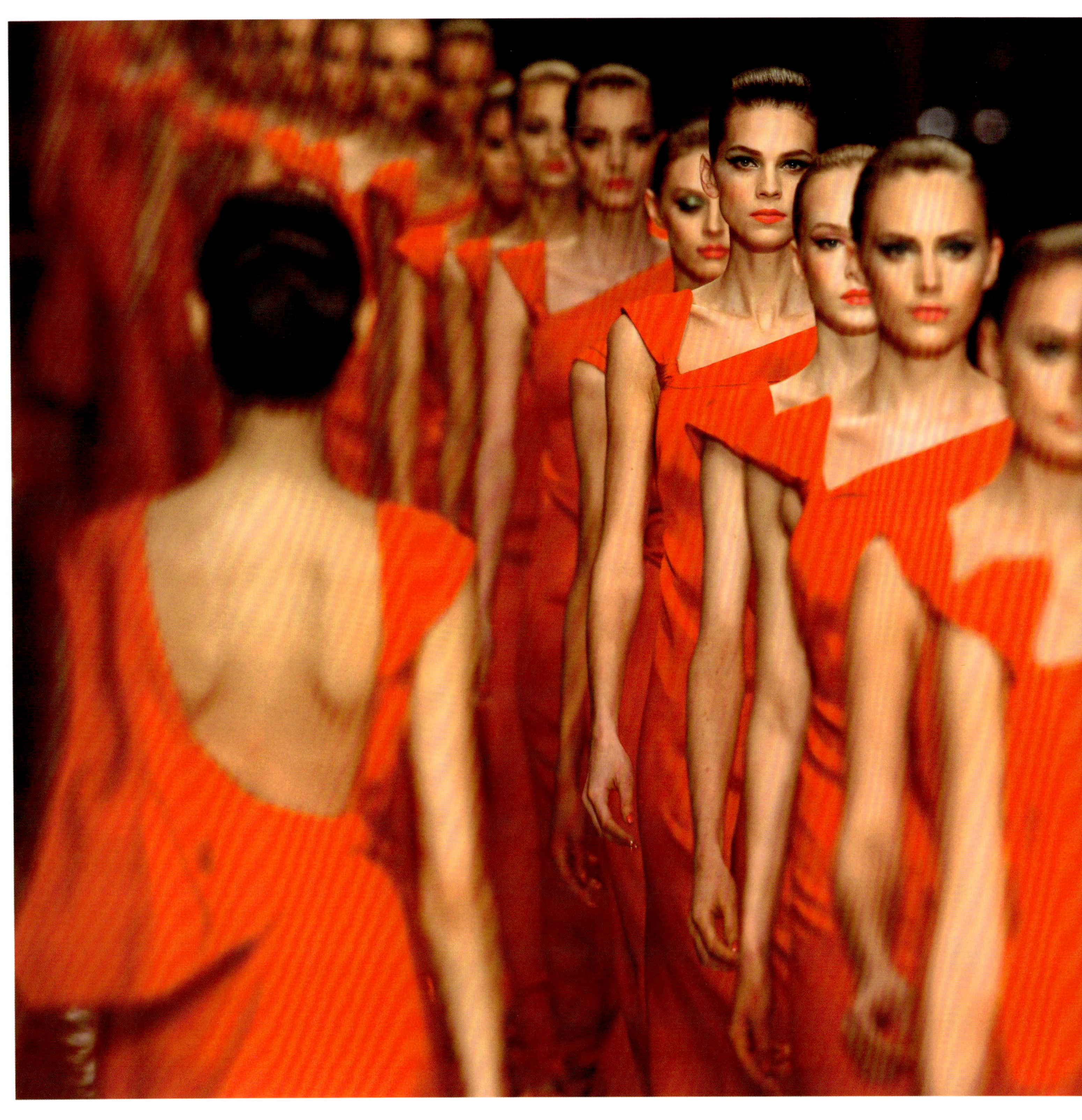

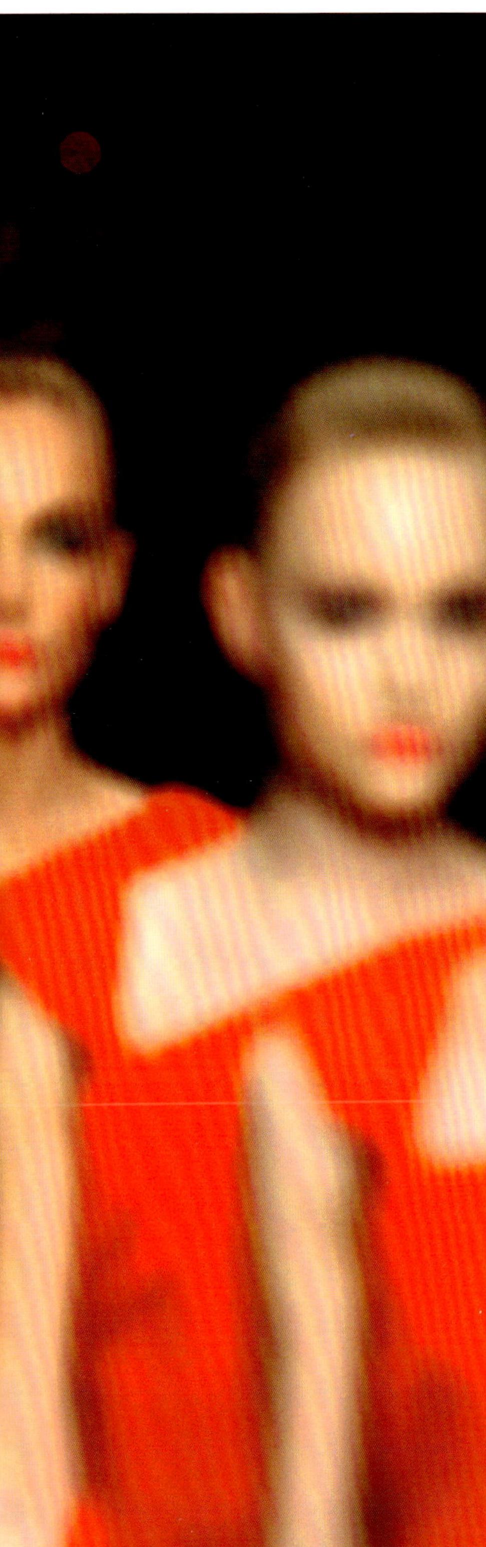

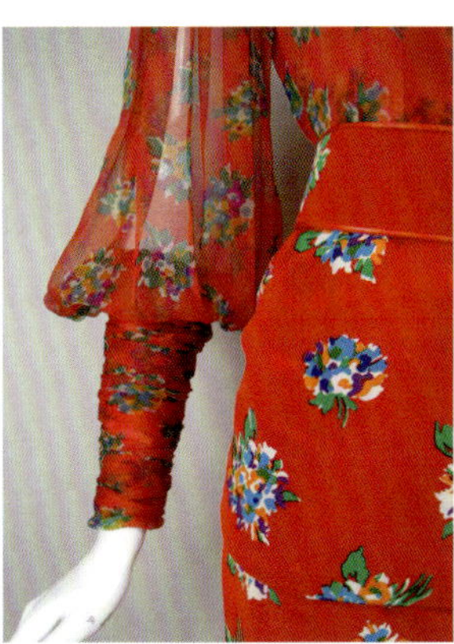

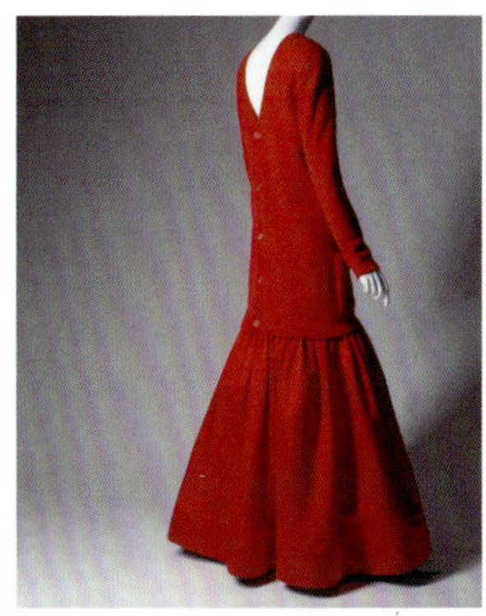

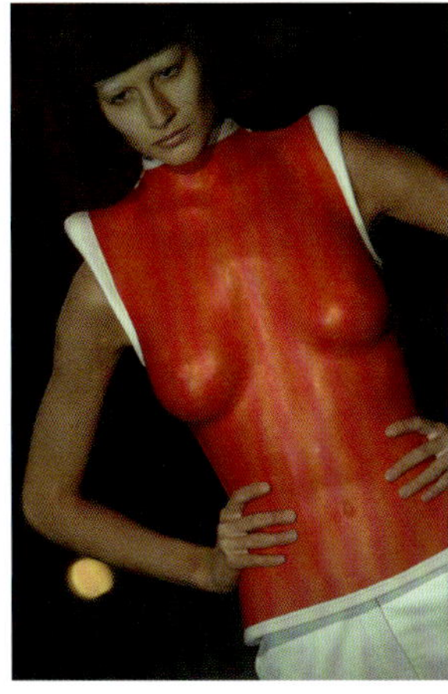

"Red is a fascinating colour; the colour of life, blood, and death, passion and love; the ultimate cure for sadness."
—*Valentino*[50]

Red is show-stopping and eye-popping. In the 1980s, First Lady Nancy Reagan was so smitten with James Galanos's designs that they became omnipresent in her wardrobe. She wore his pieces to official portraits, social functions, state occasions, and two inaugurations. As a result, "Reagan Red" came to symbolize power, conservatism, and democracy.

Designer Bill Blass worshipped red, believing it to be the ultimate go-to color. He quipped, "When in doubt, wear red." Having never worked at any of the Parisian couture Houses, Blass is known as the quintessential American designer. He was a fixture of Seventh Avenue and won over the uptown "ladies who lunch" crowd, including Pat Buckley and couture-collecting Nan Kempner, who referred to him as "like the second coming of Christ" and worshipped him.[51]

In 1999, Alexander McQueen crafted a leather torso garment in High Risk Red during his time at Givenchy. While the irascible McQueen never meshed with the heritage or the oeuvre of Givenchy, his work for the House is clearly a precursor to his eponymous label established after his departure. While McQueen's work as a whole is brilliantly inflammatory and disturbing, this specific piece is derivative of François-Xavier and Claude Lalanne–slash–Yves Saint Laurent's 1969 bronze breastplate. Yet, the fitted bodice in pressed leather illustrates McQueen's skill, ingenuity, and ability to take fashion a step further: ramping up the in-your-face sexuality of the piece by making it a devilish red.

Valentino birthed his very own shade of "Valentino Red," which combines the primary color with "notes of deep orange to intensify its tone and impact."[52] In 1949, Valentino Clemente Ludovico Garavani became infatuated with the hue during a trip to Barcelona, and it became his lifelong obsession. A decade later, he showed his first red dress, "Fiesta," a playful strapless cocktail frock made of draped tulle and adorned with four rows of rosettes. For his final haute couture show in 2008, Valentino made his eager audience wait in mounting anticipation, displaying seventy-four gowns in white, pistachio, and pale blue. For the finale of the show—and his career—his seventy-fifth look featured the entire cast of thirty models walking the runway in fiery red gowns. It was a cathartic end for "the Sheik of chic."[53]

Grenadine

Ancient cultures, from the Hebrews to the Hindus, believed the nectar of pomegranates enhanced fertility. Bartenders may use grenadine syrup for its tart, sweet taste, but designers from the Prohibition Era through today use the color for its sex appeal.

Jean Charles Worth's 1926 rhinestone-encrusted Mandarin Red dress was befitting of the era's continuous party, and its color likely masked the spills of any similarly hued beverages. And though the Great Depression instantaneously killed the mood, glamour lived on in the 1930s. In November 1934, *Harper's Bazaar* illustrator Reynaldo Luza captured a "Chinese Red" dress by Eva Lutyens (neé Lywbrinska). While the fame of her father-in-law, architect Sir Edwin Lutyens, exceeded her own over time, in 1940, Eva Lutyens was given the same repute as other London couturiers like Norman Hartnell and Victor Stiebel.

Two-time-Oscar-nominated costume designer Irene Lentz, who dressed Lana Turner and Doris Day, isn't known as well as Edith Head or Adrian, but her work possesses a timeless Hollywood allure. Lentz's ombre gown, which appeared to have been dip-dyed in Grenadine, was featured prominently in a dance scene from the 1948 film *Easter Parade* starring Fred Astaire and Judy Garland.

Starting in 1967, Elio Fiorucci quickly showed "the world a 'new' Italy, an Italy that could set trends." His New York store, considered the first concept shop, was beloved by friend Andy Warhol and nicknamed "The Daytime Studio 54."[54] In the late '70s and early '80s, Fiorucci transformed rain boots into something to love. By cropping waders to slightly above the ankles, lining them in wool, and adding a kitten heel, the second-generation Italian shoemaker's "Love Boots" in Fiesta red made women look forward to rainy days.

Vany and Thando Mangaliso's South African–based label Sun Goddess presents "a regal Africa . . . one of legends, kings and queens, gods and goddesses."[55] Though self-exoticizing, the label refutes stereotypes of a poverty-ridden continent devoid of high fashion, instead offering and defining African luxury. The pair explains, "We make African clothing for African people. As much as we follow international trends, we . . . combine them with African trends, and we make something quite contemporary and wearable for African women," like their 2008 Cherry Tomato–colored, gold-embroidered strapless dress.[56]

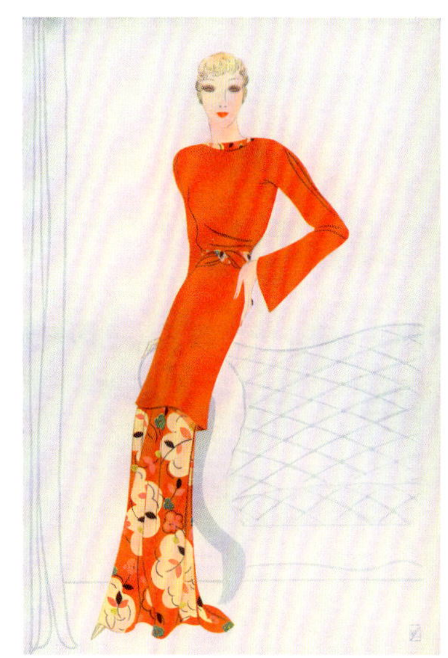

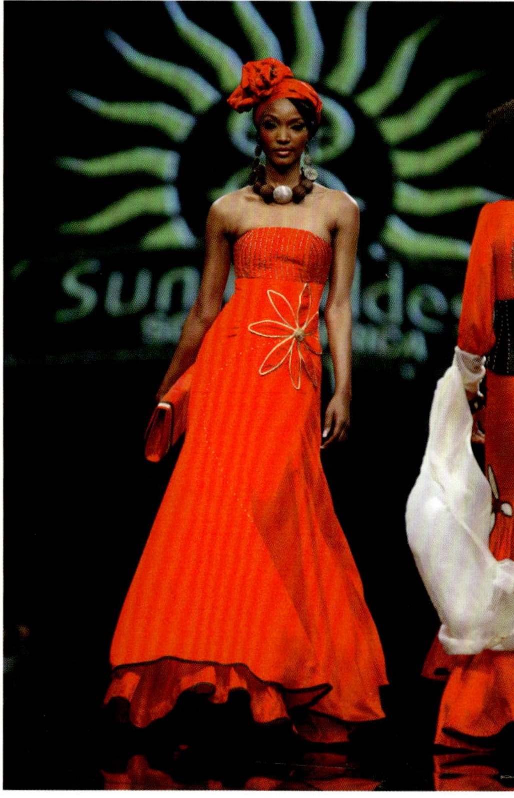

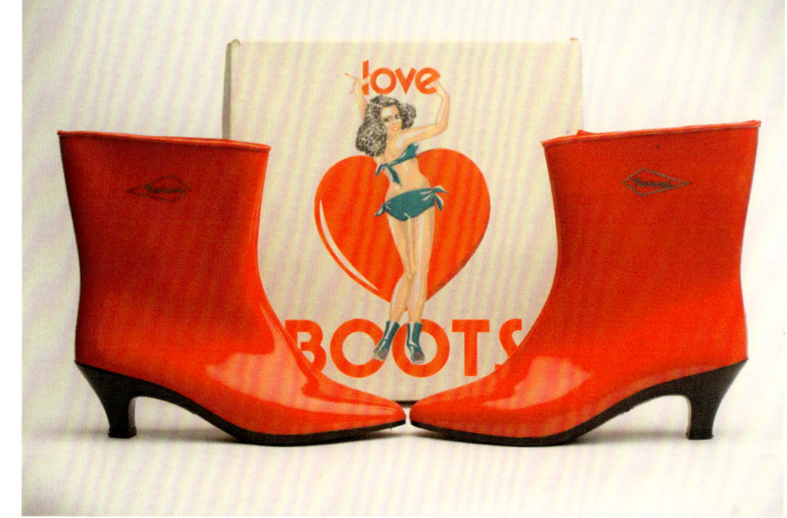

opposite, top left
Dinner gown with a tunic of heavy
chiffon romaine and a bias-cut floor-
length skirt featuring a floral pattern
that also appears along the neckline
and waist
Eva Lutyens
Illustration by Reynaldo Luza for
Harper's Bazaar
1934

opposite, top right
Silk "Bomvana Khamanga" gown
with matching purse and headpiece
Vanya and Thando Mangaliso for
Sun Goddess
Spring 2008

opposite, bottom
Rubber "Love Boots"
Elio Fiorucci
circa 1979

below
Feathered gown for Ann Miller
in *Easter Parade*
Irene Lentz 1949

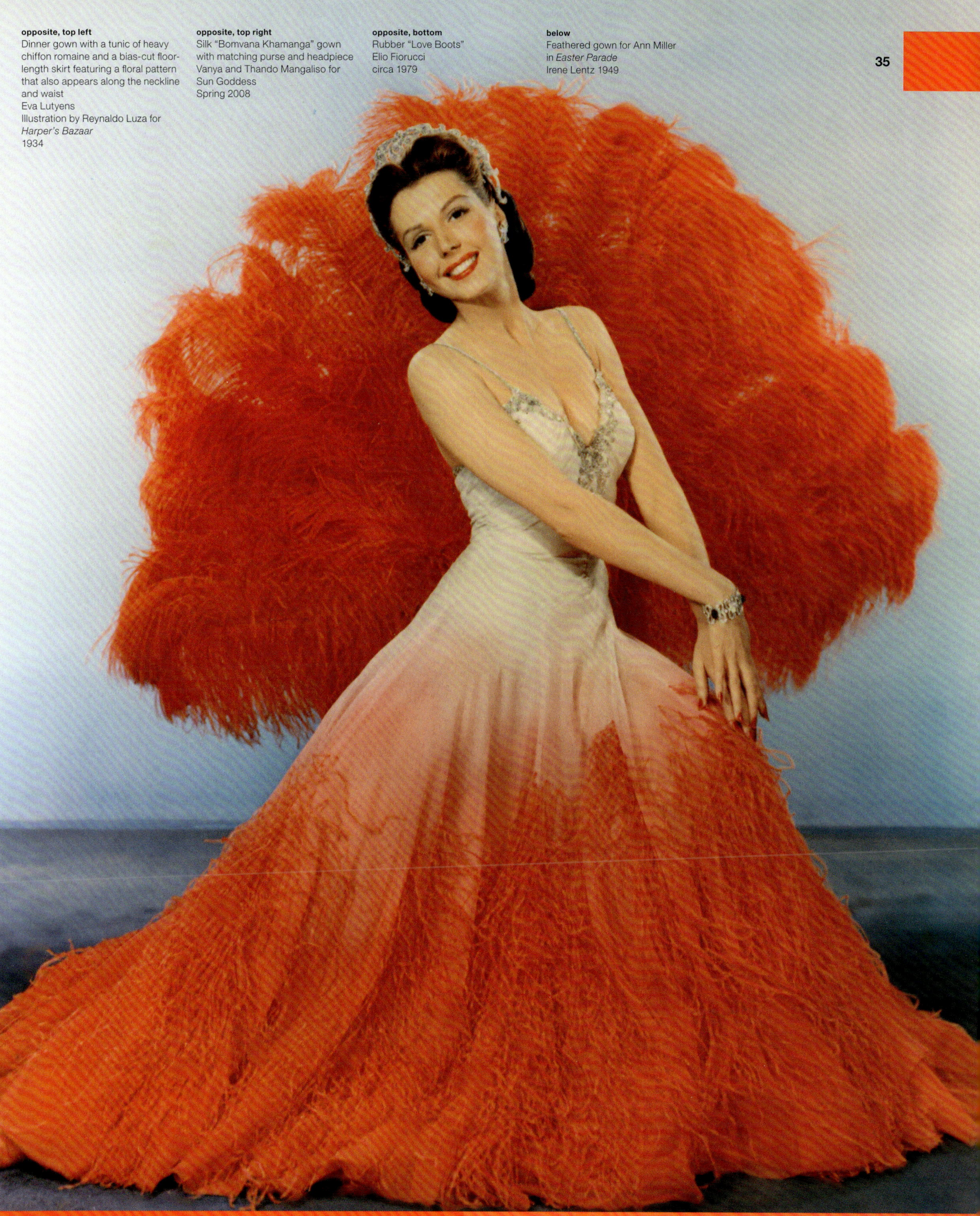

Fiesta
PANTONE 17-1564

Mandarin Red
PANTONE 17-1562

Crimson

For Fall 2004, designers began to move away from the puritanical color palette that became the norm following 9/11 by reintroducing Scarlet and Crimson. This deeper red, with its blue undertones, encompassed the darkness of the time, while simultaneously beginning to depart from it. A dramatic, pulse-quickening red (in the cochineal family) has captured hearts of textiles artists as early as the 2nd century BC and was just as fashionable in AD 2004. While New York designers didn't trace their inspiration back as far as ancient South America, their impetus for utilizing the color did stem from a past more far-reaching than usual.

The draping capes, hoods, and mantles worn by actual knights during the Crusades and the garb of Geoffrey of Monmouth's AD 1150 character Merlin inspired designer Yeohlee Teng, who aptly believes that "clothes have magic."[57] New-Zealander-turned-New-Yorker Rebecca Taylor was similarly inspired by mythological unicorns and dragons, like those featured in the AD 1440 tapestry *Wild Men and Moors*, woven with a distinct Crimson background. Wall hangings from the Renaissance also inspired nonconformist Nicole Miller; however, she eclectically mixed that inspiration with a Victorian aesthetic and "a hint of [modern] military."

Rather than pulling from medieval textiles, *Clueless* costumer Jill Stuart, Barneys-window-dresser-turned-dress-designer Douglas Hannant, and Max Azria of BCBG ("*Bon Chic, Bon Genre*") thought of brilliant gems when choosing their collections' reds. Hannant asserted that, like rubies, "it's the woman that you want to shine."[58] While that triplet equated red with the luxury of jewels, Carolina Herrera mused on 1930s Swiss luxury winter resorts and the chic garb worn near the lounge fireplaces. Duo Mark Badgley and James Mischka drew on that luxurious era in New York when El Morocco and the Stork Club were hopping with screen stars, aristocrats, and high society. Badgley's confidence in the Lipstick Red pieces overflowed, saying, "One zip and you're glamorous!"[59] A plethora of designers were enamored with Rococco Red. Peter Som was entranced by its "rich luxury,"[60] Carmen Marc Valvo by its "glamour,"[61] and Ralph Lauren by its "drama."[62] For his Louis Vuitton collection, the ever-eclectic Marc Jacobs combined the Scarlet of Scottish plaid with references to disparate painters: James Tissot and Tsuguharu Foujita. For Fall 2004, without question, red hit the mark.

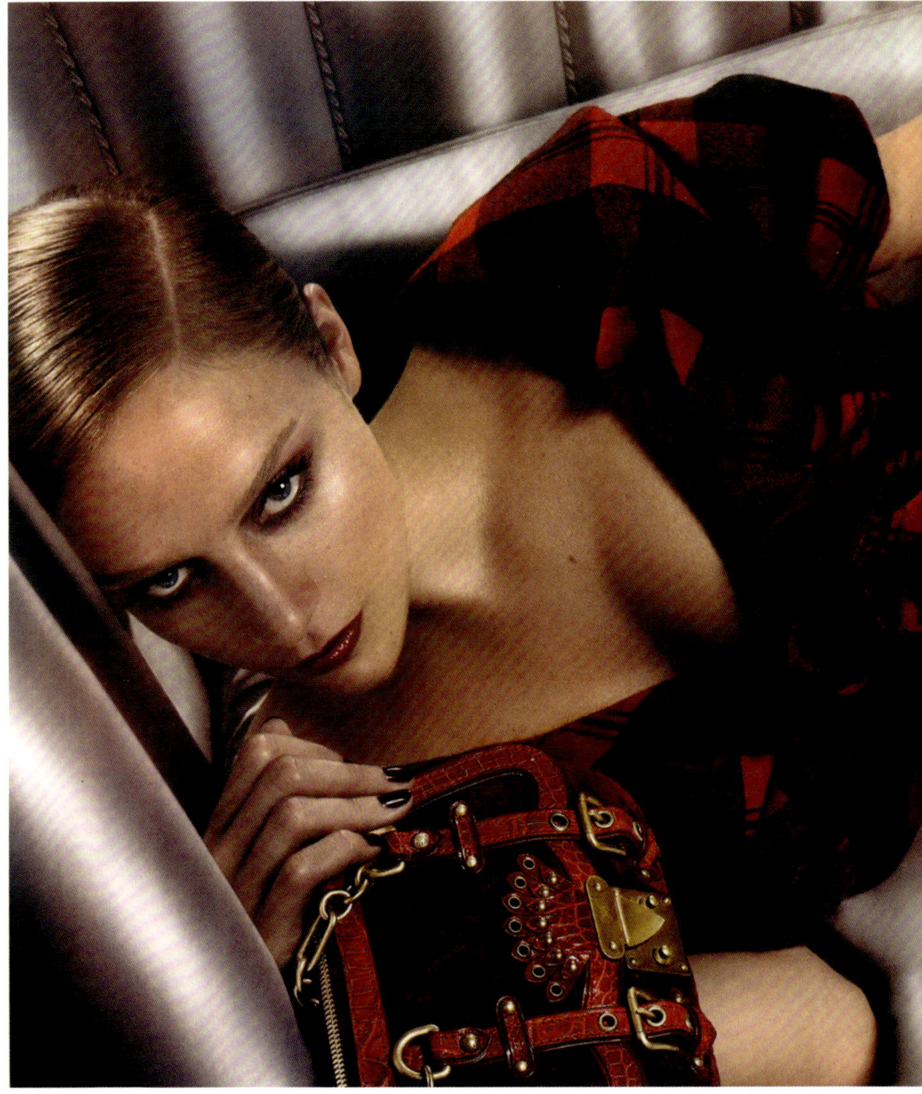

left
Print ad featuring Chloë Sevigny
Louis Vuitton
Fall/Winter 2004

right
Gown
Badgley Mischka
Fall/Winter 2004

bottom left
Coat and dress
Douglas Hannant
Fall 2004

bottom right
Jacket
Ralph Lauren
Fall/Winter 2004

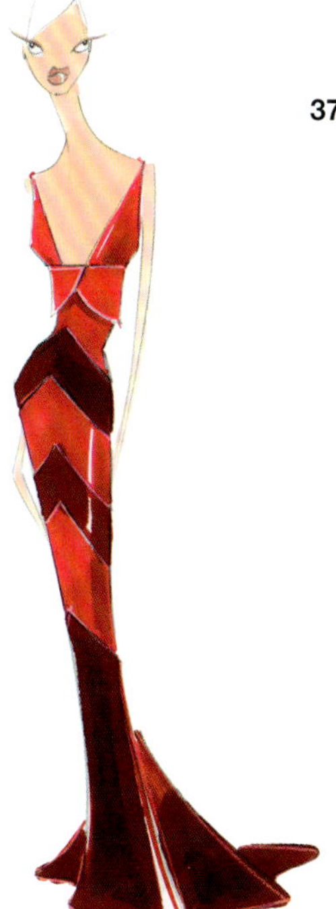

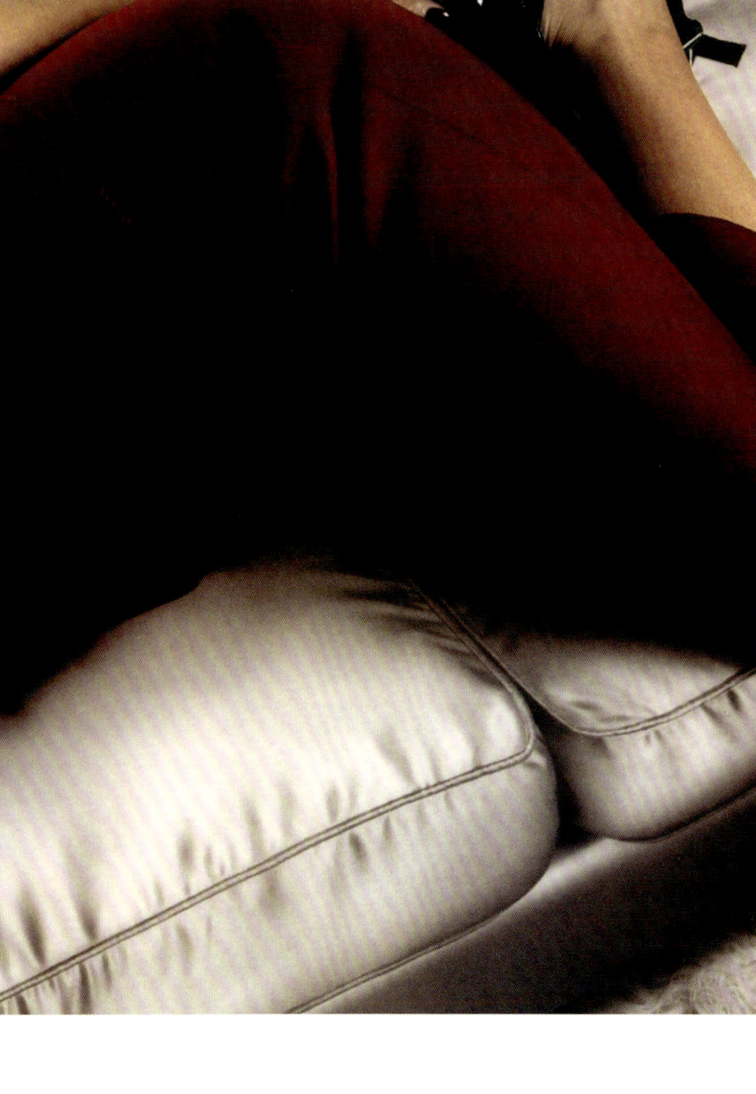

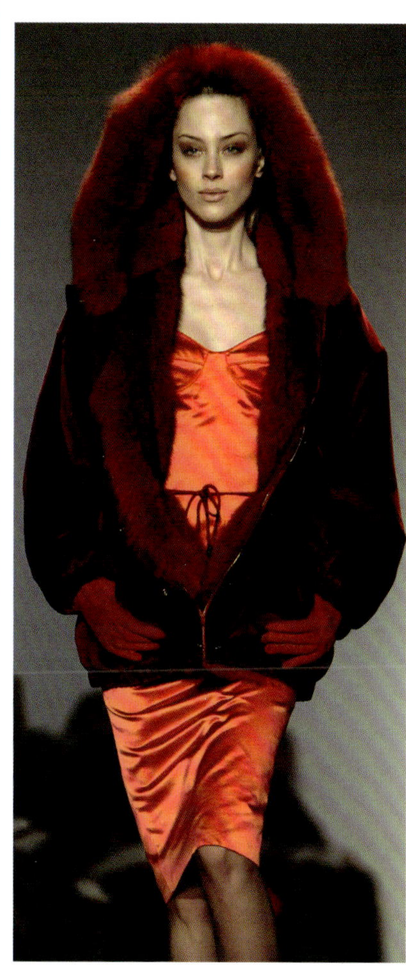

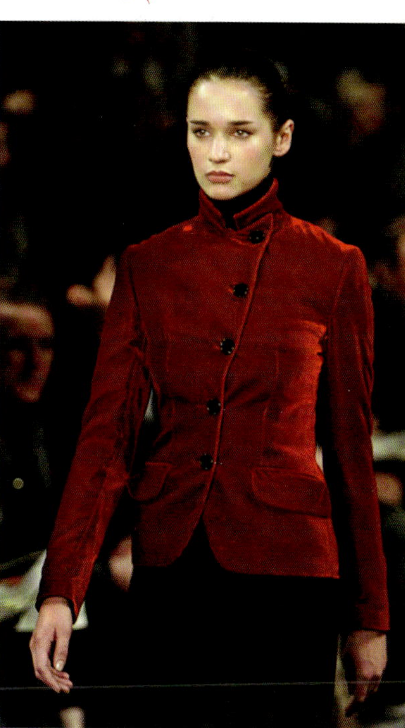

Ruby Wine

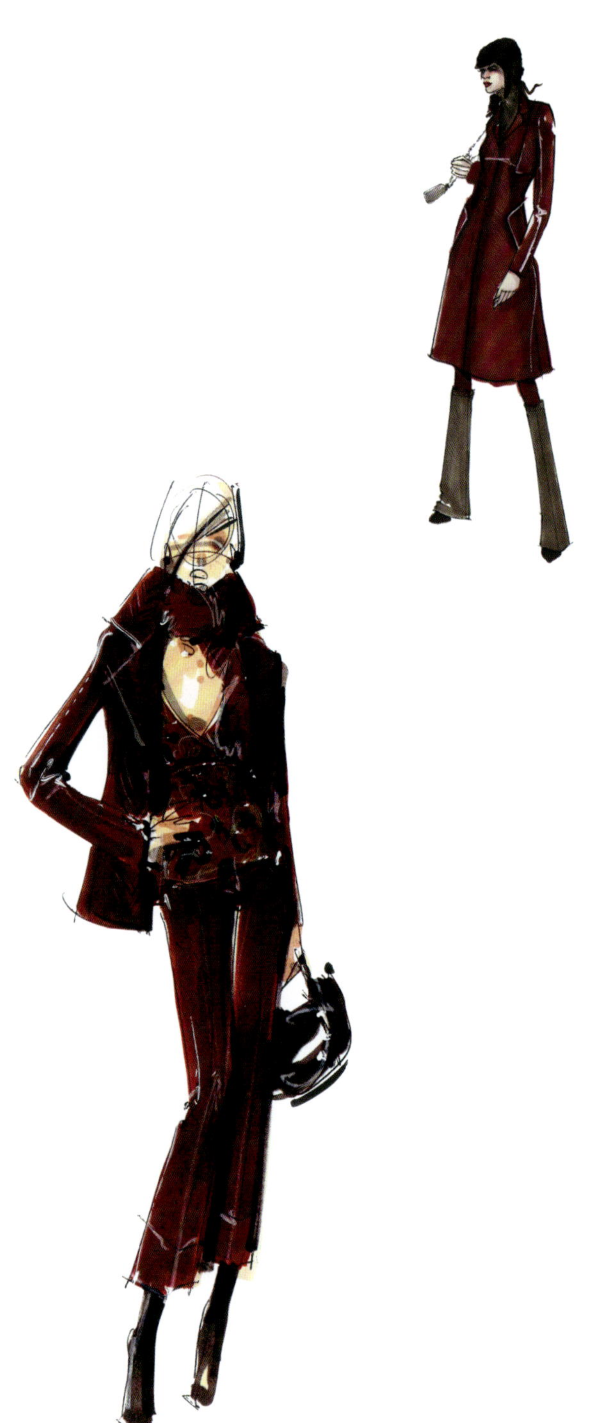

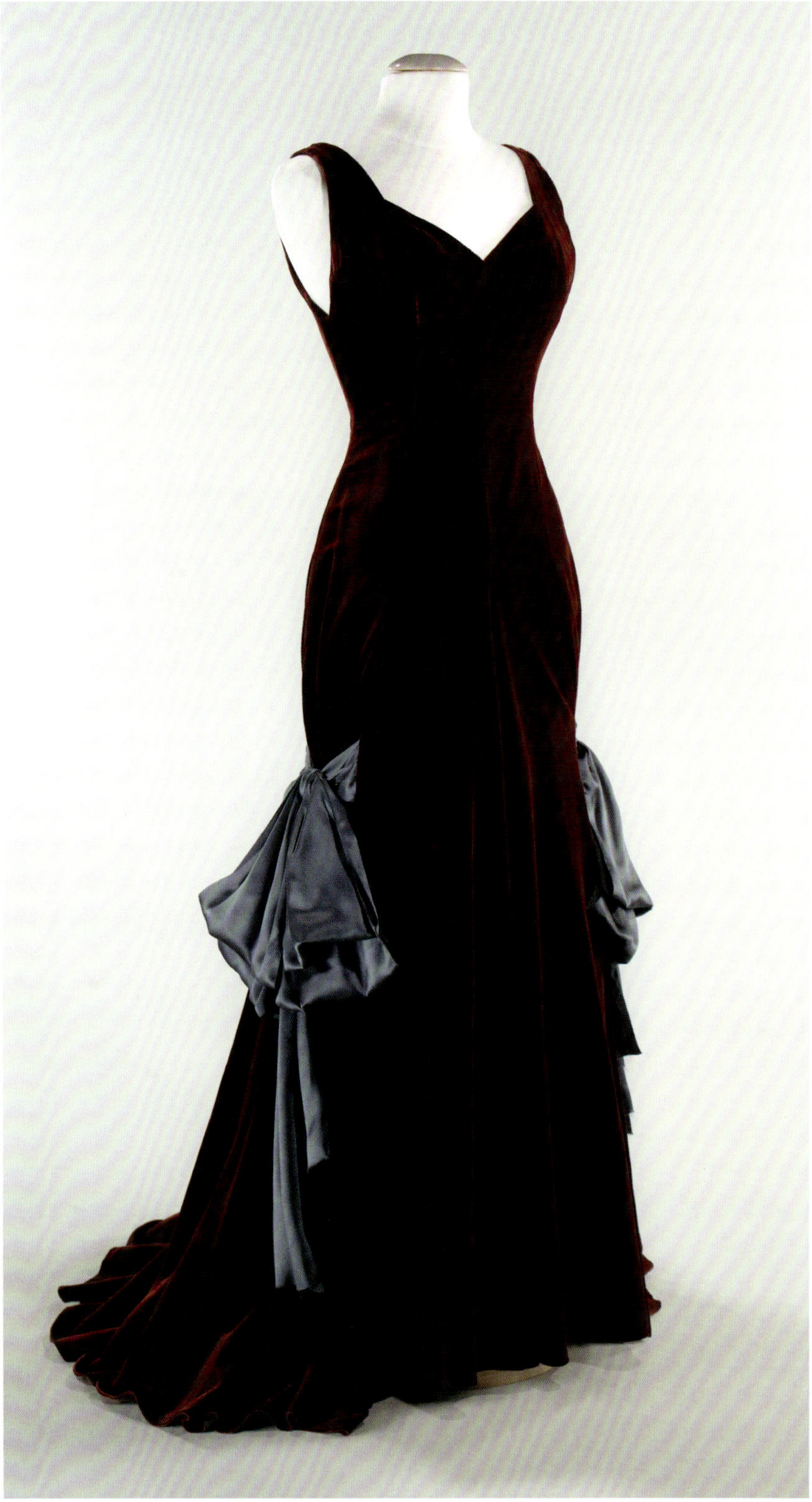

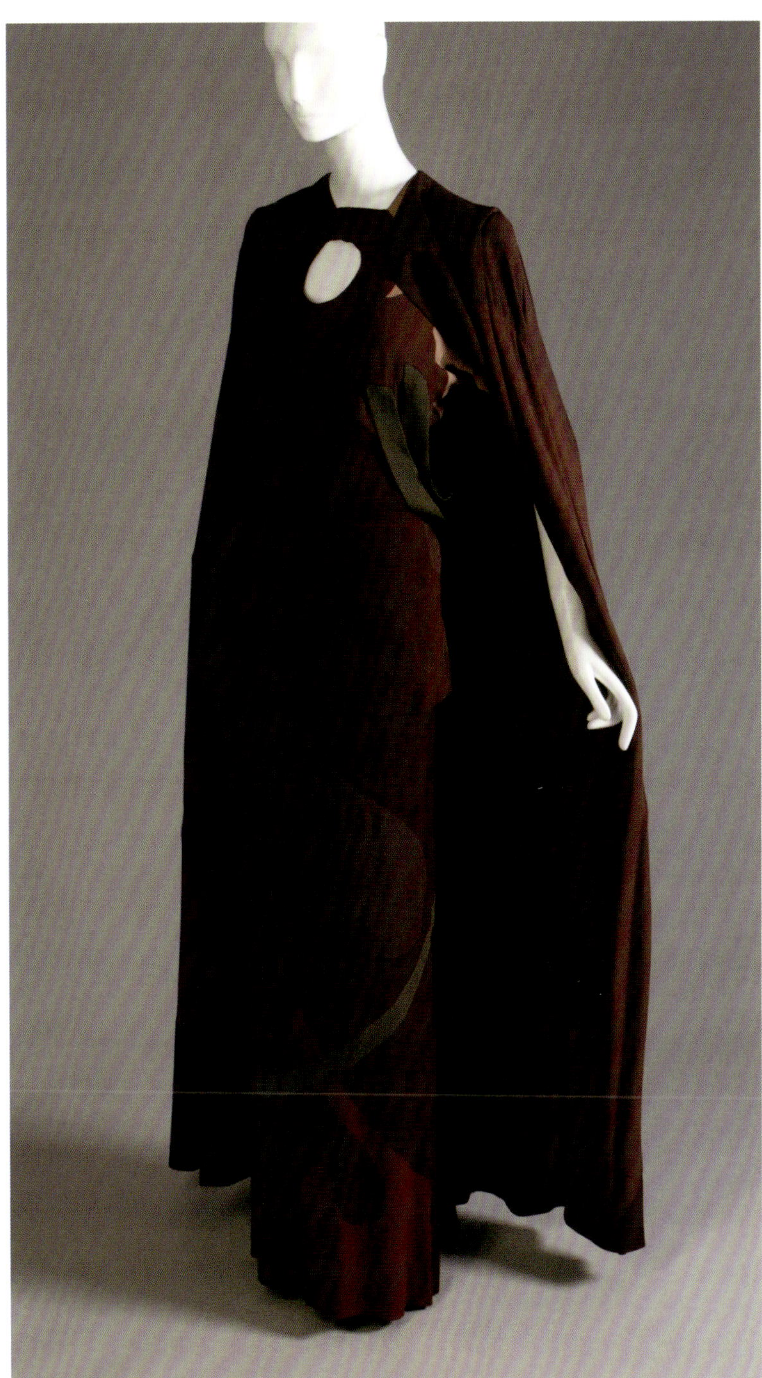

This rich jewel tone is the color most favored by designers who are nearly iconoclastic in their love of simplicity. It speaks for itself—no furbelows needed.

In the 1930s, Elizabeth Hawes outspokenly said "to hell with" Parisian fashion supremacy.[63] An outspoken advocate of American dress reform, Hawes begged the public: "Buy it because it's right . . . not because it's green or blue, not because Patou showed it last month, not because everyone in New York is wearing it, not because *Vogue* tells you it's chic. Buy it because you'll wear it with pleasure for several years." Women's rights advocate Elinor S. Gimbel heeded Hawes's advice and purchased her Fall/Winter 1937 Syrah-colored silk gown with contrasting gray-blue ties at the lower hip, which she later donated to the Brooklyn Museum.

Born Adrian Greenberg in Connecticut, Parsons-educated Adrian was a "star who dressed stars."[64] He transformed Greta Garbo, Joan Crawford, and Jean Harlow into glamorous screen goddesses, and in doing so, turned Hollywood into the Paris of America. In 1941, Adrian left MGM and established his own label. Adrian's rayon crepe dress consists of five varying shades of Cabernet reds, over-dyed to complement each other. Dated between 1944 and 1945, the gown was created during Adrian's period of fascination with modern art. In keeping with that, Adrian loathed American women's penchant for over-accessorizing. Adrian ultimately inspired designers decades later, such as Azzedine Alaïa, Christian Lacroix, Tom Ford, Elie Saab, and Thierry Mugler.

Designer Shelly Steffee, who got her start at Liz Claiborne and Tahari before launching her label in 1999, sought "pure and true" colors like Tawny Port for her Fall 2005 collection, inspired by luxury automobiles from the 1930s.

Spoiler alert: There is no Ellen Tracy. Linda Allard has designed the label since 1962, when owner Herbert Gallen hired her right out of college. Similar to the views of Elizabeth Hawes, Allard believes "the extreme end of fashion is over-rated . . . it doesn't mean anything to a lot of women."[65] Allard's conservative, wearable separates are made without "glitz or sleaze," illustrated by her Fall 2005 Ruby Wine pantsuit with matching top and scarf.

Rose Wine

Blame it on those sexy vampires. *Twilight*, *True Blood*, and *The Vampire Diaries* led to Fall/Winter 2012–2013 catwalks (from Yves Saint Laurent to Rodarte, Acne to Maison Martin Margiela) being splattered in macabre oxblood. The following autumn, there was a slight departure from the sanguine color, embracing Rose Wine hues, with grape undertones rather than muddy ones. This fermented color, which only gets better with age, symbolizes maturity, courage, and strength. Designers like Christopher Bailey, Andrew Gn, and Frida Giannini invited their clients to become indulgently intoxicated with the delicious color.

Christopher Bailey designed an empire around Burberry's iconic trench coat. Bailey, who was appointed creative director of Burberry in 2001 following a five-year stint designing womens wear for Tom Ford's Gucci, explained that when he joined, the British brand was "a beautiful jewel that needed polishing."[66] Today, it sparkles. For Fall/Winter 2013–2014, Bailey played with Burberry's 157-year-old gravitas by "making it subversive and kinky."[67] To do this, Bailey manipulated the classic cocktail sheath by using vinyl rather than fabric. The transparent piece, in a claret shade, achieved his goal of creating a fashion that "make[s] the heart race."[68]

Paris-based designer Andrew Gn drew inspiration from the Wiener Werkstätte for his Fall/Winter 2013–2014 collection. His lavish quilted parka, in a dark Malaga hue, featured patterns akin to artist Koloman Moser's, as well as kimono-esque sleeves, which illustrated his ability to incorporate the Orient and the Occident without falling into an East-meets-West cliché. Born in Singapore, Gn received an international design education at London's Central Saint Martins and Milan's Domus Academy. Afterward, Gn assisted Emanuel Ungaro before launching his own label in the Marais district. Gn's clients, as international as he, include well-to-do Asian families, aristocrats from Europe, and Middle Eastern royals.

Established in 1934 by brothers Giovanni and Giacomo, the Italian label Canali has been known for uncompromising quality since its inception. Priding itself on combining the best textiles with flawless tailoring, Canali remains unwavering in its commitment to excellence in menswear three generations later. For Fall/Winter 2013–2014, the Milan-based brand went "British," creating a double-breasted velvet Maroon coat with large fur lapels. While it was Old English, the outfit also still expressed the cheeky swagger of men today.

Zac Posen brought excitement with him when he entered the New York fashion scene in 2001. At only twenty, he was already dressing Naomi Campbell and Claire Danes with his Vionnet-inspired designs. For Fall/Winter 2013–2014 he dressed wispy model Catherine McNeil in a Dry Rose caped-gown, evoking grown-up glamour.

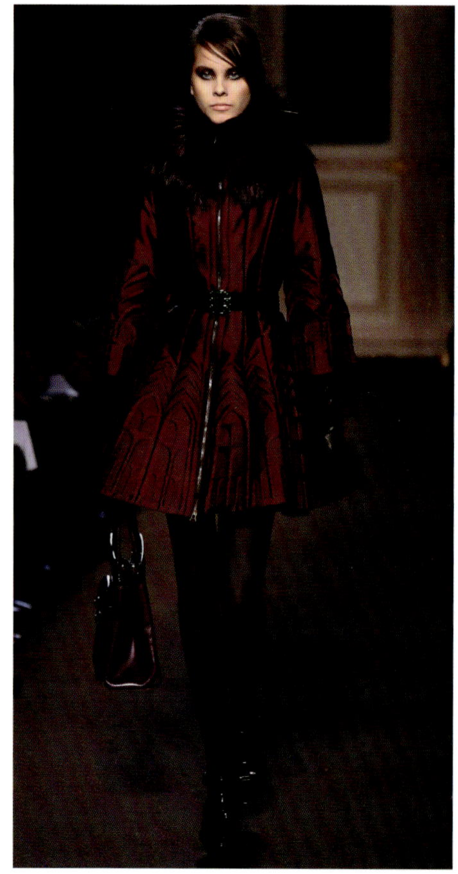

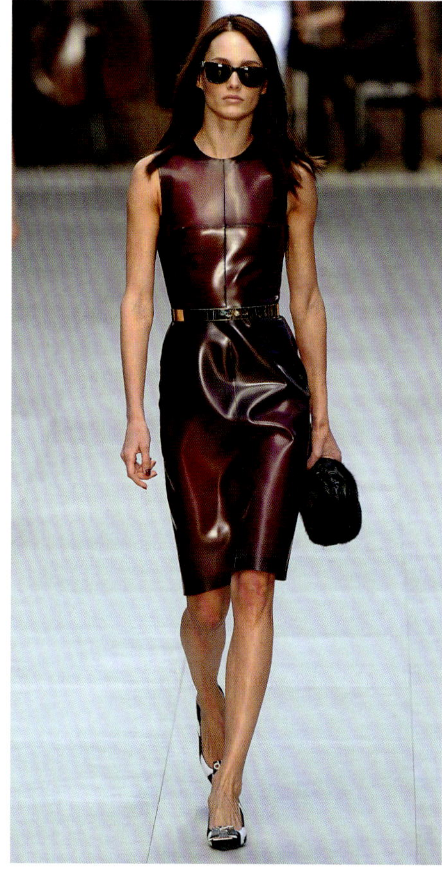

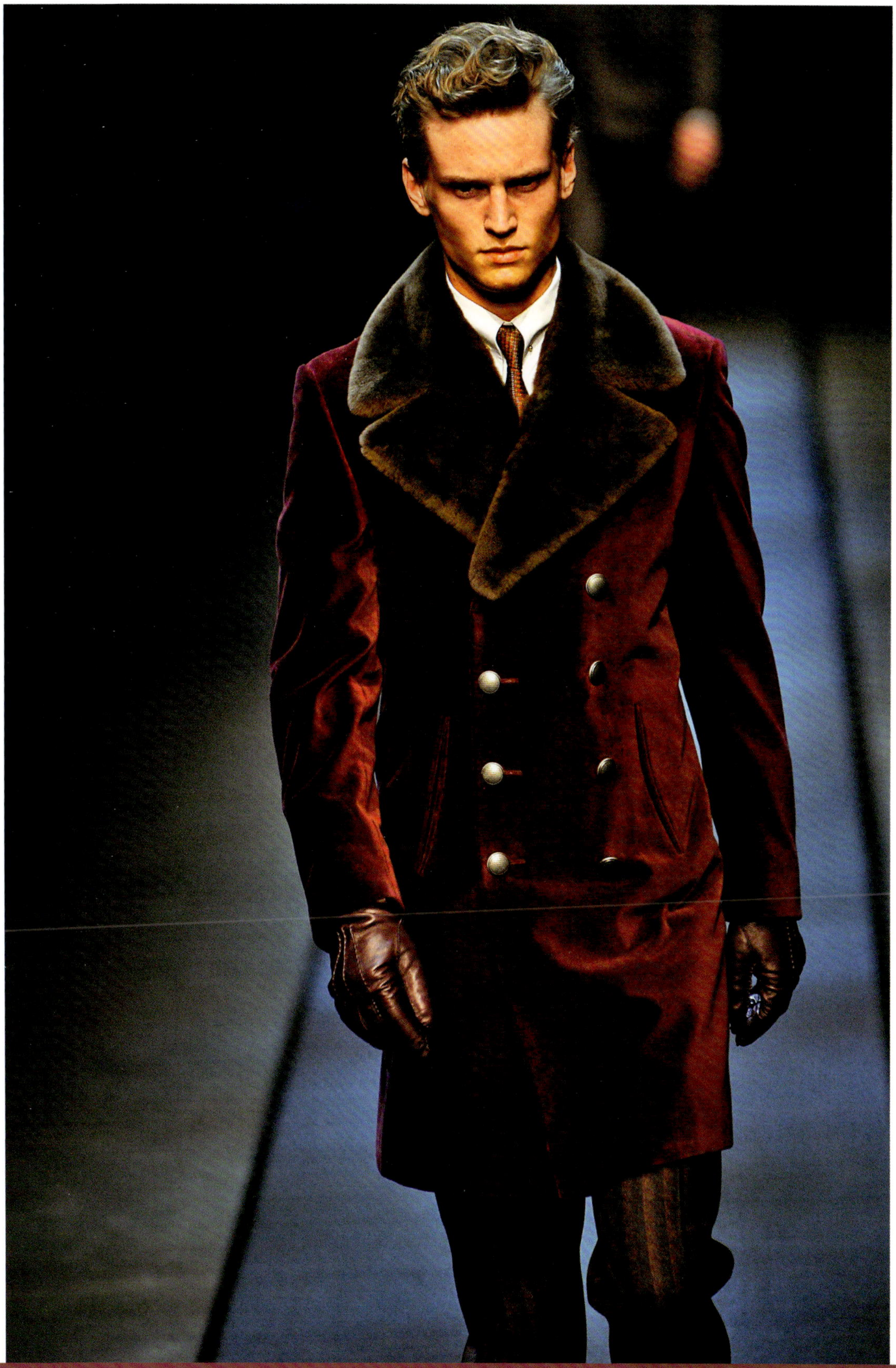

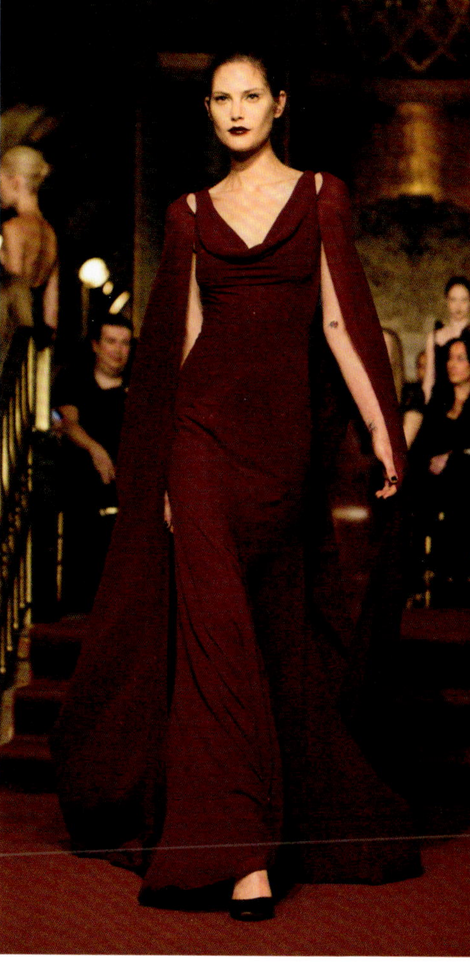

Festival Fuchsia

Fuchsia is a celebratory hue that marries regal purple and seductive red. Its emergence in WWII, aided by more readily available dyestuffs, expressed a refusal to bend to the dire realities of wartime. By 1948, it illustrated the newfound joy of a world without total war. The Baton Rouge color was revived in the early 21st century, relaying the exciting possibilities held by the new millennium.

Charles James obsessively toiled over his "soft sculptures" to the extent that, at his height, he could dress only ten women.[69] Society women like Millicent Rogers and Mona von Bismarck tolerated James's notoriously tempestuous attitude solely because of his genius. Arrogantly, James once said, "I'm a legend. A master of magic . . . Poiret said, 'I pass my crown on to you. You do with scissors what I do with color.' Madame Grès saw my work and nearly fainted."[70] Unfortunately, one look at James's 1939 Fuchsia "La Sirene" gown makes any rebuttal moot.

A lover of metamorphosis, Germaine Krebs not only transformed fashion, but also herself. She adopted the name "Alix Barton" in the early 1930s and then in 1940 "Madame Grès." Fascinated with the body in motion, Madame Grès created neoclassical Grecian *drapés* (draped dresses) for over half a century. Meticulous and obsessive, Madame Grès repeatedly attempted to create perfection: a dress that could be put on and forgotten. Her 1967 Fuchsia silk gown exemplifies her ability to use unique geometric patterns cut on the bias to effortlessly complement the female form. Despite her talent, Madame Grès's business was bankrupt by 1984. Exiting fashion, she lamented, "Today, luxury is confused with waste and excess."[71]

When Amy Smilovic fell for the fabric markets of Hong Kong (while an expat), her hobby of sketching morphed into a knack for fashion. By embracing contradictions ("youthful and sophisticated, masculine and feminine, bold and muted"), Smilovic's label, Tibi, has garnered a loyal following of trendsetters like Miroslava Duma, eager to don her Purple Orchid minidresses and the like.[72]

After Tom Ford's exit, Gucci floundered until Frida Giannini was promoted to creative director. Many doubted if she was up to the challenge, questioning how her feminine Italian personality would materialize (physically and fiscally) after Ford's hyper-masculine-American legacy of sex. It took a few begrudging seasons for the fashion world to acclimatize, but ultimately all admitted her brilliance. For Fall/Winter 2011–2012, Giannini clad model Chanel Iman in a low V-neck, high-thigh-slit gown of semi-transparent Rosebud chiffon swaths. While the dress was enticingly revealing, by pairing it with thick rectangular Gucci sunglasses, Giannini made the look and wearer seem tantalizing, but untouchable.

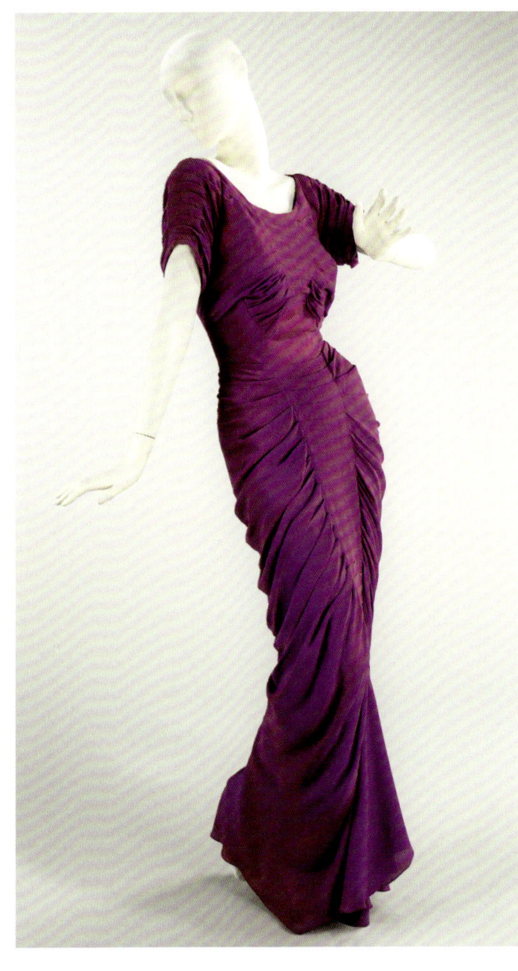

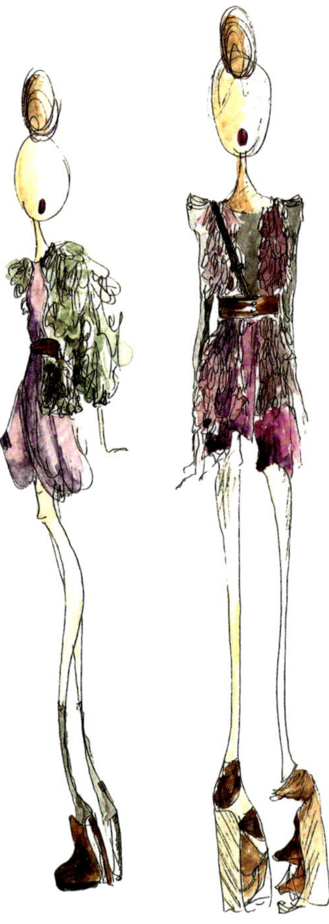

opposite, left
"La Sirene" gown of molded silk
Charles James
1939

opposite, right
Fashion sketch
Amy Smilovic for Tibi
Fall/Winter 2010

left
Gown
Gucci
Fall/Winter 2011

right
Silk evening gown
Madame Grès
1967

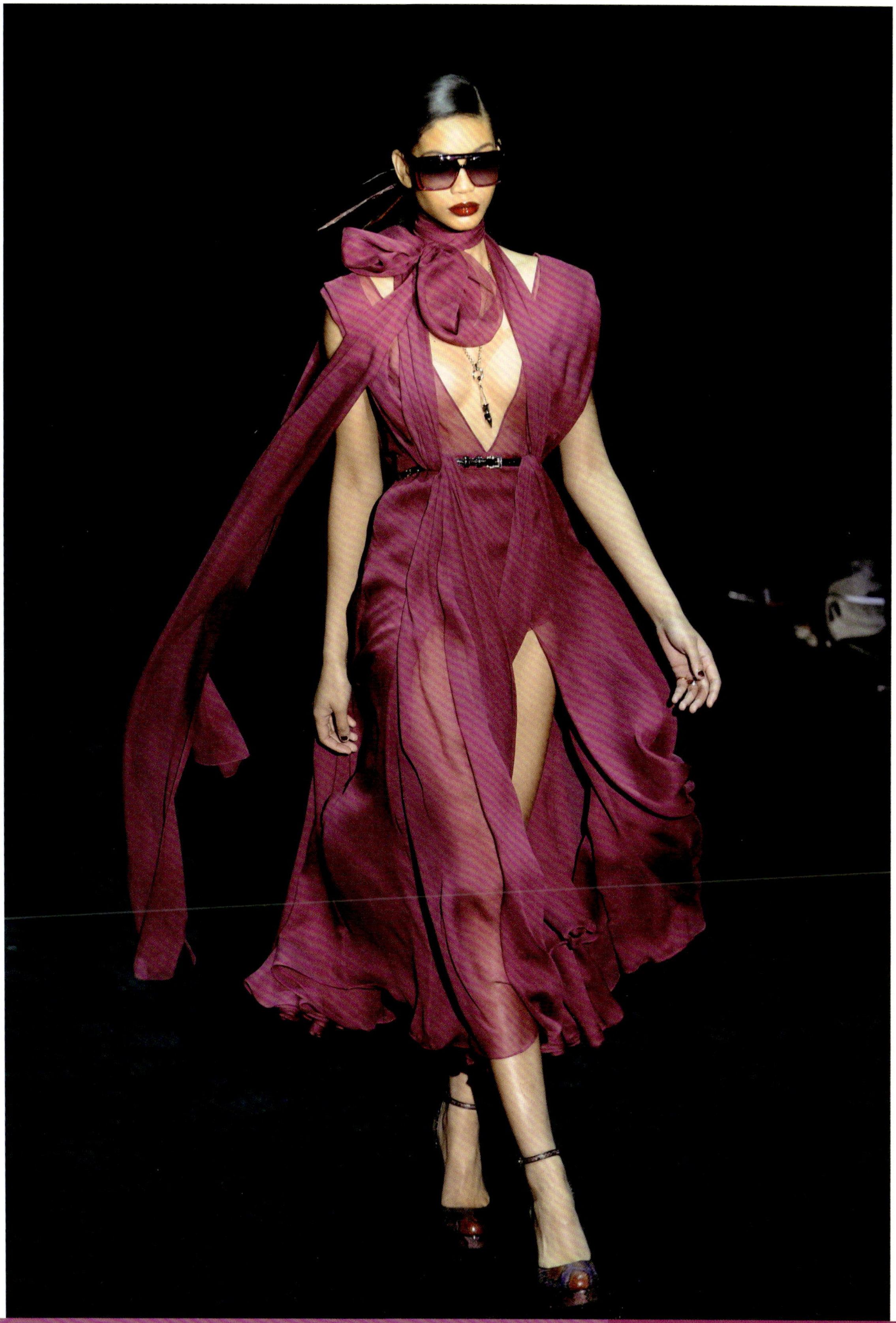

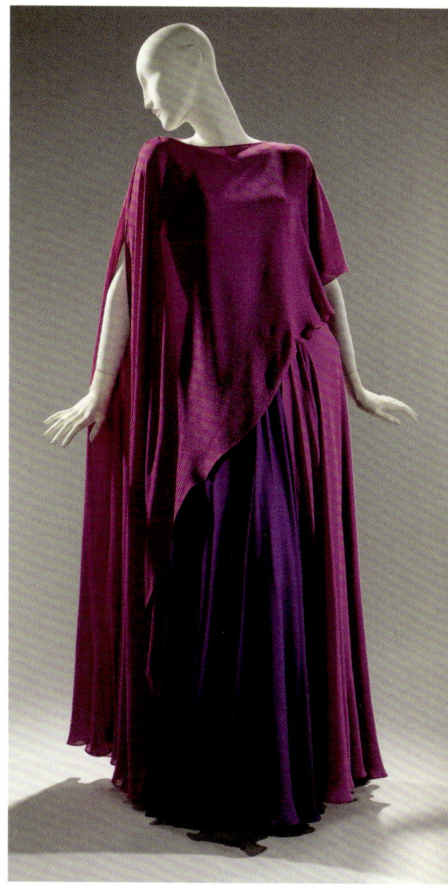

Purple Orchid
PANTONE 18-3027

Baton Rouge
PANTONE 18-2527

Mauve Shadows

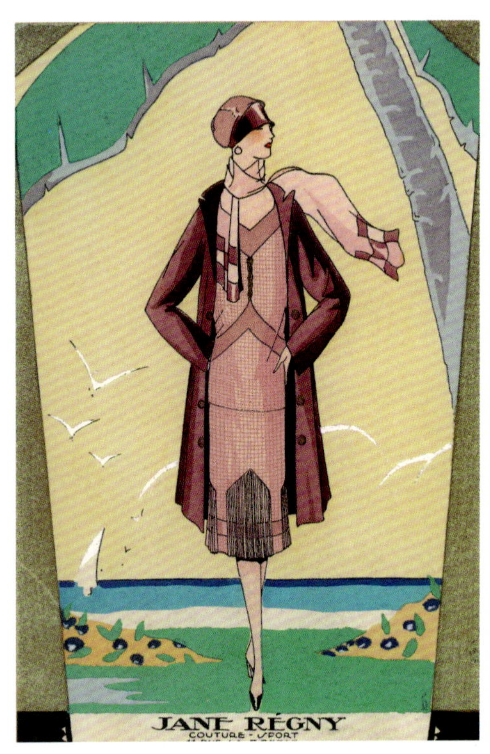

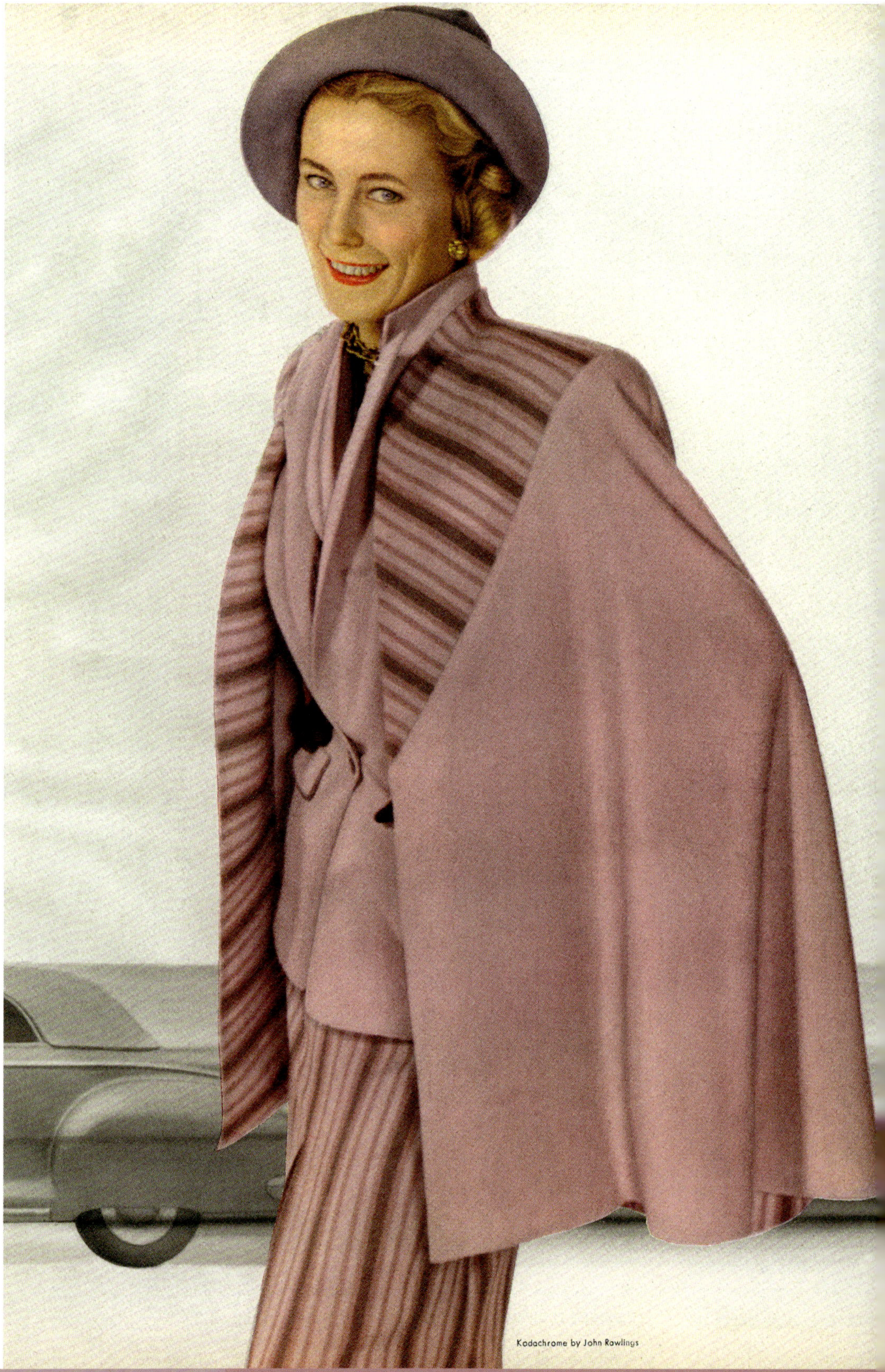

Kodachrome by John Rawlings

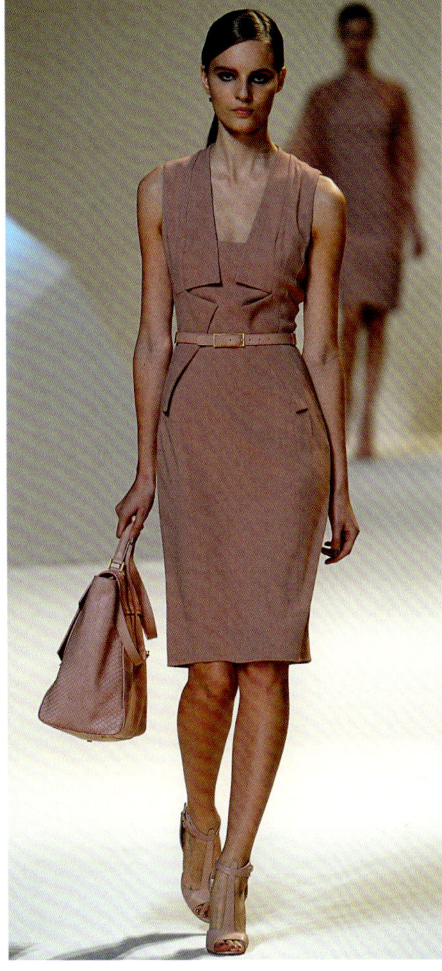

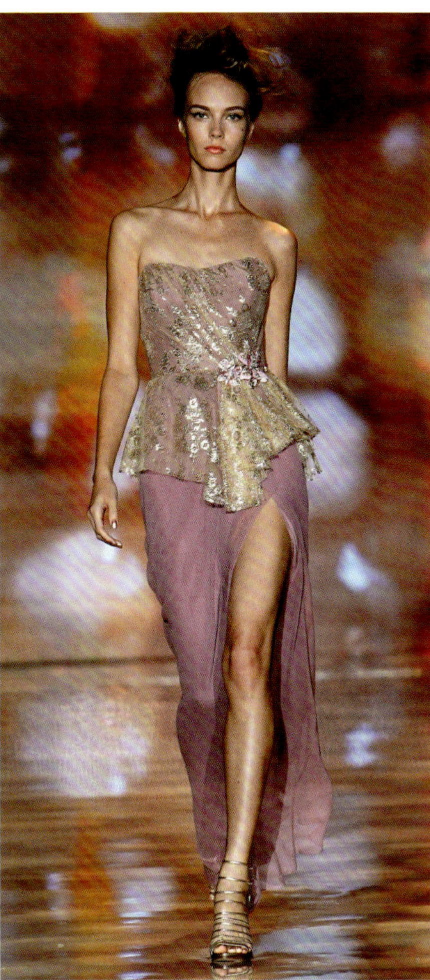

Mauve is defined as a pale purple color, but, enigmatic and versatile, it can range from grayish pink to grape. Considered the first aniline dye, invented and named in 1856 by the young chemist Sir William Henry Perkin, mauve became so popular in the 1890s that the period was dubbed the "Mauve Decade." Designers like Jean Patou, Drecoll, and Jane Regny all used the hue during the 1920s;[73] Christian Dior, Cristóbal Balenciaga, and Philip Mangone chose the color following WWII; and Badgley Mischka along with Elie Saab resurrected it early in the new millennium.

Furthered by designer Jane Regny, the "sportif" look of the 1920s became a "fashion obsession, even among those whose most strenuous physical exercise was lunching at the Ritz."[74] Attuned to the mood of the modern woman, Regny's fashions, "brilliant in color," were usually shown on women skiing, playing tennis, or golfing.[75] While Regny's 1926 mauve-wearing woman in *Art-Goût-Beauté* is merely standing at the beach, her flowing scarf and distant gaze suggest she is about to embark on an adventure, perhaps in a new motorcar.

Designer Philip Mangone best embodies having fashion in one's blood, with seven generations of tailors on his family tree. Mangone, a first-generation Italian-American, opened his own New York business in 1916. A frequent traveler, Mangone miraculously survived the *Hindenburg* explosion in 1937. He was badly burned, but the success of his business helped to cover his high medical costs. After a long recuperation, he continued his work in fashion, and in 1946 won *Fashion Trades* magazine's Golden Thimble Award as one of the top ten designers in America. Mangone's 1948 Lilas suit and cape, photographed by John Rawlings, demonstrated his distinctive adeptness with wool, his fabric of choice.

Pair of Parsons alums Mark Badgley and James Mischka once again provided fabulous formalwear for Spring/Summer 2012, outfitting Kristy Kaurova in a Mauve Orchid bustier gown.

Milan and Paris have welcomed Beirut-based designer Elie Saab with open arms, respectively naming him a member of the Italian Camera Nazionale della Moda and the French Chambre Syndicale de la Haute Couture. Saab's "well-made, cut-to-the-curve clothing," inspired by the elegance of Lebanese women, fuses Arabic and Western influences.[76] Fashion editor for *Marie Claire Arabia* Amine Jreissati explained that "the culture [of the Middle East] is in the dress, in the cut and the shape, with layers and movement and embroidery."[77] Saab's fame shot up in 2002 when Halle Berry wore his gown during her Oscar win. For his Spring/Summer 2013 "Heiress" collection, Saab clad model Tilda Lindstam in a belted Wistful Mauve dress.

Lavender Fog

In 1934 Chicago, brothers Emil, Bernard, and Maurice Adelaar set up a blouse company using Maurice's designs. In 1945, they moved their base to the Big Apple where they continued to produce women's dresses and blouses, often using union labor. The company, which also boasted a line called Adelaar's Aristocrat aimed at the aspirational upper crust, created this 1960 Lavendula belted blouse and matching tweed skirt. The outfit speaks to the increased focus on comfort and sportswear seen in post-WWII America, as well as a more "feminine" color palette embraced in the era.

During her long mid-century career, Mollie Parnis had the distinction of dressing four First Ladies—Mamie Eisenhower, Bess Truman, Lady Bird Johnson, and Patricia Nixon—which is exactly how she would have it. "I'm not interested in designing for the average housewife. I don't even know her," Parnis admitted to *LIFE*.[78] The designer, who grew up on the Lower East Side of Manhattan was a first-generation American, born to Austrian Jewish refugees. By nineteen, she was already a "smashing success," landing her name on the door of her wholesale employer. By 1933, the Depression be damned, Parnis started her own business, despite not being able to cut, sew, or draw. The brand's eye and editor, Parnis ensured that garments like her 1970s Lavender Fog Ultrasuede shirtdress possessed "quality" and "a little sex."[79]

Detroit-born designer Anna Sui names music as her muse. Sui gathered the "confidence to stage her own show" only after Madonna wore one of her dresses. Lisa Marie Presley, daughter of Elvis, considers Sui's designs "exciting, without caution . . . good ol' fashion, balls-out rock and roll." Sui's inspiration for Spring/Summer 2004 was the 1960s beach-party film series with singing teen idols Frankie Avalon and Annette Funicello. Sui liked the idea of "a girl who could not wait to get in the water," hence the top and bottom of Sui's Lavender ensemble are based on a bikini.[80]

American couturier Geoffrey Beene offered up his showroom to newcomer Douglas Hannant in the late 1990s, saving the up-and-comer money and raising his profile. The Hannant/Beene relationship was symbiotic in nature, as Hannant named Beene as his main design inspiration. Hannant's career has continued to gain momentum since. His Spring/Summer 2009 dress in Bougainvillea is classy without being ostentatious. Hannant summed up his design edict, saying, "There's a purity inherent to American style. It's not overdone or wildly extravagant."[81]

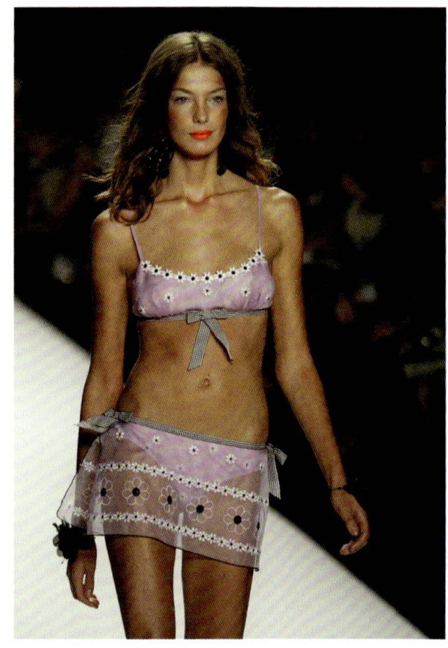

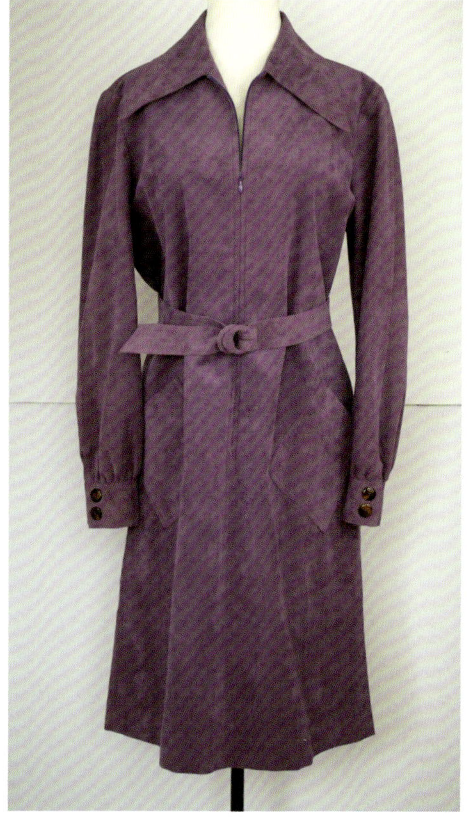

opposite, left
Bikini under a sheer miniskirt
cover-up
Anna Sui
Spring/Summer 2004

opposite, right
Ultrasuede shirtdress
Mollie Parnis
circa 1970

left
Belted top and patterned skirt
Print ad
Adelaar
1960

right
Chemise evening dress
Douglas Hannant
Spring/Summer 2009

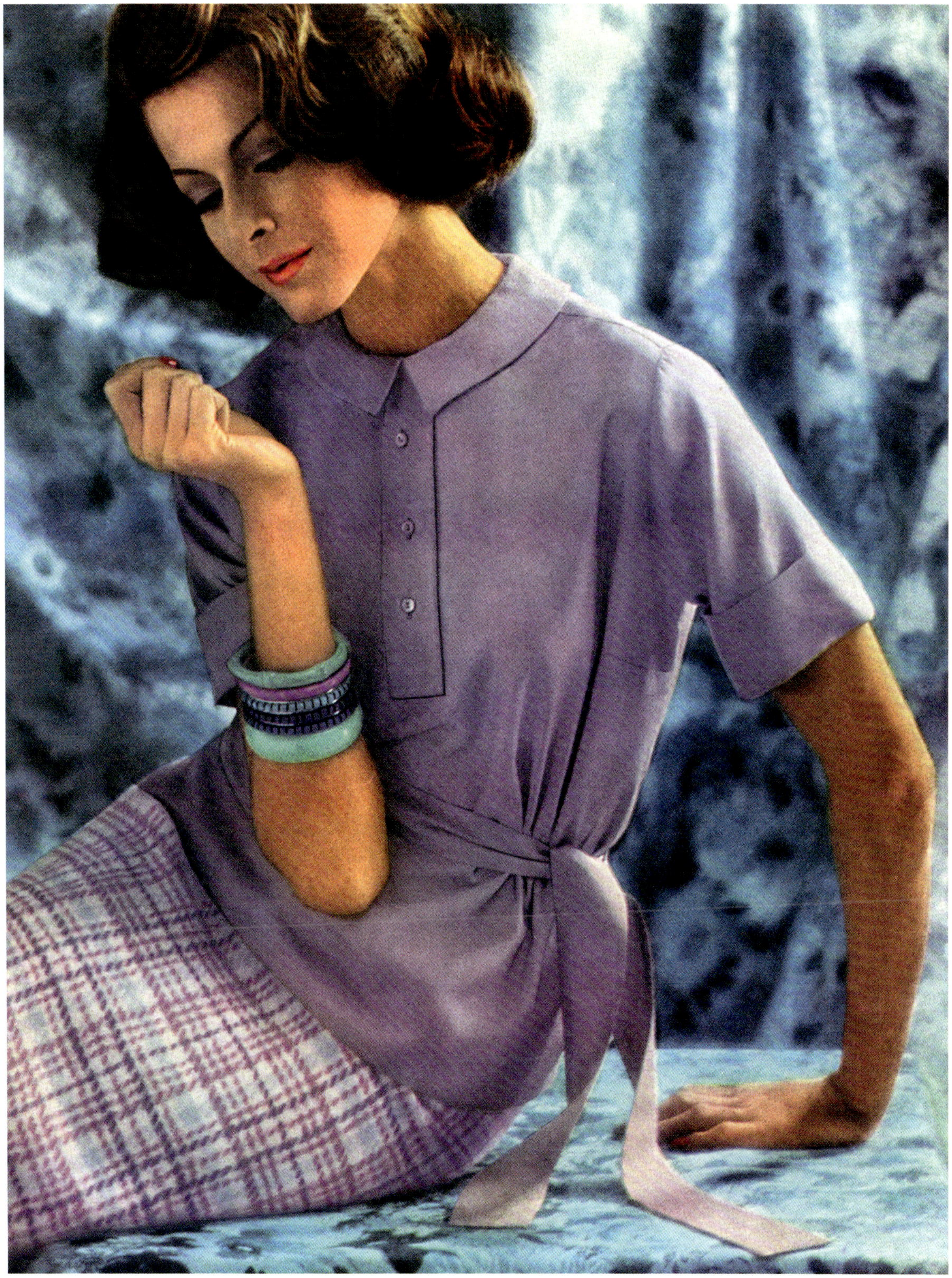

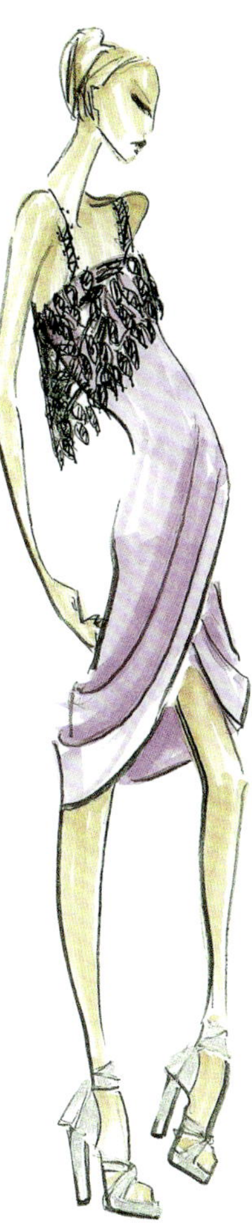

Royal Purple

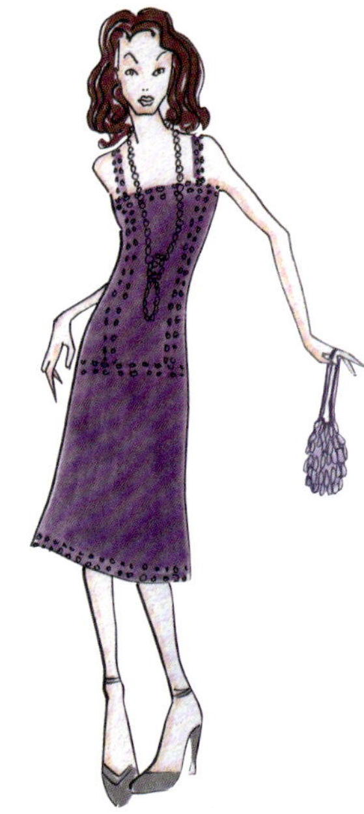

"When I am an old woman, I shall wear purple."
—Jenny Joseph

Historically, Royal Purple was the world's most precious dye. Harvested from snails' glands, it takes 336,000 mollusks to produce one ounce of purpuridae.[82] Expensive as a result, purple was a commodity affordable only to royalty and the wealthy. In modern times, synthetic dye allowed purple to become increasingly attainable, though it still exudes a level of its past drama and complexity.

In 1929, *L'Officiel de la Mode* pronounced *"Augusta Bernard est au premier plan de la création parisienne"* (Augusta Bernard is at the forefront of Parisian fashion).[83] In agreement, *Vogue* invited Rene Bouet-Willaumez to illustrate a Royal Lilac Augusta Bernard evening gown for their September 1933 issue. Most active between 1922 and 1934, Bernard gained acclaim for her neoclassical designs, considered "grand simple affairs."[84]

Apropos for the '70s era of "happenings," Halston became known for the "mad, wild, crazy parties in his showroom," where New Yorkers like "Babe Paley and a Puerto Rican drag queen" mingled.[85] Halston worked as hard as he partied, staying up half the night, "sew[ing] until his hands bled."[86] By 1975, *Esquire* wondered, "Will Halston take over the world?"[87] Halston's *raison d'être* was crafting simple—but not boring—garments, like his 1975 silk evening dress. The boldly purple disco-era "American classic" would have easily suited Halston's clientele of fashionable people like Angelica Huston and Candice Bergen.[88]

Jill Stuart's fashionable parents, who owned "Mister Pants," dressed Lucille Ball and Natalie Wood. By fifteen, Stuart was precociously following their lead, selling accessories to Bloomingdale's. After graduating from the Rhode Island School of Design, she went on to launch her own collection in 1993, which is now worn by celebrities like Jennifer Aniston and Kirsten Dunst. Her 1996 dress in Meadow Violet is better suited for Hollywood nights than grungy Seattle's rain-filled days.

The murder of Gianni Versace in 1997 could have effortlessly and understandably left the House in ruin. Determined to continue his legacy, Donatella Versace stepped up (in 160-mm heels, no less). Having worked with her brother throughout his career, Donatella deeply understood the Versace ethos, but at first she avoided the brand's classic iconography, preferring to leave it untouched as a type of "sanctuary" to her late sibling. But by Fall/Winter 2006–2007, she was ready to revisit it. Her menswear collection articulated a Miami-masculinity of the 1990s with patterned silk shirts and matching trousers in Purple Heart.

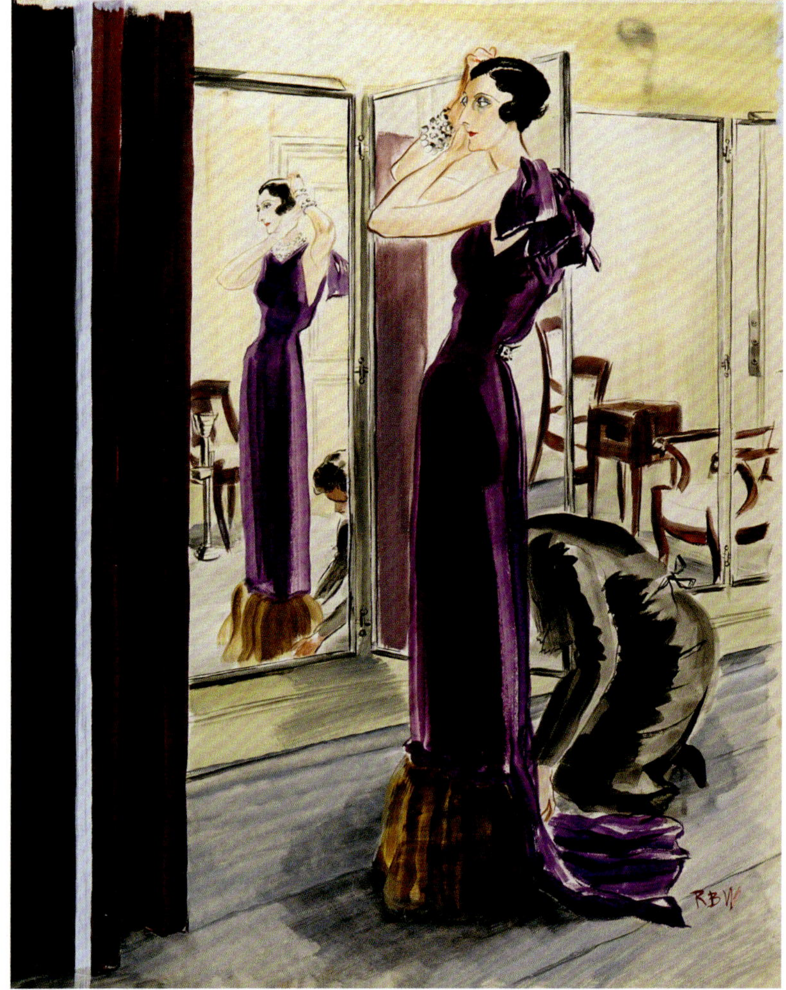

opposite, top
Spaghetti-strap dress
Jill Stuart
Fall 1996

opposite, bottom
Illustration by Renet Bouet-
Willaumez for *Vogue* featuring
the Marquise de Paris
Augusta Bernard
1933

left
Silk shirt and ascot
Donatella Versace for Versace
Fall/Winter 2006

right
Off-the-shoulder silk Grecian gown
Halston
circa 1975

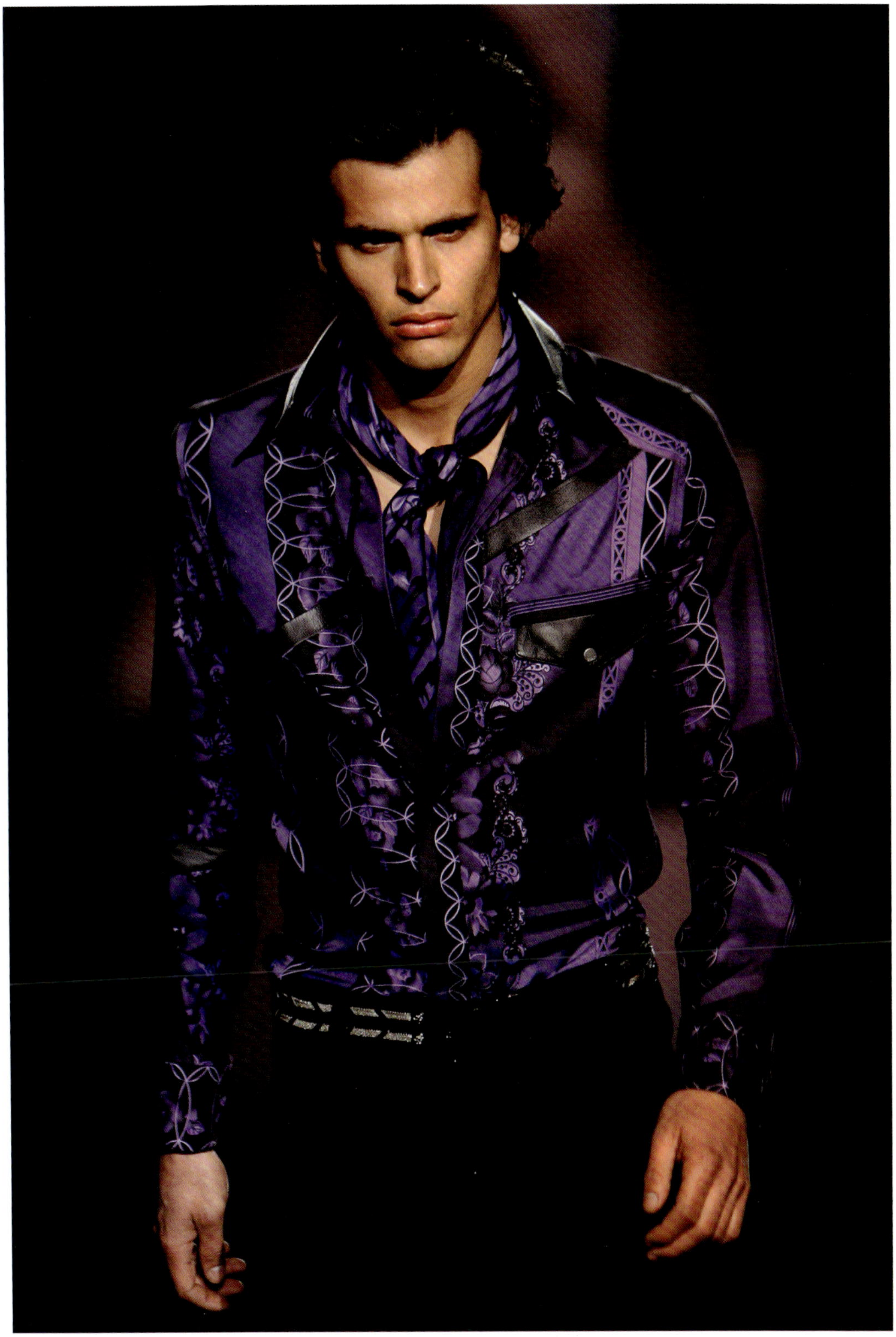

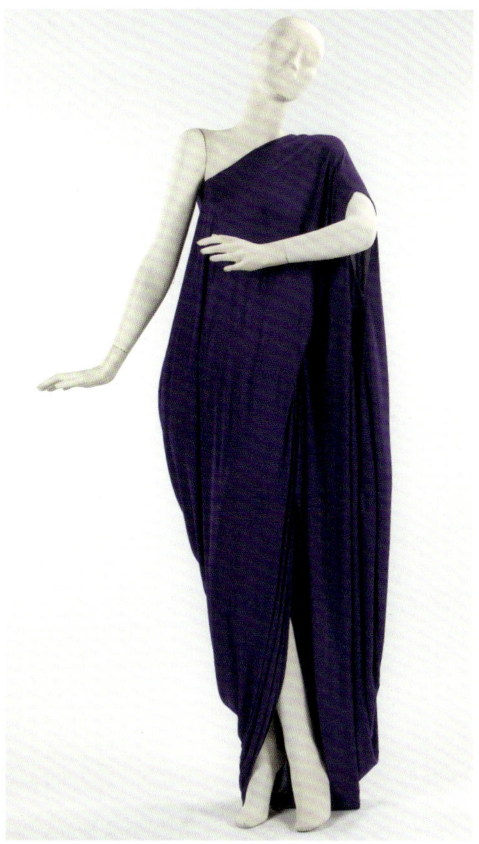

Purple Heart
PANTONE 18-3520

Royal Lilac
PANTONE 18-3531

Plum Purple

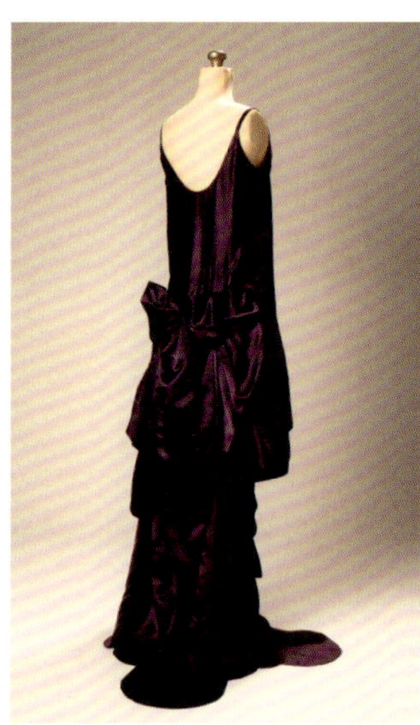

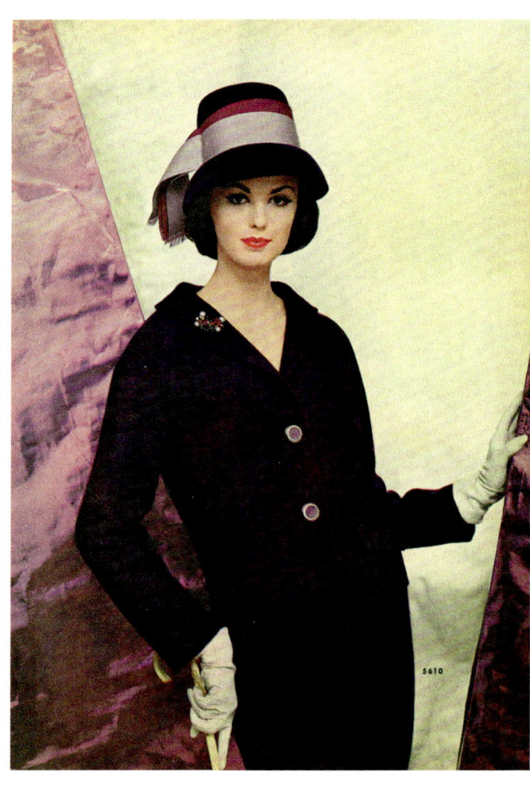

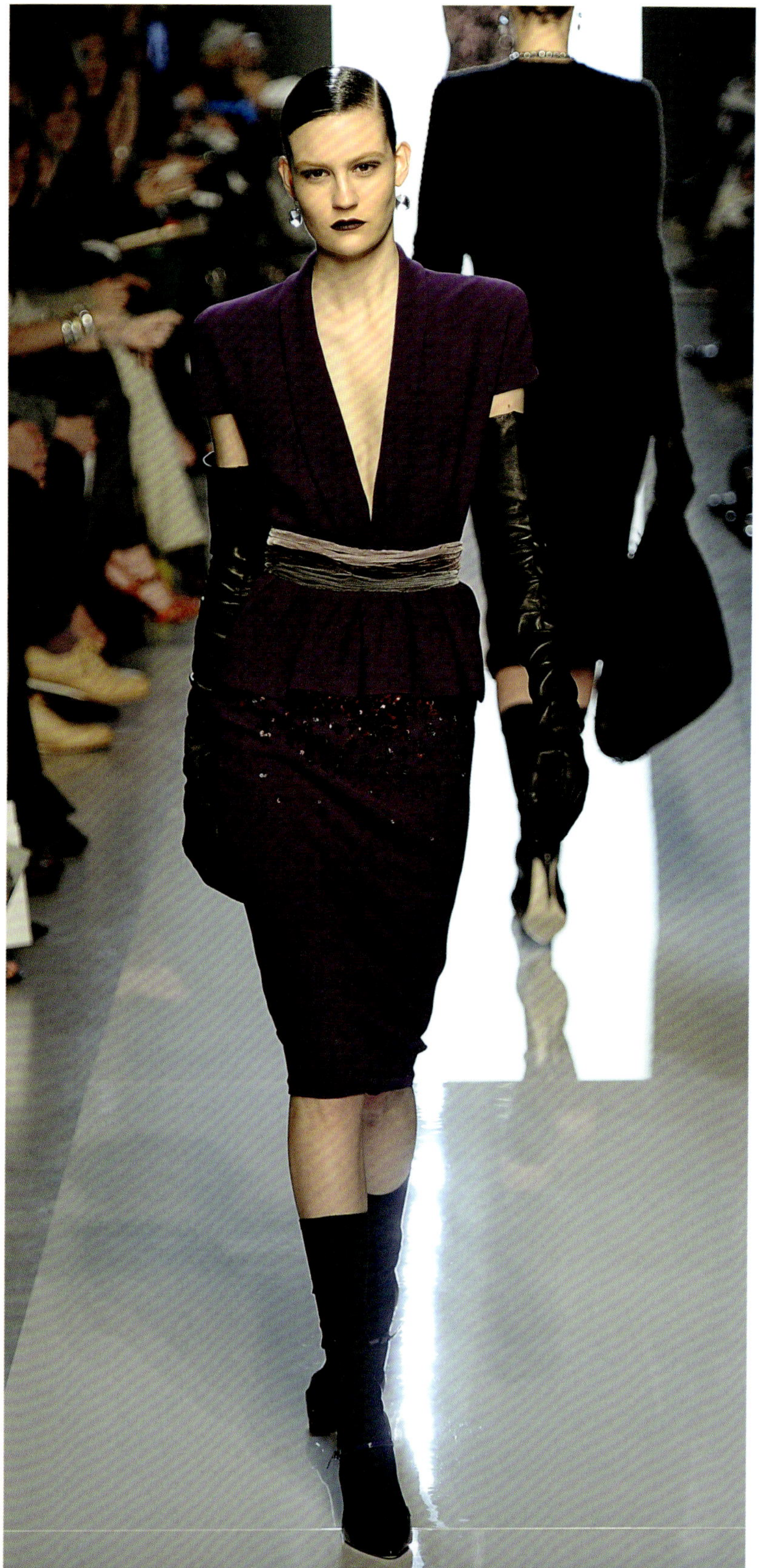

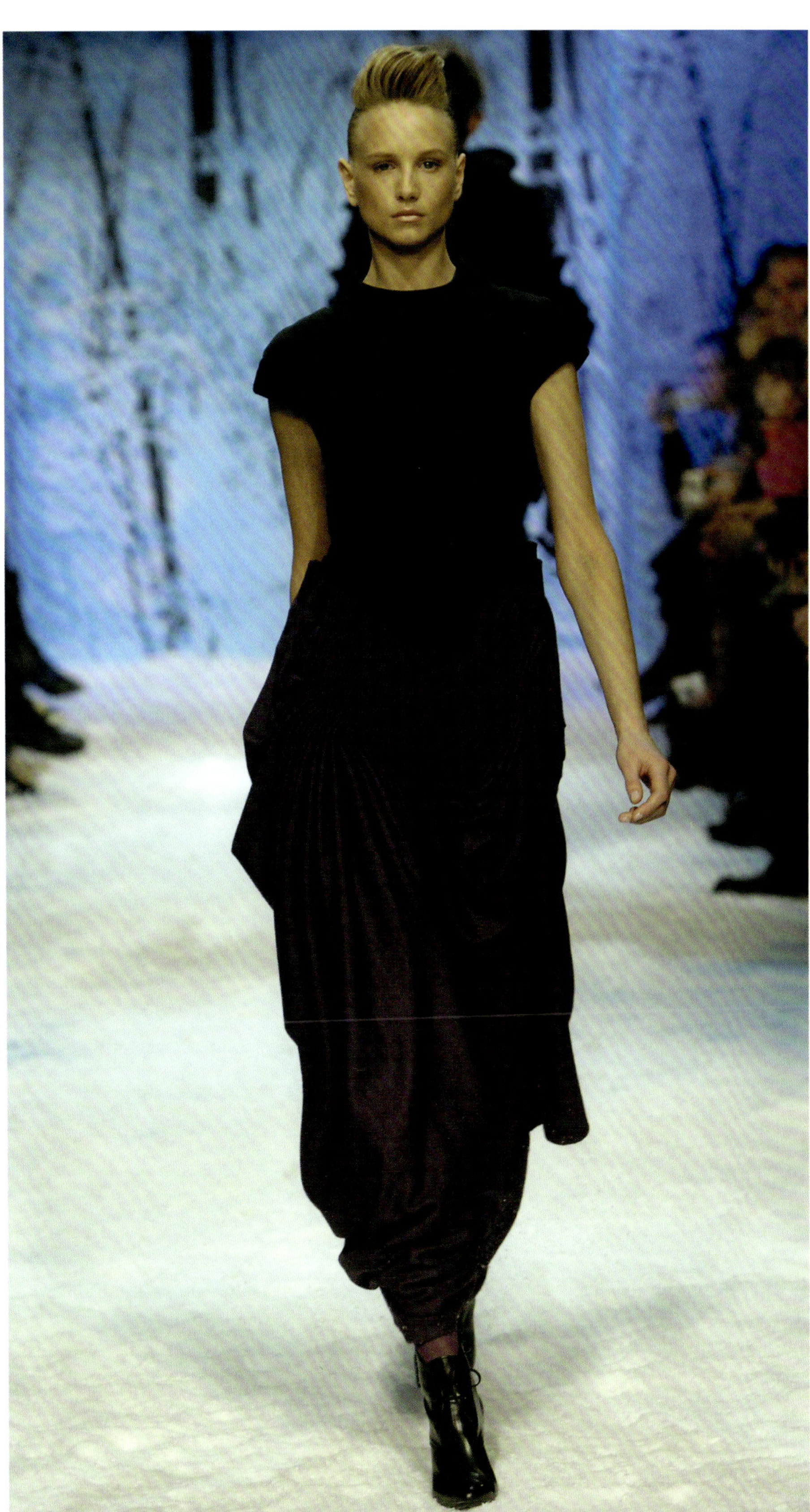

Couture's impending death is apocalyptically forecast at regular intervals. Yet, it lives, in a major part due to Lucien Lelong. During WWII, Nazi Germany, tired of being endlessly mocked for its unfashionable Fräuleins, wanted Berlin to become the center of the fashion universe, ousting Occupied Paris from its throne. Designer and president of the Chambre Syndicale de la Haute Couture, Lucien Lelong, at great personal risk, diplomatically fought, through cunning, to keep couture in Paris. This accomplishment cemented Lelong in fashion history but has since overshadowed his talent as a designer, which can be seen in his Royal Purple dress from the 1920s. Lelong has also been eclipsed by the talented designers under his tutelage: "a shy, cherubic" Christian Dior, and Pierre Balmain.[89]

Irish-American Brooklyn beauty Dorothy McGowan worked with the best fashion photographers of her time: Irving Penn, Melvin Sokolsky, and William Klein, who eventually secured the lead role for her in the 1966 cinematic fashion satire, *Who Are You, Polly Maggoo?* Before appearing on the big screen, McGowan modeled for *Vogue* and *Harper's Bazaar*, as well as in *McCall's Pattern Fashions* magazine in 1960 wearing a Grape Royale hat to match her jacket and skirt.

Lie Sang Bong, dubbed the "Korean McQueen," gained prominence in Seoul during the 1990s, earning "Best Designer of the Year," before debuting in Paris in 2002 and making the City of Light his base. Upon entering the Western fashion market, he was considered "a wonder," a sentiment still shared by fans of his work like Beyoncé and Lady Gaga.[90] Lie's garments are inspired by a variety of disparate elements, such as "Korean poetry and calligraphy, cubism, and 1930s *film noir* heroines," often concocted with a vivid palette of rich reds and plum purples.[91]

Tomas Maier's Fall/Winter 2012–2013 collection for Bottega Veneta was the strongest he had presented since joining the House in 2001. Fashion critic Sarah Mower and onlookers alike experienced an "involuntary wave of emotion."[92] The brooding collection covered up the models (high gloves, high socks), in stark contrast to the increasingly transparent garments that had been trending. Maier placed model Maria Bradley in a thick Wineberry peplum suit set, appropriate for women with unshaking confidence, but not the younger demographic of girls that the fashion world had been courting.

Deep Periwinkle

In 1925, inspired by his American models, French designer Jean Patou produced an "interesting shade of pale periwinkle with a hint of mauve in it which has won applause."[93] With Parisian approval, the color's fashionability exploded with nearly every fashion column in *The New York Times* mentioning it that year. The youthful color was inescapable! American copies abounded, as did homemade garments in the same shade of Jacaranda, like this 1920s dress by an unidentified designer. In subsequent decades, Patou's compatriot Maggy Rouff carried the color into the 1930s and 1940s when, conscious of both fashion's frivolity and its deep importance in Nazi-occupied Paris, she exclaimed, "Dear and lovely dresses, useless and foolish, it's you that I love!"[94]

For Miriam Haskell, "high quality fake" does not refer to anything nefarious or black market. Her meticulously hand-assembled costume jewelry is collected with fervor, even relished by fashion cognoscenti. Established in 1926, Haskell's New York boutique, Le Bijou de l'Heure, was brought to glory by its head of design, Frank Hess, who previously dressed windows for Macy's. Inspired by nature's lavish color schemes like wild blooms of periwinkle, Haskell's pieces were snapped up by Hollywood stars, including Lucille Ball.

Venice-based company Rossimoda produces high fashion's finest footwear, even though its label may read Givenchy, Céline, Yves Saint Laurent, or Ungaro. Established in 1942 by Narciso Rossi, Rossimoda extols the art of shoe craftsmanship. Their twelve-step process melds the best of today's computer-aided design (CAD) technology with human intervention such as manually cutting every single piece of the footwear's form from leather. Each year, nearly twenty million pairs are made in more than five hundred types of materials and colors, including the Easter Egg hue of Fendi's 1994 shoe.

Eley Kishimoto's Dusted Peri skirt is particularly conspicuous when styled with a black, white, and gray top, characteristic of their brilliantly clashing color schemes. Husband-and-wife team Mark Eley from Wales and Wakako Kishimoto from Japan joined forces in 1992 and started Eley Kishimoto in 1996. In addition to their own line, Eley and Kishimoto, who studied fashion at Brighton Polytechnic and Central Saint Martins respectively, also design for clients like Hussein Chalayan, Alexander McQueen, and Jil Sander. Known for their printed textiles, they explain, "We mix a palette as we go along every season . . . and buy stock color fabric as well as greige fabric for dyeing."[95] In a typical day, the nonstop pair "design, print, manufacture, market, communicate, and laugh," the secret to their twenty-year success.[96]

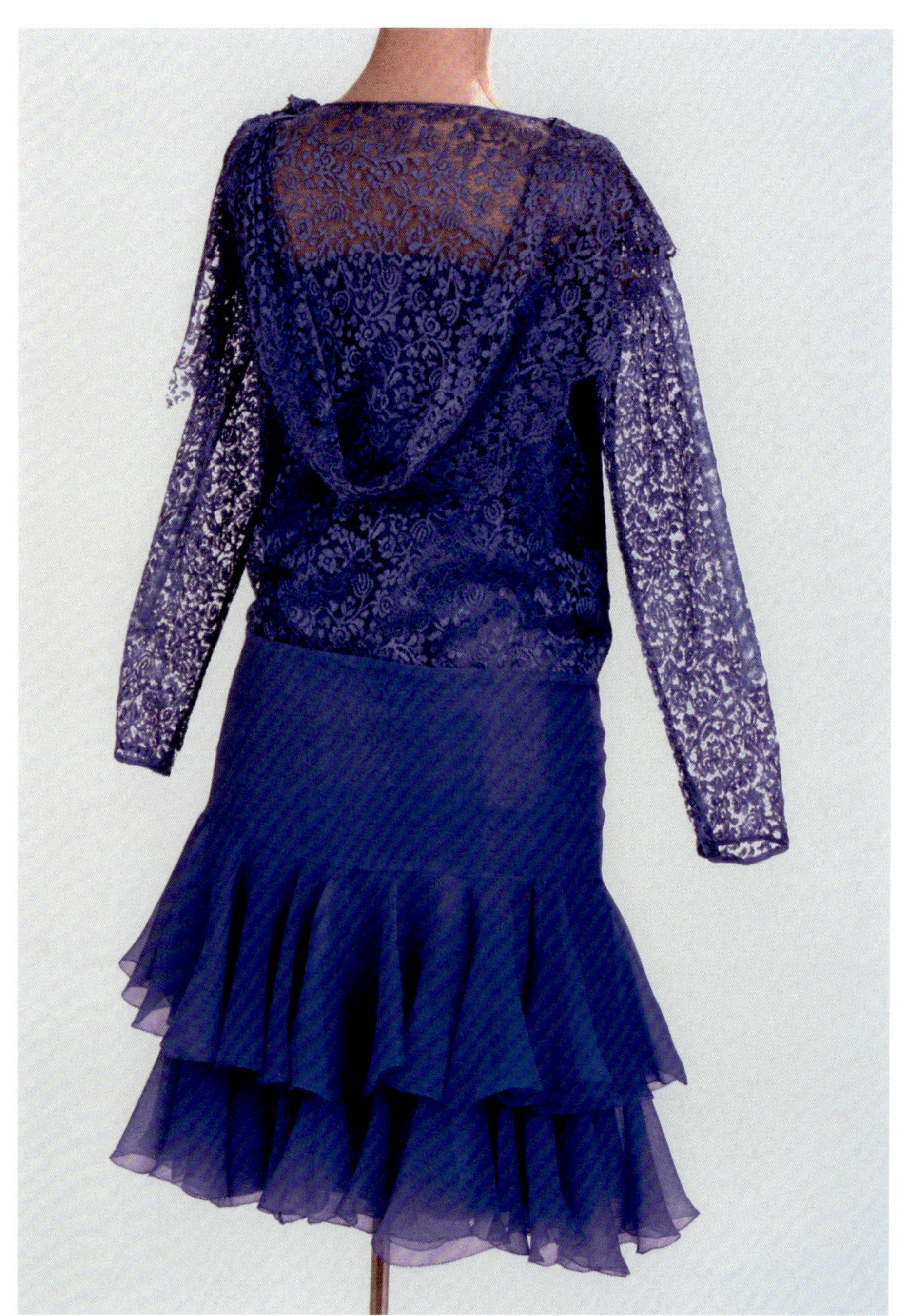

opposite
Lace and georgette afternoon frock
Designer unknown
circa 1920s

top left
Necklace (detail)
Miriam Haskell
circa 1950

bottom left
Patent leather and wood
platform shoe
Rossimoda for Fendi
Spring/Summer 1994

top right
Sheer skirt with striped top
Eley Kishimoto
Spring/Summer 2008

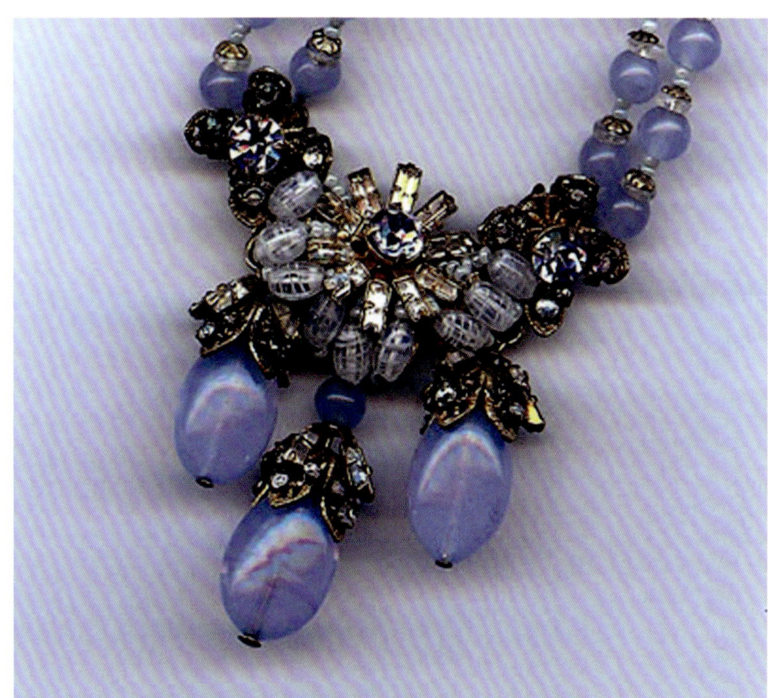

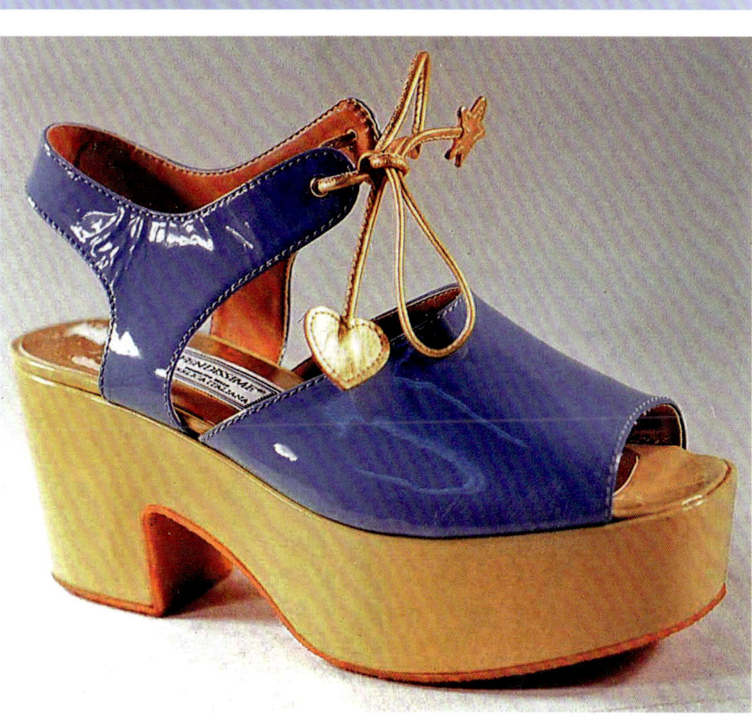

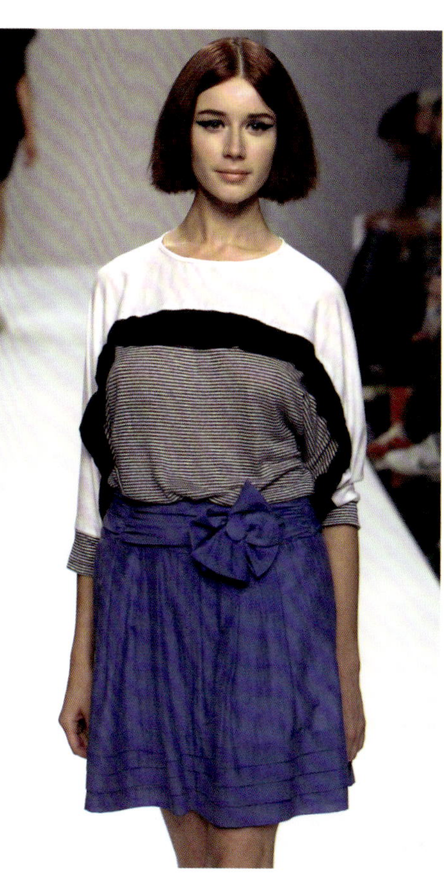

Dazzling Blue

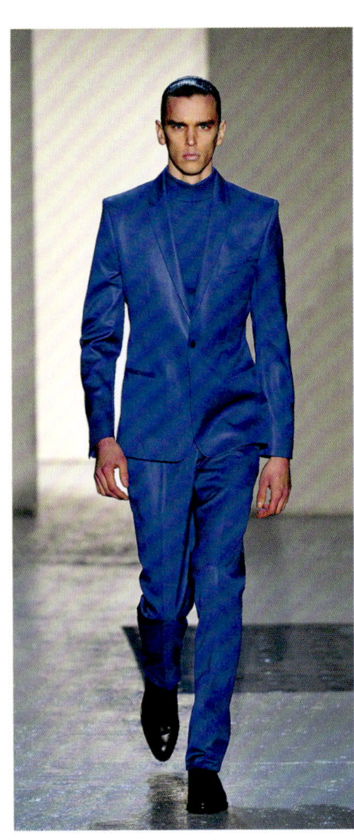

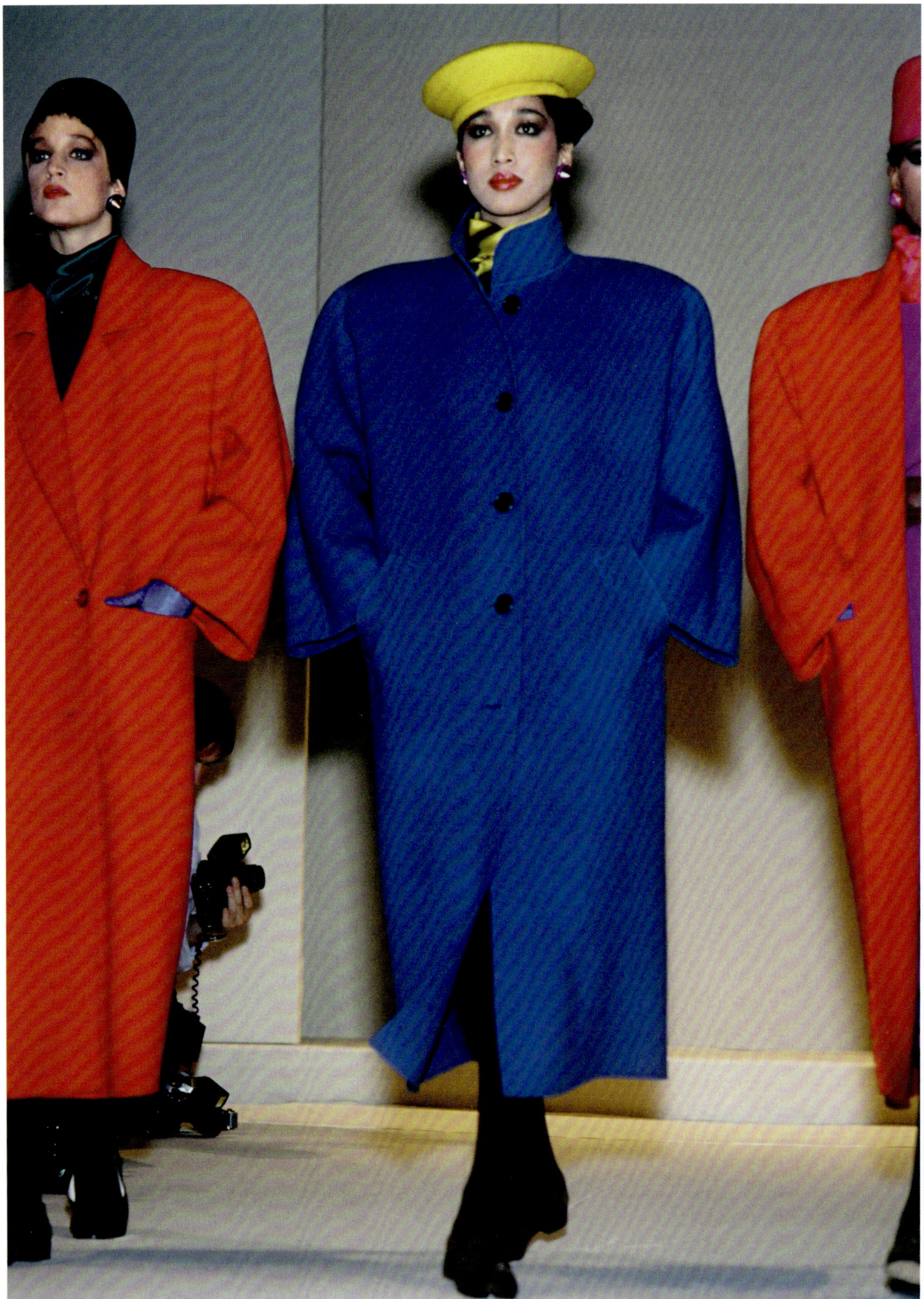

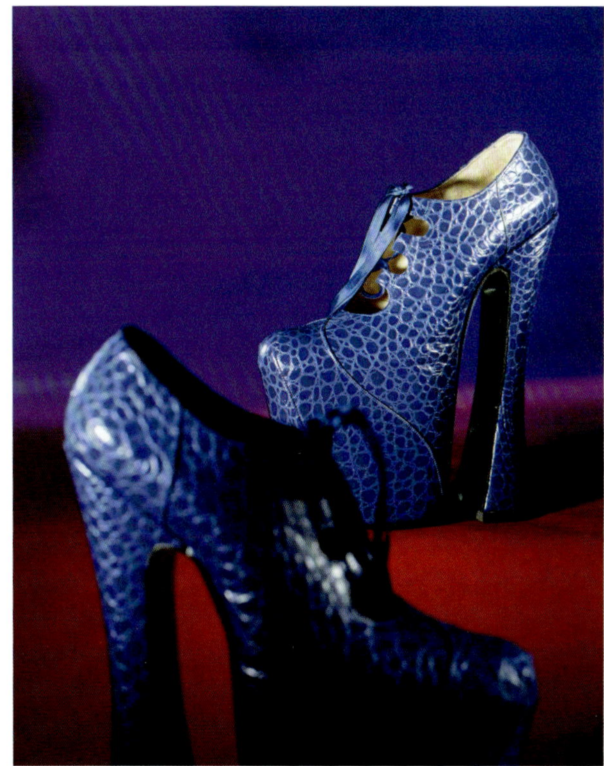

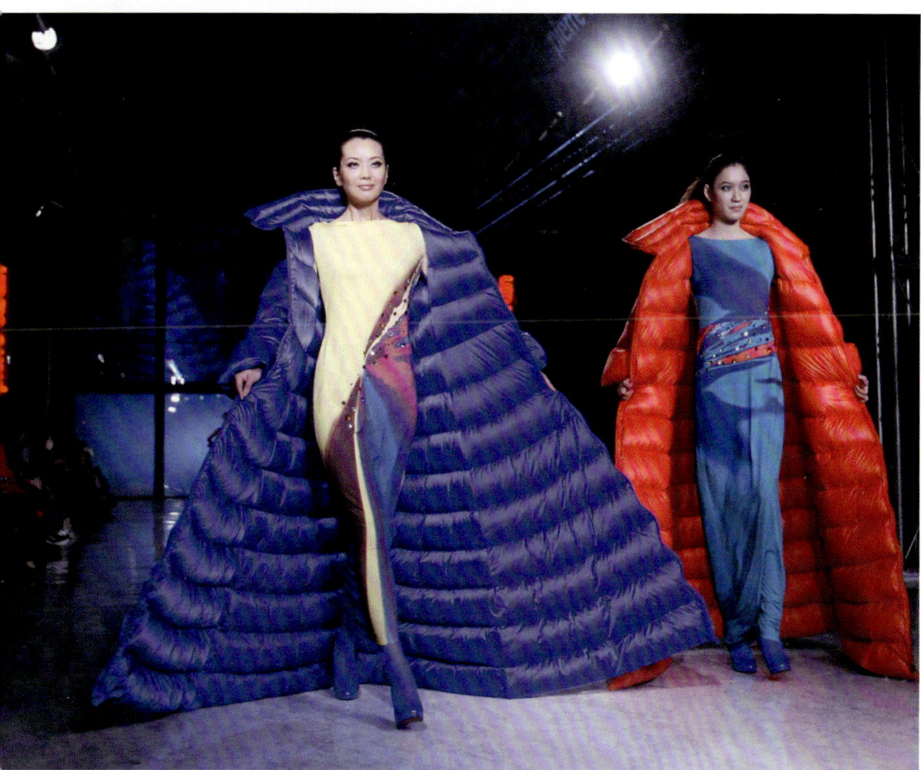

From the ocean to the sky, much of the planet is blue, yet Dazzling Blue does not come from Mother Nature. This lurid primary color flaunts its artificiality. More outlandish than heavenly, Amparo Blue found its moment in the 1980s as an alternative to Reagan Red.

For Fall 1984, Oscar de la Renta showed the nearly neon hue on his woolen coats. The power-shoulder outerwear, an unnatural shape in an unnatural color, was considered by *The New York Times* writer Bernadine Morris to be "obligatory for the season ahead."[97]

Dame Vivienne Westwood scoffed at functional footwear in 1993, creating the "Mock-Croc Super Elevated Gillie" shoe for her famous "Anglomania" collection. The 210-mm heels in affronting blue defy gravity and challenge mobility. Supermodel Naomi Campbell, known for her fierce strut, toppled completely on the runway, illustrating that even professional "walkers" are subjecting themselves to peril. The fetishistic footwear, which elevates the wearer well above the fray, is unquestionably sensational, simultaneously empowering and debilitating. Westwood's choice of blue leather bucks convention and avoids the cliché of red, often associated with such sexualized shoes.

In 2008, Deep Ultramarine resurfaced when Pierre Cardin chose it for his typically geometrical padded coat. Cardin, who studied under the great couturiers Jeanne Paquin, Elsa Schiaparelli, and Christian Dior, had experienced the height of his success forty years earlier, creating *prêt-à-porter* pieces (arguably, the first) for the space age. "The dresses I prefer are those I invent for a life that does not exist yet—the world of tomorrow."[98] The ninety-year-old designer is still looking toward the future, for example showing his 2008 collection in Beijing, China, whose economic power will surpass the United States's by 2020.

After rampant success in the 1980s and 1990s, Thierry Mugler's House was shuttered in 2003. The revamped House gained notoriety when fashion-editor-turned-Lady-Gaga-stylist Nicola Formichetti was tapped as creative director in 2010. Vocal about not being a designer, Formichetti added Romain Kremer, previously of Christian Dior Monsieur, to his menswear design team. Together, for Fall/Winter 2013–2014, they crafted a "MuglAIR" army clad in "chemical blue." *NOWFashion*'s Elisabeta Tudor considered the color alone to be "violent."[99]

Bijou Blue

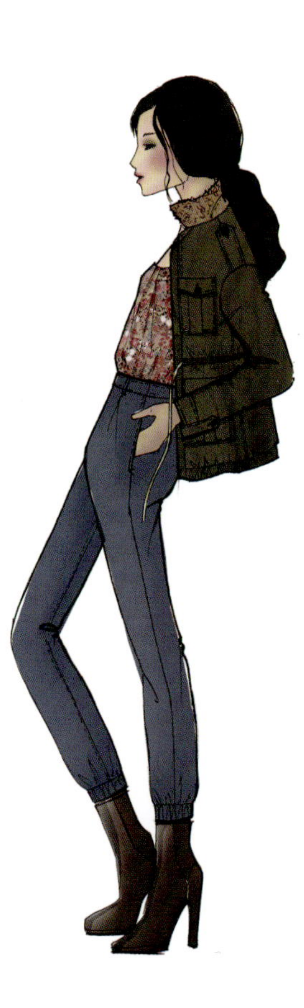

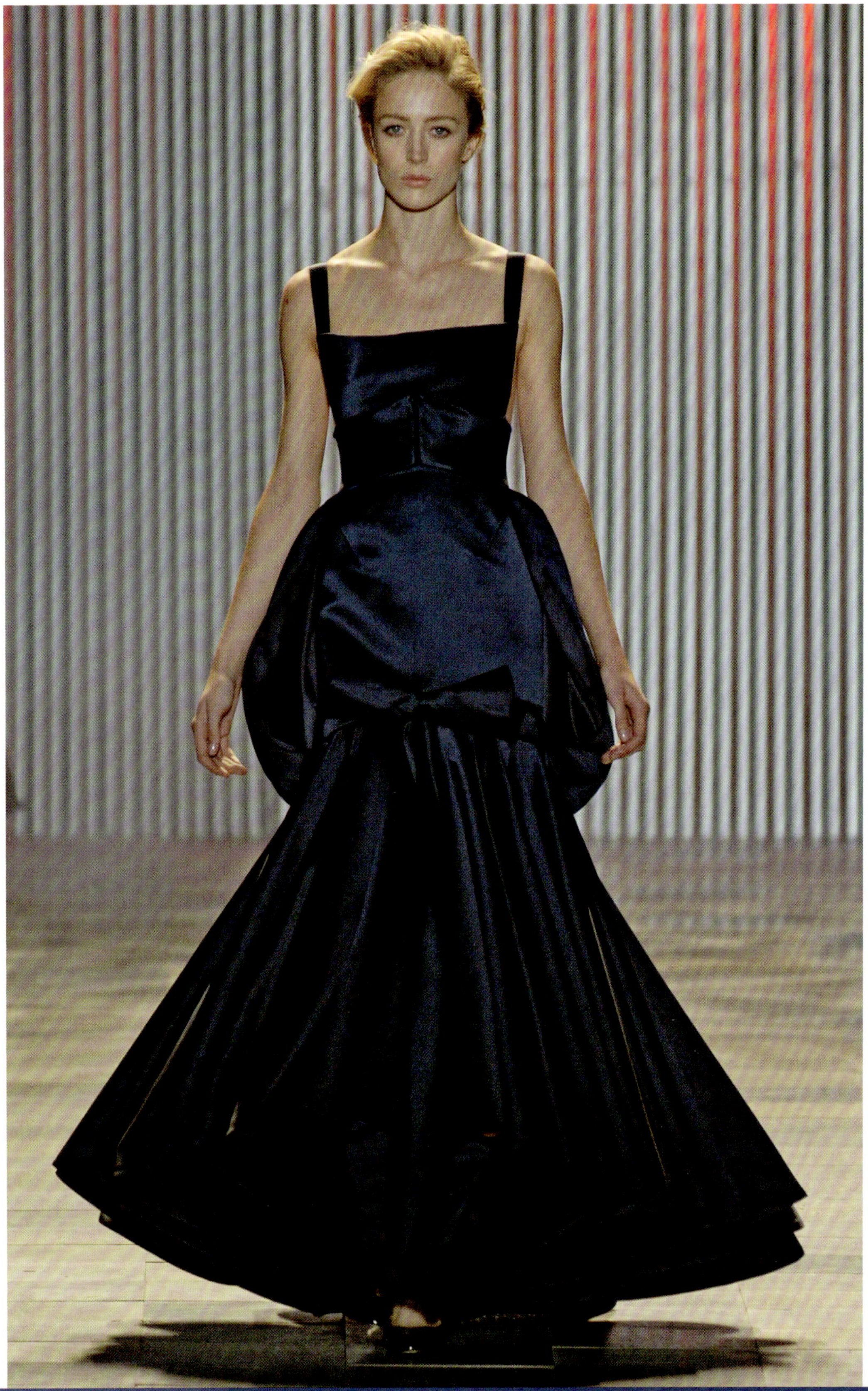

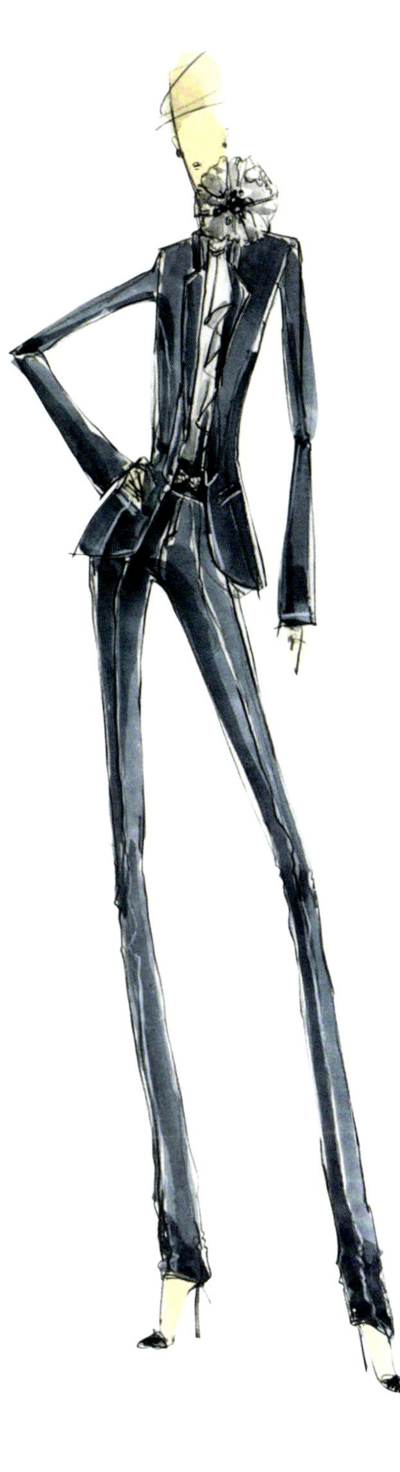

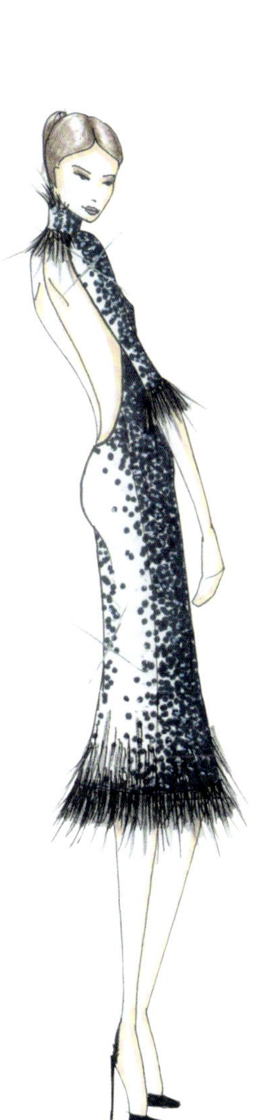

"There is nothing sexier or more real than navy and jet."
—Zac Posen [100]

Across the board, sketches for Fall 2006 were made with a thin blue line. Designers like Barneys-approved Behnaz Sarafpour, London-born Charlotte Ronson, ball gown master Naeem Khan, and Giancarlo Giammetti–mentored Yigal Azrouël all gravitated toward deep blue, incorporating hues of True Navy, Ensign Blue, Bijou Blue, and Vintage Indigo into their collections.

The wars in Afghanistan and Iraq, alongside economic concerns, cast a shadow on New York Fashion Week. As is historically common, the influence of the war found its way onto the runway. Designer Cynthia Steffe admitted her collection was inspired by a "military schoolboy" aesthetic with a feminine twist, like "menswear with a sex change." [101] Designer James Coviello drew parallels between the shifting terrain of the "English inter-war years" (between WWI and WWII) and the uncertainty of the early 21st century through his garments. [102] Designer Alvin Valley embraced True Navy and its association with the "early 70s intellectual and design movements" that arose in response to the Vietnam War. [103]

Yet, this blue was not associated solely with conflict. Pam Devos for Pamella Roland used deep-jewel-tone blue in a fondly nostalgic way, based on the work of turn-of-the-century artist John Singer Sargent, whose blue palette was used to capture budding wealth, luxurious leisure, and decidedly peaceful landscapes. Similarly, Y & Kei's use of Bijou Blue for their sharply tailored suits was meant to evoke a "crisp winter scene." [104]

In contrast, rather than romanticizing evening sky blues, "it" designer of the moment Zac Posen viewed Ensign Blue as "fierce and moody," ideal for a "perfectionistic rebel," like his regular arm candy, Natalie Portman. Reviewing the collection, Cathy Horyn, fashion critic for *The New York Times*, positively highlighted Posen's "supertight (sic) pants in navy python" as being "terrific" and "aggressive," with "tough-girl styling." [105] Rapper and business mogul Sean "Diddy" Combs agreed, giving it a standing ovation, which marked blue as unquestionably cool.

Dark Denim

Mary Lance's documentary *Blue Alchemy* attests that indigo has "captured the human imagination for millennia" and has "been in use worldwide since antiquity." The history of natural indigo is, in part, dark: time-consuming and labor-intensive, it is enmeshed with slavery (in pre–Revolutionary War America) and colonization (in Bengal under the British Raj in the mid-19th century). But it is also ubiquitous.

The first jeans made by Levi Strauss used natural indigo dye. However, in 1890, a chemical was developed that yielded a synthetic dye similar to indigo, and the cultivation of the crop significantly diminished. In 1915, the Cone Mill in North Carolina began producing denim for Levi's using synthetic indigo. The majority of indigo is now synthetic; however, small, local movements have cropped up in the 21st century to try to revive the art of natural indigo dyeing.

From the 19th through the early 20th century, denim was solely used as work wear. But from there its ascendency into popular casual wear skyrocketed. In 1934, "Lady Levi's" were introduced. By the 1950s the original Western blue jean brand suggested to women it was "Right . . . for Leisure." In 1955, "greasers" began appropriating denim after James Dean sexily sported them in *Rebel Without a Cause*. By 1977, hippies were donning denim patchwork and tie-dyed outfits, like those made by retailer Serendipity 3.

Calvin Klein was the first designer to embrace teenage sexuality, using it to brand and sell fashion in 1980, a provocative gamble that paid off in sales of as much as $2 million per month. Clad in an oversized men's shirt, singularly buttoned at the bust, and tight Calvin Klein Jeans in Dark Denim, fifteen-year-old model Brooke Shields breathlessly asserted, "You want to know what comes between me and my Calvin's? Nothing." After all, Calvin Klein didn't start selling skivvies for women until 1983.

Rei Kawakubo for Comme des Garçons regularly transforms the banal into the beautiful (or in some cases, the grotesque). In doing so, she engages the viewer and wearer in existential philosophical questioning about the purpose of fashion and the ideals of society. Comme des Garçons designer Junya Watanabe, who has been with the brand since 1984, shares this type of approach. Watanabe began showing his own line under the CdG umbrella in 1992. Intensely private, Watanabe is not the cult icon Kawakubo is, and while his work fits in with the label's ideology, it is unique. Ironically, unlike Kawakubo, Watanabe neither shies away from nor confronts the idea of femininity. His Spring/Summer 2002 dress mimics the silhouette of a ball gown, freeing the denim from its singularity of purpose.

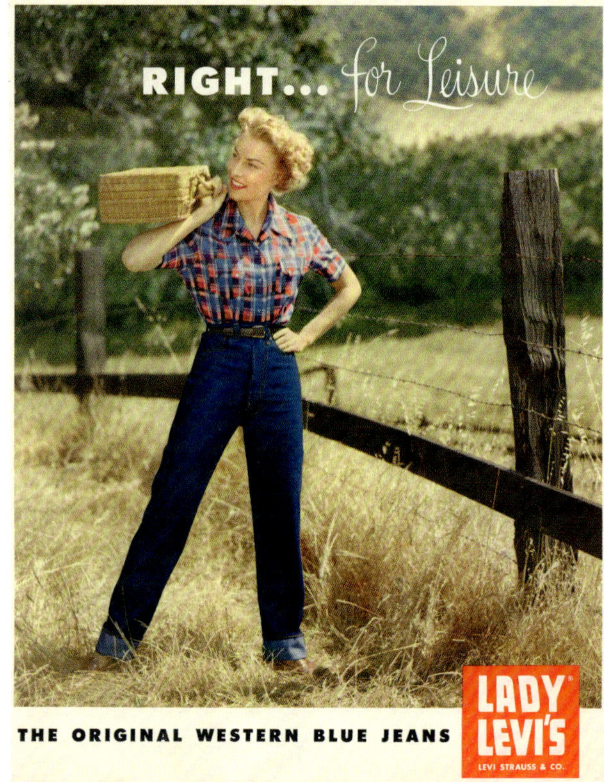

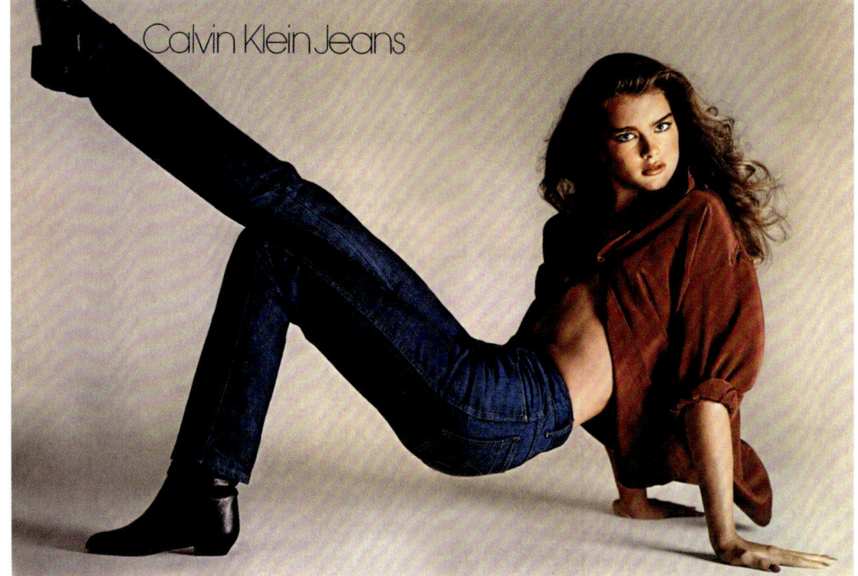

opposite, top
Jeans
Print ad
Lady Levi's
circa 1950

opposite, bottom
Jeans and shirt
Print ad featuring Brooke Shields
Calvin Klein
Early 1980s

left
Distressed denim dress
Junya Watanabe
Spring/Summer 2002

right
Multicolored denim dress
with snake motif
Serendipity 3
1972

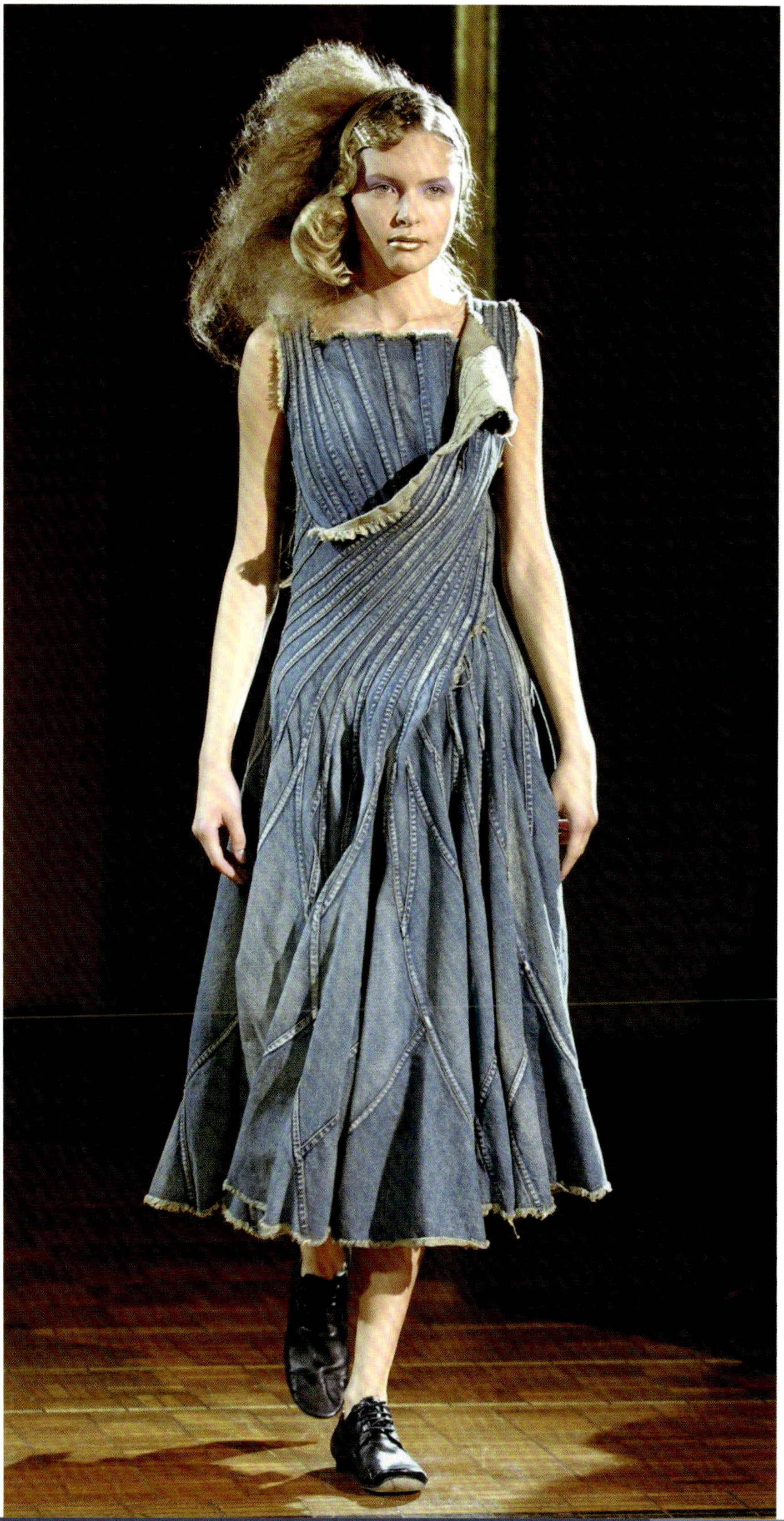

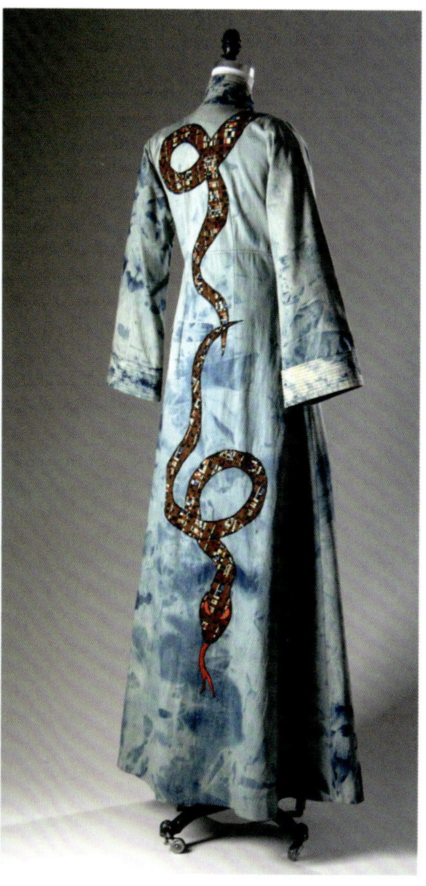

Midnight Navy

"Among all the colors, navy blue is the only one which can compete with black; it has all the same qualities."
—*Christian Dior*[106]

Navy is the go-to blue hue that, despite its connection to maritime pursuits, withstands sea change. Navy blazers made their first appearance in 1920s menswear, which women adapted and appropriated. After Muriel King clad Katharine Hepburn in Navy "lounging pajamas" for the 1937 Hollywood film *Stage Door*, American women, having noted the color in posters and lobby cards, clamored to copy the look. During WWII, Navy returned to its military roots as men in blue sailed off to fight. Understandably, the popularity of Navy diminished after the war; the American public was more interested in "blue suede shoes" and blue jeans in the 1950s. But in the 1980s *The Official Preppy Handbook* brought mainstream attention to the upper-class leisure activities of yachting and nautical sports and the Navy garb that accompanied them. From the 1990s through the early 21st century, Navy was repeatedly proclaimed "the new black," and was worn with similar frequency.

Educated as an illustrator in Paris, Muriel King became a New York designer and sometimes Hollywood costumer, despite her inability to cut, drape, or sew. King became known for outfitting Katharine Hepburn with "cautious daring" on and off stage, indulging the star's unconventional penchant for trousers.[107]

In 1967, fashion god Yves Saint Laurent cut a thin, mod Navy pinstriped suit with a Navy polka-dot button-up. While the suit may appear conservative in retrospect, at the time its gender-bending style was anything but. More revolutionary than Hedi Slimane's 2002 razor-thin menswear for Dior Homme, Saint Laurent's suit outlandishly expressed "the youthfulness of the Sixties . . . beautiful and damned."[108] Before the idea of androgyny was bandied around, Saint Laurent's mod attire for ectomorphic men and/or women bridged the gap between the boxy masculinity and hourglass femininity of the 1950s. Fascinated with the "world in awesome transition," Saint Laurent aided the era's evolution, in part through the use of gender-blind Navy.[109]

In the early 21st century, Navy has been an ever-present classic, from Coach bags to J.Crew jackets. Indeed, in 2013 the classic Navy blazer was reworked again and again, as *Seinfeld*-referenced catalog J. Peterman offered a "Lady Mendl" Navy blazer, using witty copy to educate its audience about America's first female interior decorator. And Caroline Smiley's cheeky British brand Moloh offered Midnight Navy outerwear that was "rather sporty with a hint of military theatrics thrown in."[110]

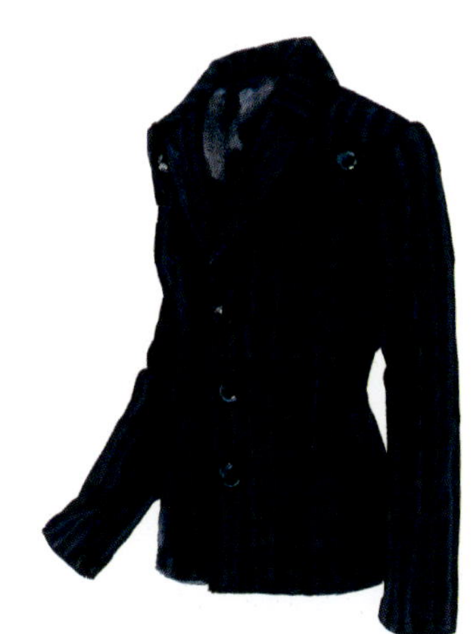

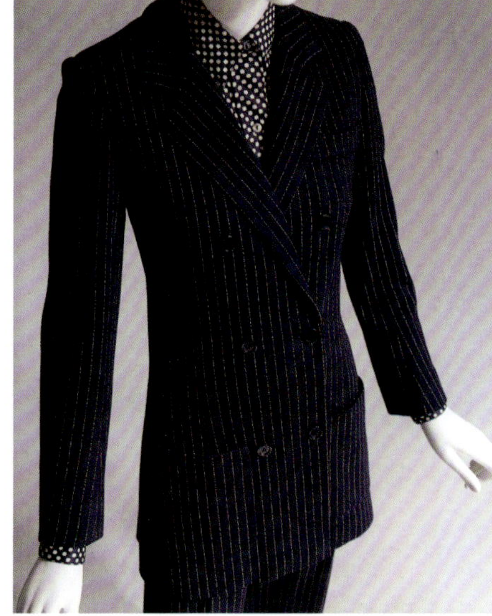

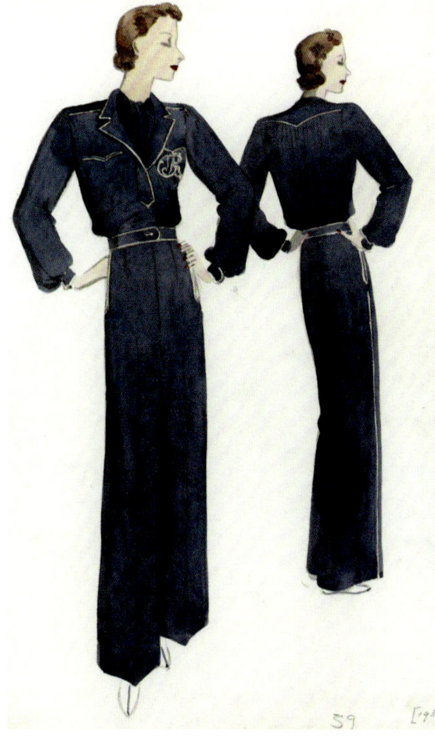

opposite, top left
Elsie's Blazer
J. Peterman
2013

opposite, bottom left
Double-breasted wool suit
Yves Saint Laurent
1967

opposite, right
Lounging pajamas designed for
Katharine Hepburn
Muriel King
1939

below
Stamp jacket and tassel wrap skirt
Moloh
2013

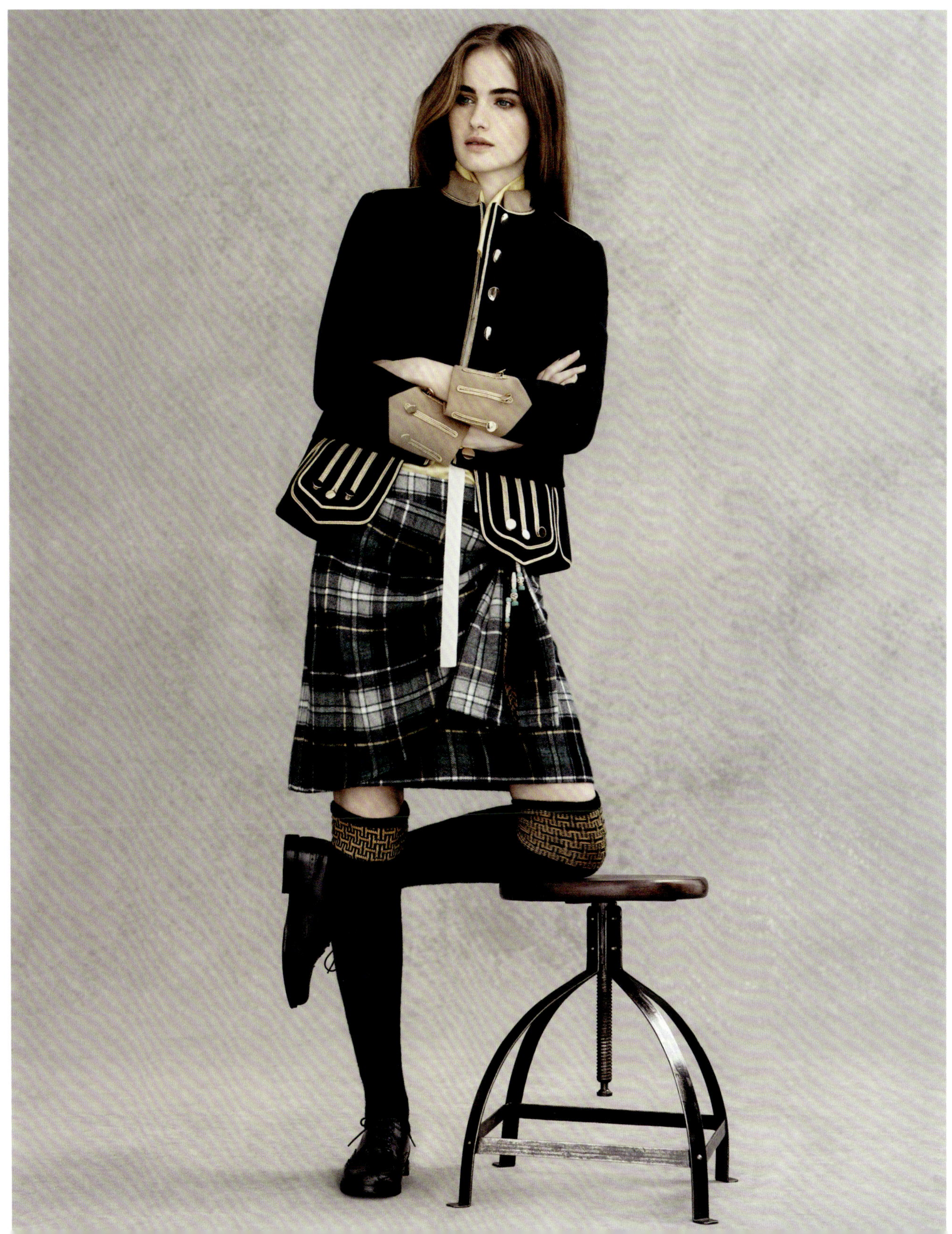

Sky Blue

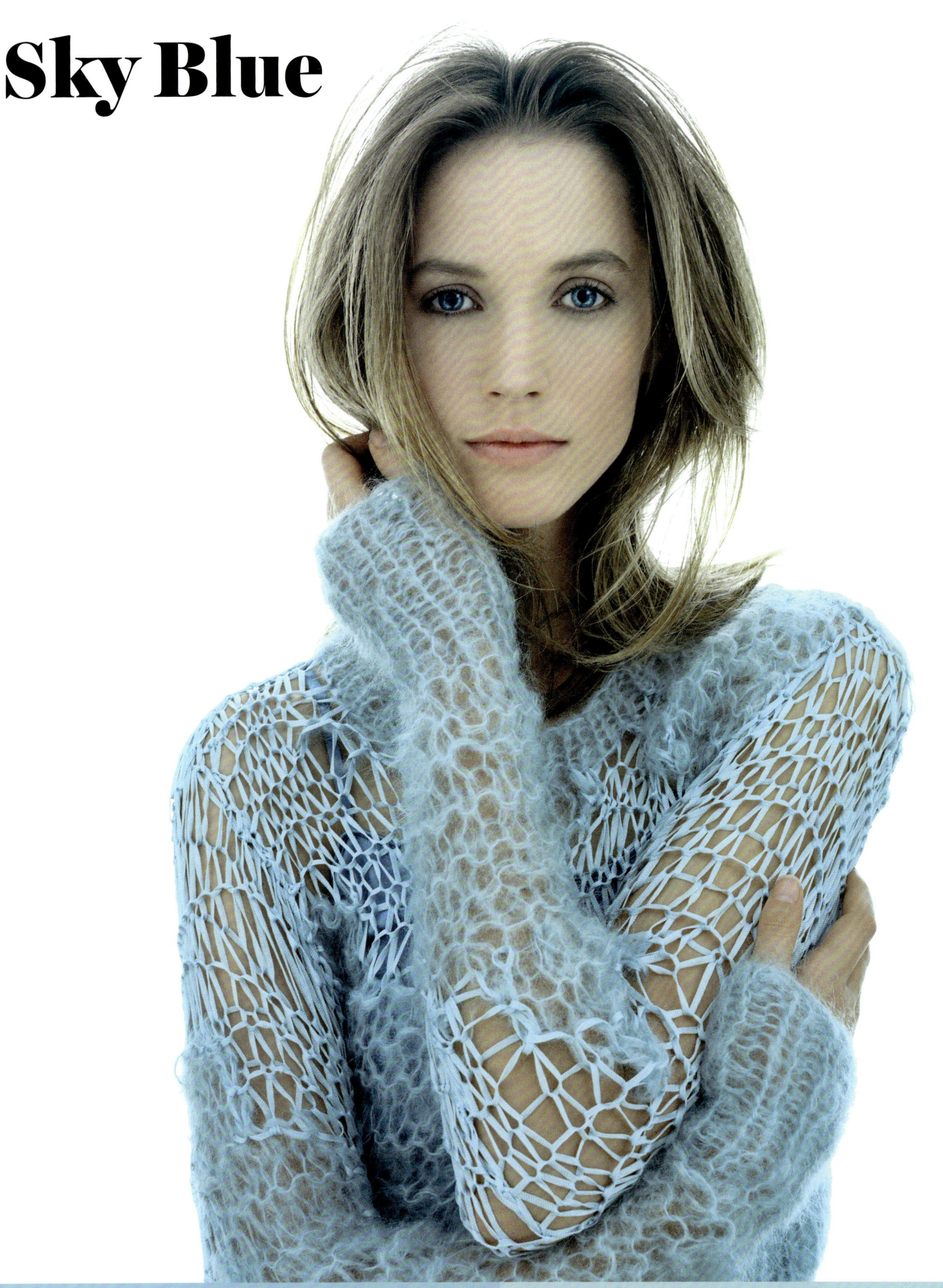

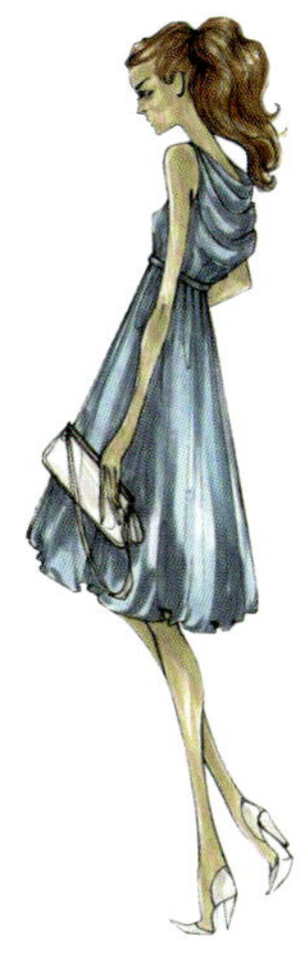

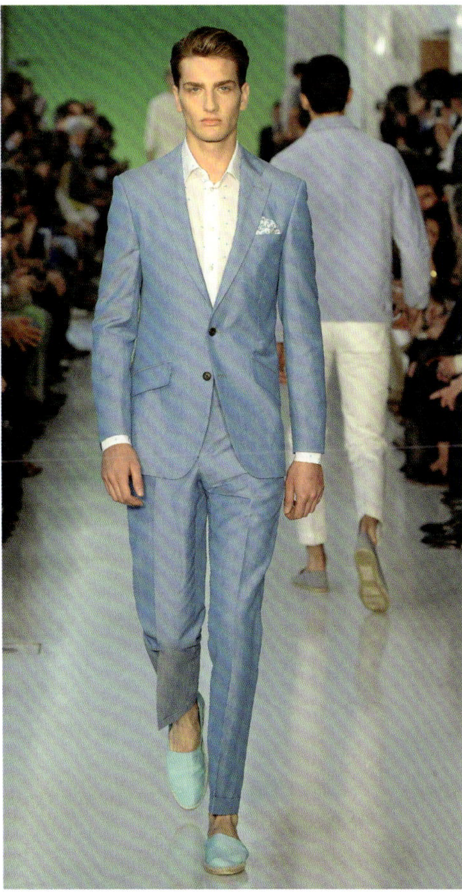

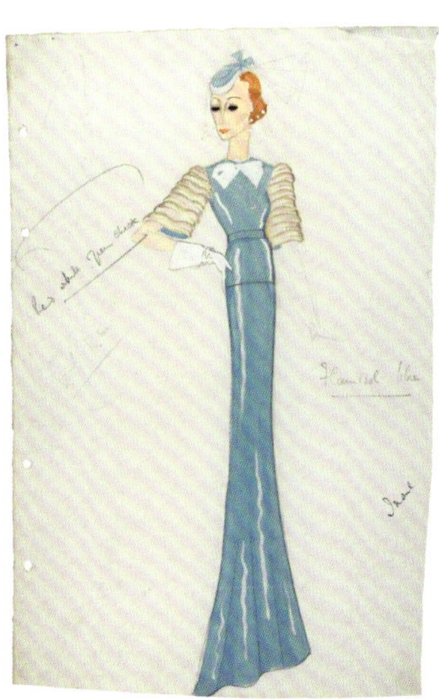

"Pale blue is one of the prettiest colors, and if you have blue eyes, no color is more becoming."

—*Christian Dior*[111]

In the 1920s and 1930s, the newly embraced allure of the beach and its waves brought Sky Blue down from the stratosphere and onto the body. Coco Chanel and her coterie transformed bronzed skin into a status symbol of the wealthy leisure class, and in 1930, *Harper's Bazaar* dedicated an entire issue to the French Riviera. While "the name of Victor Stiebel is synonymous with romantic evening gowns and impeccable tailoring,"[112] Stiebel was just as adept at designing for the beach, evidenced by his long cotton dress with crisscrossing back straps and a matching jacket in Sky Blue. While a quintessentially English designer, Stiebel's childhood upbringing in South Africa undoubtedly aided him with designing for warm weather between the wars.

While Seattle's damp gray weather influenced Nirvana's choice of apparel, 1990s fashion designers introduced color into the grunge aesthetic. Anna Sui showed a Sky Blue version of a grubby moth-hole sweater for her Spring/Summer 1994 collection. Nicole Miller, educated at Rhode Island School of Design and L'École de la Chambre Syndicale de la Couture Parisienne in Paris, reinvigorated traditional mackintosh rainwear by swapping out Burberry's signature tan for a soft glacier blue. Donna Karan New York's "DKNY" line, targeted at a younger demographic and priced more affordably, featured silky light blue pajama pants on the runway, her Spring/Summer 1999 version of the "just rolled out of bed" look.

The promise of a new century and increased concern for the environment caused light blue to continue its reign into the 2000s. Tracy Reese's namesake line, known for "eccentric color combinations" and "lush fabrics and embellishment" has not only cultivated a loyal following of celebrities like Gabrielle Union and Veronica Webb with pieces like her Spring/Summer 2007 empire-waist Aquamarine frock, but also that most sought-after customer, First Lady Michelle Obama.[113]

In the 1990s, Richard James was the "new boy causing a stir," setting up a Saville Row shop without a background in tailoring. While tradition is honored in Britain, the new guard is equally appreciated, and James's knowledge of high-fashion, when paired with a staff fluent in bespoke, quickly earned him a Menswear Designer of the Year Award from the British Fashion Council. James is still fearless twenty years later, using colors not typically associated with menswear, like celestial blue, which encapsulated the Spring/Summer 2014 idea of a "cool, color-drenched hour when the summer sun slips away."[114]

Blue Turquoise

"Your friends are used to you in navy blue. They hardly look twice. But if navy blue changes to turquoise, you can be certain it will be noticed."

—*Claire McCardell*[115]

"Turquoise" describes both the distinctive mineral and its color. While found in ancient cultures from Persia (Iran) to Mexico, the French came across it in Turkestan, referring to it as *pierre turqueise* (Turkish stone). It became Anglicized to "turquoise" in AD 1567. In North America, the Anasazi mined turquoise as early as AD 1000, and the Pueblo in AD 900. The Zuni and the Navajo also used turquoise in their jewelry, the Navajo using more silver and the Zuni characteristically carving it into shapes for mosaics.

After 9/11, a monochromatic neutral palette dominated, but color began to trickle back onto the runway for Spring/Summer 2005. Turquoise began to have its moment in the sun.

Michael Kors, the jet-setting American golden boy and *Project Runway* TV personality, based his collection on the magnificent Mediterranean blue of the Greek Isles. The line, considered "as smooth as a moonlight sail," included a mermaid gown in turquoise as part of its finale.[116] While the color is louder than most of his "quiet" minimalist work, it still exemplifies Kors's distinctive "clean lines" and classical nature. Kors, whose work has a wide appeal, prides himself on being able to cater to a spectrum of women, from Barbara Walters to Jessica Simpson.

Parsons alum and Bill Blass's protégé Peter Som chose "washed and cool shades of green with blue undertones," to reflect the "relaxed, carefree culture of Northern California beaches."[117] Narciso Rodriguez loosened up his characteristically close-cut clothing for the season, showing seven ensembles in Blue Turquoise.

In 2005, Ralph Lauren debuted a new perfume, "Pure Turquoise," a theme on which he also based his collection. Lauren's interest in the Southwest surfaced in 1978, when he put forth his "Westernwear," a bohemian mixture of cowboy and *Little House on the Prairie*. Lauren made his billions by branding American lifestyles, from the polo prepster to *The Great Gatsby*. Born in the Bronx to two poor Jewish immigrants, he embodies Horatio Alger's "American dream." However, like the work of many designers who appropriate tropes drawn from native cultures, Lauren's embrace of Native American visuals "has also come under criticism."[118]

Italian-born New York designer Luca Orlandi of Luca Luca was first drawn to "exquisite colors"[119] like the blue of Caribbean waters in the mid-aughts. And nearly a decade later, in the Spring/Summer 2012 collection, the brand revisited Lake Blue again for a light, airy goddess dress.

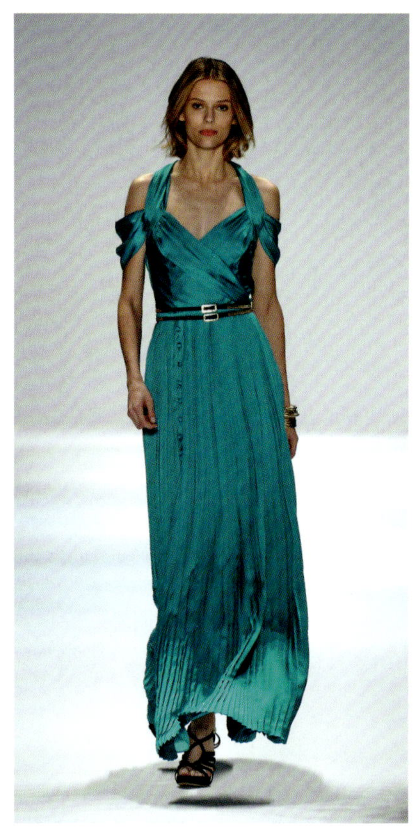

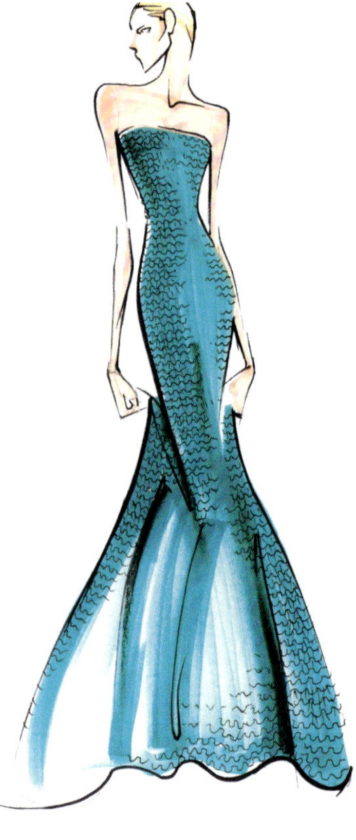

opposite, left
Dress
Raul Melgoza for Luca Luca
Spring/Summer 2012

opposite, right
Strapless gown
Michael Kors
Spring/Summer 2005

left
Necklace, earrings, cuff,
and conch belt
Ralph Lauren
Fall 2004

right
Zuni needlepoint Sleeping Beauty
bracelet
Durango Silver Company
circa 1953

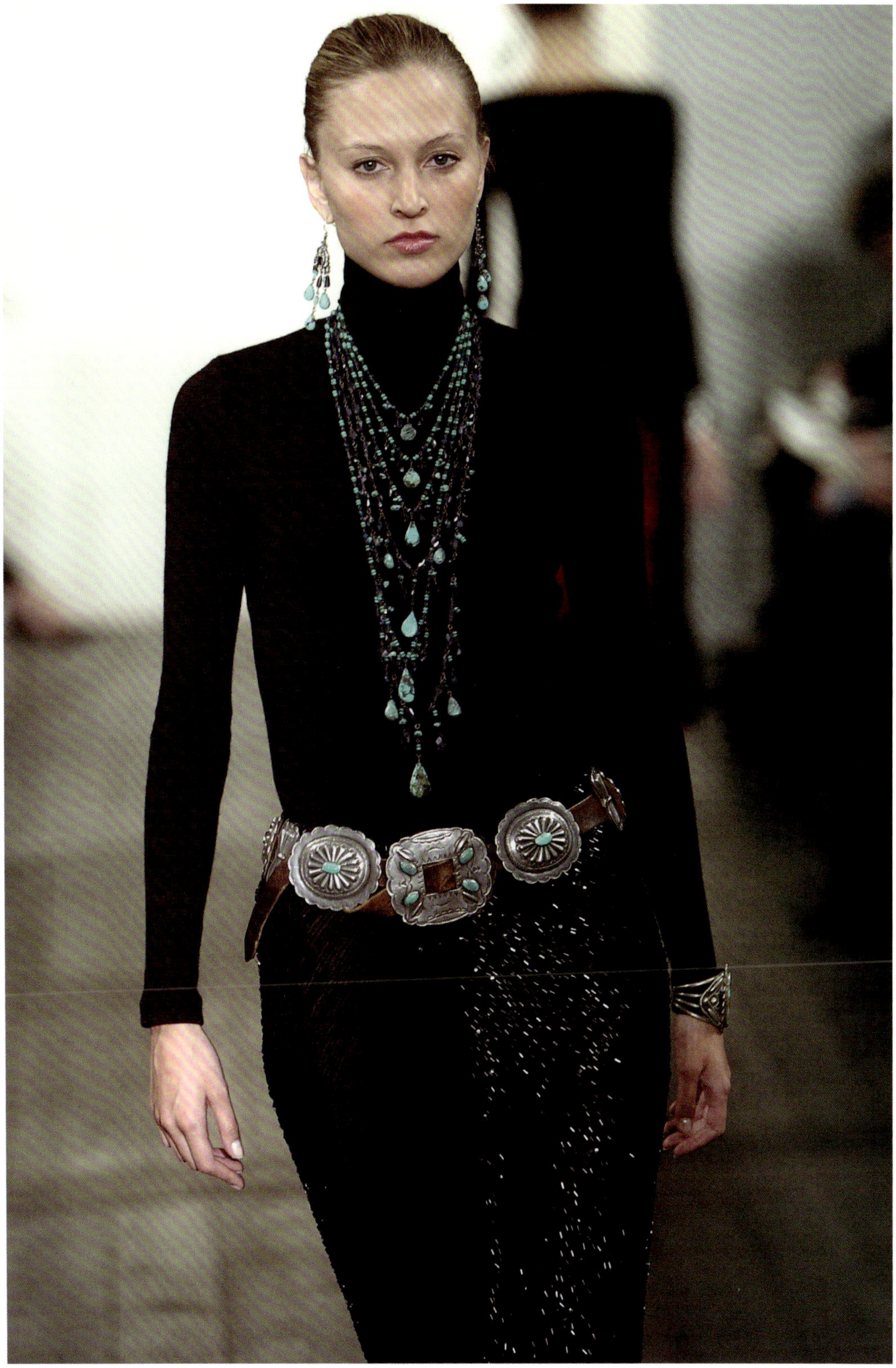

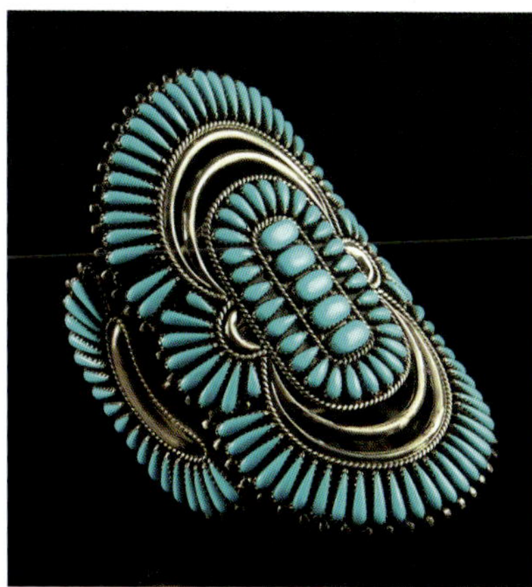

Deep Teal

Deep Teal is a resplendent color inspired by various ornithological shades, from blue-toned peacocks to green-toned drakes. Teals, also present in darkening skies and deepening waters, portray the transitions of nature and thus humanity.

Following the end of the German Occupation, self-taught German-Jewish artist Ursula Sternberg-Hertz (who, despite being hunted, miraculously survived) used teal to represent a colorful emergence from darkness in her watercolor entry for an art contest held by London's Ascher Studio. Sternberg-Hertz's depiction of a fashionable postwar woman with a large Deep Teal hat and matching vibrant blouse won third prize and landed her a job freelancing for the House. This original submission, along with some of her other pieces, is now part of the collection of the Victoria & Albert Museum. Gallery owner Carol Schwartz considers Sternberg-Hertz's work to be "primitive and surrealistic at the same time, displaying charm, joy, and whimsy,"[120] a type of art that, after WWII, was in high demand.

In her Fall 2008 collection, Japanese designer Akiko Ogawa celebrated a combination of teals: iridescent, indigo-tinged, and mixed with jet black for her collection inspired by the "glittering arc of the Milky Way Galaxy."[121] Ogawa, who graduated from Kuwasawa Design School, worked for Japanese clothing manufacturer Onward Kashiyama before beginning her own brand in 2001. Cosmopolitan women in Tokyo, Paris, and New York have snapped up her flirty, party-ready pieces aimed at high-end scenesters.

Teal was used with zeal in 2011 at New York Fashion Week. Tommy Hilfiger, Tadashi Shoji, and Shaun Kearney for Cynthia Steffe all opted to use it in their differing lines. British-born designer Kearney crafted an exaggerated funnel-neck wrap coat in an Everglade hue for Cynthia Steffe's label. Kearney, who has personally designed for celebrities like Jennifer Aniston, desires to continually create clothing that "evoke[s] an emotional response in the person who wears them."[122]

A. F. Vandevorst sent models down the runway with their faces obscured by Stephen Jones fedoras and bundled scarves. For Fall/Winter 2012–2013, the Belgian duo mused on choreographer Pina Bausch, mashing together Bausch's everyday masculine attire with the hyper-feminine garb typically worn by dancers. The result was effectively a faceless mannequin in a silky Deep Lake vest, caught in mid-metamorphosis. The high-cut black trousers highlighted the fact that the piece was not quite a ball gown.

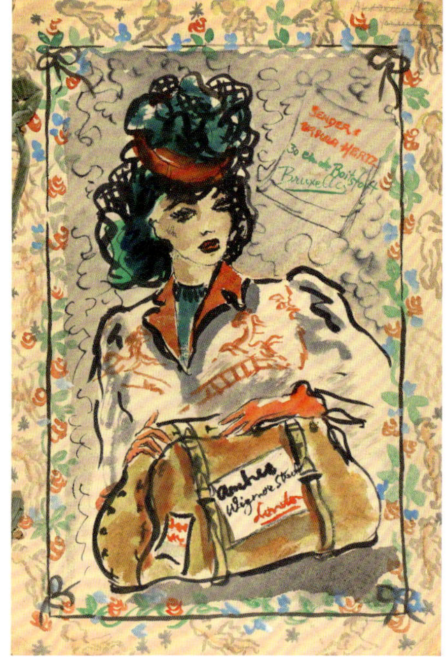

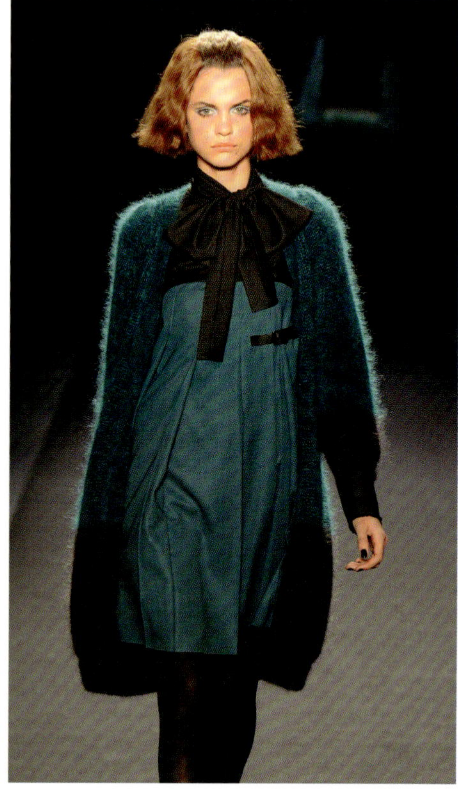

opposite, left
Painted sketch
Ursula Sternberg-Hertz
1947

opposit, right
Dress with bow under
a long sweater
Akiko Ogawa
Fall/Winter 2008

left
Vested cape over shirt and trousers
with matching boots, hat, and scarf
A. F. Vandevorst
Fall/Winter 2012

right
Wrap coat
Shaun Kearney for Cynthia Steffe
Fall/Winter 2011

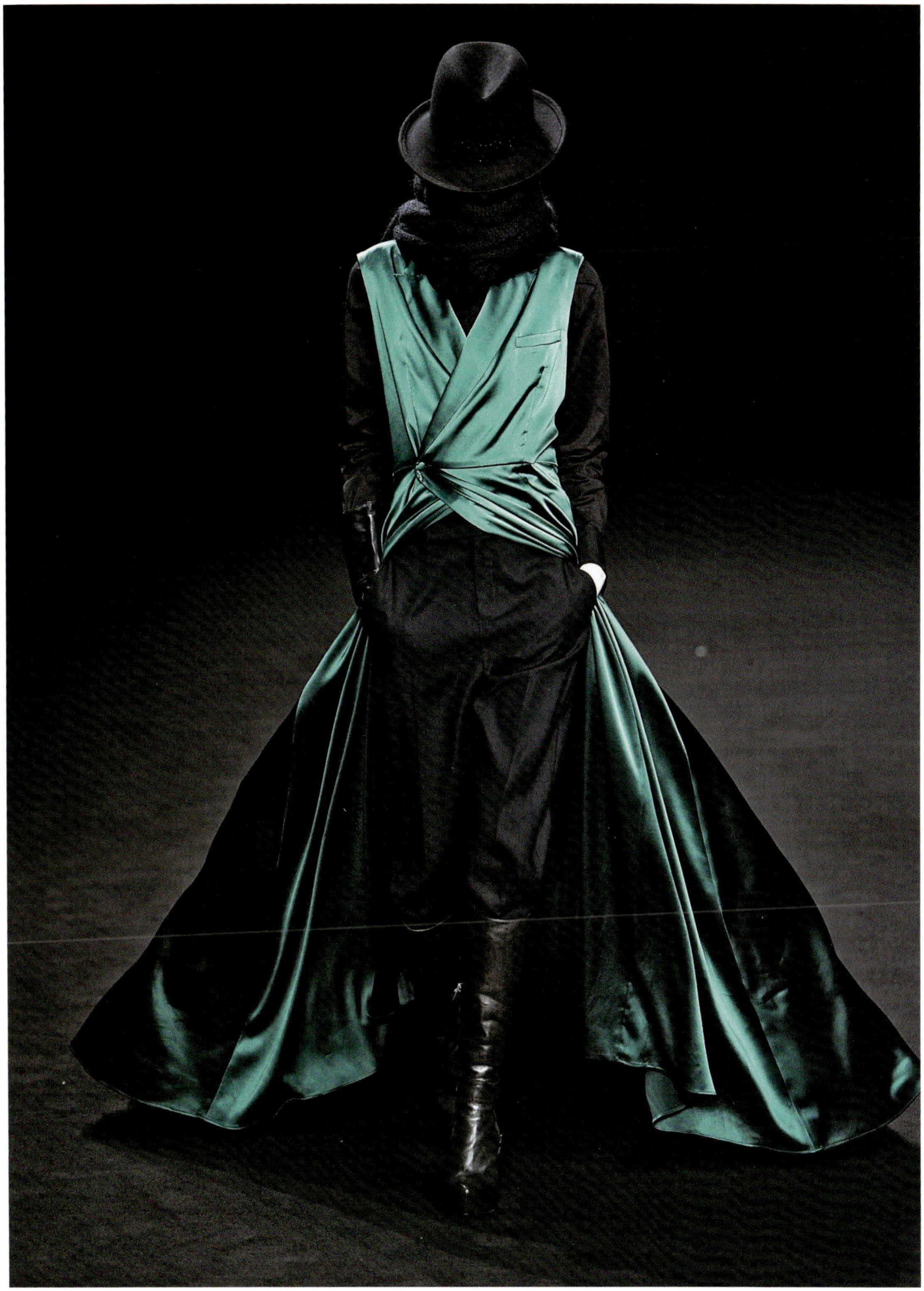

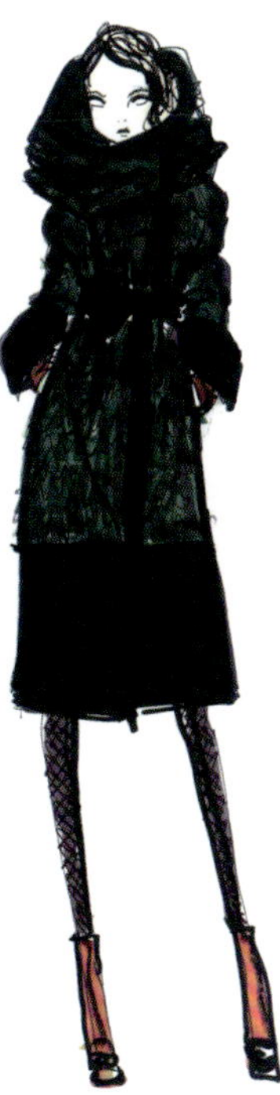

Hunter Green

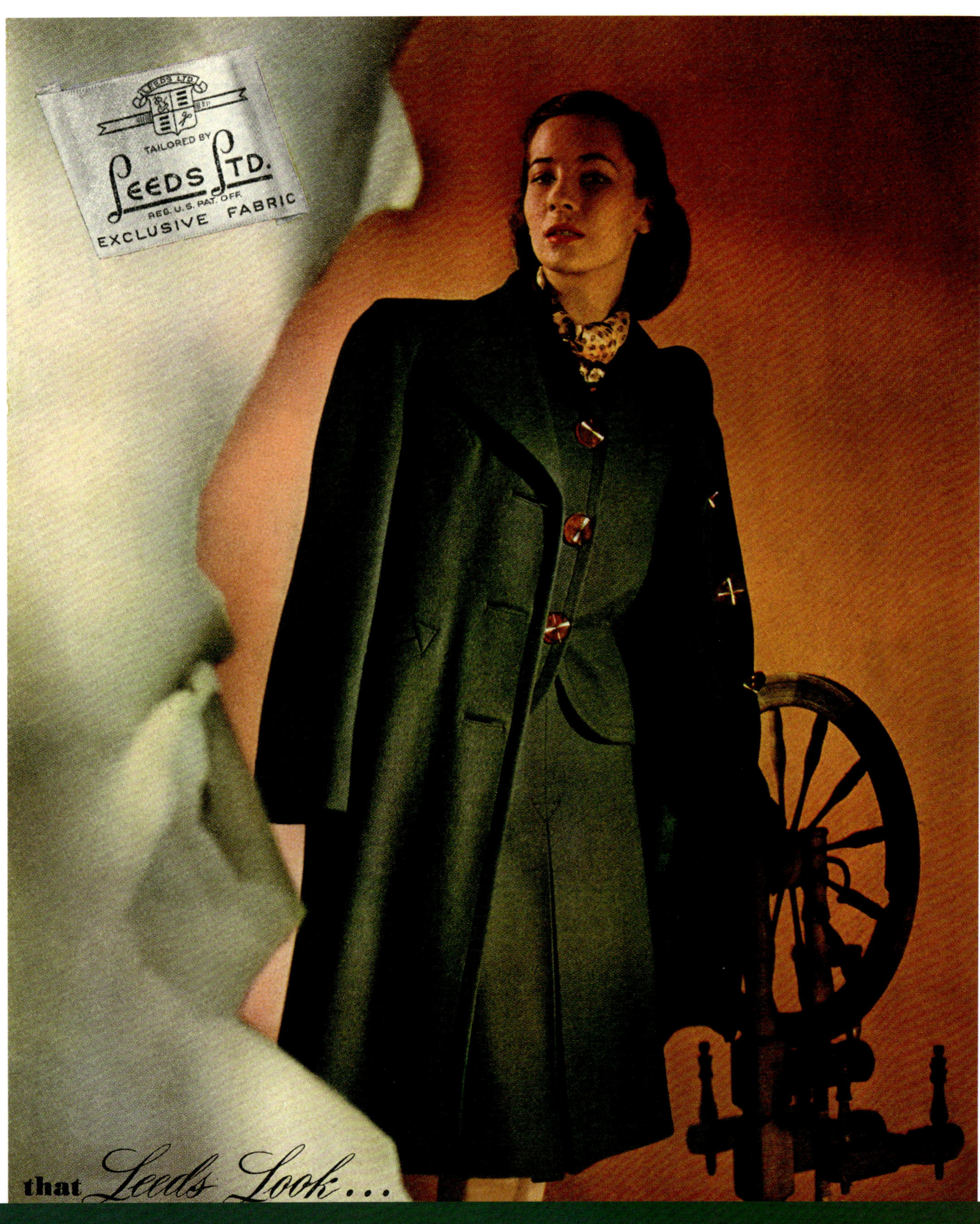

Hunter Green
PANTONE 19-5511

Dark Green
PANTONE 19-5513

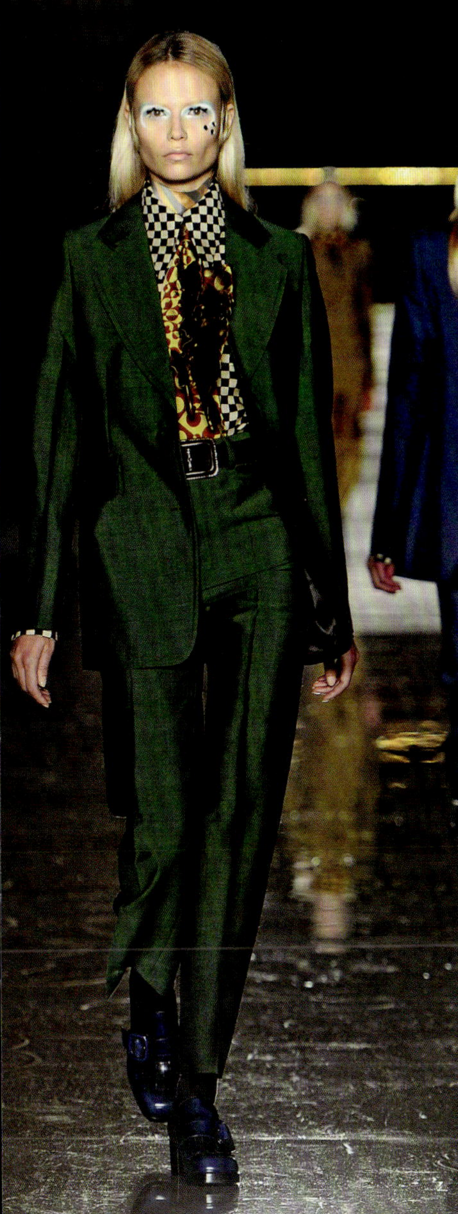

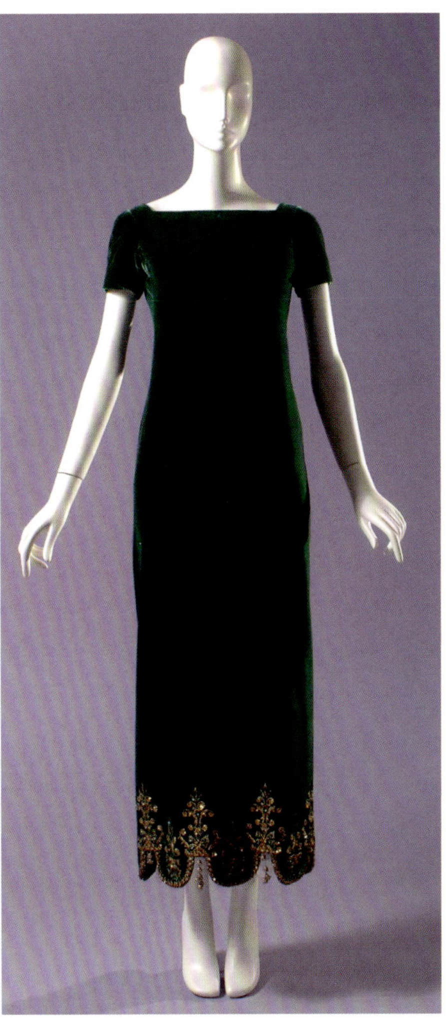

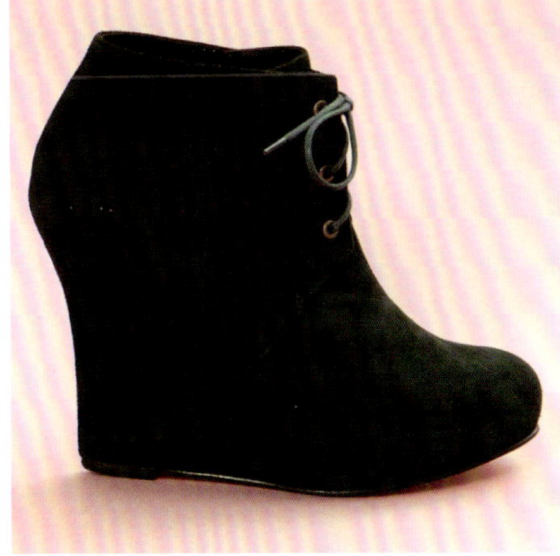

Hunter Green has a long history, as the deep sylvan dyes were readily accessible in many countries. In the 1920s, the dark Evergreen was appropriated by *la garçonne* (a boyish girl); today's 21st-century neo-*garçonne* has recently followed suit. In the 1930s, Mariano Fortuny heightened the romanticism of his classical Grecian gowns with the forest-inspired hue. Women in the 1940s wore the color as a symbol of unity with the troops, though it was quickly abandoned post-victory. In the 1960s, Baby Boomer teenagers delighted in the newly deemed "unisex" color. In the 2000s, Opening Ceremony die-hards became similarly taken, enamored with the idea of bygone vintage, but desiring something actually new.

In 1932, Mariano Fortuny immaculately crafted a Hunter Green silk tea gown, using a pleating device he created. Fortuny's avant-garde indoor robes furthered the casualization of fashion, as women desired to flaunt them around town.

After tempestuous starts-and-stops at Christian Dior where he butted heads with boy wonder Yves Saint Laurent, Marc Bohan became chief designer of the venerable House in 1960. A smashing success, Bohan presented a Dark Green velvet dress with rhinestone flourishes on the hem for Dior's Fall 1963 line.

During WWII, women unable to contribute to the war effort adopted Dark Green ensembles as a way of showing solidarity with the troops. This 1944 British advertisement for a Hunter Green ensemble by Leeds Ltd. uses photographic techniques usually seen in fashion editorials, but also somewhat incongruously includes a spinning wheel. While women certainly weren't spinning their own fabric during the war, they were using sewing machines to make and mend their own clothing, as well as favoring sturdy fabrics that resisted wear.

Opening Ceremony's owners/designers Carol Lim and Humberto Leon have been the arbiters of everything "major" for the last decade. Their store carries the world's hippest labels, including their own—which amps up downtown New York street trends. Their 2010 Evergreen suede wedge boot was higher and clunkier than other labels', and its minimalism (three grommets, and two cut pieces of leather) conspicuously stark in comparison, which made them an ideal statement piece for cool kids like Chloë Sevigny.

After years of skirts, Miuccia Prada's Miu Miu label featured Pineneedle green matching pantsuits for Fall/Winter 2010; modish and metallic, they were ideally suited for modern-day *garçonnes* like Kate Lanphear.

Ultramarine Green

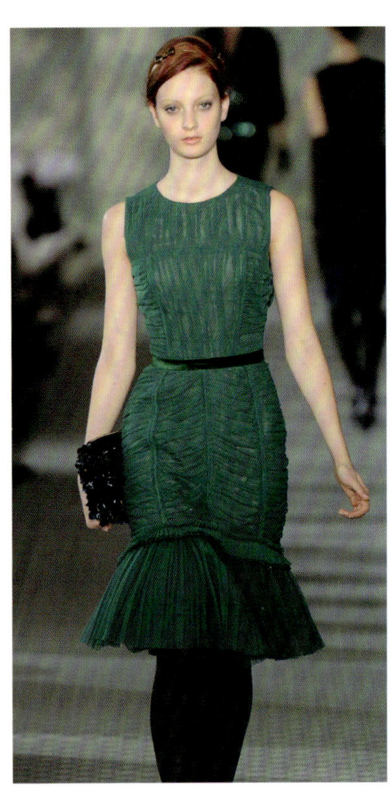

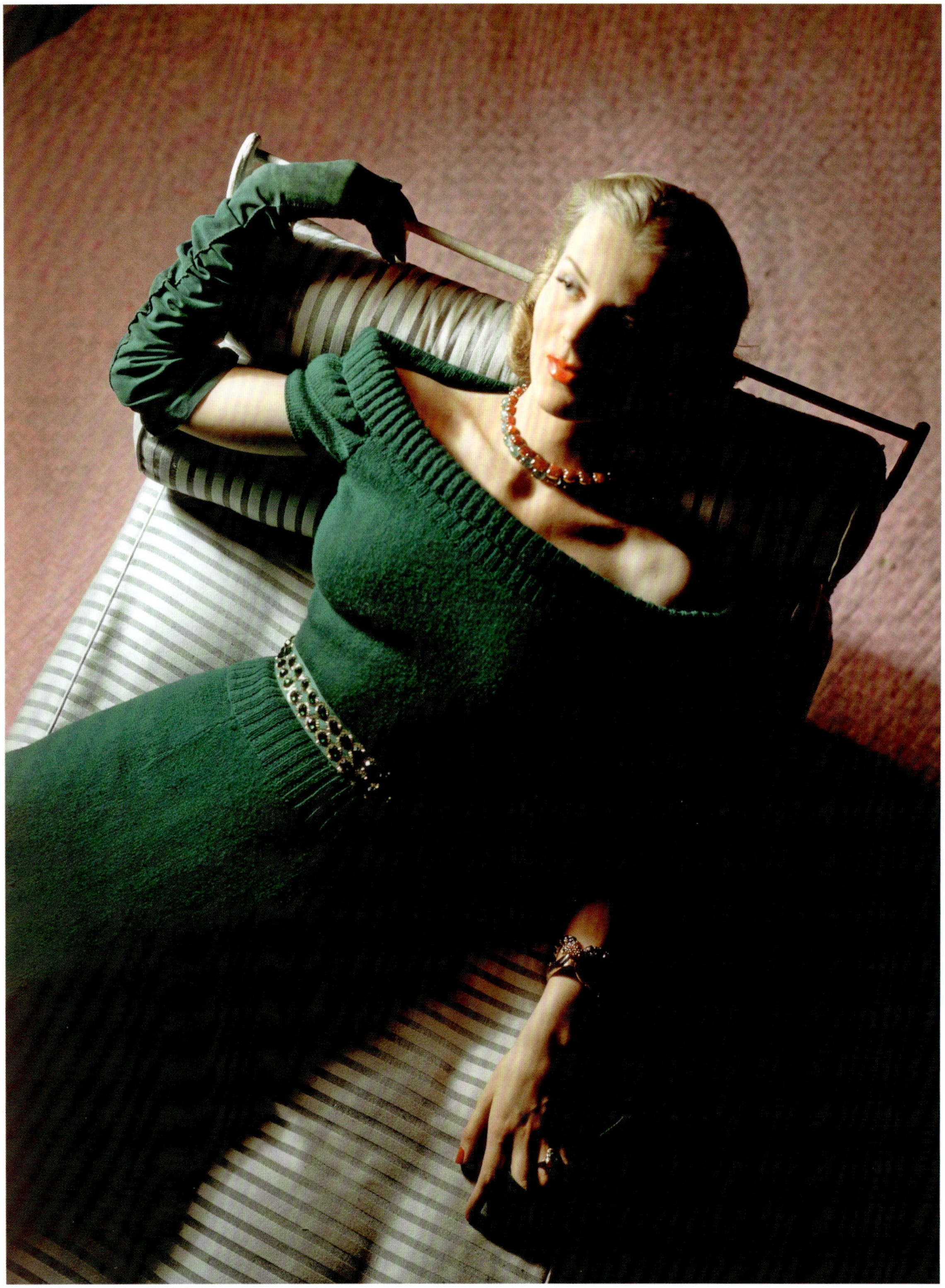

Ultramarine Green
PANTONE 18-5338

Shady Glade
PANTONE 18-5624

Harnessing the strength of an emerald, eye-catching Ultramarine Green exudes confidence, making it a regular fashion favorite.

In 1947, Nancy Berg ran away from home and began modeling. Three years later, Berg remembers making her way to New York, "I checked into the Plaza hotel and in six months, I was on the cover of *Vogue*."[123] In 1955, Berg modeled a boxy "Capri" blazer in Viridis for Talbott. Five years later, Nancy Berg was raking in $40,000 a year as a "glamour girl" and "enjoying every minute of it."[124] American-born Berg later transitioned into acting as a new crop of London models—Twig, Cod, and Tree—leapt in front of the lens.

Henrietta Kenengeiser, better known as Hattie Carnegie, became incredibly successful in the fashion industry in spite of the fact that she could neither sew nor draw. After years of working at Macy's, nineteen-year-old Carnegie opened her own hat shop in 1909. By 1940, Hattie Carnegie Inc. employed over 1,000 people. Carnegie's Originals, based on Parisian designs, were created by means of Carnegie communicating style ideas to those with the ability to make them a reality. In 1943, the "tiny, tempestuous, and talented" Carnegie sold an Ultramarine Green boatneck knit dress, photographed by John Rawlings.[125]

Whenever a socialite tries her hand at fashion, insiders scoff and snicker. Even Carolina Herrera suffered this fate at the beginning of her career. Yet, like Herrera, Tory Burch has built a glorious empire with a strong foundation. Since 2004, Burch's classic, yet modern American sportswear—with foreign flourishes from her travels thrown in here and there—has charmed. Burch's WASPy beauty and connections have been given more notice than her serious industry credentials, despite the fact that, before launching her own line, she worked for Ralph Lauren, Vera Wang, and Narciso Rodriguez at Loewe. For Fall/Winter 2012–2013, Burch based her line on the film *In the Mood for Love*, including prim pieces with a bit of spunk, like her knee-length ruched frock in Shady Glade on model Codie Young.

Born in the Philippines, Monique Lhuillier moved to Los Angeles to attend the Fashion Institute of Design and Merchandising (FIDM). Like Vera Wang, Lhuillier was disenchanted with wedding dress options and began her business to craft dream dresses for special events; like those of Randolph Duke, Lhuillier's gowns are most often seen at award shows on celebrities like Kerry Washington and Lucy Liu. For Fall 2013, Lhuillier chose model Elsa Sylvan to display her sequined art-deco-referencing Emerald gown, worthy of Oscar-wear.

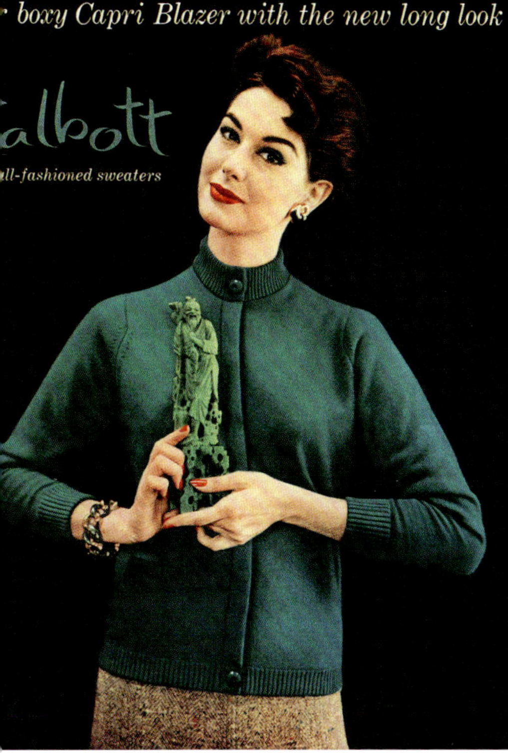

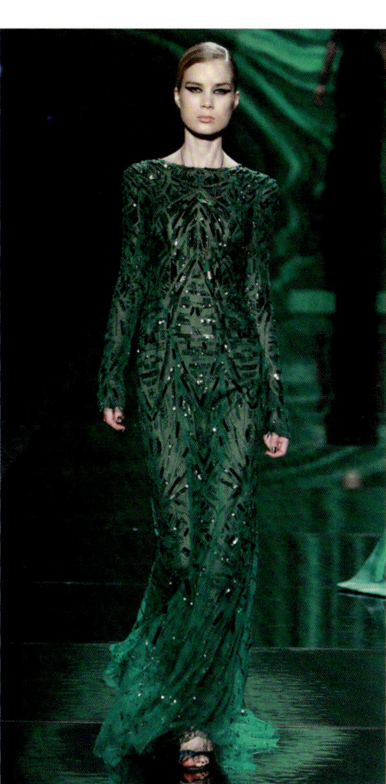

Opal

Named after the gemstone, the color Opal is hard to pin down. Ever-changing in the light, Opal has a magical quality that evokes childlike wonder. This soft green lacks aggression and exudes vulnerability, which is evident in *Vogue*'s accessible 1970 mod coat pattern and Van Beirendonck's Spring/Summer 2012 menswear. In contrast, Thierry Mugler chose the gentle shade for his overtly sexual garment in the late 1990s, a juxtaposition that heightened its incendiary nature.

Even in 1899, *Vogue* knew that not all its readers would be able to afford the garments featured within its pages, and began selling sewing patterns. In 1970, *Vogue Patterns* offered a Cardin-esque mod Brook Green coatdress. By selling do-it-yourself "designer" looks for nearly nothing, *Vogue Patterns* continues to exist, despite the exponential decrease in American home sewing.

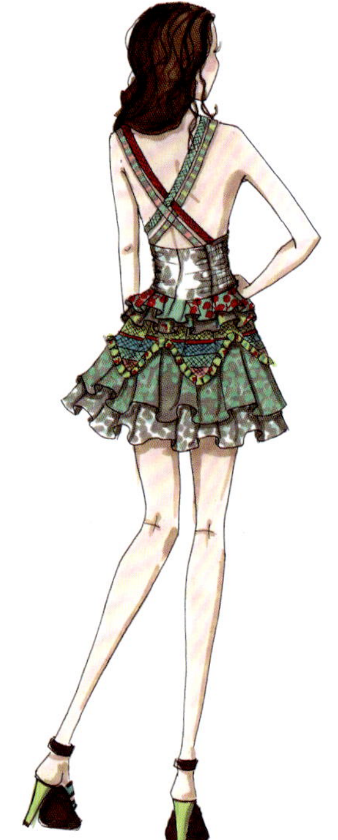

Thierry Mugler provocatively uses eroticism in his designs. For Spring/Summer 1999, Mugler outfitted model Ester Cañadas in a transparent Lucite Green chiffon peignoir that revealed a corresponding thong. Justifying his design, Mugler quipped, "the majority of the world's population would put cleavage over practicality every time."[126]

Nanette Lepore knows what it takes to make it in New York: "a wardrobe like armor and battle heels."[127] Since launching her successful label in 1992, Lepore has been creating feminine, boho pieces that, despite their cool vibe, cause catfights among insatiable customers and celebs alike, including Blake Lively and Leighton Meester. For Spring/Summer 2009, she produced a flirty floral frock in Opal, made in the city's Garment District.

Part of the "Antwerp Six," Belgian-born Walter Van Beirendonck has been causing a ruckus since 1983. Van Beirendonck introduced the sweet green in his Spring/Summer 1998 show, "A Fetish for Beauty," where he accessorized an Opal tulle dress with a matching gas mask. For Spring/Summer 2012, he subversively placed the delicate Honeydew hue in his menswear collection. The ensemble is surprisingly wearable for Van Beirendonck. Taken out of context, the blazer would work for a Hamptons benefit, excluding the complementing face paint of course. The pastel palette made the deconstructed, destroyed, oversized, and ruffled pieces seem less abrasive. "From day one, when I started to study fashion, I liked and used colors a lot. For me, they are part of how I express my ideas in the collections," Van Beirendonck explained.[128]

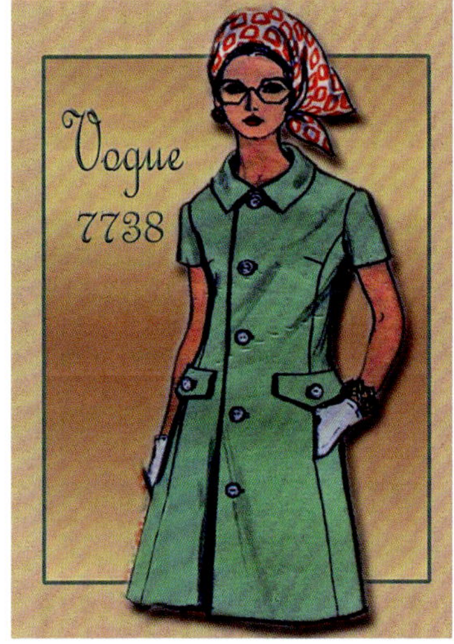

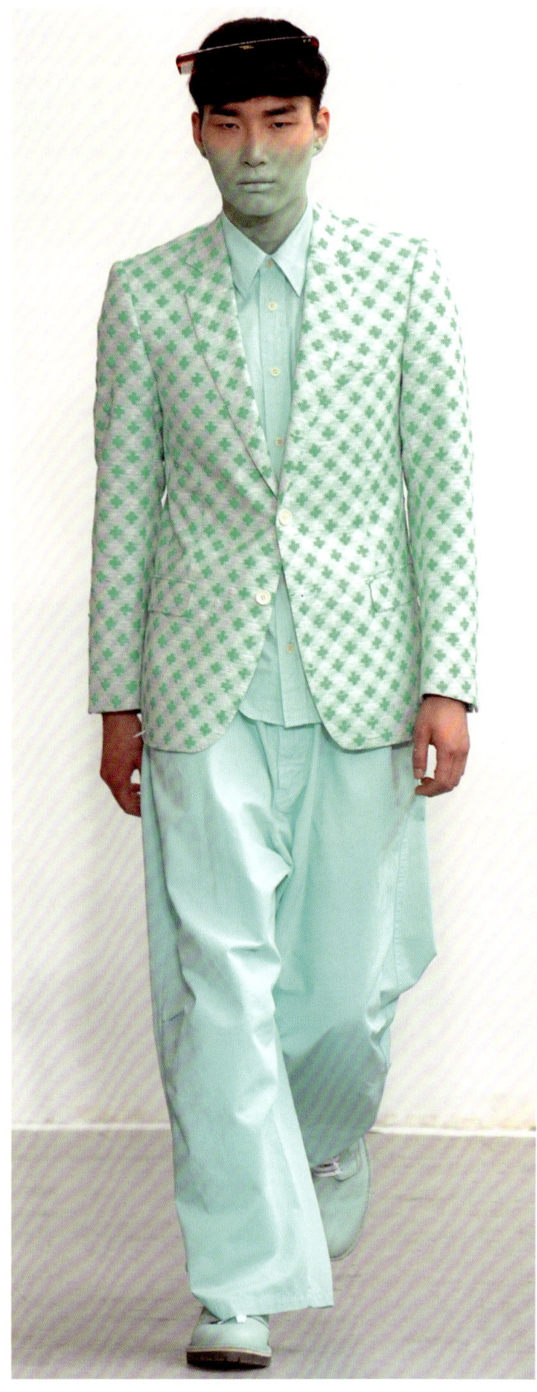

opposite, top left
Dress with ruffles
Nanette Lepore
Spring/Summer 2009

opposite, bottom left
Coatdress
Vogue® Patterns
1970

opposite, right
Patterned blazer with shirt,
trousers, and shoes
Walter Van Beirendonck
Spring/Summer 2012

below
Chiffon peignoir with ruffles
over matching panties
Thierry Mugler
Spring/Summer 1999

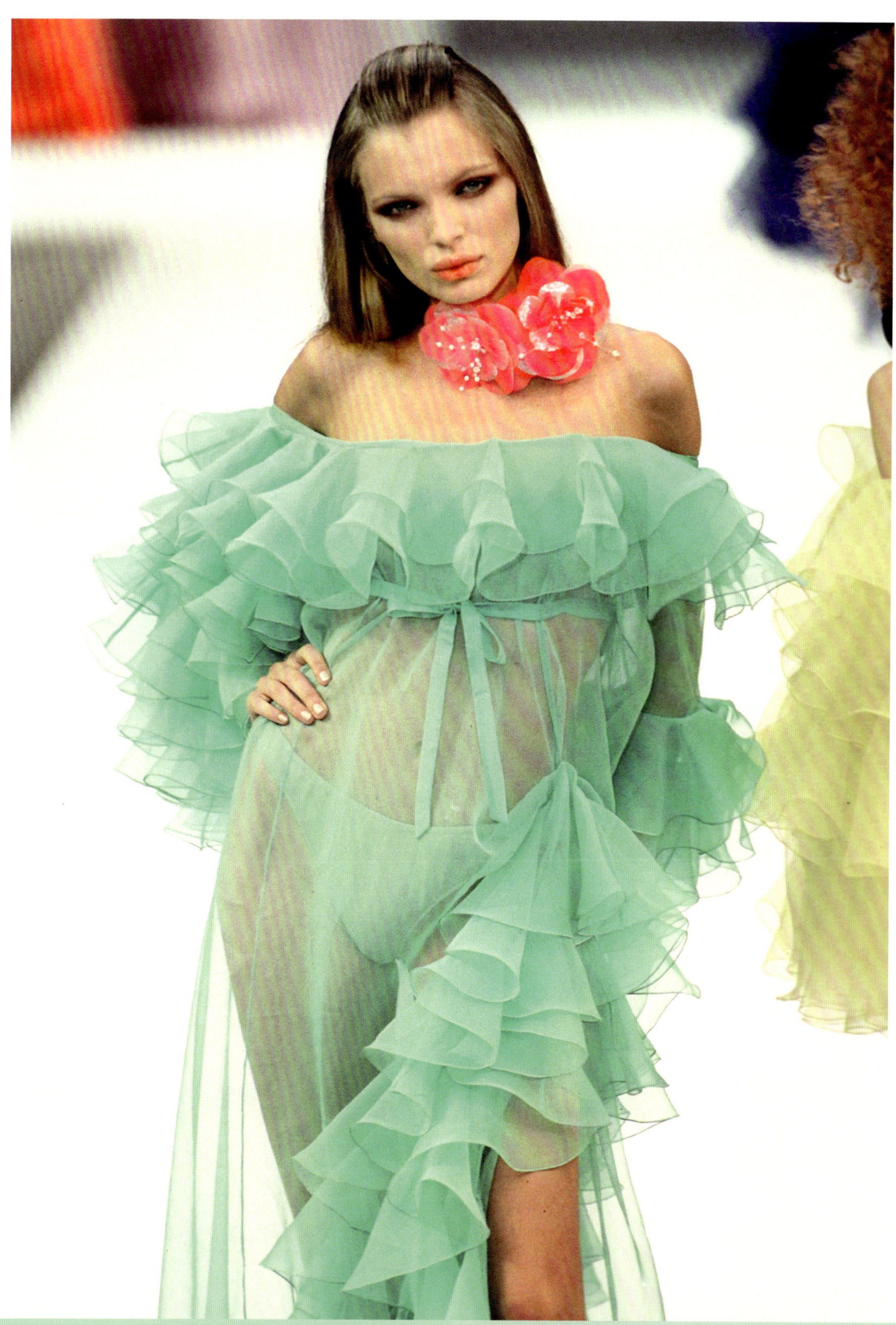

Brook Green
PANTONE 13-6009

Honeydew
PANTONE 12-5808

Hemlock

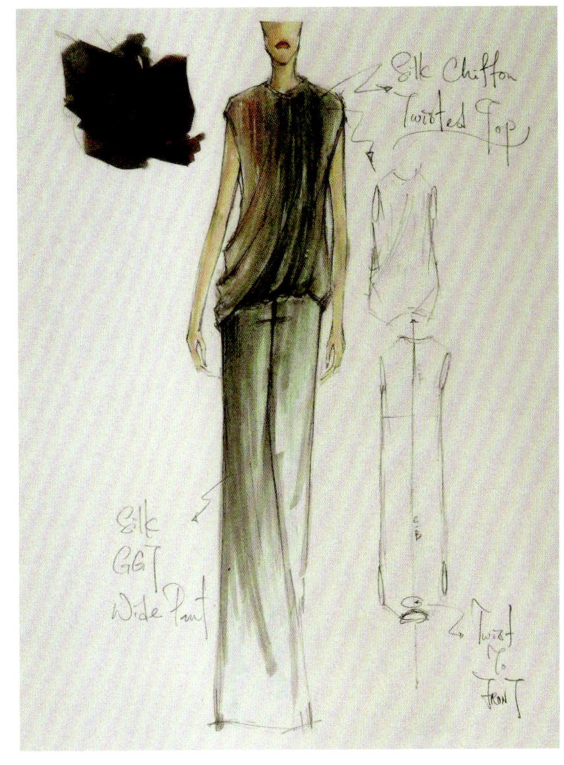

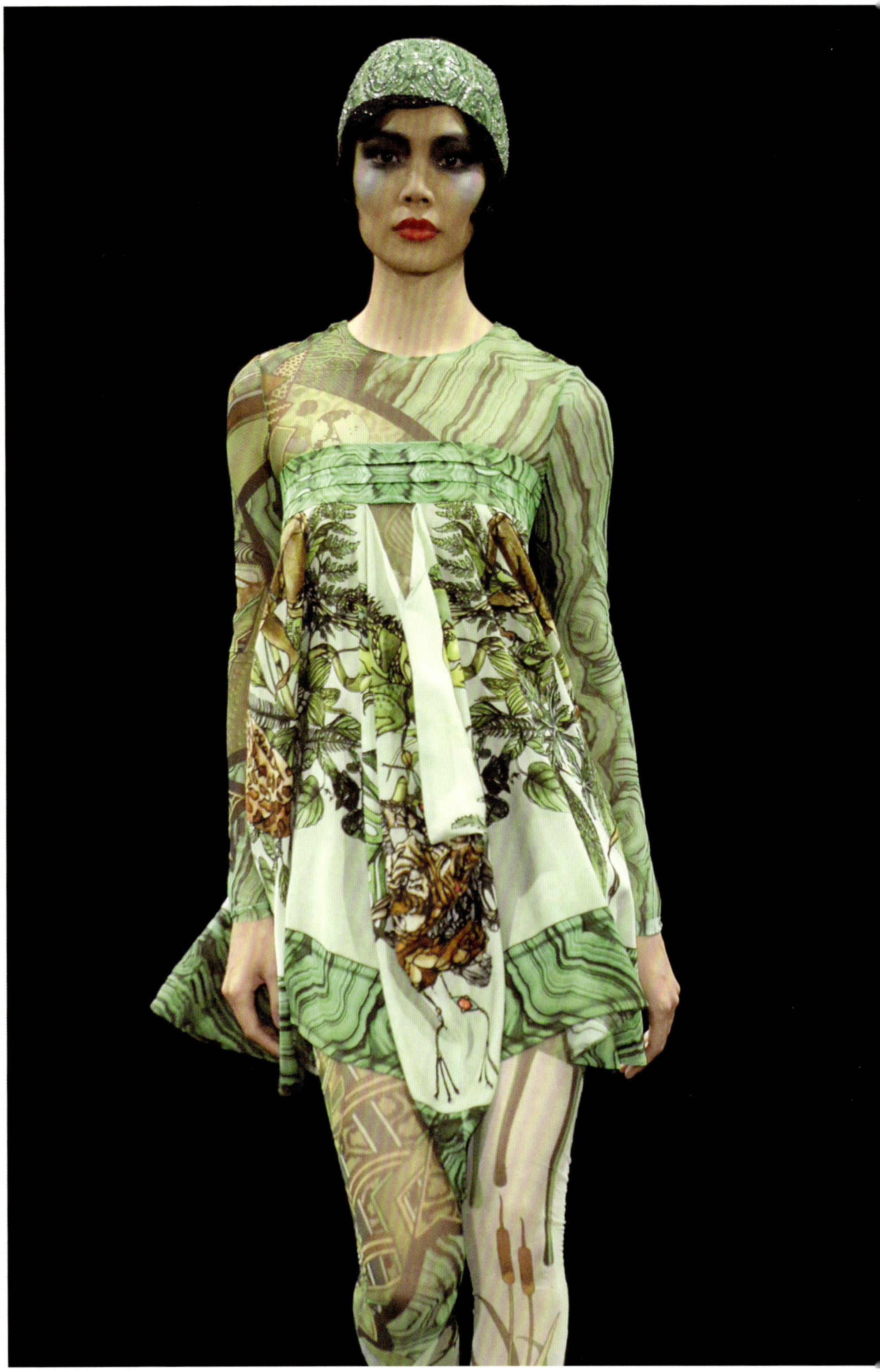

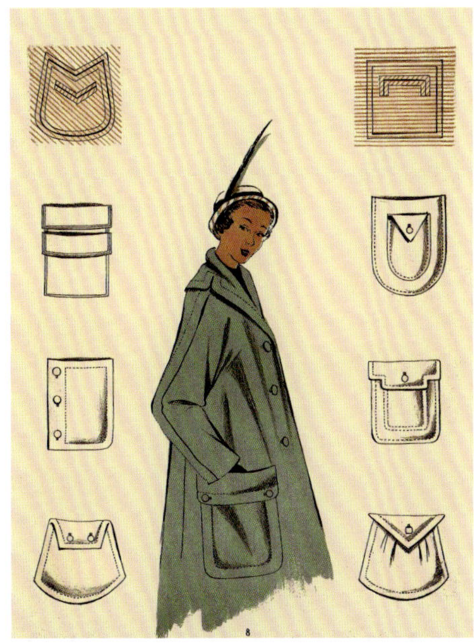

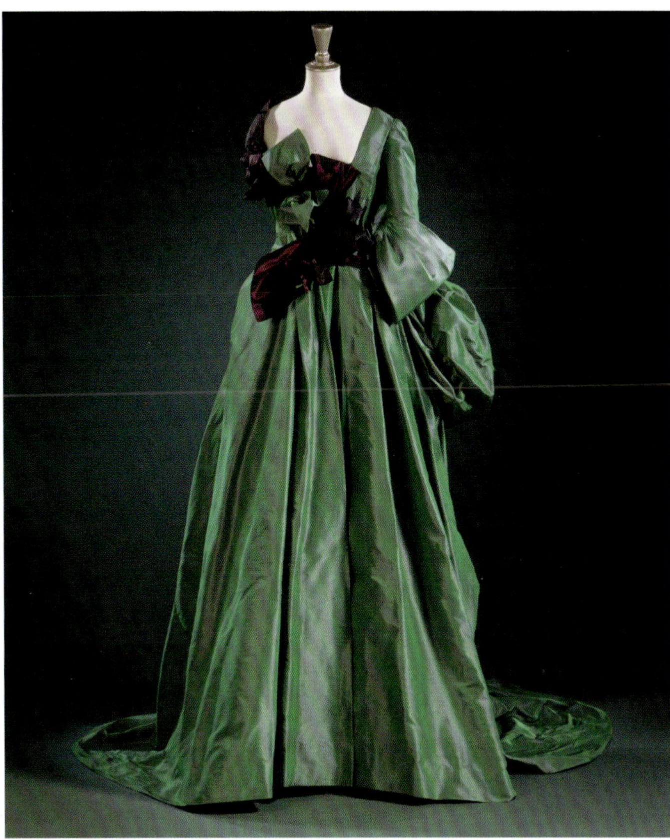

"The taste for the refinements of the eighteenth century had led all women into a sort of deliquescence . . . all that was soft, washed-out, and insipid, was held in honour. I threw into this sheepcote a few rough wolves . . . greens . . . that made all the rest sing aloud."

—Paul Poiret [129]

This friendly shade of green is named for a notoriously lethal plant. The subtle shade of Hemlock is naturally nuanced, one of Mother Nature's most neutral colors. Designers from Vivienne Westwood to Basso & Brooke have recognized its versatility and appeal.

Established in the 1930s, *Idées: Détails-Couture* was an early, limited-edition fashion industry publication with hand-colored pochoir prints, perhaps a precursor to trend forecasting. Anticipating future fashions in the 1950s, the 1949 issue ran a Meadow green couture coat with an early version of the A-line silhouette, which Christian Dior premiered to rave reviews in Spring 1955.

The queen of reinvention, Vivienne Westwood has "Let It Rock," promoted "Sex," and called on "Seditionaries" to gather before the "World's End." In her continued upheaval of English norms, Westwood dove into 17th-century literature and 18th-century art, inspired by Jean-Antoine Watteau's *fête galante* and the maxims of François de La Rochefoucauld. Made for *Les Femmes ne connaissent pas toute leur coquetterie* (Women who do not understand the full extent of their coquettishness), Westwood's Spring/Summer 1996 "Watteau" gown co-opts idyllic clothes from days gone by and destabilizes them. The asymmetrical ruffle and pouf appear as the unnatural lumps and bumps they are, stressing the malleability of the silhouette in the hands of a master designer like Westwood. The gown's Hemlock hue is brilliant, simultaneously sweet and sinister.

In 2004 Brazilian digital artist Bruno Basso and British fashion designer Christopher Brooke, who comprise the London-based duo Basso & Brooke, made history with the first 100% digitally printed collection. As Dr. Cathy Treadaway from the Cardiff School of Art & Design points out, "Computer monitors . . . are capable of producing up to 16.4 million colors, far more than the human eye can see,"[130] which, Basso notes, allow for a "very precise, very millimetrical way" of working.[131] Basso & Brooke's Spring/Summer 2007 collection comprised colors too numerous to count, but did rely on Sprucestone hues throughout.

Since 1986, Blanc de Chine had created garments that fold Chinese design values into luxury fashion goods. The silk chiffon top and wide silk trousers in Jadesheen designed in the late 2000s by Kin Yeung embody the Blanc de Chine philosophy of subtlety, functionality, and comfort.

Poison Green

The fashionable shade known as "Paris Green" suddenly turned deadly in the 19th century when arsenic became a component of its manufacture. The sinister hue garnered the nickname "Poison Green," which stuck even after harmless elements replaced the deadly addition. There are various other names for similar tones, such as Kelly, Fern, or simply Vibrant Green, but none convey the shade's same threat and intrigue as well as Poison Green.

Today, Gabrielle "Coco" Chanel is a legend, an icon, an idea, whose persona eclipsed her personhood. Ten years after her entrance into couture, Georges Auric remembers, "Paris in 1925 was a perpetual party. And Coco Chanel was the living symbol of every luxury and every extravagance of the period."[132] Chanel is so famous for her Little Black Dress that her remarkable use of color is often overlooked. In 1927, Chanel melded art deco and *Japonisme* for her Vibrant Green and black silk crepe theatre coat with chrysanthemums in gold brocade. Loelia Ponsonby observed, "[Chanel's] clothes, simple and uncomplicated, were considered the height of chic."[133] While the success of Chanel's post-war "comeback" was still being debated in 1960s Paris, American consumers were in the grips of Chanelmania. Those unable to buy her suits (or even copies) could indulge in her colorful costume jewelry, such as this gilt bracelet with Fern Green glass and faux pearls.

Manolo Blahnik's lifelong obsession with shoes manifested in 1971 at the behest of *Vogue* editor-in-chief Diana Vreeland. Blahnik recalls, "She looked at my drawings and then started to scream. . . . She said, 'Go make shoes.' It was like a commandment from God."[134] Obeying, Blahnik quickly rose to footwear fame. For Ossie Clark's 1971 show, Blahnik avoided the trend of platforms, instead crafting strappy Poison Green high heels with decorative cherries. Dangerous and delicious, "Manolo Blahnik's shoes are about sex—bold, even slightly menacing sex."[135]

"We like beautiful, flattering color!"[136] Tracy Reese beamed, summing up the collections of her career. Dada artists like Man Ray inspired Reese's Spring/Summer 2009 collection. Reese wanted the collection to "make you dream, to make you happy and optimistic."[137] Her Kelly Green sleeveless mini-frock undoubtedly brought joy to many a cocktail-party attendee, including New York socialite Tinsley Mortimer.

For Spring/Summer 2013, Gucci's Frida Giannini clad massively-major-model-of-the-moment Ondria Hardin in a caped Vibrant Green dress. Pairing it was a gaudy statement necklace, a faux reference to Liz Taylor's '60s jewelry. Giannini's willingness to include bright colors is strengthening the label's popularity during sweltering summers.

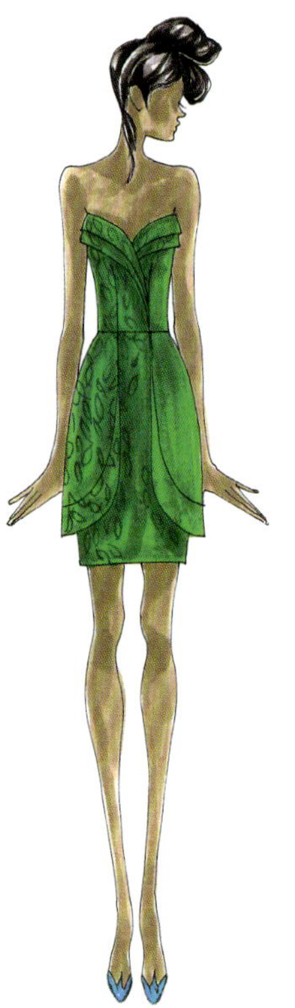

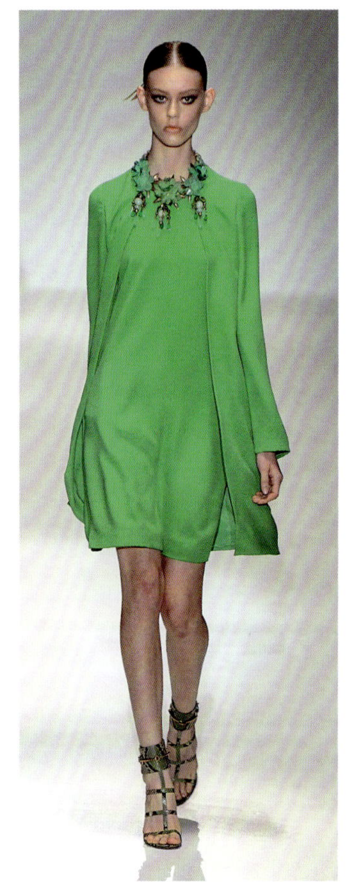

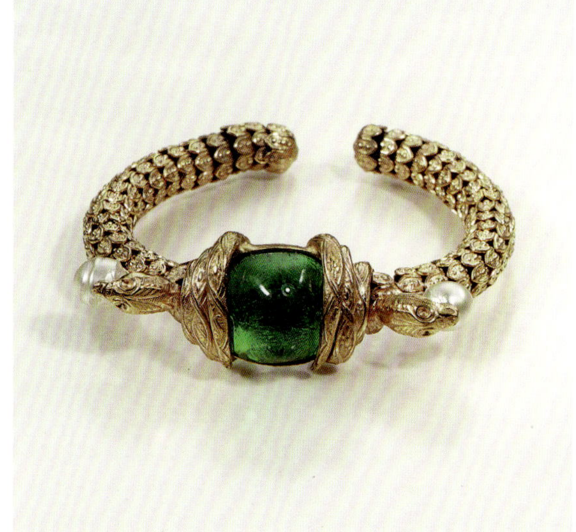

opposite, left
Dress with matching overcoat
Frida Giannini for Gucci
Spring/Summer 2013

opposite, center
Strapless dress
Tracy Reese
Spring/Summer 2009

opposite, right
Bangle bracelet made from gilt
metal, green molten glass, and
simulated pearl
Chanel
circa 1960

below
"Ivy" cherry shoe
Manolo Blahnik for Ossie Clark
1971

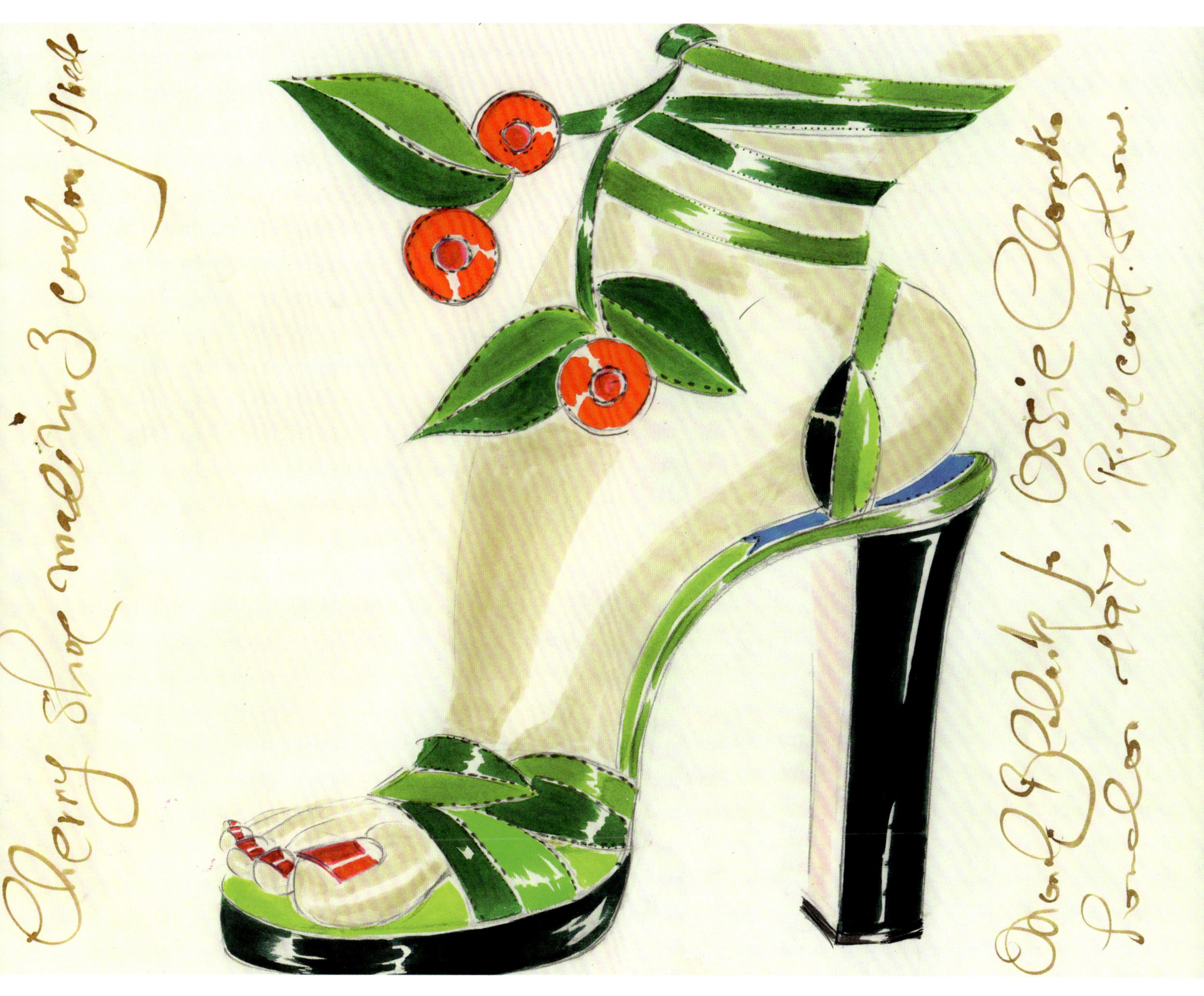

Kelly Green
PANTONE 16-6138

Fern Green
PANTONE 17-6153

Daiquiri Green

The vivid color of the pucker-inducing lime-and-rum punch (regularly imbibed by both Ernest Hemingway and John F. Kennedy) emerges in fashion sporadically. In the psychedelic '60s, punk-fueled '80s, and bright new millennium, fashion designers around the globe, from Russia to Korea, have dared to craft garments in the intoxicating hue.

When Alena Akhmadullina made her 2005 Paris debut, she wanted to prove that her native Russia was not a country "far from fashion."[138] Her Spring/Summer 2007 Daiquiri Green ensembles (replete with a Philip-Treacy-worthy head-dress) asserted her talent, as well as her country's fashion relevance. Combining "Russian audacity and Paris sense of style,"[139] Akhmadullina crafts clothing inspired by Russian Constructivism, late-19th-century photographs, and Polish art deco painter Tamara de Lempicka for clients like Eva Green, Naomi Campbell, and Moscow's elite.

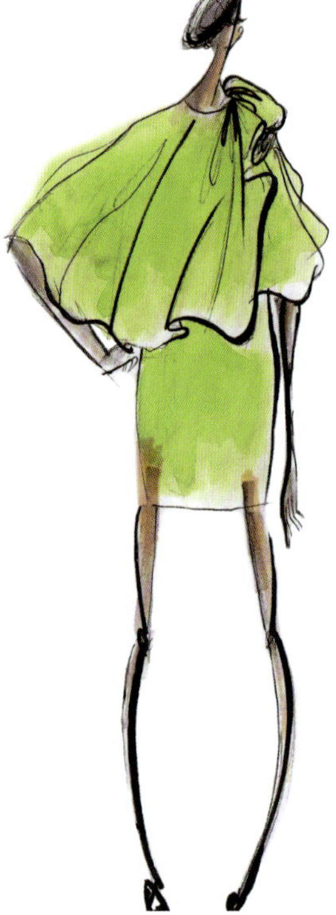

Whether it's his impeccable garments, his empowering philosophy, or his good looks that rival Tom Ford's, something about designer and surfer stud Yigal Azrouël turns women's heads. His dictates, like the epitome of luxury is "confidence"[140] and that one "doesn't need to show too much skin," become immediately followed.[141] For Fall/Winter 2007–2008, Azrouël stuck with a New York color palette of blacks, browns, and grays with the exception of a loose jersey tunic in Sulphur Spring worn layered over leggings and a tee.

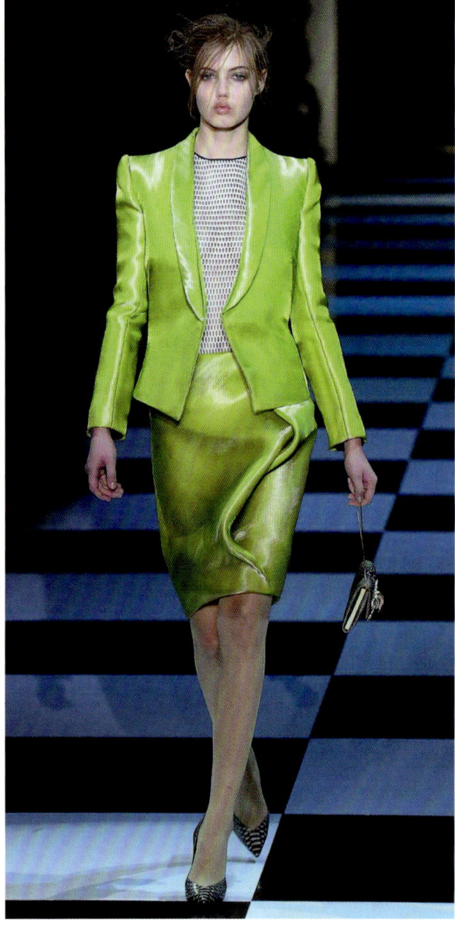

Husband-and-wife team Gene Kang and Hanii Yoon admit they are "true workaholics" who are "the happiest when designing," which explains their helming not one, not two, but three labels: OBZEE, O'2nd, and Y & Kei.[142] Kang and Yoon began Y & Kei in 2001 and shuttered it in 2008. For Y & Kei's final show, they punctuated the concise collection with a single Limeade piece. Originally imagined as a cocktail dress, the realized creation was a blindingly bright loose trench dress.

For Spring 2012 Couture, Giorgio Armani reneged from his usual "clean and functional"[143] modernist aesthetic, instead suggesting glistening "statement silhouettes" in Wild Lime.[144] The collection, inspired by metamorphosis, featured models with mussy hair, as if they'd just emerged from cocoons. The line's "absinthe-bright" mesh garments transcended their athletic association, instead appearing snakelike.[145] Armani's "imagination, use of fabric and design" over nearly forty years has fascinated not only consumers worldwide, but also film directors like Martin Scorsese.[146]

opposite, left
Caped suit
Y & Kei
Spring/Summer 2008

opposite, right
Sculptural blazer and dress
Giorgio Armani Haute Couture
Spring/Summer 2012

left
Dress
Yigal Azrouël
Fall/Winter 2007

right
Long skirt, top, and headdress
Alena Akhmadullina
Spring/Summer 2007

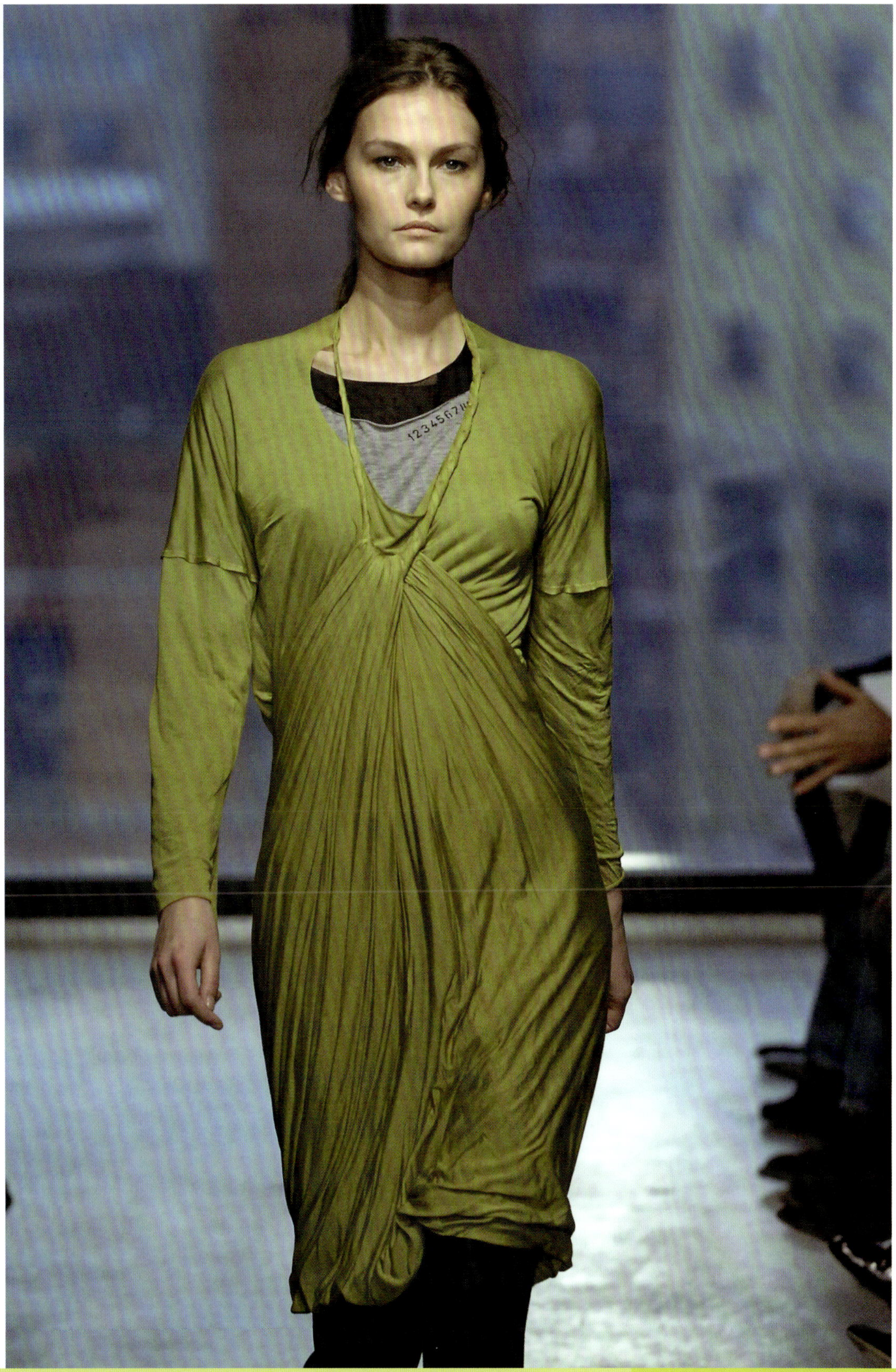

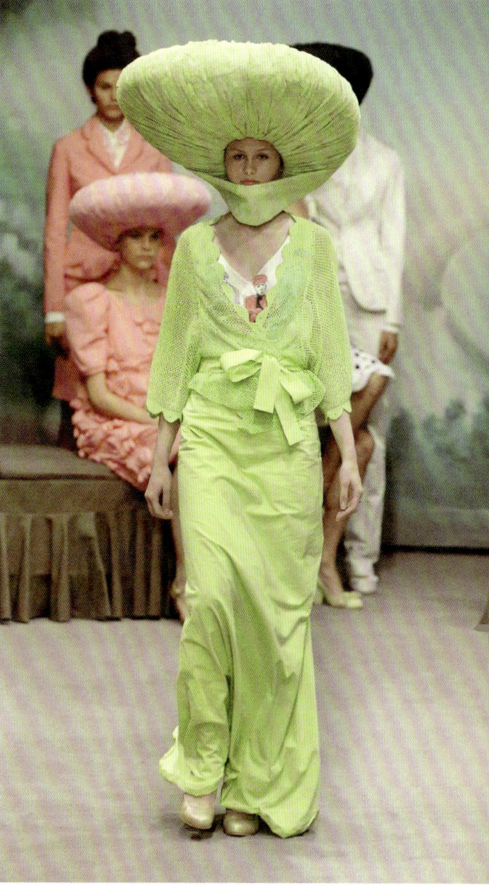

Limeade
PANTONE 13-0645

Sulphur Spring
PANTONE 13-0650

Macaw Green

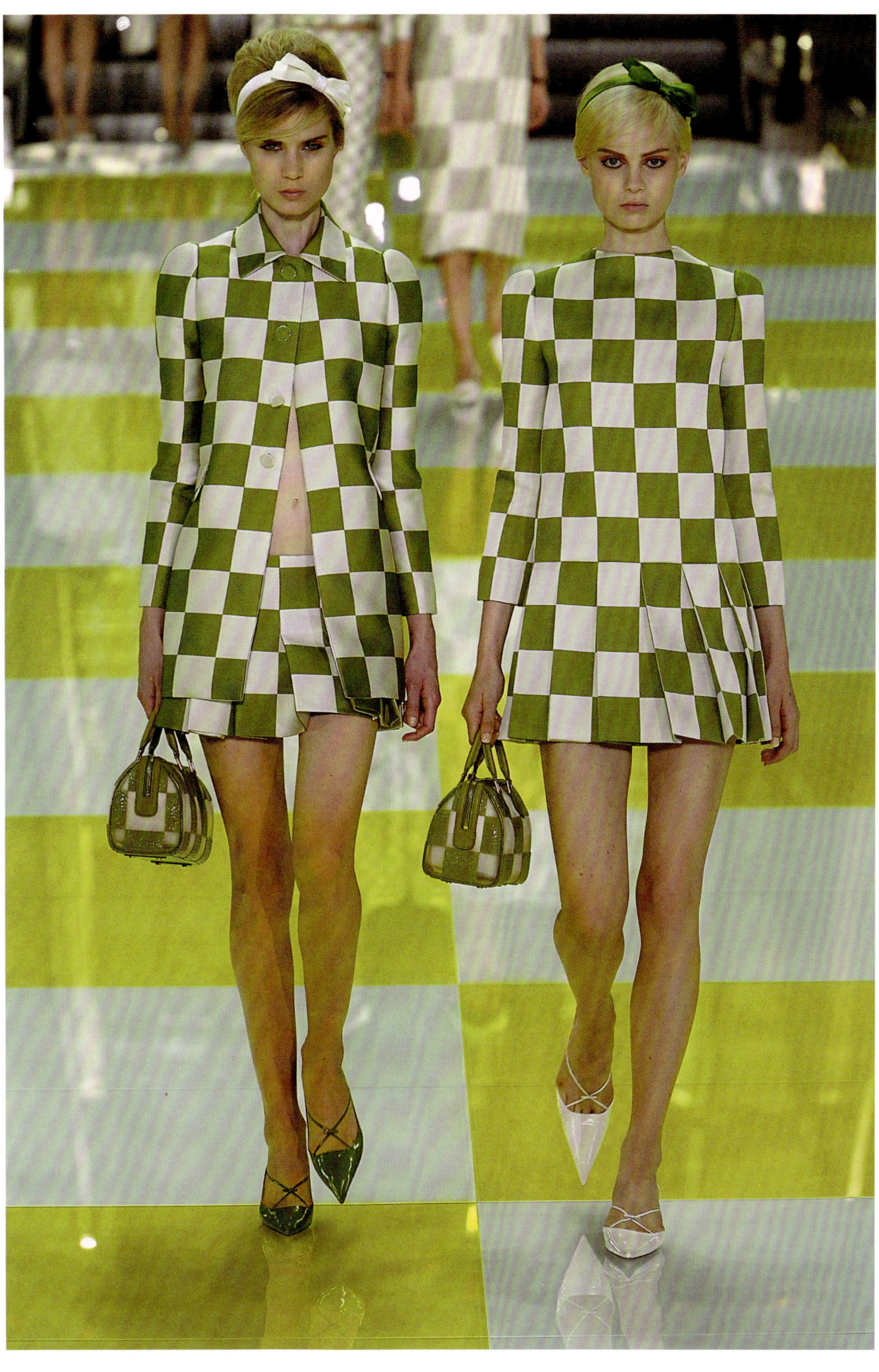

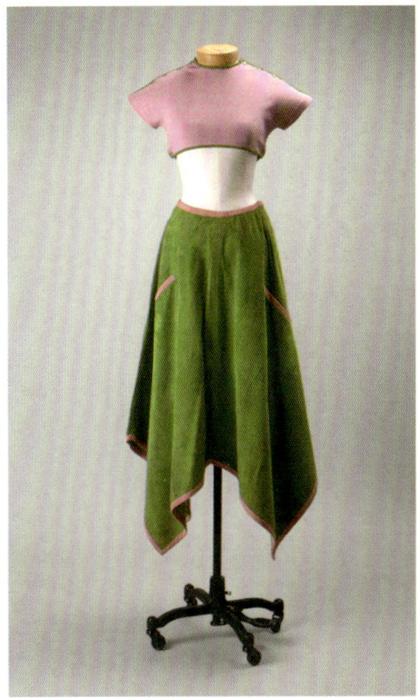

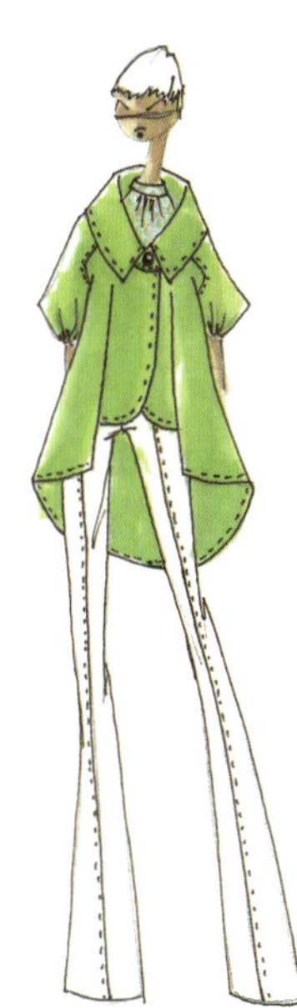

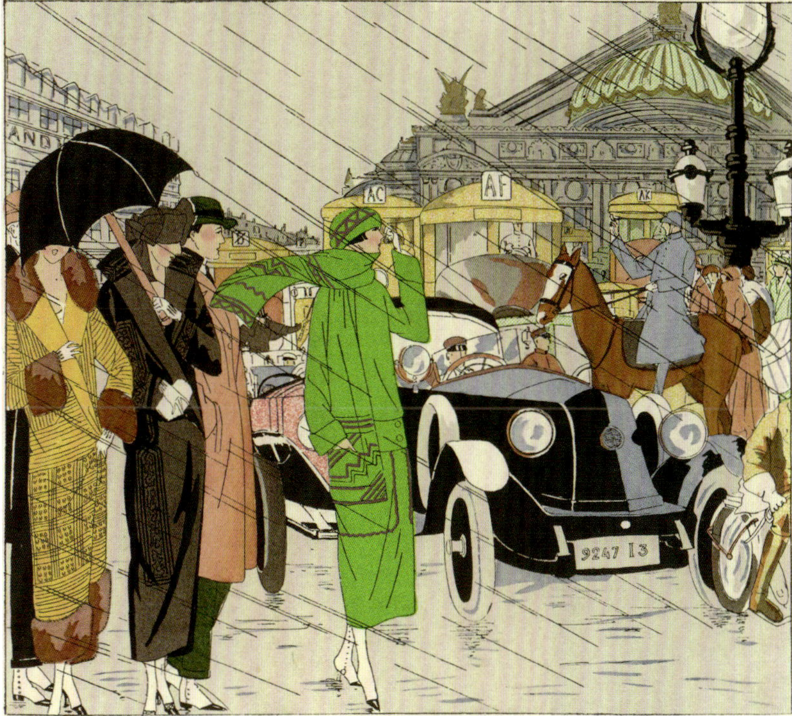

Between 1920 and 1933, elegant Parisian women consumed the periodical *Art-Goût-Beauté* (Art-Taste-Beauty), absorbing the latest fashions through the breathtaking art deco pochoir prints in vivid hand-painted colors. Christoff von Drecoll's 1924 illustration for the publication featured a gamine model with rouged cheeks, earlobe-revealing hair, and matching Macaw Green ensemble of a slim-silhouette, drop-waisted coat, hat, and scarf. Undeterred by the inclement weather, this modern woman exuded the vivavious *esprit du temps*.

A true modernist, Bonnie Cashin loathed what she saw as fashion's "arrested development" and was always searching for new ideas that could promote functionalism.[147] Her 1973 double-knit jersey top reveals the midriff, while the bright Parrot Green suede midi-skirt conceals most of the leg. Brazenly, the top has mother-of-pearl buttons along the shoulder line that serve as fasteners . . . or easy access should one indulge in an "Afternoon Delight."

Fashionable characters on the hit TV shows *Friends* and *Sex and the City* wore David Rodriguez's garments from the late 1990s through the early 2000s, causing viewers to quickly copy their style. For Spring/Summer 2009, Rodriguez created an oversized Dark Citron jacket, partially cropped in front and longer in the back. The warm-weather coat elongates the legs, clad in flared trousers. The outfit reveals Rodriguez's background at both Chanel and Richard Tyler. The hair and jacket are as Parisian-perfect for their own era as von Drecoll's were eight decades before, but the trousers are pure 21st-century Hollywood.

From the 1970s until his death in 1986, Perry Ellis found success making casual clothes for women who were "just out of jeans who weren't ready to dress for success." Father of the "slouch" look, Ellis broke tight garments' monopoly on sex appeal. Fashion journalist Carrie Donovan explained, "[W]hen worn by the women who understand them, they are as sexy as those that cling."[148] Ellis wished to convey "the ease of life today and the humor of it."[149] Ellis's Leaf Green "Burren" tweed suit also featured a fez, guaranteeing no one will take it too seriously.

For Spring/Summer 2013, Marc Jacobs showed checkerboard outfits in "an intense almost sickly citrus" green for Louis Vuitton.[150] The collection, based on the work of "French national treasure" Daniel Buren, was an ode to the artist's "minimal, mathematical, architectural" work. For the show, Buren (at the behest of Jacobs) transformed the Palais du Louvre's courtyard, installing escalators for the models to descend. After seeing the LV Collection, Buren called it "beautiful, extremely strict, almost cubist; not designed for the sake of design," the highest of compliments.[151]

Olive Drab

Associated with war uniforms, Olive Drab has worked its way onto the catwalk and into civilian wardrobes, evoking environmental consciousness, earthy sexiness, and (of course) classic military chic.

Over 150,000 women served in the Women's Army Corps (WAC) during WWII. Many of these women "handled highly classified material, worked long hours with few days off, and were exposed to a significant amount of danger."[152] Despite their dedication to their country, because the WAC challenged gender norms, debates ensued over how a woman could be a "lady" and also serve her country, with bizarre rumors flying that the WAC was full of prostitutes. Yet, that did not stop devoted women who believed that "This is my war, too" from signing up and wearing the Olive Drab uniforms.

The Fall/Winter 2007–2008 Olive belted tunic by Igor Chapurin ("the Russian Armani") sexes up the former Soviet Union's military aesthetic, playfully confronting clichés about Russian society. Combining unique elements of Russian culture with "modern rich chic," Chapurin explains, "I want to show the Russia that belongs to Chagall and Kandinsky, to make Russia famous for creativity and style, rather than caviar and vodka."[153]

Tia Cibani could easily be called an international woman of mystery, and her designs for New York–based label Ports 1961 were aimed at world-traveling ladies like herself. Born in North Africa, the designer of Turkish and Italian heritage was raised in Vancouver, British Columbia, and has lived and worked in China and the United States. Of her 2008 collection she explained: "This season we are on another journey to another place. This time we are in Scotland. We are under the spell of a Scottish winter. It is very dark and moody, very rich with enchantment, mysticism, and magic."[154] The fabrics are "tough Shetland wools, rustic tweeds." Color-wise, there are "jewel tones . . . hits of intense shades in the green." While her Mosstone sketch for the Pantone *Fashion Color Report* didn't make it into the collection, it illustrates her inspiration and the direction of the line.

While today's generation is unlikely to see trench warfare, the "trench" coat is still present, and Christopher Bailey continues to update the Burberry mac season after season. Keeping its utilitarian purposes intact, Bailey tries not to reinvent it, but rather to simply add stylish and often nostalgic elements, like the wartime color of Elm.

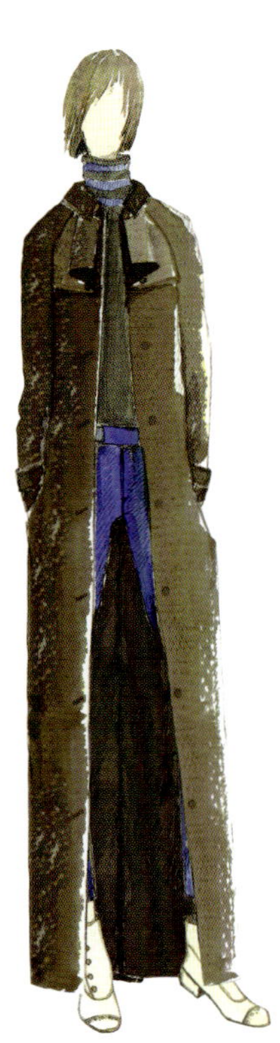

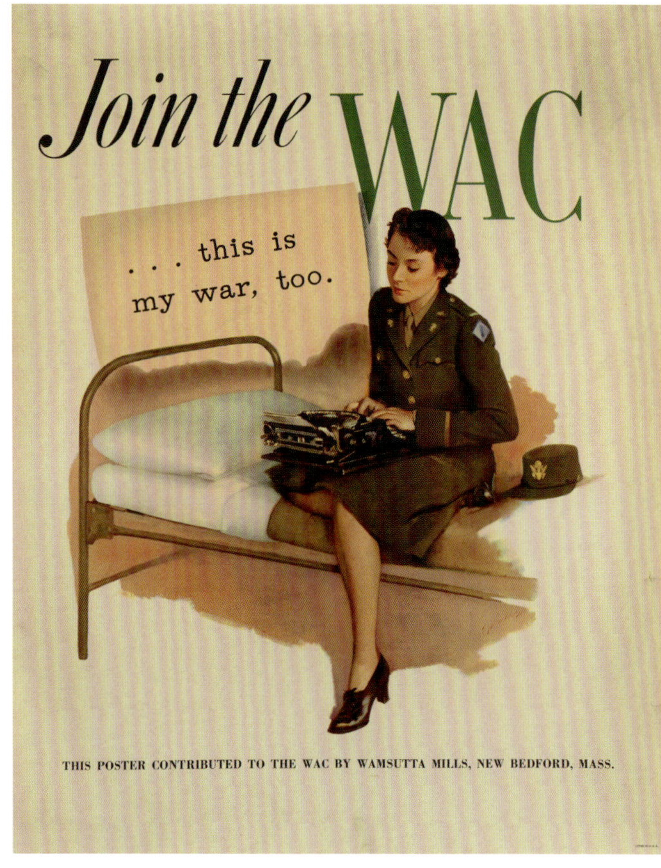

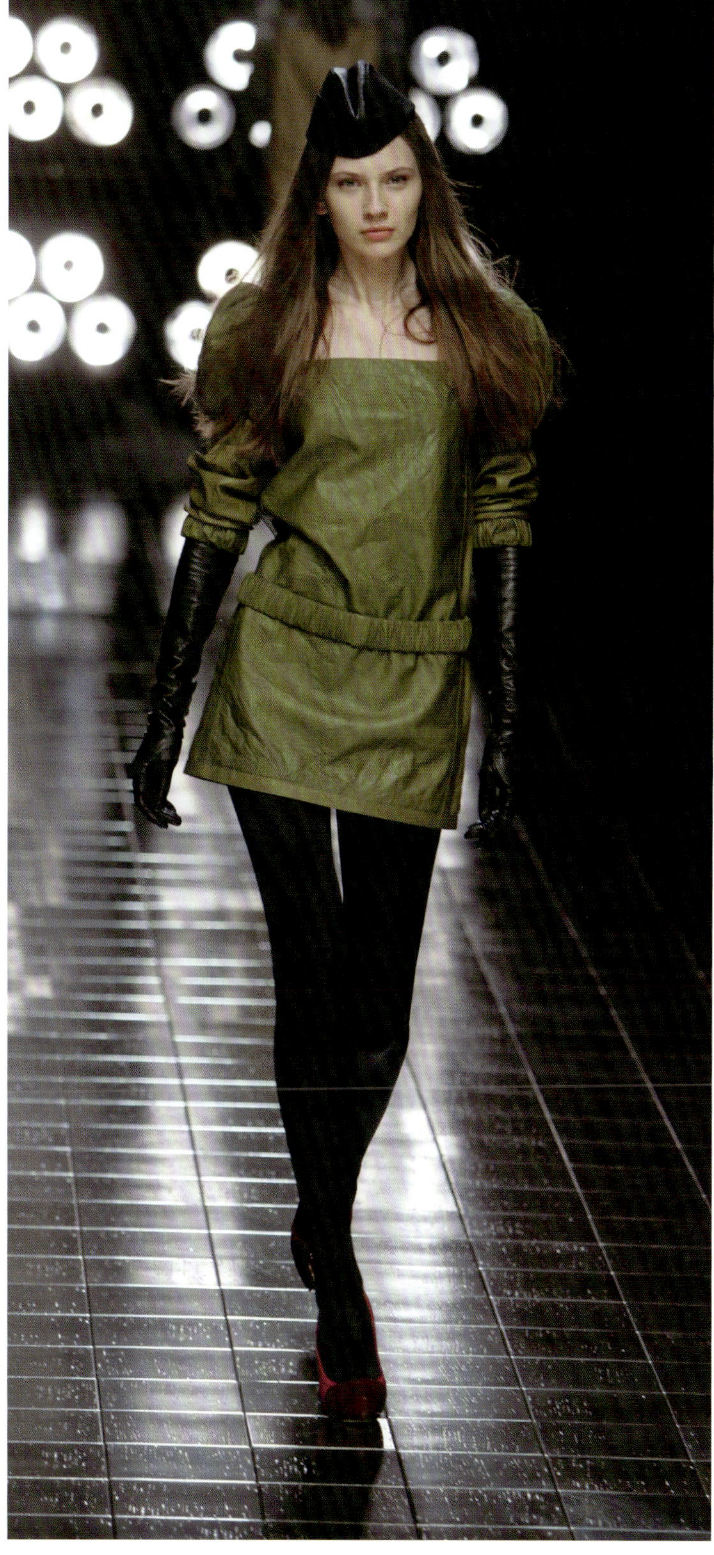

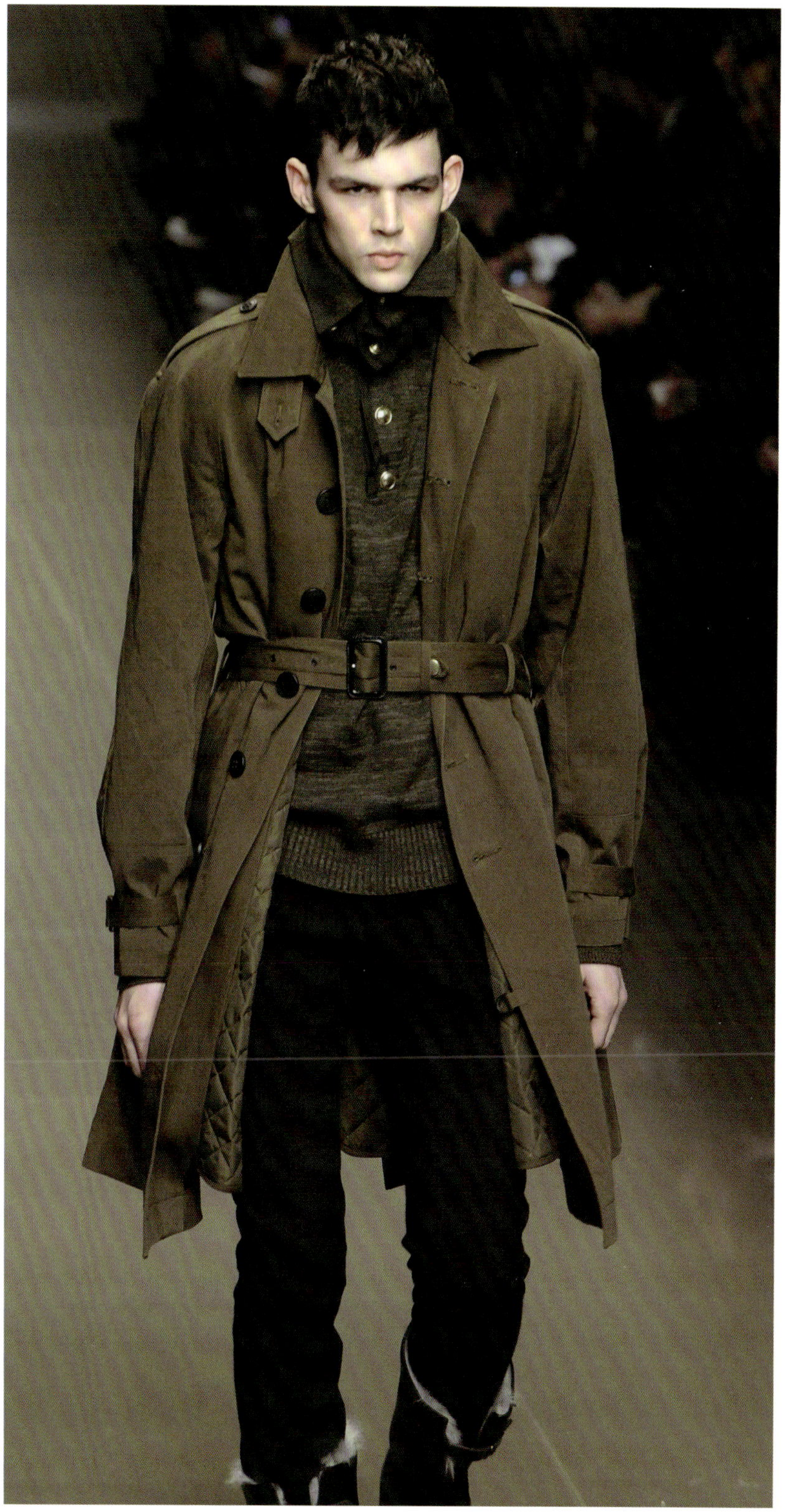

Mosstone
PANTONE 17-0525

Elm
PANTONE 16-0613

Khaki

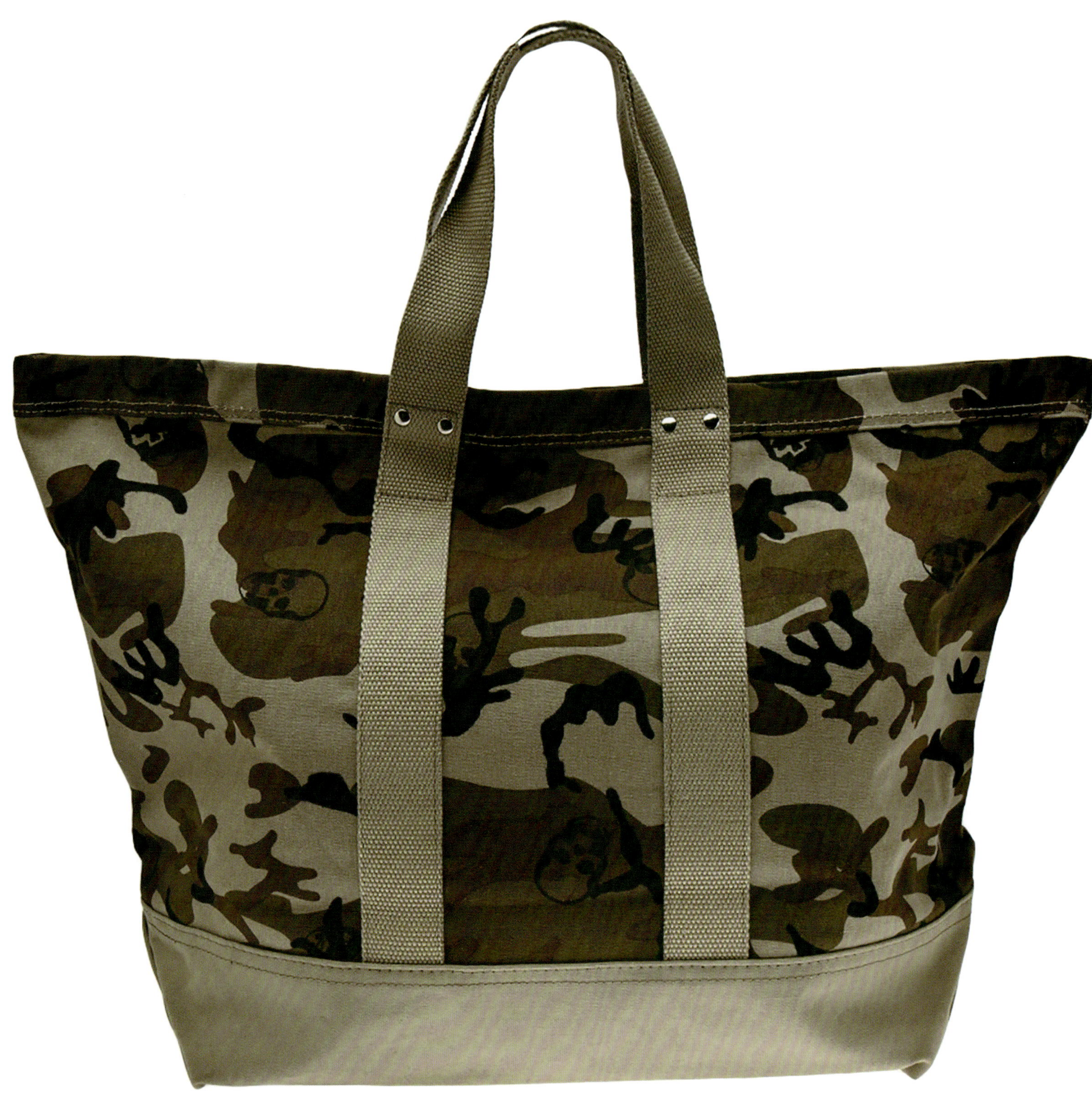

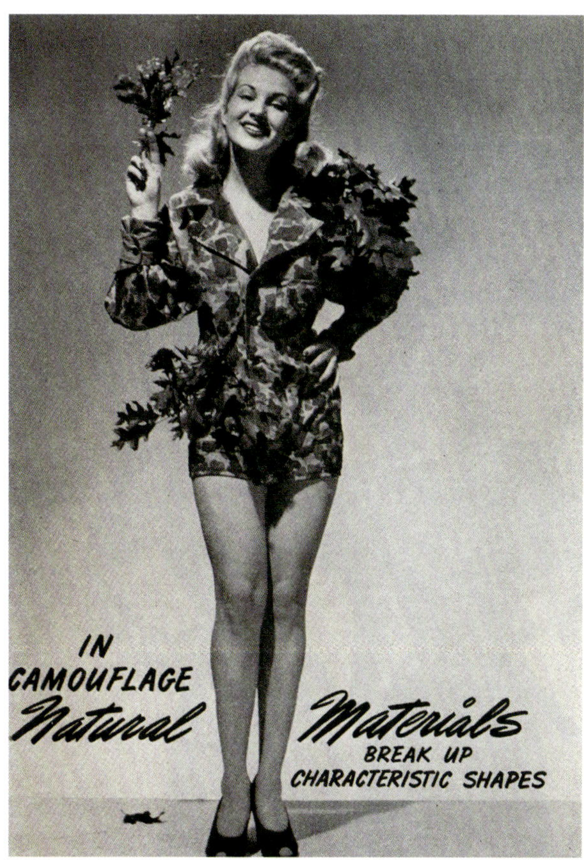

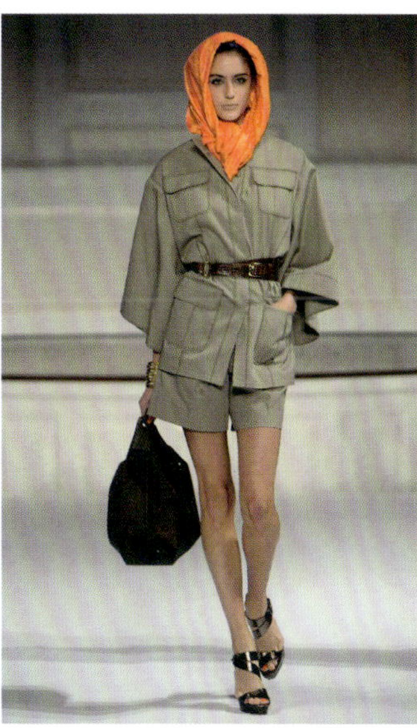

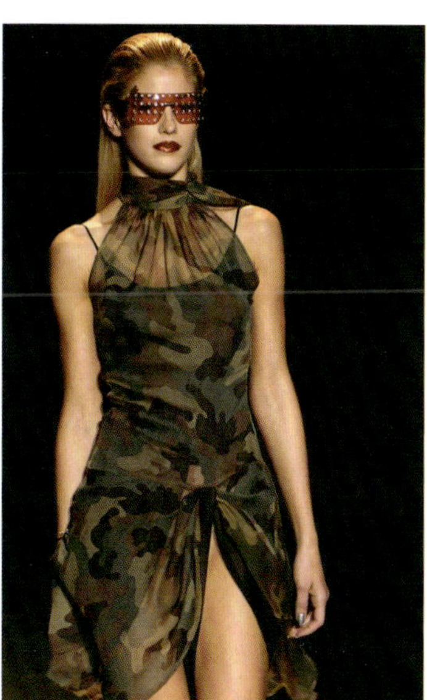

Whether inevitable or not, war has plagued humanity since its inception. Continual conflict bleeds its way into every aspect of life. The uniforms of combat crossed over into fashion during the Renaissance when sleeves were deliberately sliced to expose the undershirts, mimicking sword-damaged garments. In 1846, Punjab-based English lieutenant Harry Lumsden, tired of casualties caused by the bright red British uniforms in a desert region, dyed his using mud. Other infantrymen followed suit, some using ink, coffee, tea, or tobacco juice as dye instead. While not the first to use the earth as camouflage, Lumsden is responsible for the birth of "khaki," the Urdu word for "mud," as the name for a color of clothing. In 1884, khaki dye was patented. What originated as army fatigues slowly made its way into the everyday.

To entertain troops during WWII, pinup girl Chili Williams put on short camo shorts and a matching shirt with a few leaves as embellishment, mimicking Eve. The sexiness of Ewing Krainin's photo, which ran in *LIFE* magazine on April 10, 1944, was seen as raising morale.

During the 1960s through the 1980s, the meaning of Khaki, military uniforms, and camo became subverted. Rather than symbolizing the courage of soldiers, it was adopted by anti-war protestors to bring visibility to the Vietnam War halfway around the world. Rockers like Frank Zappa and Jimi Hendrix "disrespectfully appropriate[ed] the United States's iconic military dress" as a visual way of capturing the "youth disillusionment with politics, foreign policy, and suburban consumer culture."[155] In postmodernity, the sign became removed from its signifier, with military uniforms mostly stripped of meaning. Richard Geist, the owner of an Army-Navy outfitter, referred to civilians procuring the items as being like "buying a character."[156]

Manchester-born John Richmond's Covert Green "street chic" skirt from Spring/Summer 2003 references rock 'n' roll, not the Gulf War. Japanese designer Akiko Ogawa does not hark back to WWII with her Khaki dress; she is merely "pushing the usual edgy envelope" with it.[157] Wayne Lee's Fall 2010 outfit of green and Khaki camo is in the same postmodern vein. Lee, who left war-torn Vietnam as a child, is not making a statement with the army garb, only offering a "look" for consumption. Oscar de le Renta's Khaki army jacket and shorts for Spring/Summer 2010 is not targeted at female soldiers, but wealthy women on a jaunt to Dubai. Lucien Pellat-Finet's 2013 camo man-bag is more fit for a weekend trip to the Amalfi Coast than Iraq or Afghanistan.

Bright White

As if to confront the eternal blackness of space, the main "color" of NASA was bright white. The Space Race captured not only headlines, but also the imagination of French designer André Courrèges, who created fashions for the space age. Courrèges, who worked for Cristóbal Balenciaga for a decade, opened his own House in 1961 but did not come into his own until 1964, when he launched his "Moon Girl Collection" with its flat-leather-and-Velcro ankle boots. The futuristic collection was so *volte-face* that it received no applause. Aghast, the editor of *L'Officiel de la Couture* even sent Courrèges a letter: "You were crazy . . . boots in the summer. It won't work. What were you thinking?"[159] At first in tears, Courrèges received the last laugh when his collection skyrocketed, being worn by star Catherine Deneuve.

A sensual King Midas, everything Tom Ford touches drips with sex. Ford's 1996 Gucci collection disregarded Labor Day taboos and embraced Blanc de Blanc for fall, making white hot. The tough hardware that adorned the matte jersey dresses added a tactile component: the body naturally heats the cold metal. Ford's peek-a-boo cutouts plead for stolen kisses in unexpected places. Under Ford's reign, Gucci (previously near bankruptcy) became a $10-billion phoenix, and white lost its innocence.

Most brides still wed in white, regardless of its original symbolism. *The* name in designer bridal wear is Vera Wang, who designed her first wedding dress for her own nuptials in 1989. Linda Wells of *The New York Times* described the "hand-beaded, full-skirted" gown with a "tumbling train and a long swoop of veil" as fitting for a "fairy-tale event."[160] Nearly a year later, Wang opened her Madison Avenue business, banking on her sixteen years of experience at *Vogue* and the design knowledge she accrued at Ralph Lauren. Two successful decades later, writer Ron Alexander joked that Wang and her staff are able to speak about bridal trends for longer than most marriages last.

In stark contrast to her usual fifty shades of black, Donna Karan debuted an entirely Snow White look for DKNY's Spring/Summer 2013 collection. DKNY offered only a few fresh whites for the season, which were mainly there to accentuate the taxi cab–yellow elements of the show.

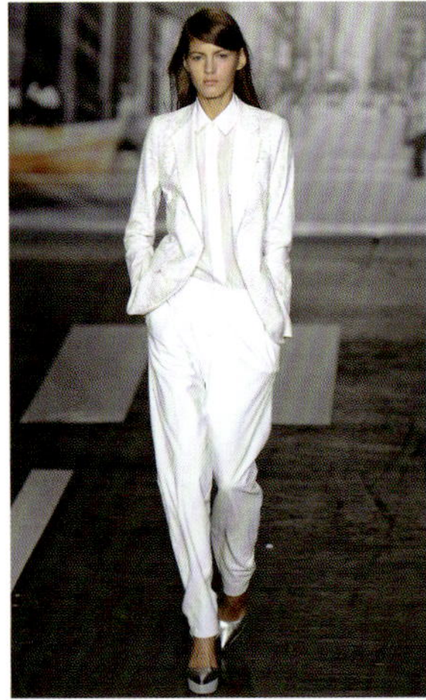

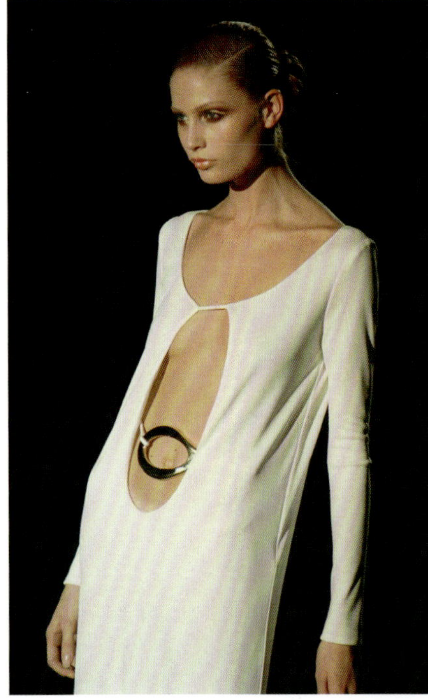

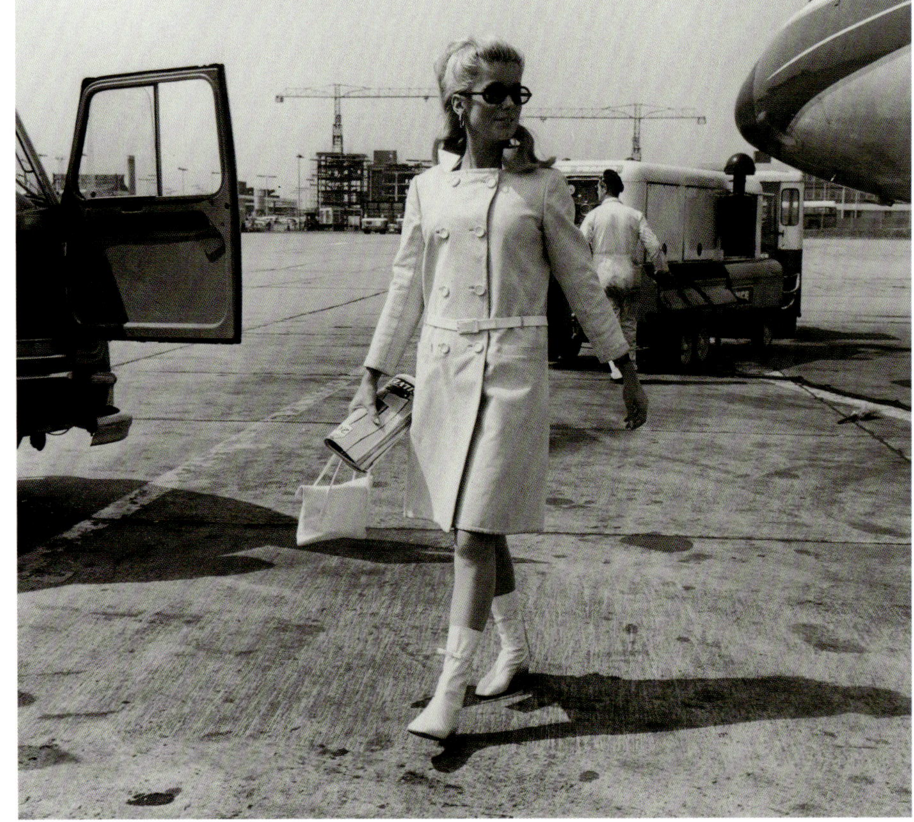

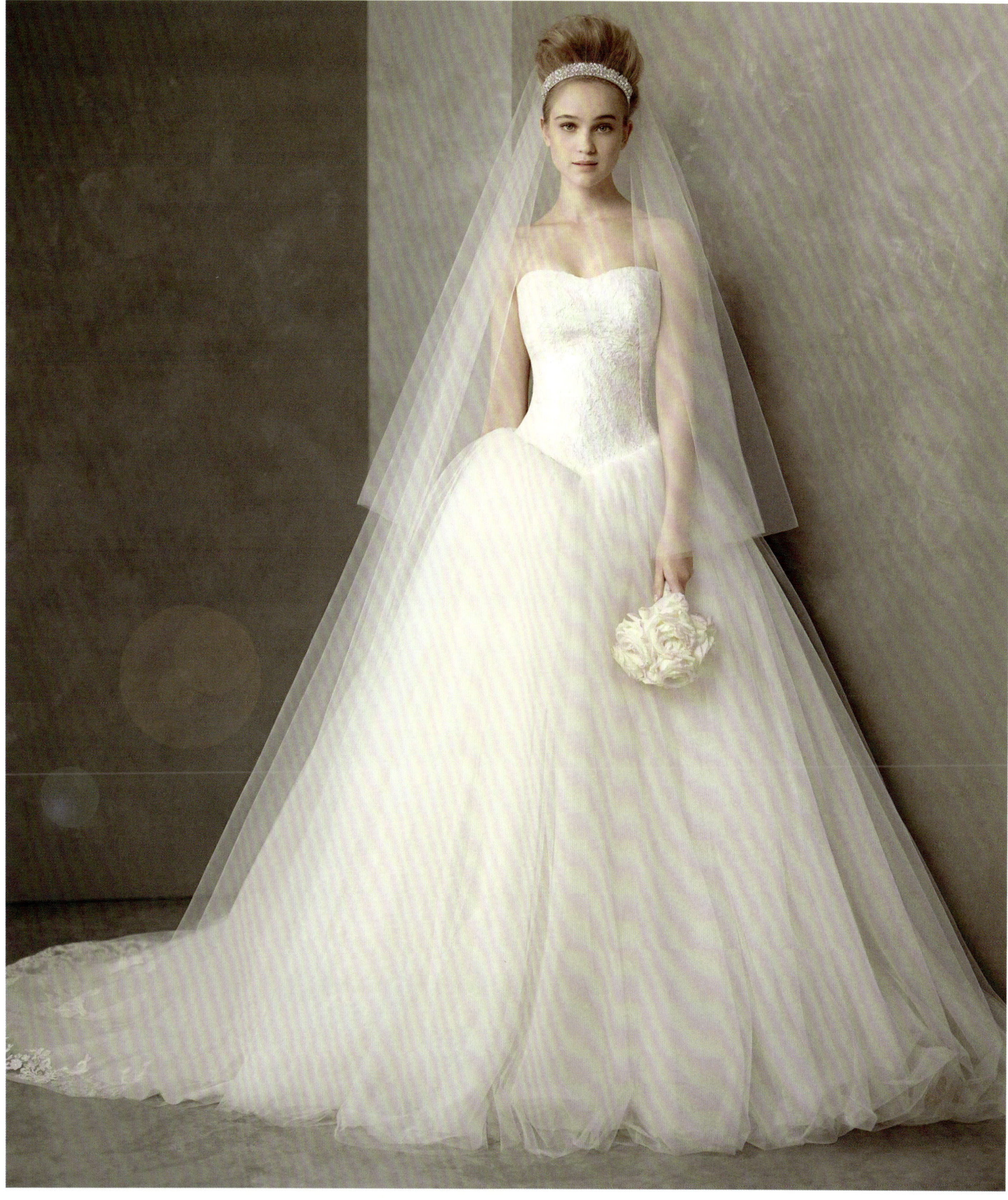

Cloud Cream

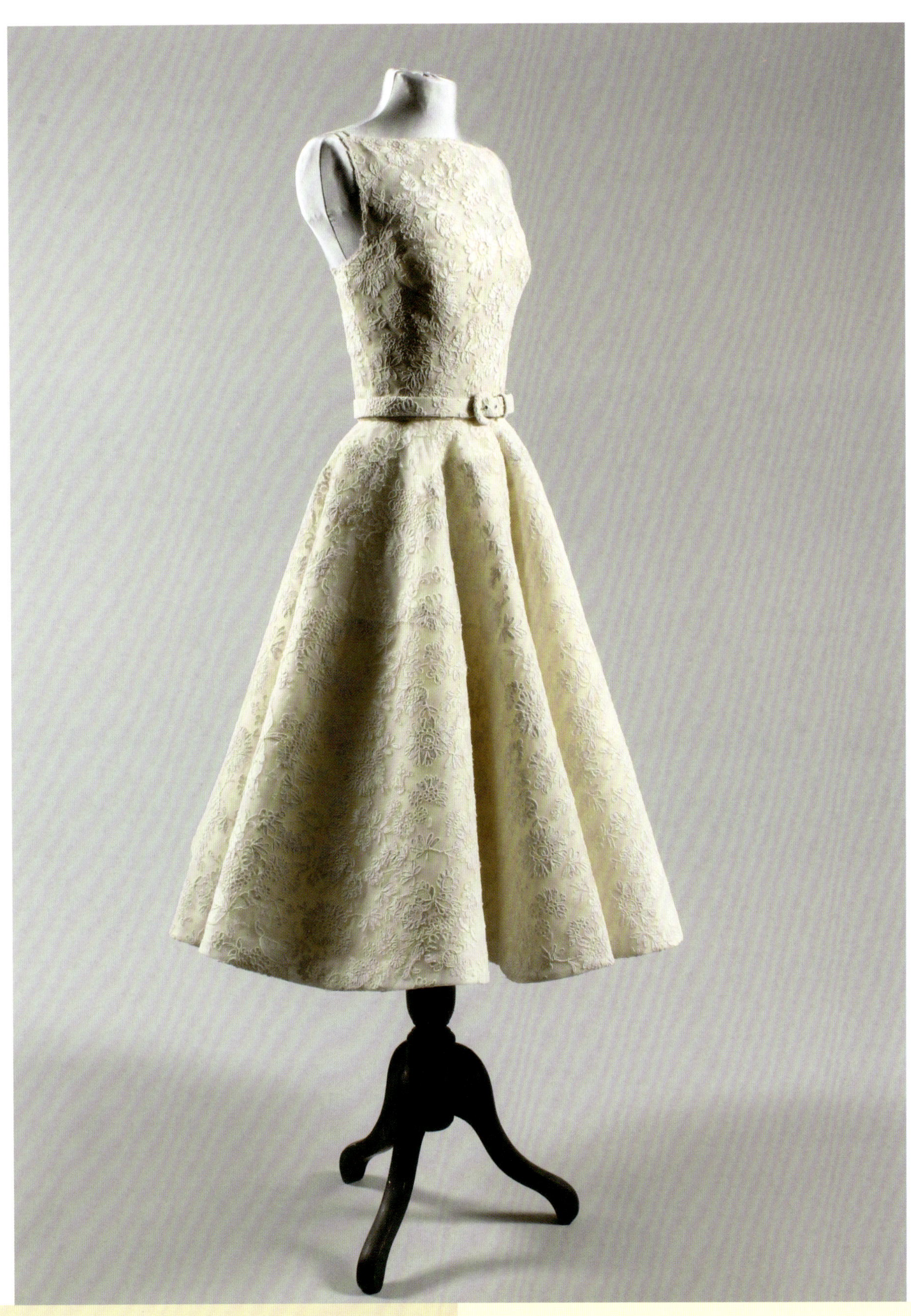

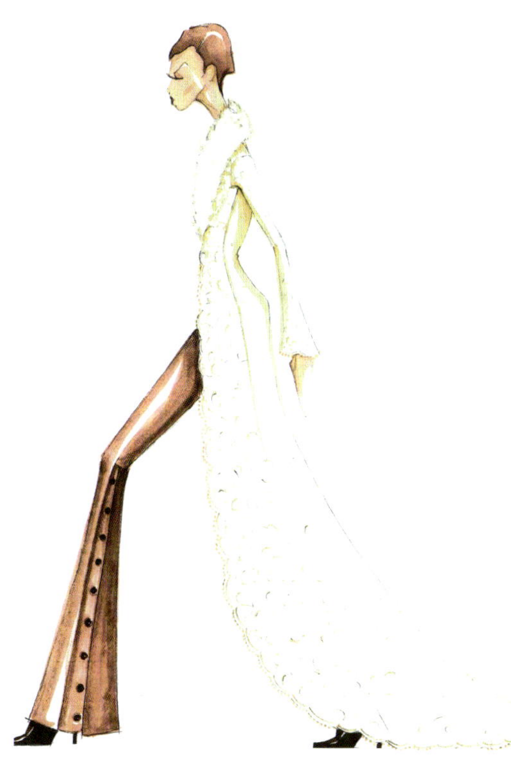

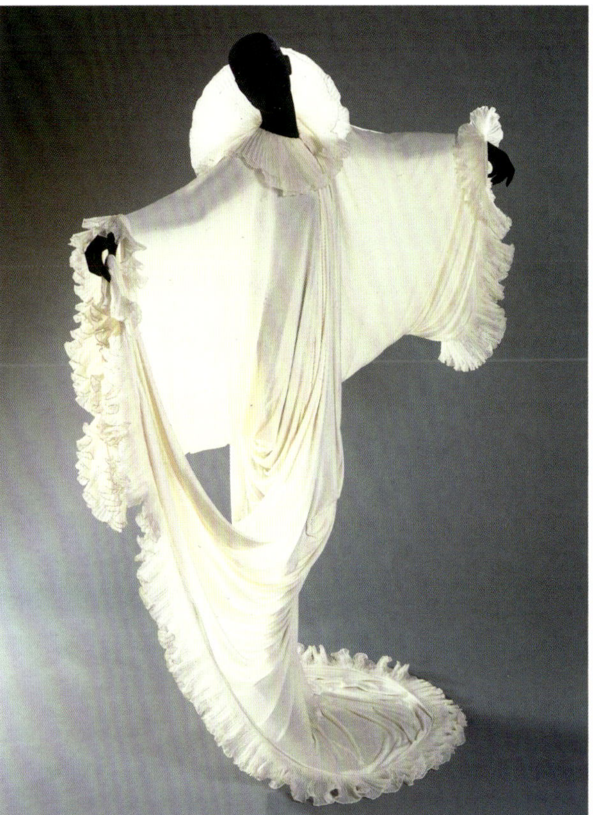

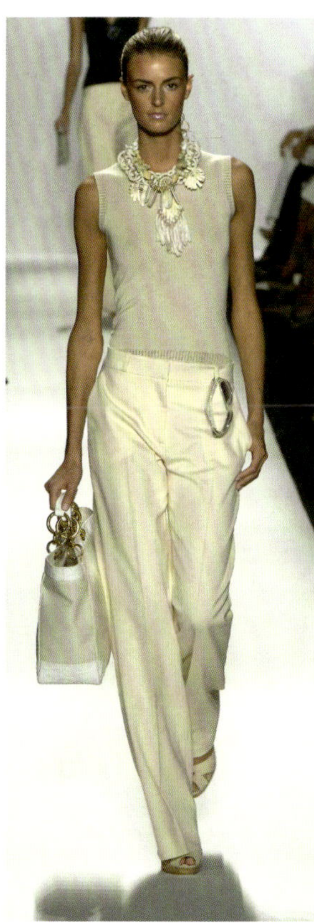

The naturally off-white togas of ancient Greece led to the association of cream colors with antiquity. Fast-forward to the early 20th century, where Hollywood costumers adeptly used creams in place of white to soften its starkness on screen. From the mid-20th century to today, creamy colors have been praised as being "friendlier" than the cool, austere modern whites.

Costume designer extraordinaire Edith Head (whose 58-year career included 546 screen credits, 35 Oscar nominations, and 8 wins) knew pure white costumes in black-and-white films were visually abrasive, and outfitted Audrey Hepburn in an Antique White dress for *Roman Holiday*'s final scene. After minor alterations, Hepburn wore it to the Academy Awards, where both she and Head won. In 2011, the frock was purchased at auction for £84,000 ($131,292).

Despite designing for over half a century and dressing Princess Diana among others, Japanese designer Gnyuki Torimaru ("Yuki") has not been given his due, perhaps because he made England (and not France) his base. While Yuki's background includes Japanese anime, textile engineering, and architecture, he ultimately chose to pursue fashion. After learning tailoring from Norman Hartnell and finishing from Pierre Cardin, he launched his own company in London in 1973. In 1977, a year after nabbing his first *British Vogue* cover, Yuki created a Winter White rayon jersey evening cloak with pleated organdie. Reminiscing, Yuki remembers choosing the "unpretentious" and "cool" color because it conveyed a "take it or leave it" attitude.[161]

For Spring/Summer 2006, Oscar de la Renta began with a clean Cloud Cream slate: a slim-cut tank top, slouchy oversized trousers, and matching accessories in Antique White on model Jaquetta Wheeler. The Dominican designer began by apprenticing at Balenciaga and assisting Antonio del Castillo at Lanvin, before wowing the New York fashion world with his designs for Elizabeth Arden in 1963. That year, he told *The New York Times*, "I just want to make beautiful clothes."[162] For nearly fifty years, he has been doing just that at his own House.

David Rodriguez crafted a long lace coat with matching fur collar in Papyrus for Fall 2003. While the outerwear evoked Old Hollywood, it was purchased and worn by New Hollywood heroines, like Kirsten Dunst and Jessica Alba, both fans of Rodriguez's.

Bleached Sand

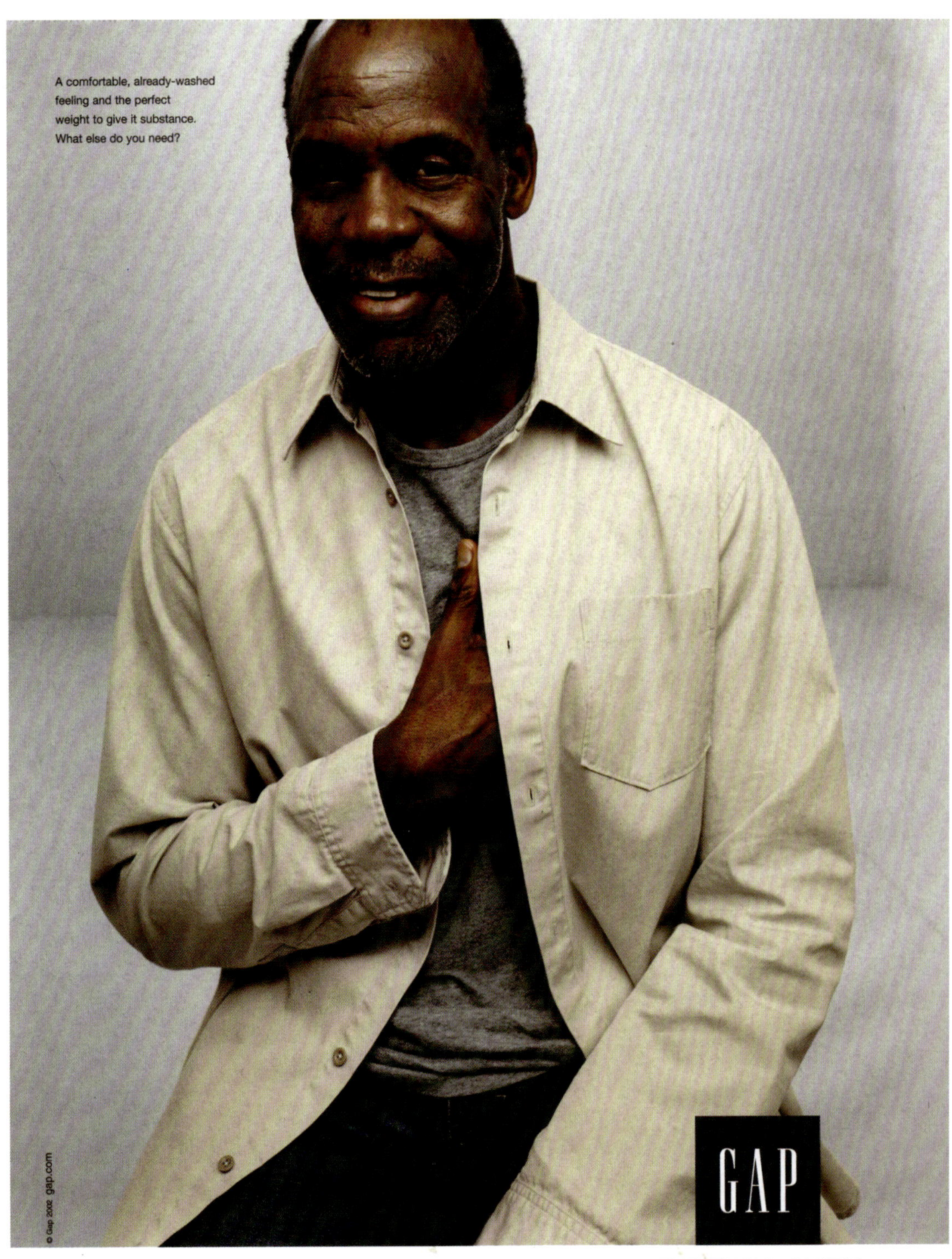

THE TWILL SHIRT

ACTOR DANNY GLOVER

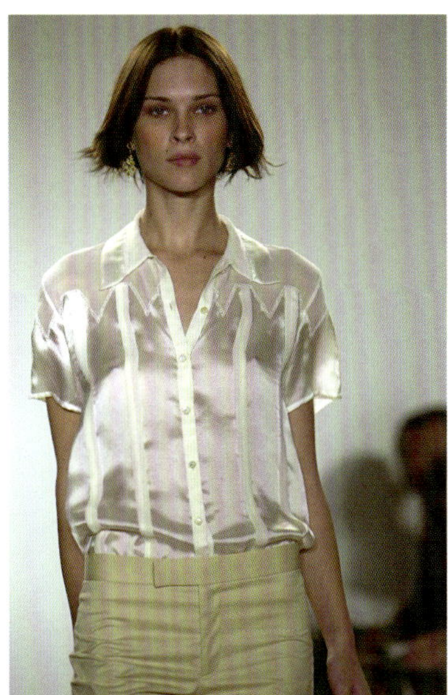

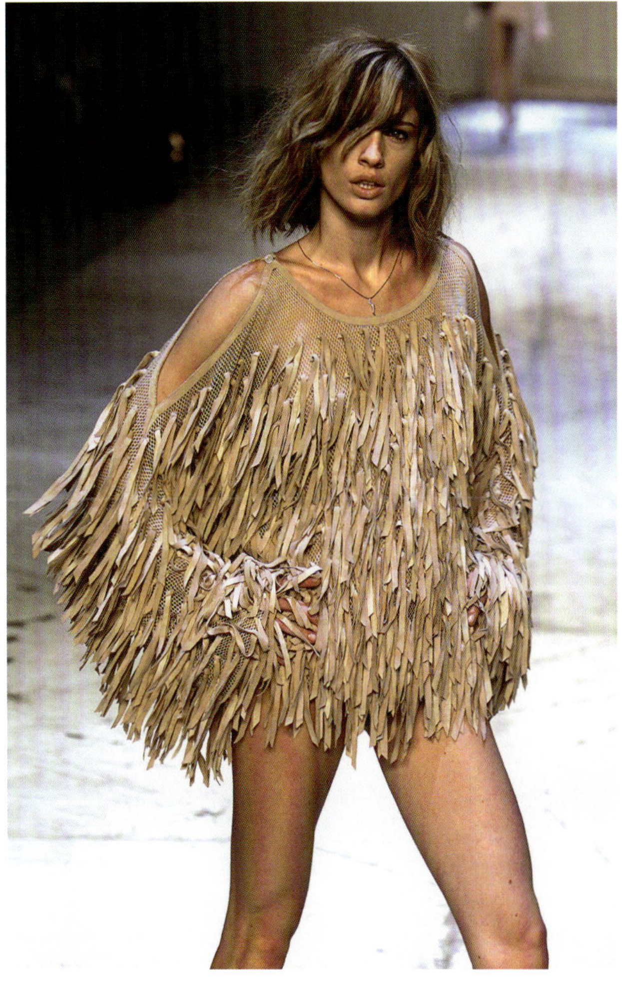

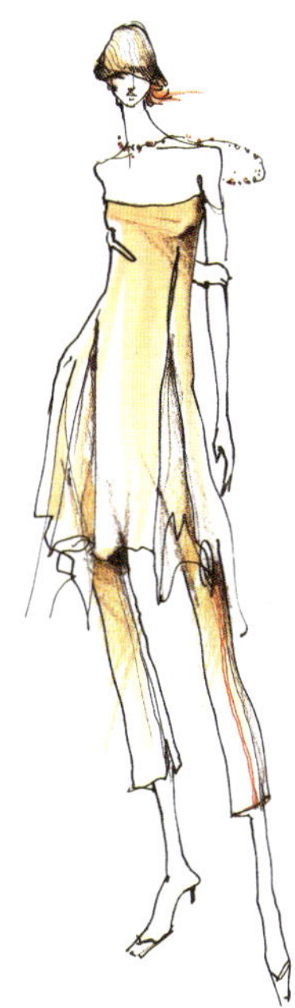

Fashion designers must time-travel between the past (a treasure trove of inspiration) and the present culture in order to create the fashions of the future. Designers, who show collections at least nine months before consumers are able to procure them, must conjure concepts, sketch them, and source materials prior to that. They often live at least a year ahead of the rest of the world. However, predicting the future requires the waves of time to be relatively smooth, which leaves little room for an abrupt storm (on a clear day) that immediately changes the course of history, as was the case on September 11, 2001.

The beginning of September is calendared as New York Fashion Week, meaning that thousands of well-dressed glitterati were shuffling between Bryant Park, Chelsea, and SoHo to see Spring/Summer 2002 fashions created by New York designers. Many were still clucking over Imitation of Christ's presentation on September 9, where seated models mimicked snotty editors while actual journalists were herded onto the catwalk, as comedian Tracey Ullman made mocking comments at them over the loudspeaker. That laughter, irreverence, and frivolity immediately halted two days later, in a way no one could have predicted. Whatever future had been anticipated, by fashion or the country, had changed. Fashion Week was canceled.

It would have been understandable if the whole season for all designers across the board and globe became irrelevant and unsuitable, needing to be completely scrapped. Interestingly, that was not entirely the case. Garments in Bleached Sand took on a new level of importance. Under different circumstances, the neutral shade may have been overlooked, but following the catastrophic events of that September morning, the uncontroversial tone became a touchstone for the fashion world. Swedish designer Lars Nilsson for Bill Blass saw the color as representing "perfect balance."[163] Carmen Marc Valvo referred to the "dusty, sunbaked, diaphanous" color as being both "sophisticated and humble."[164] New York heavyweight designer Ralph Lauren and British newbie Phoebe Philo for Chloé both drew on the romanticism associated with Parchment. Lauren's loose ruffles were a Victorian ode, whereas Philo's flowing garments alluded to the '70s. Cynthia Steffe brought the '20s to mind by adorning her models with cloche hats, long strands of beads, and slim-cut slinky garments. The ever-accessible brand GAP, under the creative direction of Jerome Jessup, chose unobtrusive Sandshell for its twill shirts. Designer David Rodriguez used the "light, feminine" color to "convey a respite from all negativity," because it simply "make[s] you smile."[165] And come spring that was exactly what was needed.

Beige

Neutral, natural, and nonchalant Beige is a touchstone for the greats, from bygone couturiers like Jacques Fath, Cristóbal Balenciaga, and Gabrielle Chanel to today's fashion prophets like Phoebe Philo for Céline and Christopher Bailey for Burberry.

In 1872, Aaron Montgomery Ward revolutionized American consumption by creating the first mail-order catalog. New York's prestigious Grolier Club later honored it, saying: "The [Montgomery Ward] mail-order catalog has been perhaps the greatest single influence in increasing the standard of American middle-class living."[166] As a fashion resource, the publication offers insight to consumption practices and historical truths; Montgomery Ward's 1943 catalog communicates the wartime zeitgeist selling military play garb for boys and girls, as well as uniform-inspired Beige suits for women.

With made-to-measure couture, the garment's story is not just one of the designer, but also the wearer. From 1947, Lady Alexandra Henrietta Louisa Howard-Johnson (neé Haig) wore only couture from Jacques Fath. Since a white gown would have been seen as inappropriate for her second marriage, Lady Alexandra wore an Almond Buff suit embroidered with gold Lurex thread for the nuptials. Thrilled with the result, she noted that the dress was "worn and worn." The outfit was alluring not only because of its elegance and romantic symbolism, but also because it was one of Fath's last. The couturier died roughly a month after Lady Alexandra's wedding day. Only then did she don another designer: Jeanne Lanvin.

To exuberant fanfare, Phoebe Philo took over as creative director at Céline for Spring/Summer 2010. Despite a cacophony of inspiration (Bob Mackie–clad Cher and early '90s David Sims and Melanie Ward editorials), Philo's work for Céline is crisp and practical, her debut a "strict palette of black, white, and varying shades of stone."[167] Fashion editor Penny Martin mused: "[A]s the creative director of Céline, Phoebe has cut through fashion's tired fantasy, turning the dust-gathering Parisian House into a platform for sharp reality and hyper-luxurious clothing."[168] Founded in 1945 by Céline Vipiana, the House was originally known for its "subdued luxe."[169]

At the behest of the British War Office in 1914, the inventor of gabardine, Thomas Burberry, fashioned his breathable, waterproof fabric into coats for soldiers in the trenches, known since as "trench coats." Today, Burberry's creative director Christopher Bailey honors that the brand's Tan coat with its Beige, black, white, and red check interior is "one of the most potent badges of Englishness," but does not shy away from modernizing it.[170] Choosing British actress Emma Watson as the face of the campaign, Bailey imbued the coat with Watson's megawatt energy.

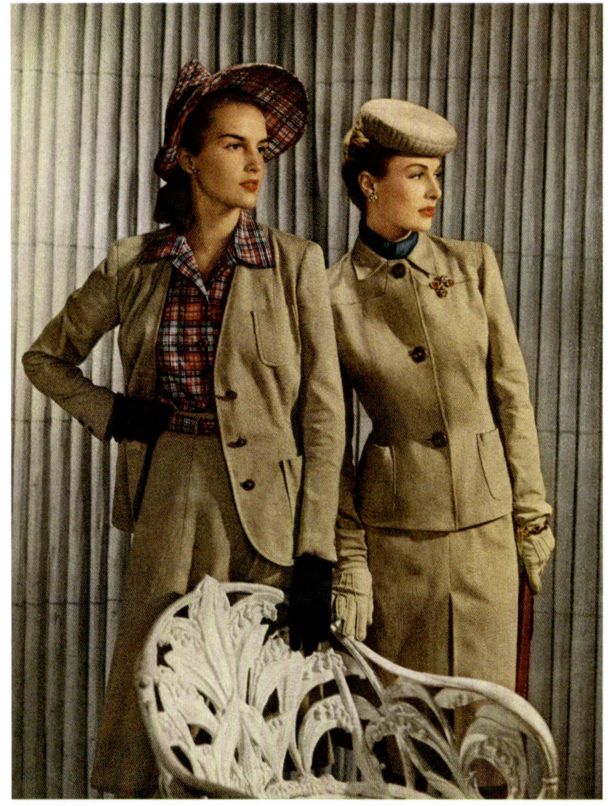

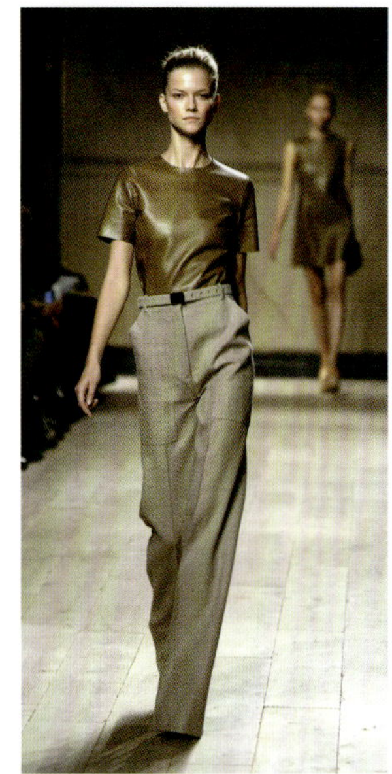

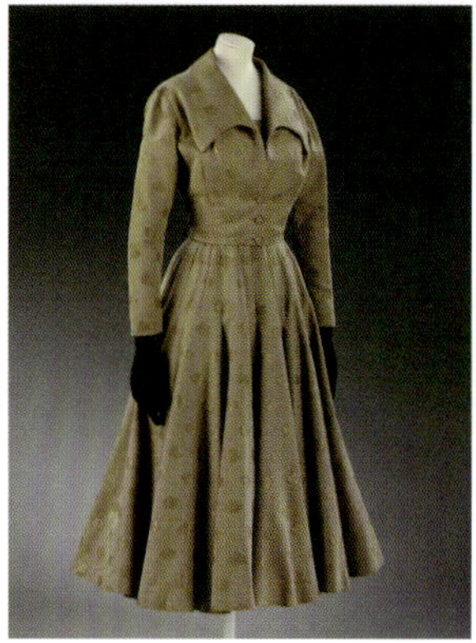

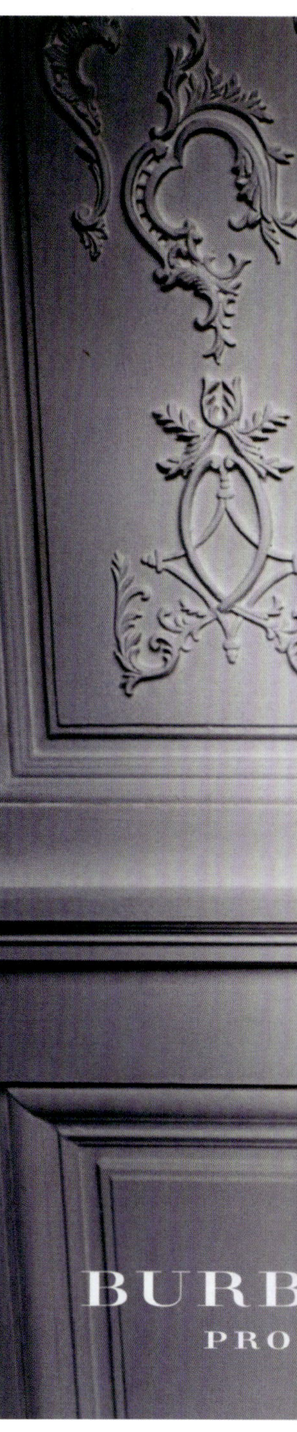

opposite, top
Cover Girl cotton dress suits
Page from the Montgomery Ward®
Spring/Summer catalog
1943

opposite, bottom left
Top, trouser, and belt
Phoebe Philo for Céline
Spring/Summer 2010

opposite, bottom right
Worsted cotton and thread dress
Jacques Fath
circa 1954

below
Trench coats
Print ad featuring George Craig
and Emma Watson
Burberry
2010

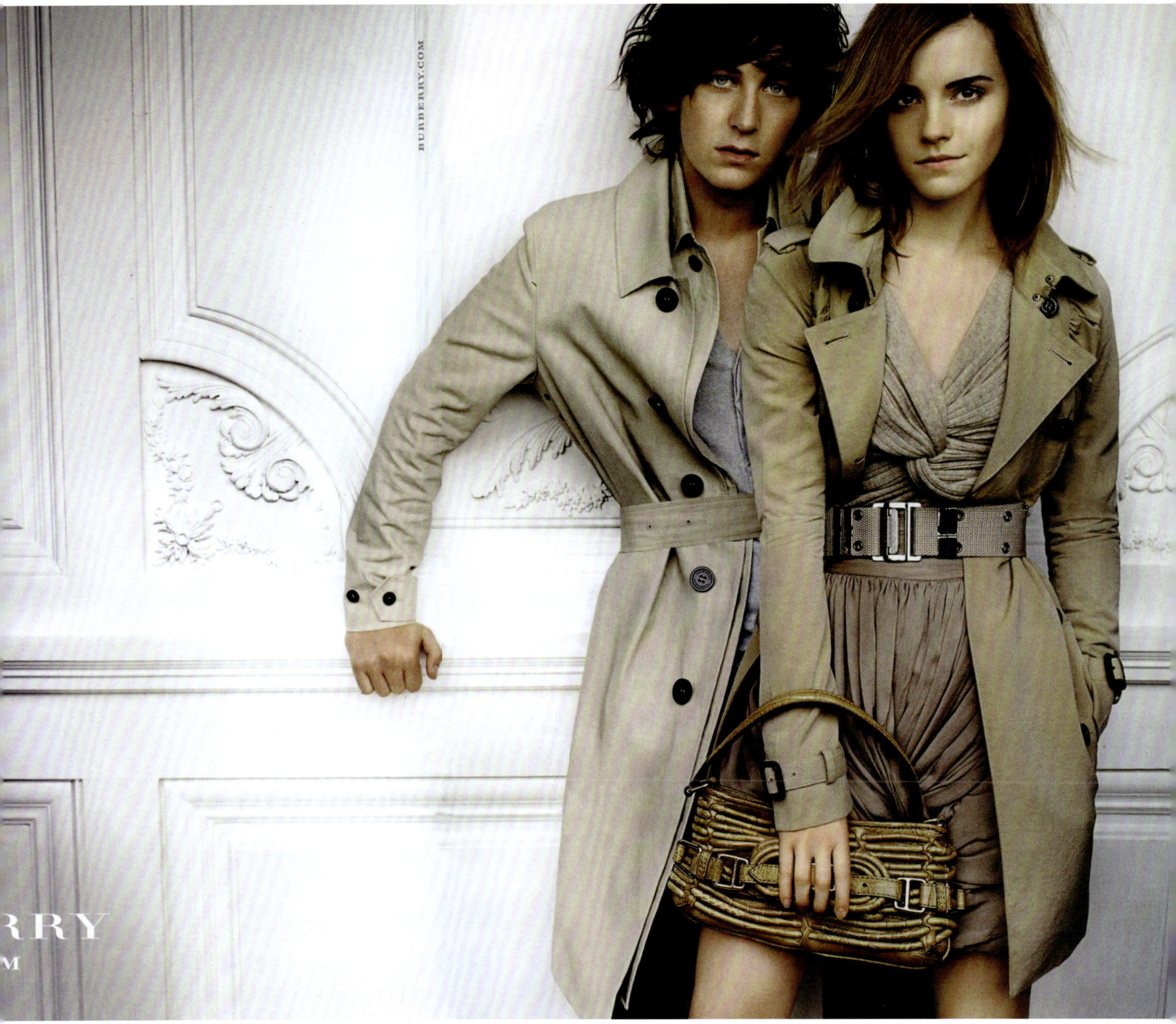

Lattè
PANTONE 15-1220

Tan
PANTONE 16-1334

Mushroom

"People have become more nuanced in their understanding of subtle organic tones; there are millions of subtle organic tones and a million ways to be sludgy."
—*Simon Doonan of Barneys*[171]

The warmer-toned derivations of the taupe family, like Mushroom, are exceedingly versatile and flattering to nearly all skin tones. Classic trousers, like "khakis," often come in timeless and wearable shades of taupe, which have the ability to "go with everything" without looking dated.

American sportswear maven Claire McCardell designed leisurely, functional clothes. While the full-skirted, nip-waisted "New Look" continued to influence 1950s fashion, McCardell's garments, like her 1952 clean-line Mushroom coat and matching skirt, stayed true to her more wearable characteristic style, which complemented women without overtaking them.

After the loud, logo-heavy 1980s, Calvin Klein smartly shifted his previously successful strategy, designing for multiple demographics in the 1990s: young adults interested in grungy androgyny (CK One) and adult women looking for "refined, sexy, and ultimately daring" dresses.[172] Klein's Spring/Summer 1992 lace slip dress takes Jean Paul Gaultier's conical corset look and pares it down to an elegant boudoir eveningwear look.

Brian Atwood may not be as well-known as Blahnik or Louboutin, but women with those two in their closets likely have shoes from him as well. Atwood's sky-high heels combine sex appeal and craftsmanship, the two essential ingredients for lust-worthy shoes. Atwood, who got his start at (Gianni) Versace, designs shoes for his label that are less vampy—more for the trophy wife, less for the mistress. His Warm Taupe slouchy ankle boots of 2010 easily pair with any fall look, as would similar ones from Tory Burch or Jimmy Choo.

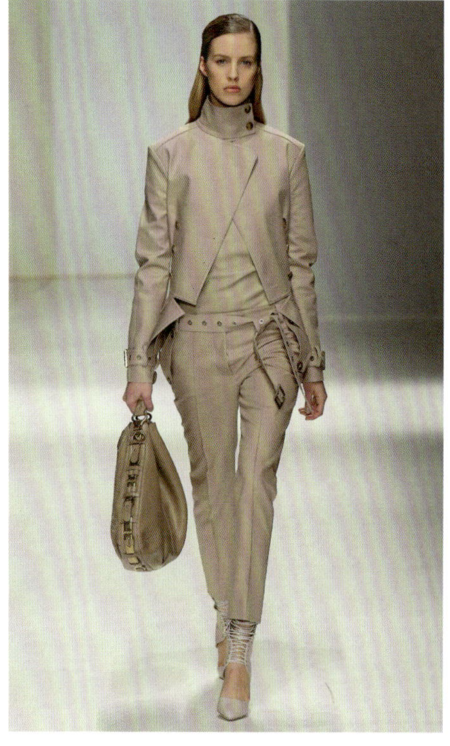

The subject of footwear naturally leads to Ferragamo, shoes being the cornerstone on which the brand is built. Between 1927 and 1960, Salvatore Ferragamo designed over twenty thousand shoes, for the likes of Audrey Hepburn, Sophia Loren, the Duchess of Windsor, and Eva Perón. After he stepped down, his six children continued to run the brand in varying capacities, increasing its reach well beyond shoes. For Spring/Summer 2013, designer Massimiliano Giornetti offered a head-to-toe look in shades of Portabella and Chanterelle, with corset-inspired shoes, a tan hobo bag, jacket, and trousers, all in lightweight, butter-soft leather. Ferragamo once said, "Elegance and comfort are not incompatible, and whoever maintains the contrary simply doesn't know what he's talking about," an ideology still held by the label today.

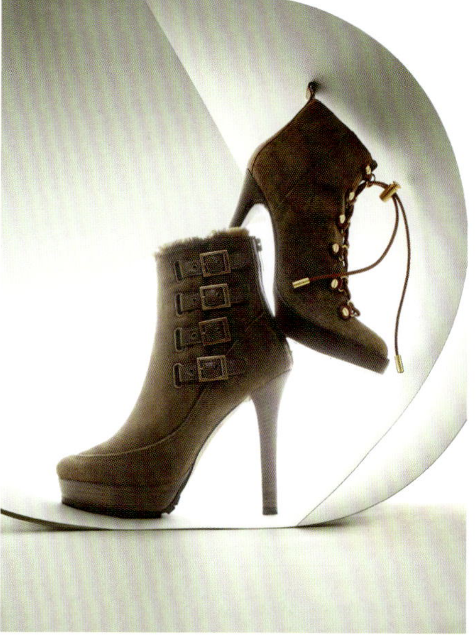

opposite, left
Leather jacket, top, and pants
Massimiliano Giornetti for
Ferragamo
Spring/Summer 2013

opposite, right
Suede ankle boots
Jimmy Choo (left) and
Tory Burch (right)
2010

left
Metalic, chantilly lace, and
chiffon evening dress
Calvin Klein
Spring/Summer 1992

right
Ensemble featured in
Vogue magazine
Claire McCardell
1952

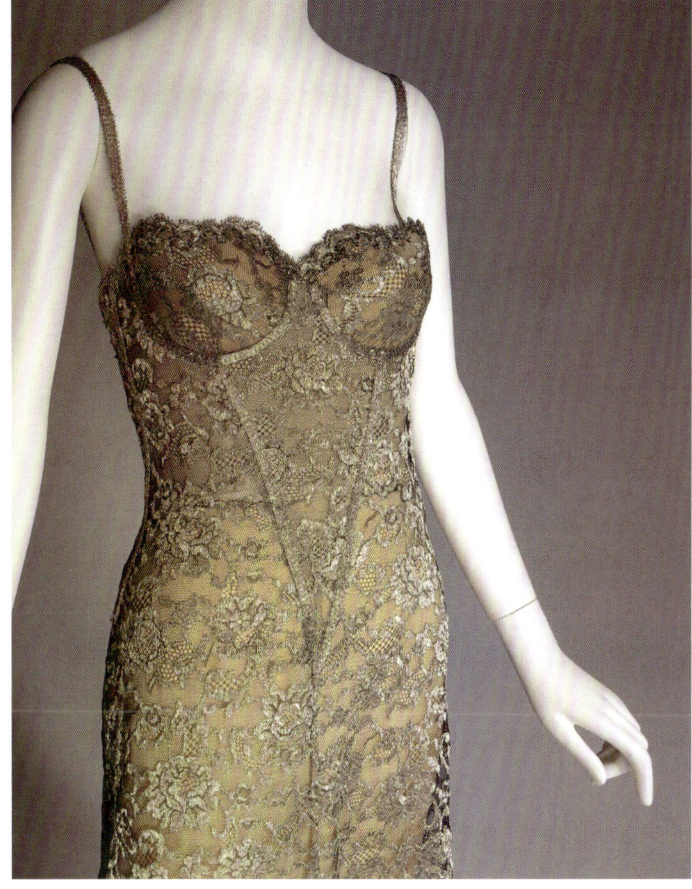

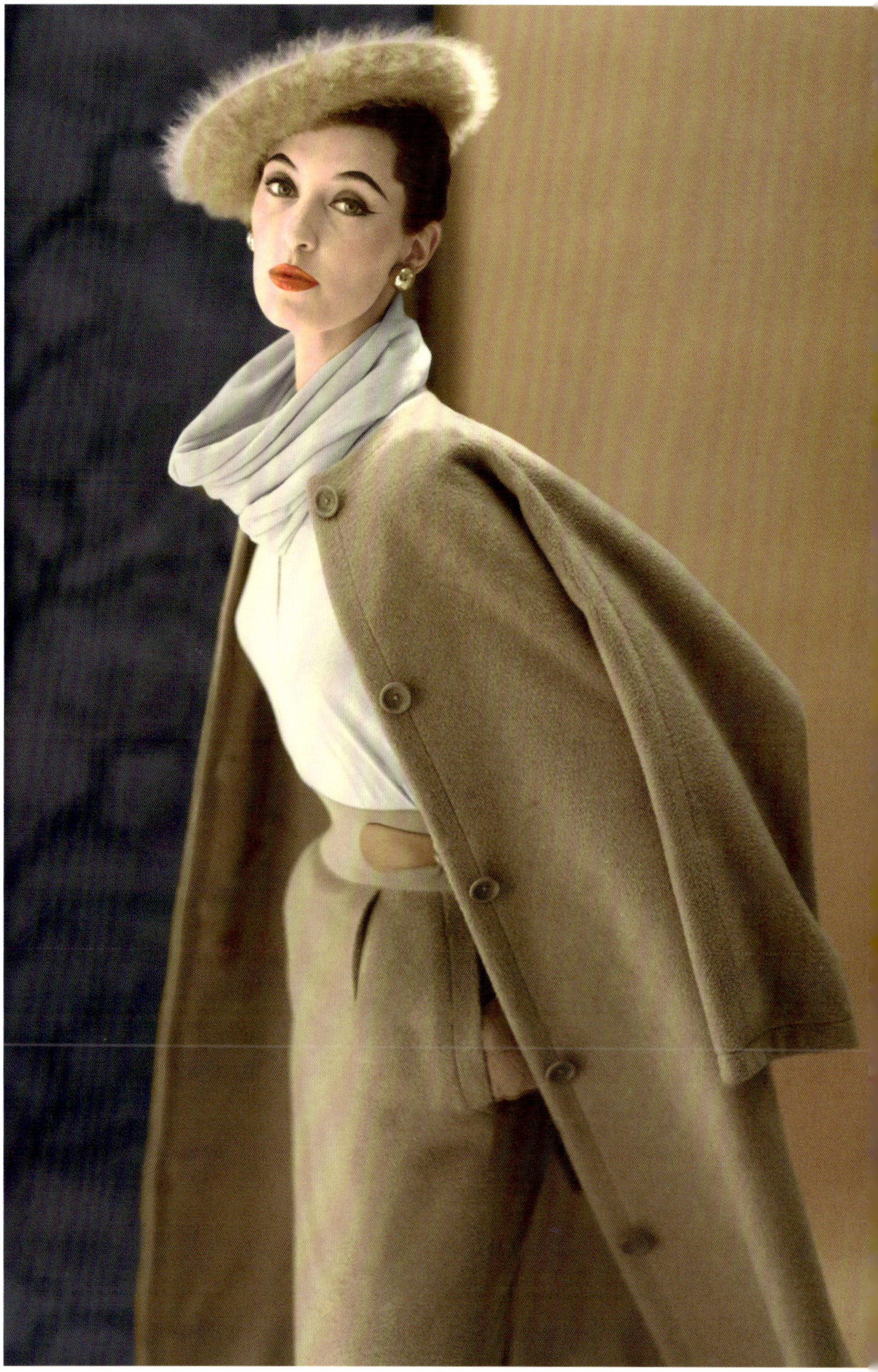

Simply Taupe

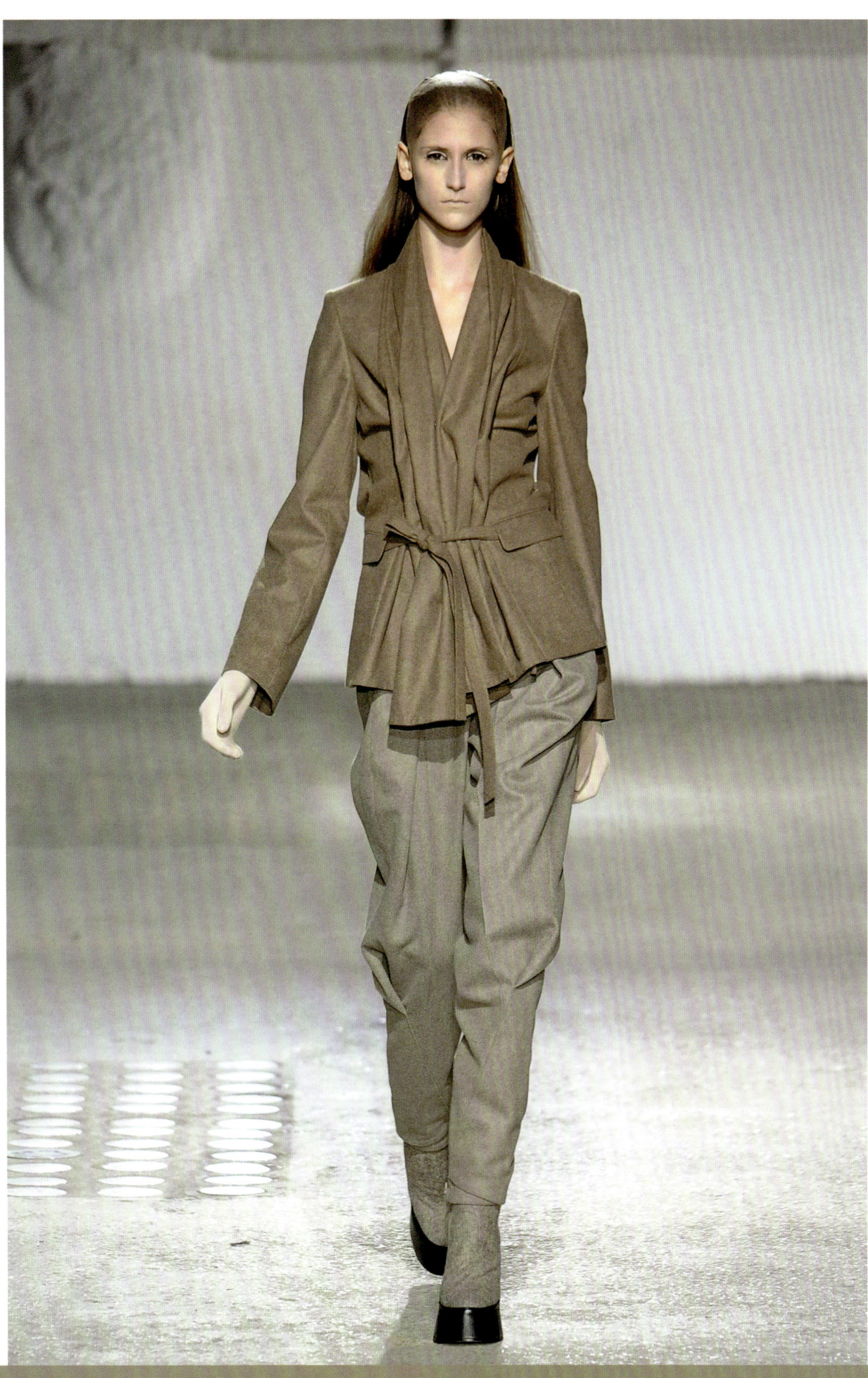

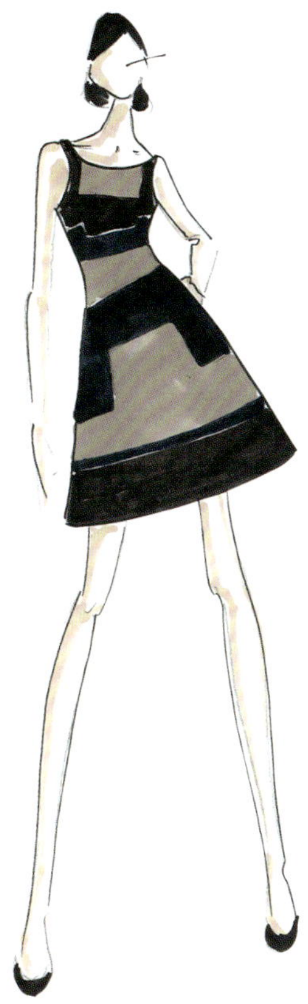

"I've become successful with eight different shades of beige."

—*Giorgio Armani*[173]

Giorgio Armani blurred gender lines by producing "soft and flowy, hence feminized" men's clothing and "sturdily tailored and subdued, hence masculinized" women's clothing.[174] Armani launched his own label in 1975. By the 1980s, workplace women clamored to nab his fluid suits, as did men who wanted to brandish their sexuality, *American Gigolo*–style. Using the same neutral palette of Simply Taupe across his men's and women's collections exacerbated Armani's lack of distinct gender boundaries.

Belgian designers sent a seismic shock through Paris fashion in the 1990s, like the Japanese did in the 1980s. Pair An Vandevorst and Filip Arickx of A. F. Vandevorst are part of the second generation of Belgian designers to gain notoriety, behind the "Antwerp Six," which included Walter Van Beirendonck, Dries van Noten, and Ann Demeulemeester. A. F. Vandevorst, established in 1997, immediately incited a commotion with its exponentially fetishistic corset belt that doubled as a saddle. For Fall 2009, the brand continued interpreting cliché fashion concepts with humorous literalism: equestrianism (horse-hoof shoes) and nomadism (sleeping-bag coats). "Look 21," one of fourteen Light Taupe outfits, reinterprets the blazer, exaggerating the lapels with excess fabric, making the singular piece appear as a jacket with matching scarf.

Raised in Paris, Rio de Janeiro, and New York, Laura Poretzky's life alone gives her the necessary cred to make it in fashion. The Rhode Island School of Design graduate launched ready-to-wear line Abaeté in 2004. For Fall 2006, Poretzky mixed Plaza Taupe with Manhattan Black for the ideal day-to-night frock. Though she closed Abaeté in 2010, her newest endeavor, *Vogue*-approved Été swimwear, suits off-duty island-hopping career women beautifully.

Clare Waight Keller is only now receiving the spotlight she deserves. After stints at Calvin Klein, Ralph Lauren, Tom Ford's Gucci, and Pringle of Scotland, Keller was named creative director of Chloé in 2011. Chloé, started by Gaby Aghion and Jacques Lenoir in 1952, began with the cotton poplin dresses beloved by Maria Callas and Grace Kelly. Since then, Chloé has had some of the world's best designers at the helm, including Karl Lagerfeld, Martine Sitbon, Stella McCartney, Phoebe Philo, and Keller. For Fall/Winter 2012–2013, Keller showed a belted Greige dress with large, ample pockets. Unlike other brands, which have been negatively rocked by different design personalities, Chloé has managed to maintain a "constant thread" true to Aghion's vision of accessible *prêt-à-porter* (a term she coined) with an air of freedom.

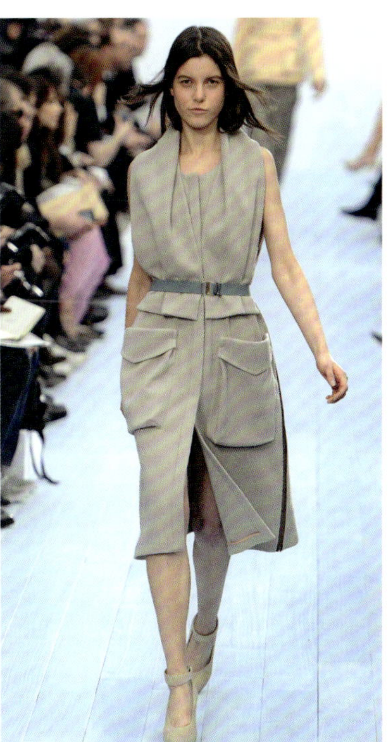

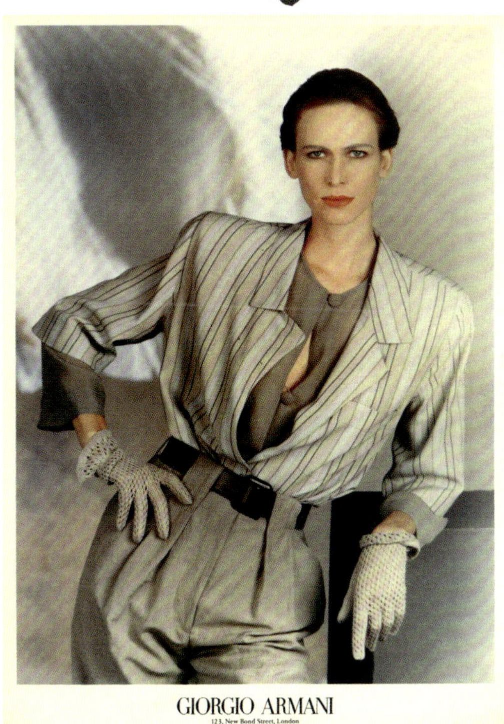

Glacier Gray

"Gray will prevail."

—*Christian Dior*

The association of gray with cloudy days and the eternally depressed (such as the *Winnie the Pooh* character Eeyore) overshadows its history of hopefulness and luxury. Toward the end of the 1800s, technological innovations like safe elevators and glass curtain walls, coupled with affordable steel, allowed buildings to touch the clouds. In 1928, *Femina* magazine's *Under the Eyes of New York Skyscrapers* shows a woman with a *la garçonne* bob in a tiered white, blue, and gray Lanvin dress standing near a window with the city's visible skyline. The art deco influences in both the illustration and architecture are immediately evident, as are the parallels between the model's lithe body and the silhouette of the buildings, all of which represent the promise of modernity. While designer Jeanne Lanvin, the matron of couture, was sixty-one when the dress was designed, her daughter and muse, by then Marie-Blanche de Polignac, was thirty-one and on the pulse of high society.

World War II caused luxury to become "a half forgotten shadow."[175] Yet, Pierre Balmain, Cristóbal Balenciaga, Christian Dior, and Jacques Fath brought extravagance back into the spotlight of post-war Paris by polarizing menswear and womens wear. Jacques Fath, couture's original *enfant terrible*, saw the optimism of gray, using it for his 1949 evening gown. The nipped-waist dress with its excess of fabric shares similarities with Dior's 1947 "Corolle" collection. However, Fath's ancestry clearly illustrates the reality that there was nothing new about "The New Look"; his great-grandmother had assisted with the dressmaking for Empress Eugénie. The Second Empire influence is evident in Fath's evening gown, as the oversized bow almost mimics a bustle.

After Monsieur Fath, Central Saint Martins alums John Galliano and Alexander McQueen vied for the coveted title of *enfant terrible*. In 1996, Galliano was made head designer at Christian Dior, where he remained until his Icarus-like fall from grace in 2011. His psychological implosion has sadly incinerated his legacy as a design talent. Like Fath, Galliano loved larger-than-life opulence, theatricality, and historical dress. Yet, his gray suit for Dior in the late 1990s is a rare example of Galliano's restraint. The harsh lines of the jacket encompass both Orientalism and fetishism while still remaining true to Dior's structured "New Look," which earned it a place in the Kyoto Costume Institute.

New York designers Yigal Azrouël and Jen Kao were both drawn to the softness of Frost Gray, eschewing its chilly associations and using it for Spring 2009 and 2010, respectively.

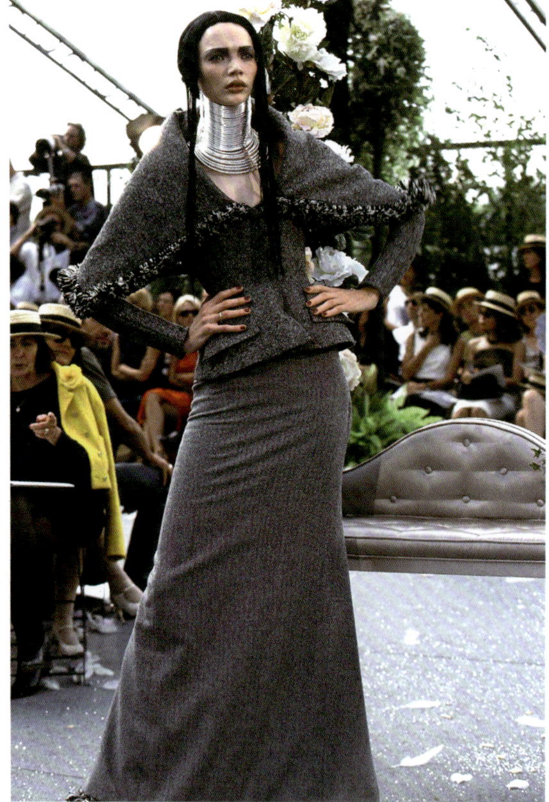

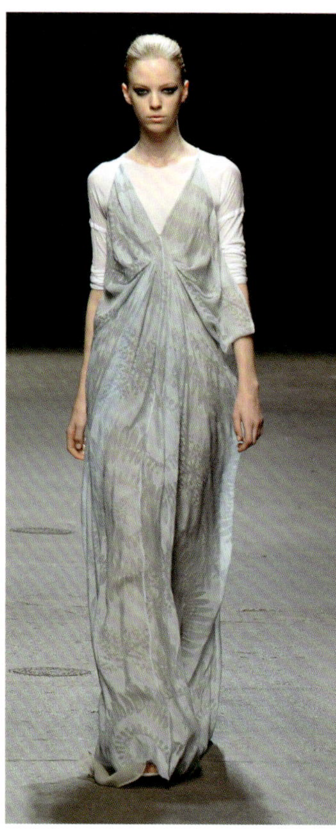

opposite, left
Jacket, skirt, and choker
John Galliano for Christian Dior
Haute Couture
Fall/Winter 1997

opposite, right
Dress
Yigal Azrouël
Spring 2009

left
*Under the Eyes of New York
Skyscrapers* lithograph by
Leon Benigni for *Femina*
Jeanne Lanvin
1928

right
Long sheer gown
Jen Kao
Spring 2010

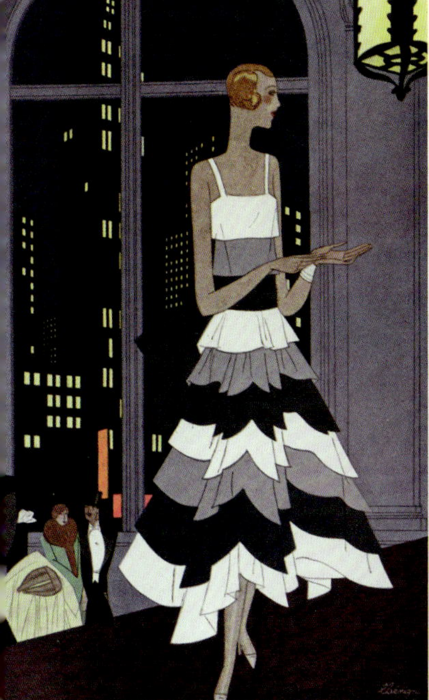

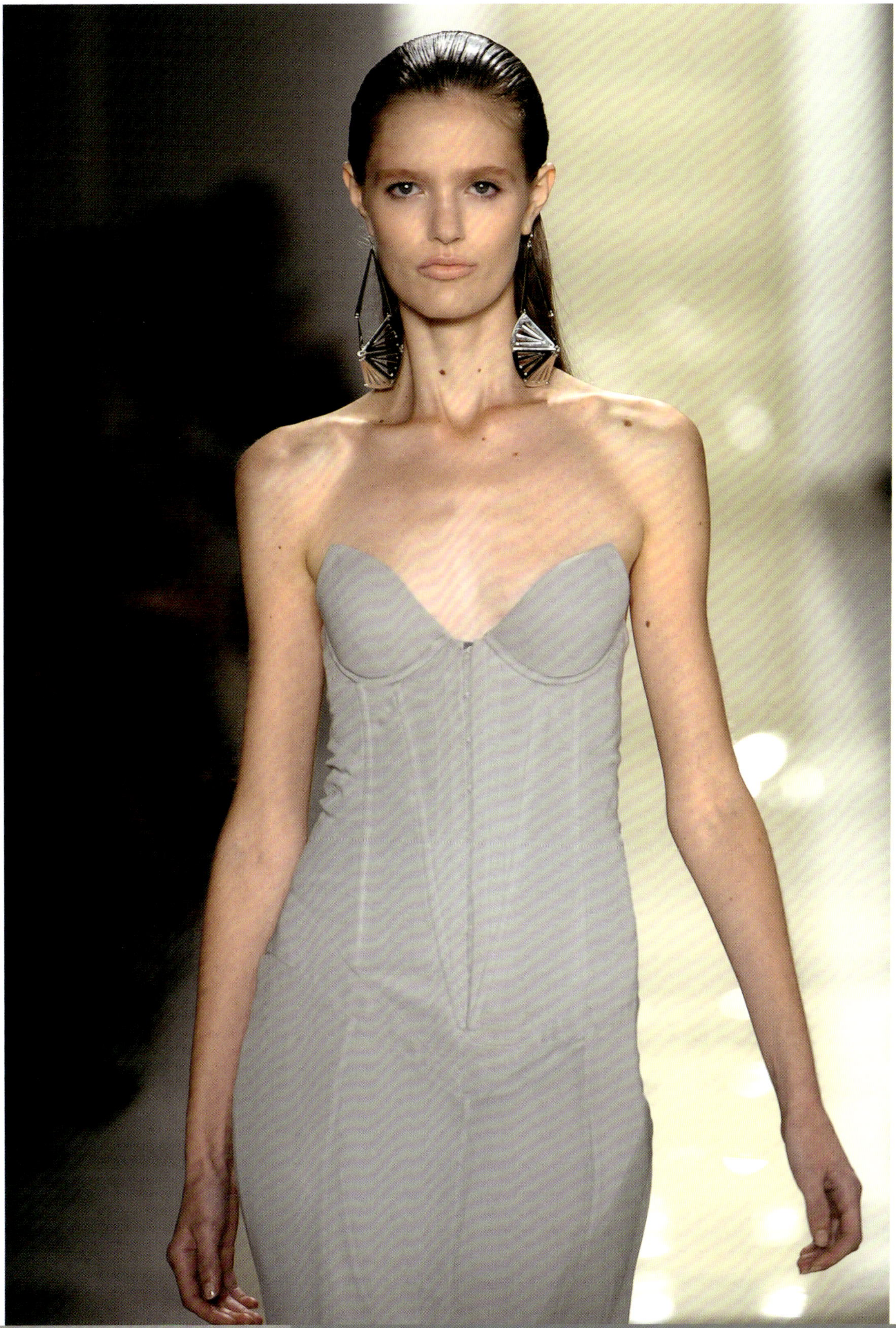

Paloma
PANTONE 16-0000

Frost Gray
PANTONE 17-0000

Silver

Sleek Silver conveys advancing technology and futurism, a vibe the American Enka Company, Paco Rabanne, and Iris Van Herpen all harnessed. But with patina, Silver can also express the passing of time, as ably demonstrated by Isaac Mizrahi.

With silk necessary for WWII parachutes, fashion turned to synthetics like rayon, which the American Enka Company provided. To help with the war effort, fashion leaders from *Harper's Bazaar* to Bloomingdale's hyped the fabric, selling it as a wearable technological advancement, rather than merely artificial silk. In 1944, the American Enka Company offered fashionable, war-conscious consumers a belted Quicksilver evening gown with matching gloves.

Spanish-born French refugee Francisco de Rabanne de Cuervo (known as Paco Rabanne) had the mettle to literally use metal. Using unconventional materials like aluminum and plastic, Rabanne infused his designs with an air of experimentation, leading fashion journalist Madge Garland to call him one of "the most inventive and original designers in Paris in the late Sixties." [177]

Before Isaac Mizrahi started designing anything and everything (cheesecake for QVC anyone?) he was the talk of the town in 1990s New York. *The New York Times* called Mizrahi's debut "one of the most promising beginnings." [178] His Fall/Winter 1997–1998 Collection was strong: his "Rouge Chic" clothes were up-to-the-minute while still referencing the "Naked City" of Old New York. His Silver Filigree sweater gleamed under the catwalk lights, emphasized all the more by its pairing with matte Silver trousers, which fashion journalist Amy M. Spindler recalled "looked loved." [179] Explaining his impetus to design, Mizrahi explained, "I don't do clothes to be influential. I do them because they're beautiful and I can't help it." [180]

After gathering experience at Alexander McQueen and Viktor & Rolf, Iris Van Herpen began designing her own fashions that could put one "in a different mood or sometimes even in a different identity." [181] Though it utilized new technology, Van Herpen's Spring 2012 couture collection also explored the emotional hunger and emptiness fertilized by the digital world. Model Elsa Sylvan showed a one-sleeved Silver 3-D-printed dress "that seems to reflect its own surface." [182] The complexity of the printing, which looked like a rain forest fungus, made the sheath appear unfinished. Fashion icon Daphne Guinness and musician Björk, both known for fashioning their identity, admire Van Herpen's glowing work, as does Rem Koolhaas, architect extraordinaire and creative director for impressively sculpted United Nude shoes.

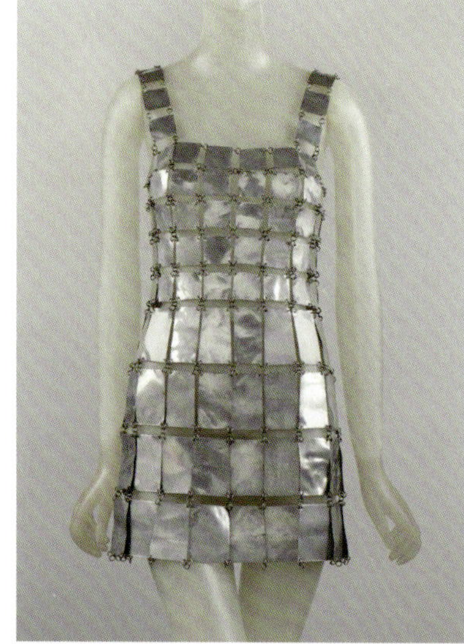

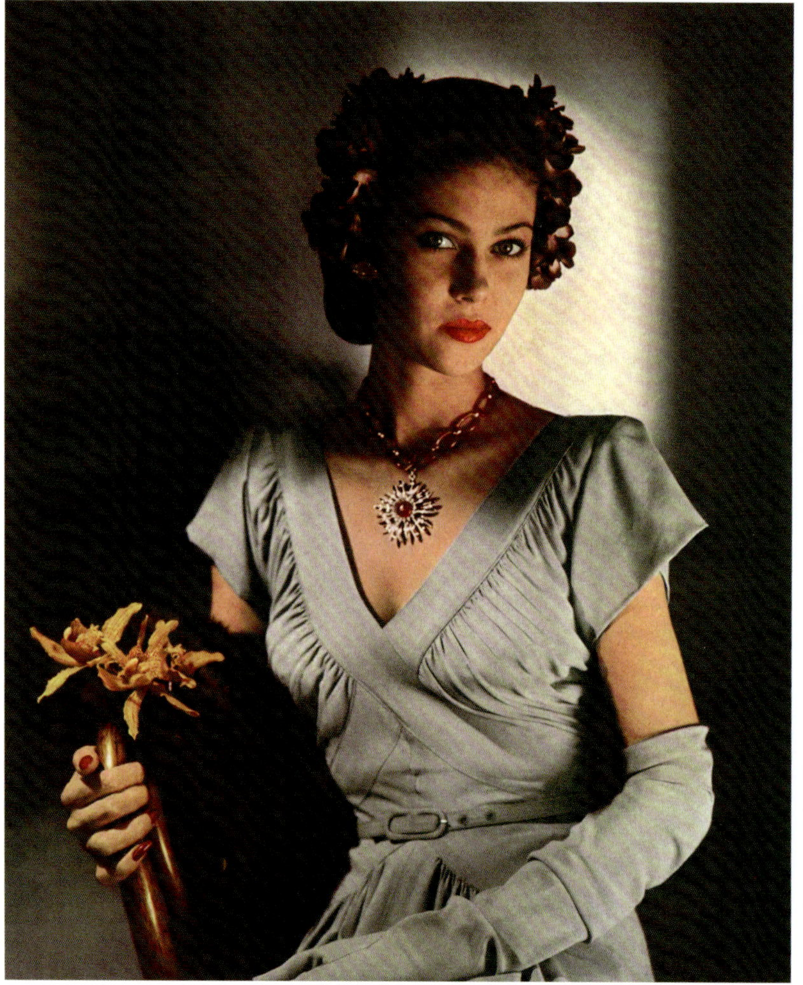

opposite, top
Metal minidress
Paco Rabanne
1967

opposite, bottom
Dress and matching gloves
print ad
American Enka Company
1944

left
Sweater with trousers
Isaac Mizrahi
Fall/Winter 1997–1998

right
Minidress with ruffles
Iris Van Herpen
Spring 2012

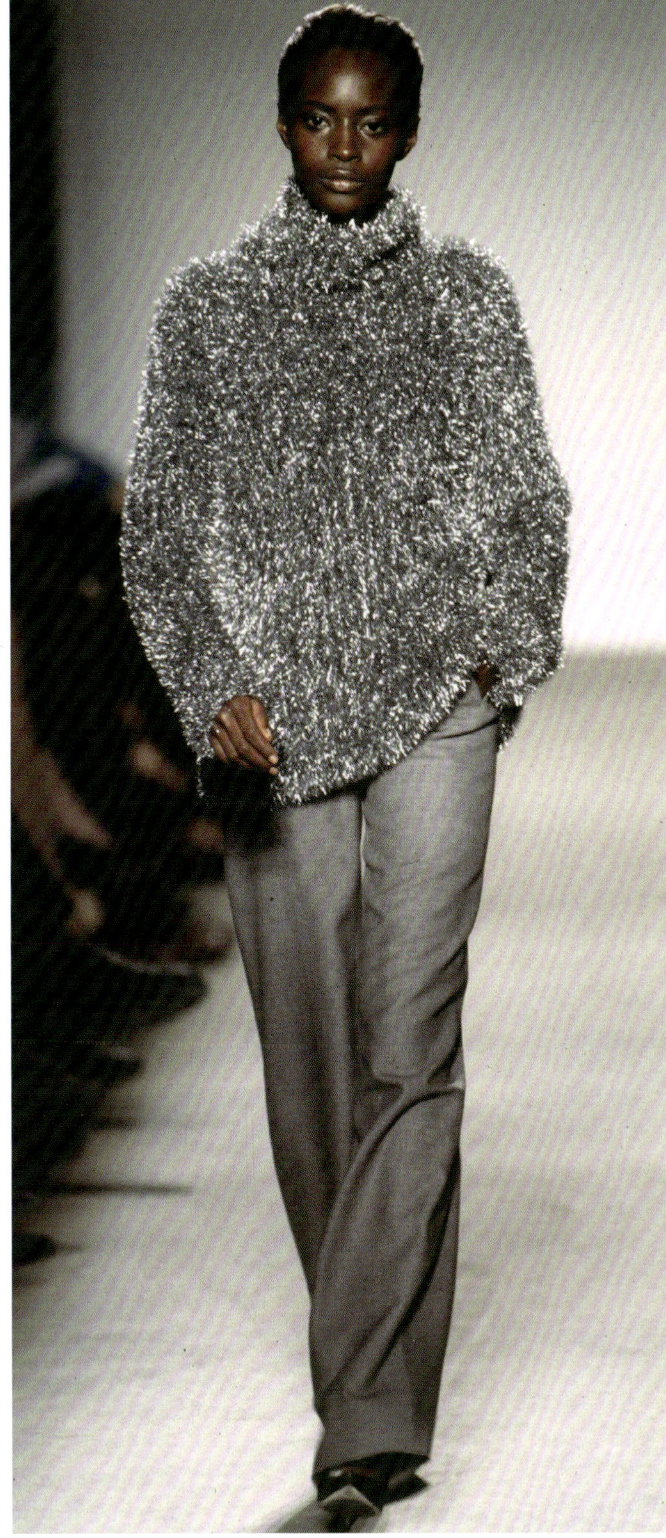

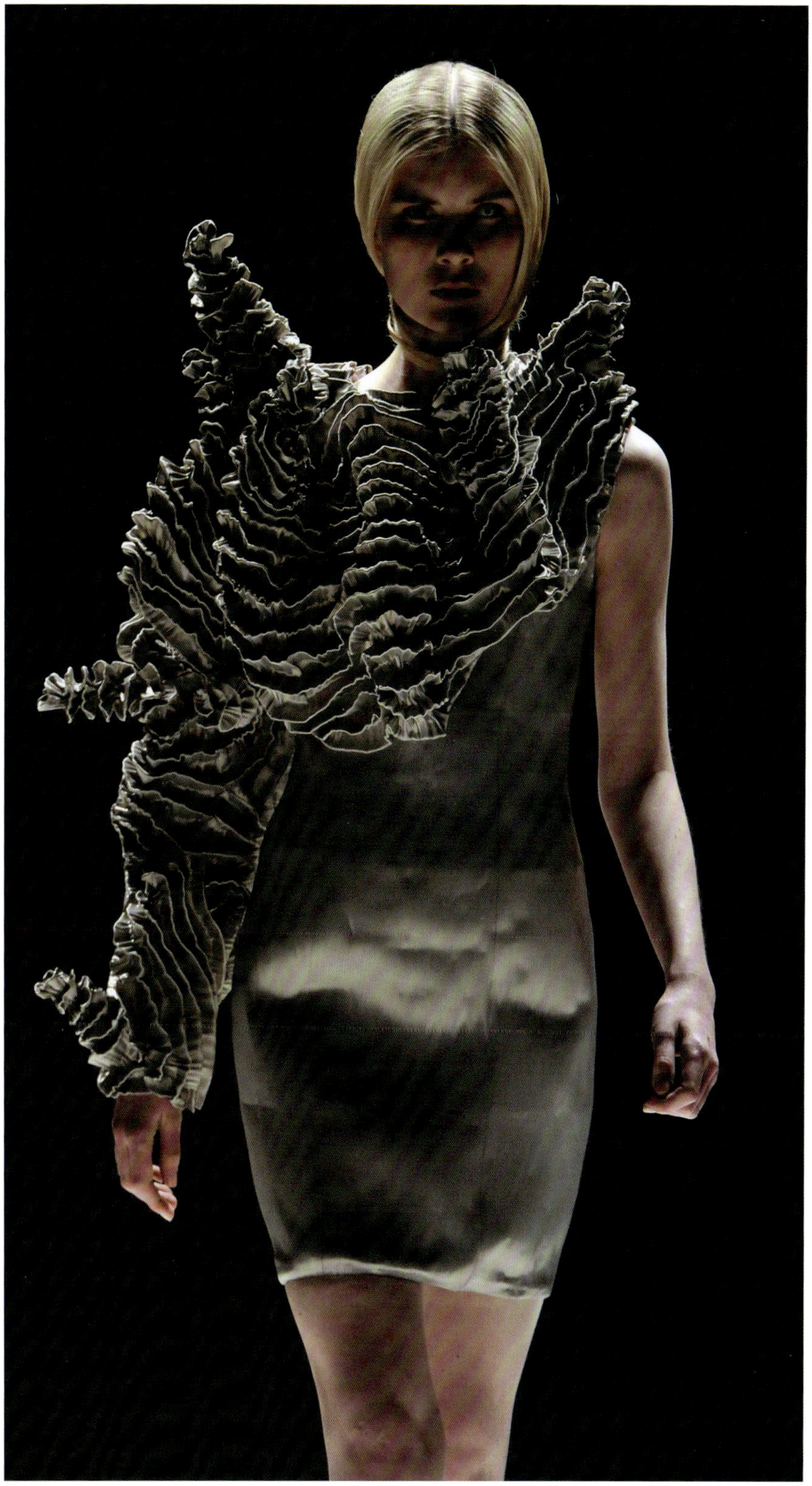

Charcoal Gray

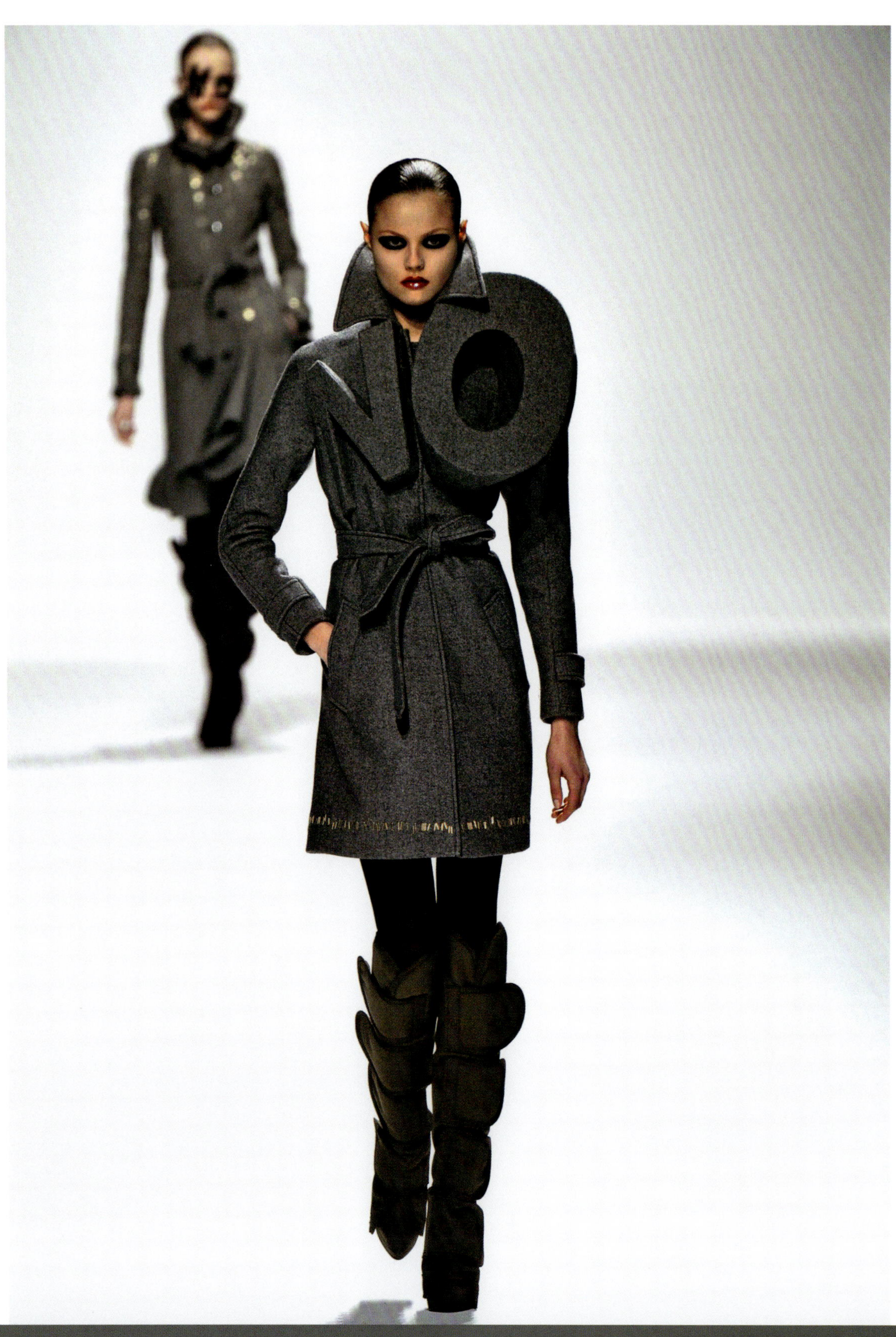

Charcoal Gray
PANTONE 18-0601

Steel Gray
PANTONE 18-4005

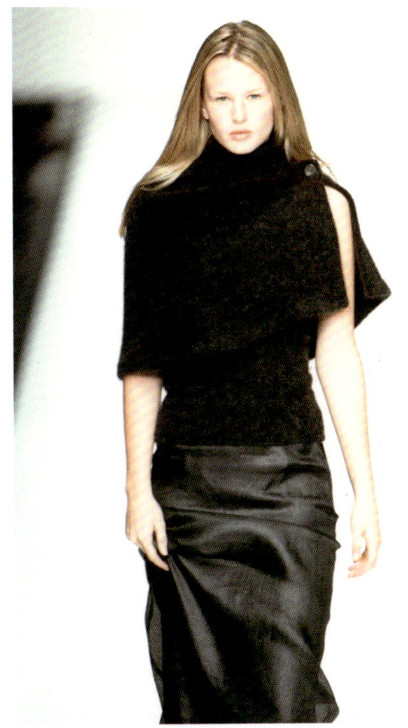

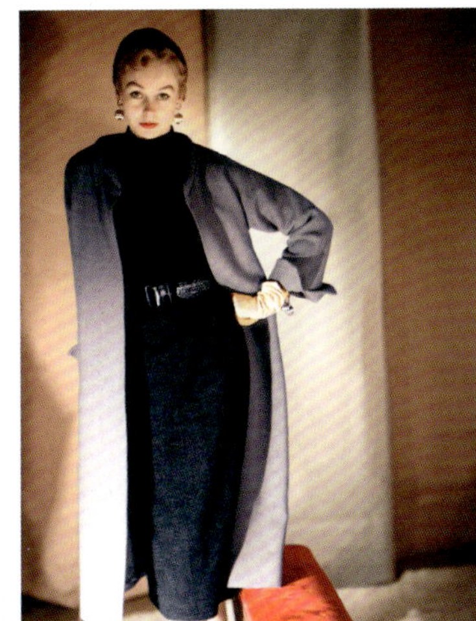

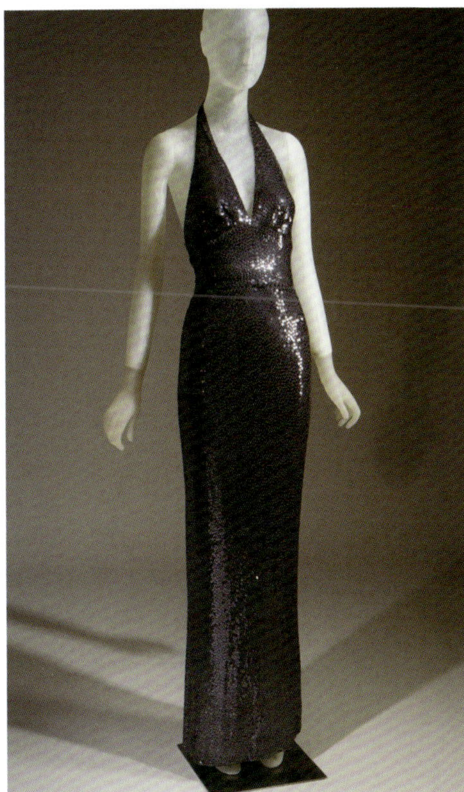

As gray inches toward pitch black on the color spectrum, it gains intensity, commanding respect and attention, which Sydney Wragge, of B. H. Wragge, understood. An early pioneer of American sportswear and separates, Wragge was known for being "undeniably the best at presenting the public with interchangeable wardrobes."[183] Inspired by the watercolors of Gordon Grant and the landscape of America, Wragge was prone to using slate grays and the color of "shingle" to outfit his demographic: stylish wives. In 1957, Wragge won the Coty American Fashion Critics' Award, fashion's Oscar, and is remembered fondly by Bonwit Teller's Ira Neimark as one of "the nobility of fashion who visited" the department store.[184]

"The acknowledged dean of American designers,"[185] Norman Norell believed a woman "can never be too plain during the day or too elaborate at night."[186] In the 1940s, Norell transformed ashen gray into a glistening, molten silver though his use of sequins (not rationed during WWII), bringing frisson to his eveningwear. Wildly successful, Norell continued to make variations of the dress, which "just never seem[ed] to go out of style," until his death in 1972.[187] Fashion critic Marilyn Bender wrote of Norell's showstoppers, "His incomparably sexy dresses cling to the body like mermaid's skin through the sleeves, then whisper of easiness at the waistline to the ankle."[188] Bender's description stuck, and Norell's "mermaid" gowns have gone down in history as his most famous, in part because of Marilyn Monroe's fondness for them.[189]

South-African-turned-New-Yorker Mark Eisen made an instantaneous name for himself in 1988 with the launch of his "Couture Denim" collection. When Eisen bowed out in 2009, his line had been featured in over 800 stores in 18 countries. This urban gray look from his Fall/Winter 1998–1999 collection shows his distinguished ability to make sportswear tailored, sleek, and easy.

Doppelgänger duo Viktor Horsting and Rolf Snoeren have had a love/hate relationship with the fashion world since moving to Paris in 1992. The pair, who met at and graduated from the Arnhem Academy of Art and Design, began by deconstructing the fashion industry more so than garments. Collected by galleries and museums, their wares seemed destined to be confined behind glass. Angered by their lack of commercial success, they went on strike for Fall/Winter 1996–1997. Similar frustration led to their Pewter-hued "NO!" collection over a decade later. Exhausted by the nonstop merry-go-round of the fashion calendar, Viktor & Rolf literally sewed their emotions into the garments. Like employees of *Office Space* gone postal, they used thousands of staples to hem the garments, expressing their frustration with fashion's overt commercialism. Ironic, given their previous strike.

Moonless Night

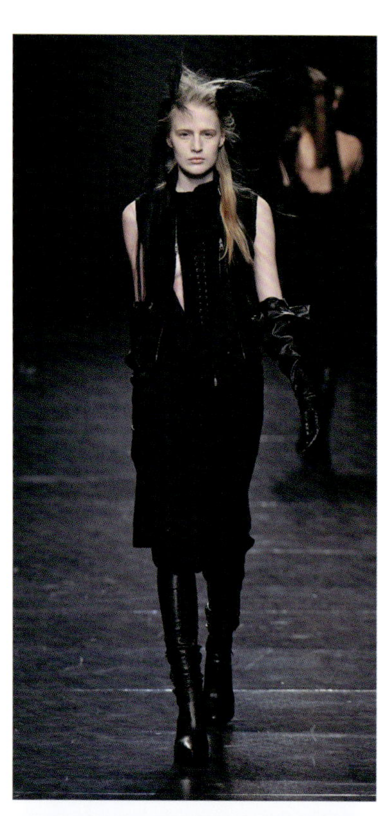

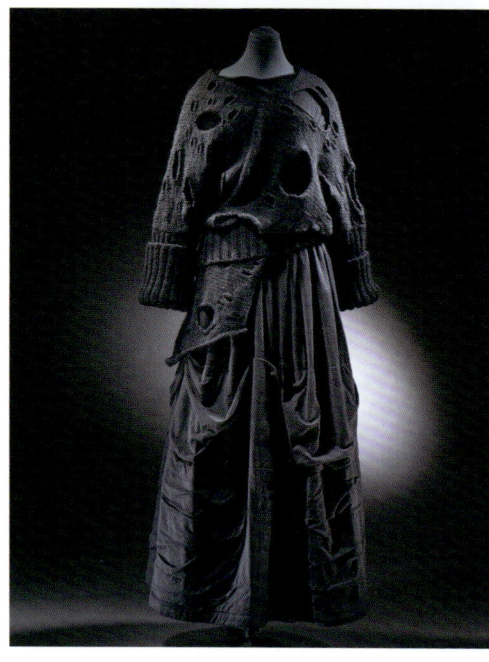

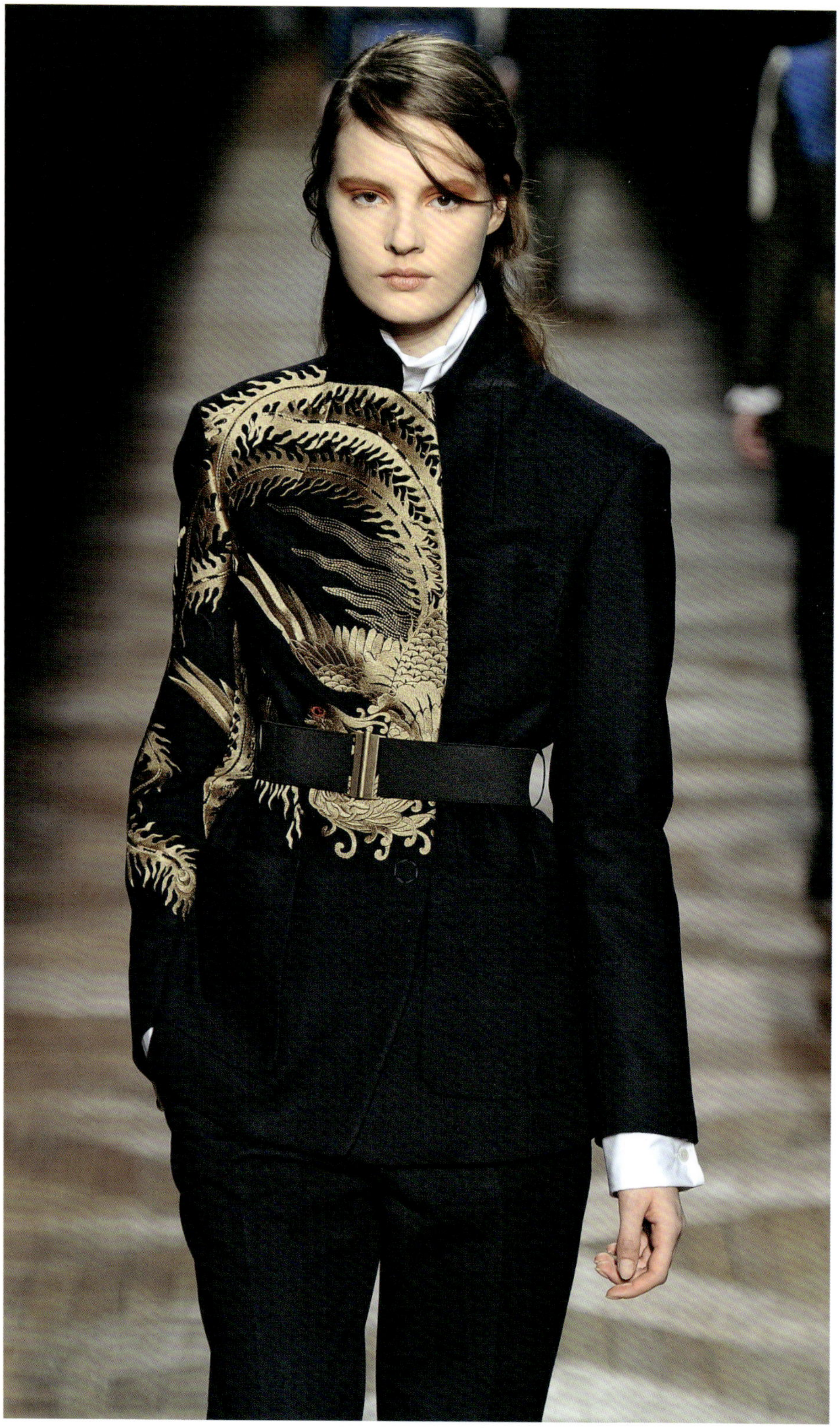

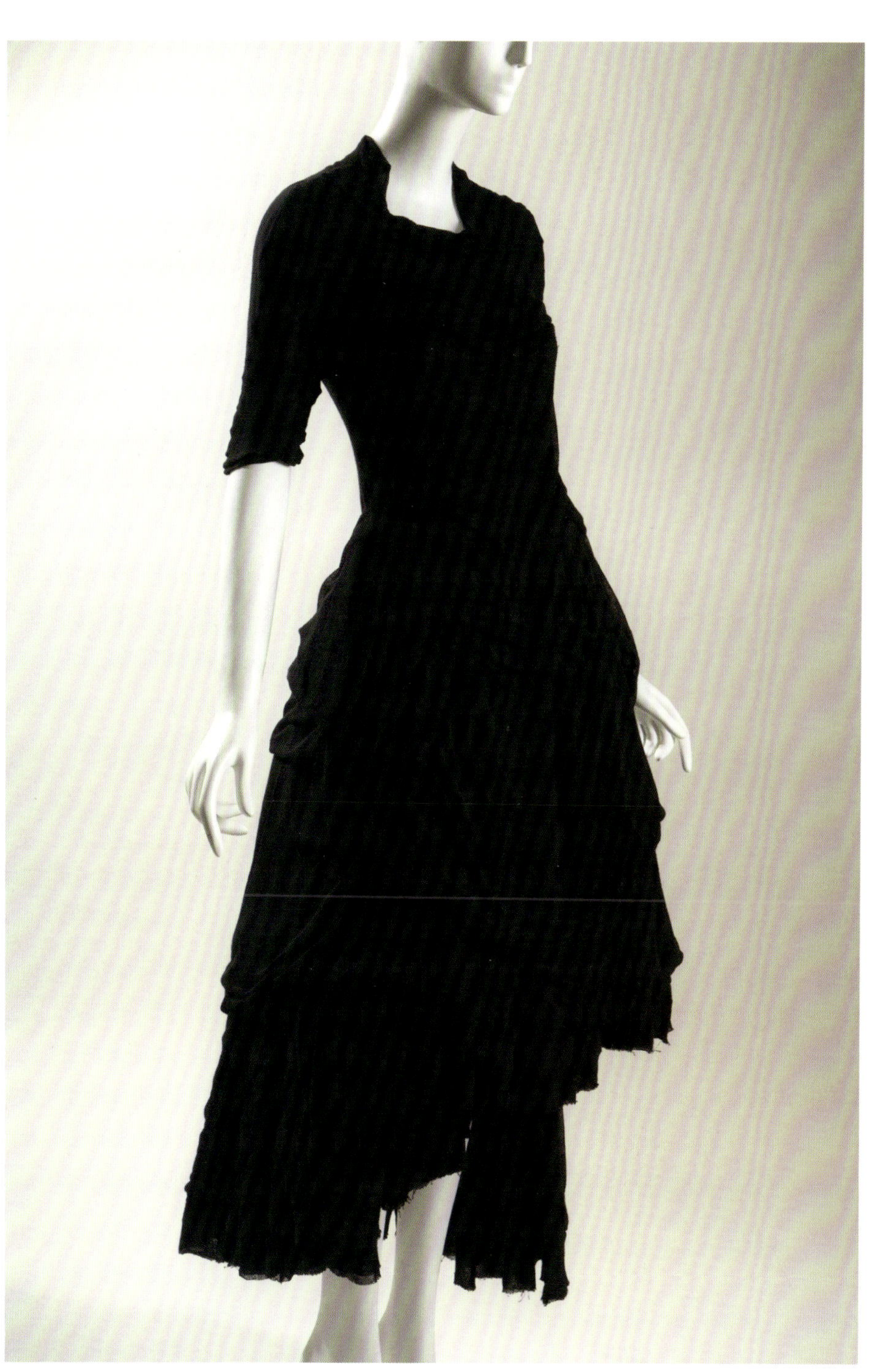

"Black is modest and arrogant at the same time. Black is lazy and easy—but mysterious. But above all black says this: 'I don't bother you—you don't bother me.'"
—*Yohji Yamamoto* [190]

This soft naturalistic black with a hint of Charcoal Gray was the color of "the Japanese Revolution in Paris" during the 1970s and early 1980s. [191] While the aesthetics of Issey Miyake, Yohji Yamamoto, and Rei Kawakubo of Comme des Garçons differ tremendously, they all dismantled notions of Orientalism by relying on the "steadfast principles of traditional Japanese design." [192]

Kawakubo's Pirate Black sweater from 1982 may appear ratty. However, the intentionality behind its creation paired with its meticulous construction shows the genius of the designer and the intricacy involved in creating destruction. The black, oversized knitwear disguises the anatomical body and simultaneously reveals it through purposeful holes, made by loosening screws on the loom. When Kawakubo was asked why she uses so much black, she replied, "I see enough colors in life." [193]

In order to craft Issey Miyake's permanently pleated polyester "Bouncing Dress" of Spring/Summer 1993, upwards of four people twisted and then "cooked" the garment, a process invented by Miyake alongside his creative director, Dai Fujiwara. [194]

Upon first seeing Yohji Yamamoto's muted work, former editor of French *Vogue* Irène Silvagni exclaimed, "The age of black is here!" [195] Regarding his affinity for black, Yamamoto explained his designing stream-of-consciousness: "I love women, the impression, the silhouette, cutting, motion, action, fabric. . . . That's why I sometimes forget to put color on it." [196] Yamamoto himself has a penchant for wearing the Moonless Night color (earning him the nickname, "The Monk") and dressing other men, like singers Sting and David Bowie, in it. [197]

Like the Japanese "Big Three," the "Antwerp Six" were moved by the possibilities of black. The Belgian contingent shot onto the London fashion scene in 1986, immediately securing orders from Barneys New York. While both Ann Demeulemeester and Dries Van Noten share similar origin stories, their work differs dramatically. Demeulemeester, whose work expresses unapologetic strength, explains her dark creations: "When I'm working with a new shape, I don't want to be distracted by color." [198] Dries Van Noten, cerebral and experimental, often melds incongruent themes like florals and patterns. His Fall/Winter 2012–2013 black suit is anything but basic with his postmodern take on *Japonisme*.

Jet Black

Between 1883 and 1884, John Singer Sargent painted *Madame X* in a black gown with a deep-V bodice and a slipping shoulder strap, but the world was not ready for the funereal color to be sexualized, and the painting garnered "more ridicule than praise."[200] Yet thirty years later, Gabrielle "Coco" Chanel created her first black dress, drastically altering its association with mourning. In 1926, *Vogue* ordained it "the frock that all the world will wear"[201] and still considers this "Ford" of a fashion the "*ne plus ultra* of understated chic."[202] Chanel's Little Black Dress (now so ubiquitous it is abbreviated by the fashion media as "LBD") has indeed become a wardrobe staple across the globe, in part because of its slimming properties and ability to conceal the grime of urban living.

In 1961, Audrey Hepburn as Holly Golightly in *Breakfast at Tiffany's* yearned for a life out of her reach, doing everything in her power to grab it and fake it until she made it. Hubert de Givenchy's dress represented Golightly's glamorous aspirations and visually conveyed an elite status—while covering Hepburn's protruding collarbones, which she hated! Ironically, Golightly's desire for an extravagant (unaffordable) life, illustrated by her costume, has since come to represent the ultimate picture of luxury, selling for $923,187 at Christie's 2006 auction (the highest price paid for a dress used in a film). Whether the dress is "pure" Givenchy is up for speculation: rumor has it Hollywood costumer Edith Head lengthened the dress, as its original Parisian shortness was too racy for the big screen.

Black has transitioned over the 20th century from Chanel chic to Givenchy glamorous to salaciously sexy, courtesy of the body-con master Azzedine Alaïa. His 1984 dress, which cupped every contour, transformed women into masterpieces of topography. Alaïa's obsession with black became cemented when he requested all 1,186 attendees of his 1985 show to wear it. Most of his admirers did, including Andy Warhol, Stephen Sprouse, and model/icon Tina Chow.

Donna Karan was integral not only in putting New York on the fashion map, but also in making black the go-to color in New Yorkers' wardrobes. Donna Karan's work, unlike Alaïa's, does not possess an overt sexuality, making it ideal for cosmopolitan working women like herself. Karan, who built her brand on the idea of "seven easy pieces" in 1985, believes that dressing should be simple. One of her essential looks is the bodysuit, worn under a skirt or pants. A practitioner of urban zen, Karan also notes it can be worn to do yoga in— one of her favorite ways to find calm in the city's chaos.

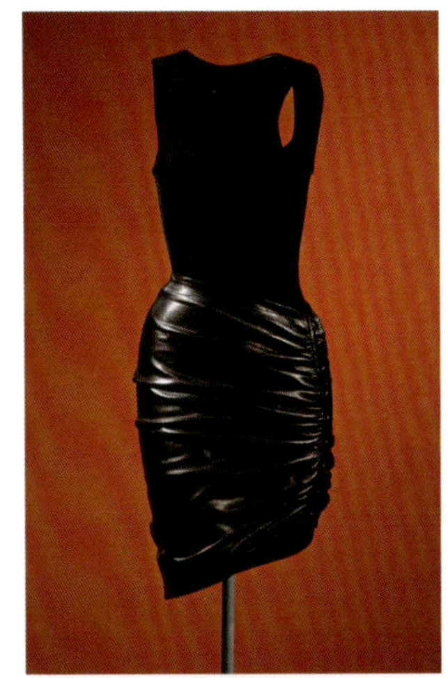

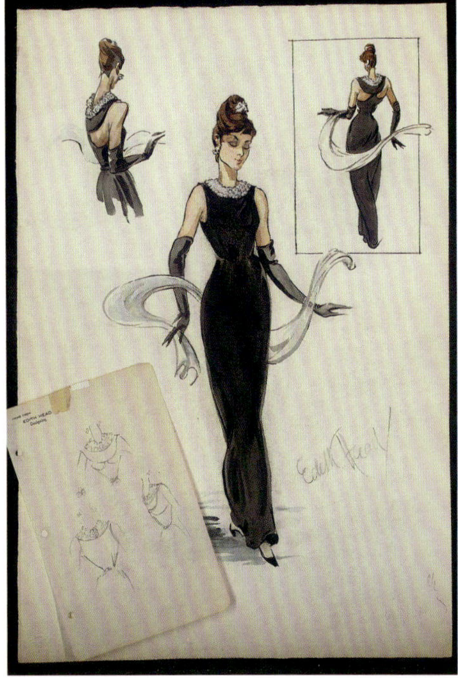

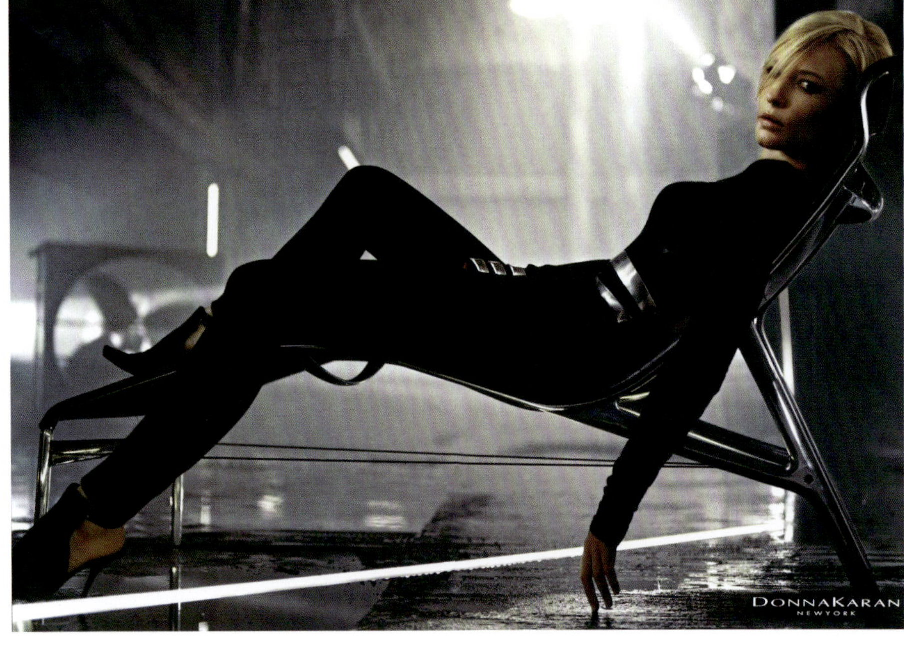

opposite, top left
Leather dress
Azzedine Alaïa
1984

opposite, top right
Dress for Audrey Hepburn in
Breakfast at Tiffany's
Sketched by Edith Head
Hubert de Givenchy and Edith Head
1961

opposite, bottom
Bodysuit
Print ad featuring Cate Blanchett
Donna Karan
2003

below
Portrait of Coco Chanel
by Man Ray
1935

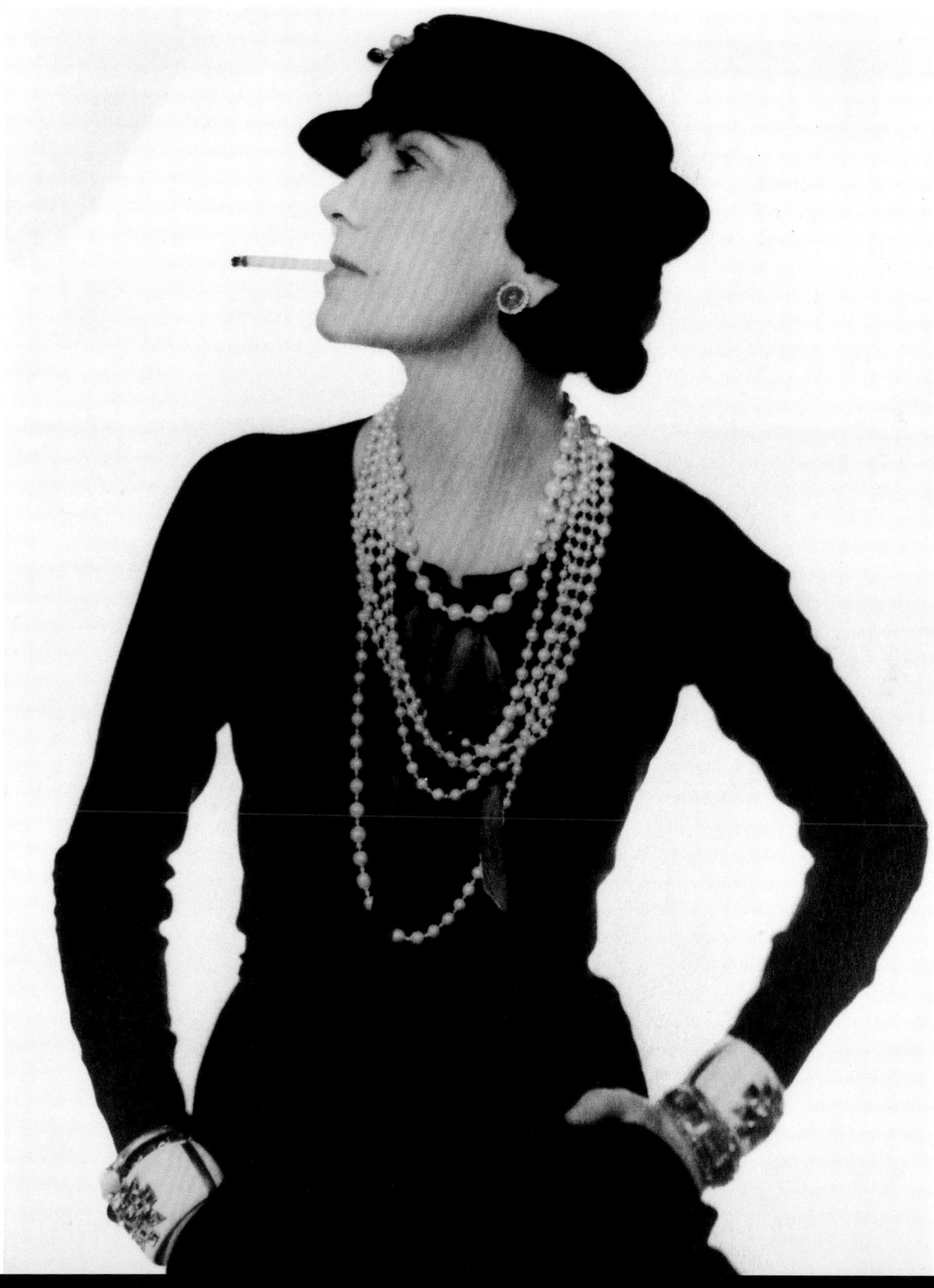

PANTONE Color of the Year

At the start of each year since the dawn of the new century, Pantone has selected a Color of the Year. This is the shade that best encapsulates the spirit of the times, and that can be expected to pop up everywhere throughout the coming months, both in fashion and in other areas of design and daily life. Here are the first fifteen iterations of the Color of the Year, as captured in Pantone's annual press release on the subject, gathered together for the first time ever.

2000
PANTONE 15-4020
Cerulean
The millennial moment raced toward an exhilarating but uncertain future, yet was also tinged with nostalgia. Solace, inner peace, and spiritual fulfillment were desired in this stressful, high-tech age, and Cerulean offered calm.

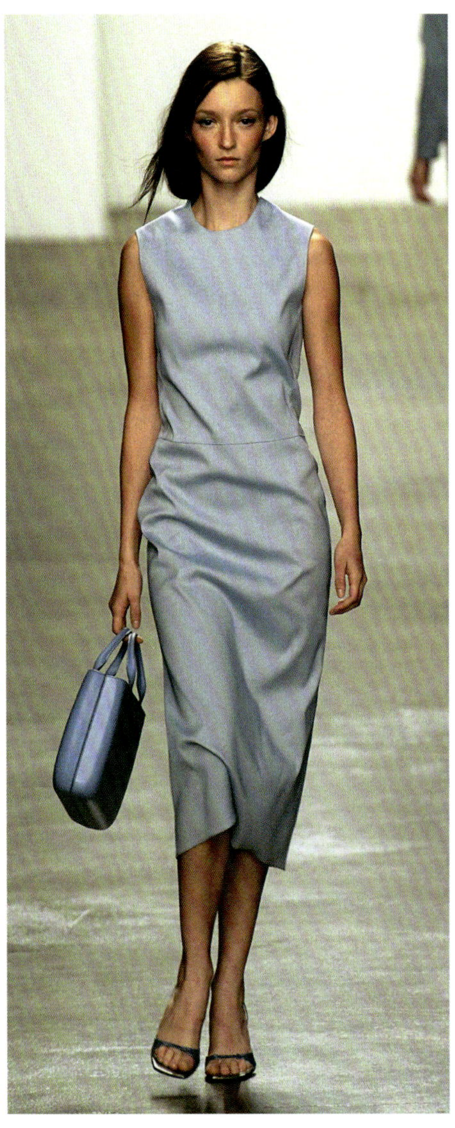

2001

PANTONE 17-2031

Fuchsia Rose

Past the consternation of the millennium, Fuchsia Rose celebrated the dawn of a new era. As 2001 began, the future was anticipated with great excitement, with no way of knowing the tragic changes that year would bring.

2002

PANTONE 19-1664

True Red

True Red is the color of patriotism—not only in the United States, but in many nations around the world. Evocative of passion and adrenalized energy, it reflected the wave of emotion that swept the globe in the months following 9/11.

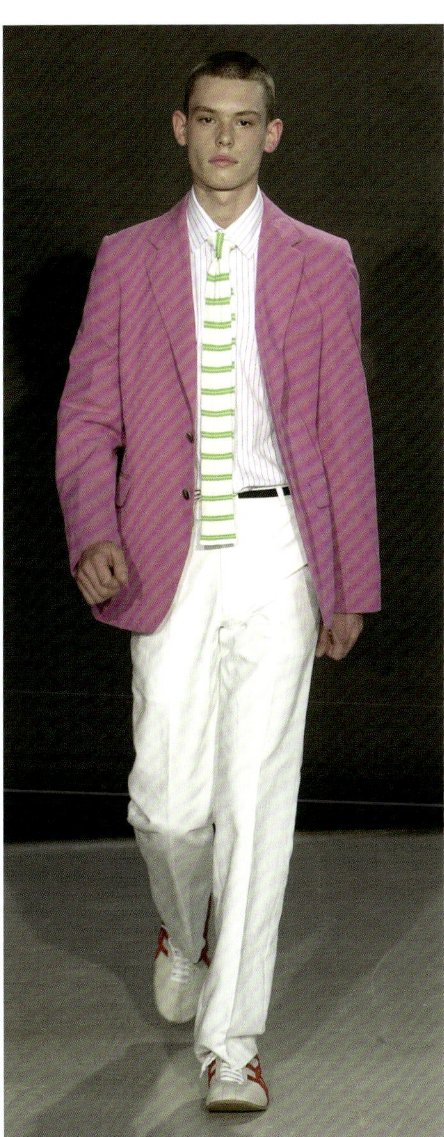

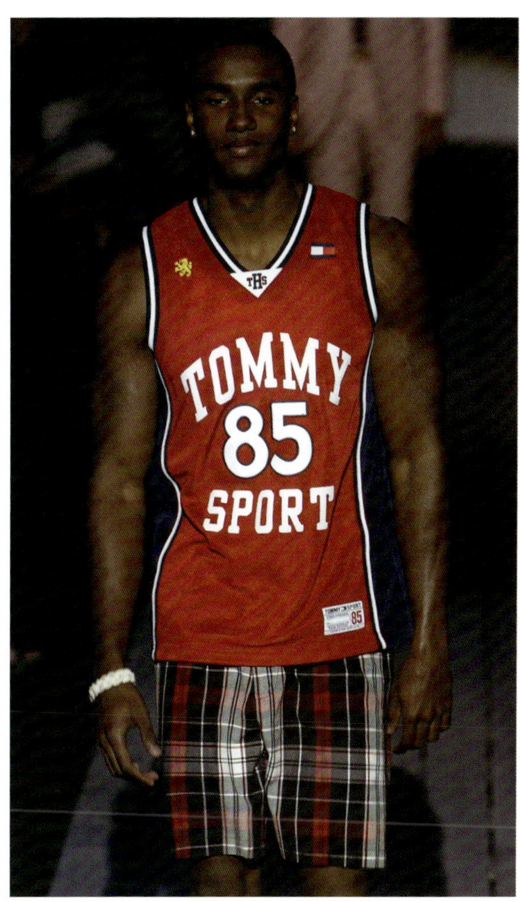

Fuchsia Rose
PANTONE 17-2031

True Red
PANTONE 19-1664

2003

PANTONE 14-4811

Aqua Sky

Anxiety remained high in 2003. Aqua Sky met the need for constancy, serenity, and dependability felt by many in this epoch. Like a tranquil sea or firmament, this hue offered peace and comfort in uncertain times.

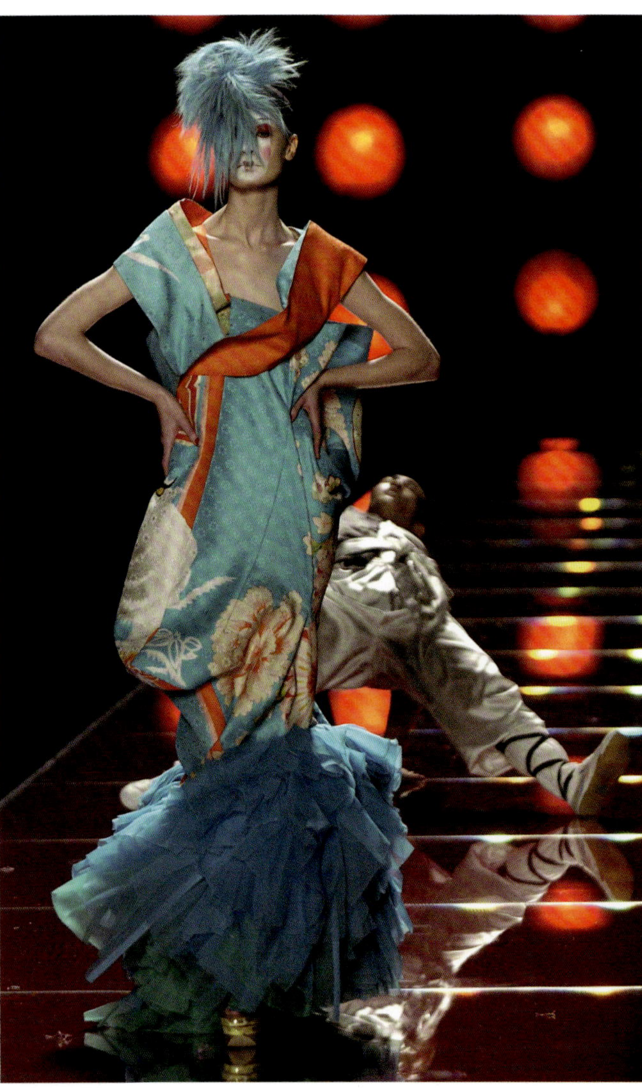

2004

PANTONE 17-1456

Tigerlily

The worse things get, the more people need color to lift their moods. In the shadow of global terrorism, a sluggish economy, and ongoing wars in Iraq and Afghanistan, a shade of warmth and cheer like Tigerlily provided a much needed boost.

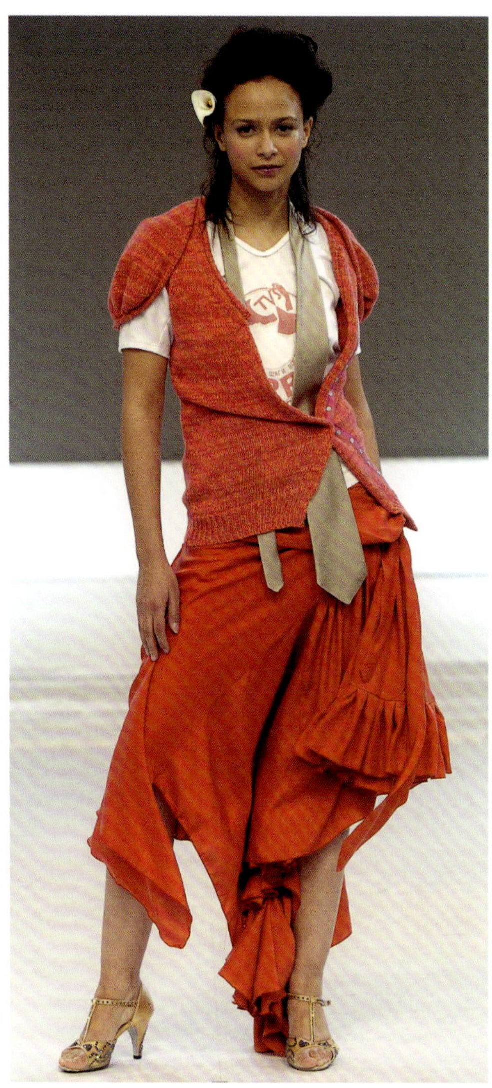

Aqua Sky
PANTONE 14-4811

Tigerlily
PANTONE 17-1456

opposite, left
"Hard-core romance" kimono
John Galliano for Christian Dior
Haute Couture
Spring 2003

opposite, right
Ensemble
Tim van Steenbergen
Fall/Winter 2004

left
Spaghetti-strap tiered dress
Jason Cauchi for Alice Roi
Spring 2005

right
Dress
Proenza Schouler
Spring/Summer 2006

2005

PANTONE 15-5217

Blue Turquoise

Once again the reassurance of a calming blue was required. But new in 2005 was the hint of excitement that Blue Turquoise, like many tropical blue-greens, suggests. Perhaps things were starting to look up.

2006

PANTONE 13-1106

Sand Dollar

Sand Dollar, a reliable neutral, spoke of solidity. As the era started to look toward more natural and organic ways of living, tones that evoked the natural world were the order of the day. Color was toned down.

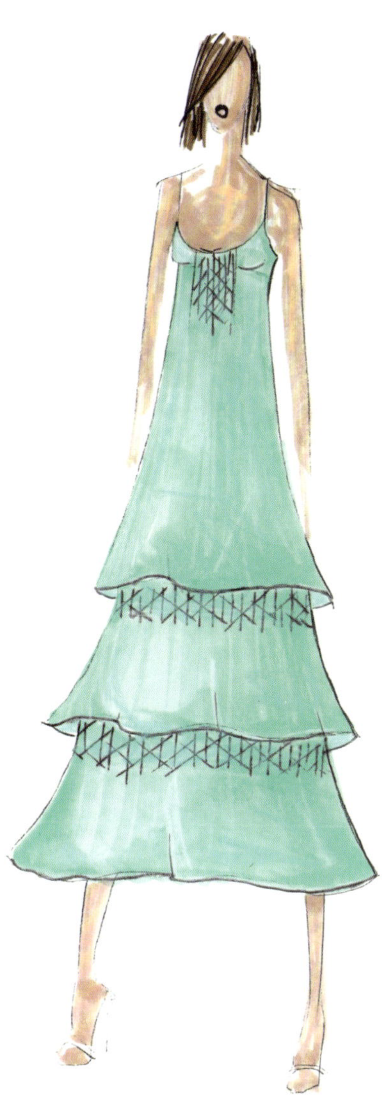

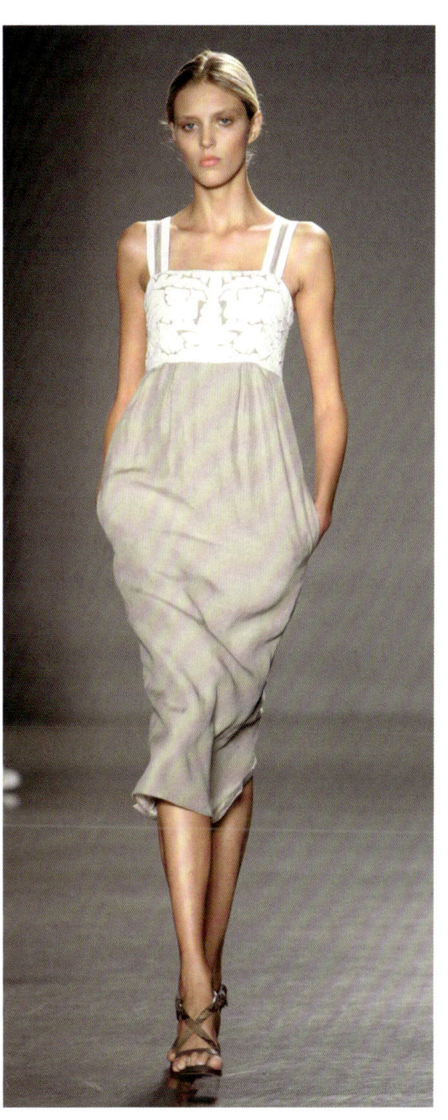

Blue Turquoise
PANTONE 15-5217

Sand Dollar
PANTONE 13-1106

2007

PANTONE 19-1557

Chili Pepper

This year saw an increased awareness of diverse cultural influences. Chili Pepper, with its connotations of spicy exoticism both in flavor and color, called to mind the intimacy of the global world and the melding of traditions.

2008

PANTONE 18-3943

Blue Iris

Combining the stable and calming aspects of blue with the mystical and spiritual qualities of purple, Blue Iris satisfied the need for confidence in a complex world, while not ruling out the possibility of mystery and excitement.

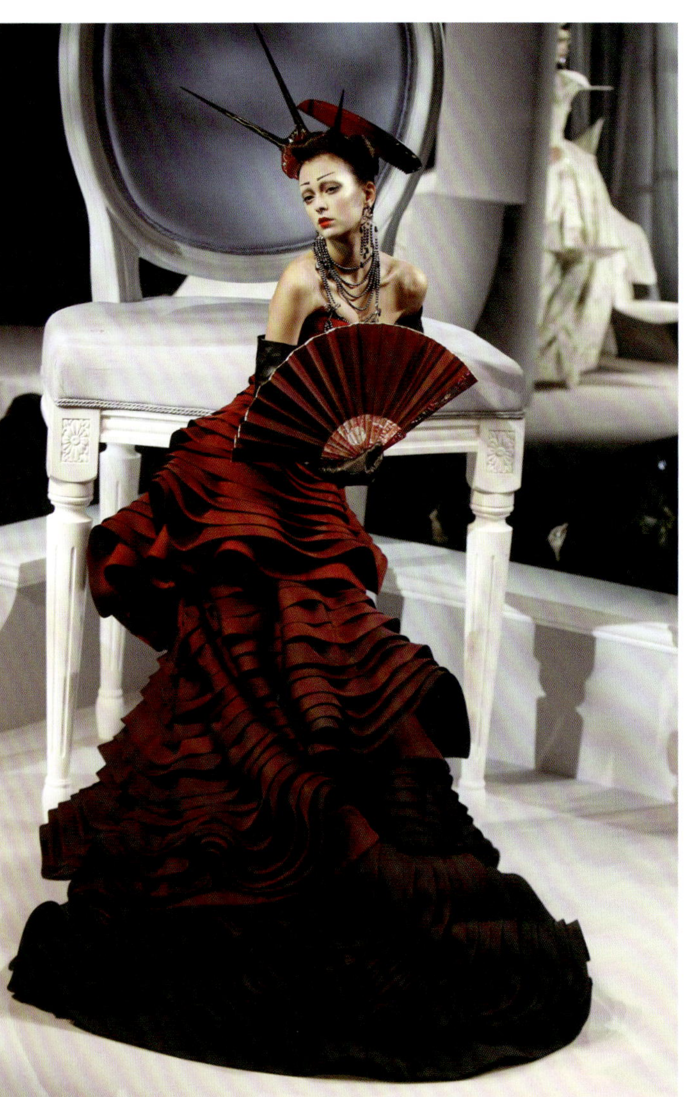

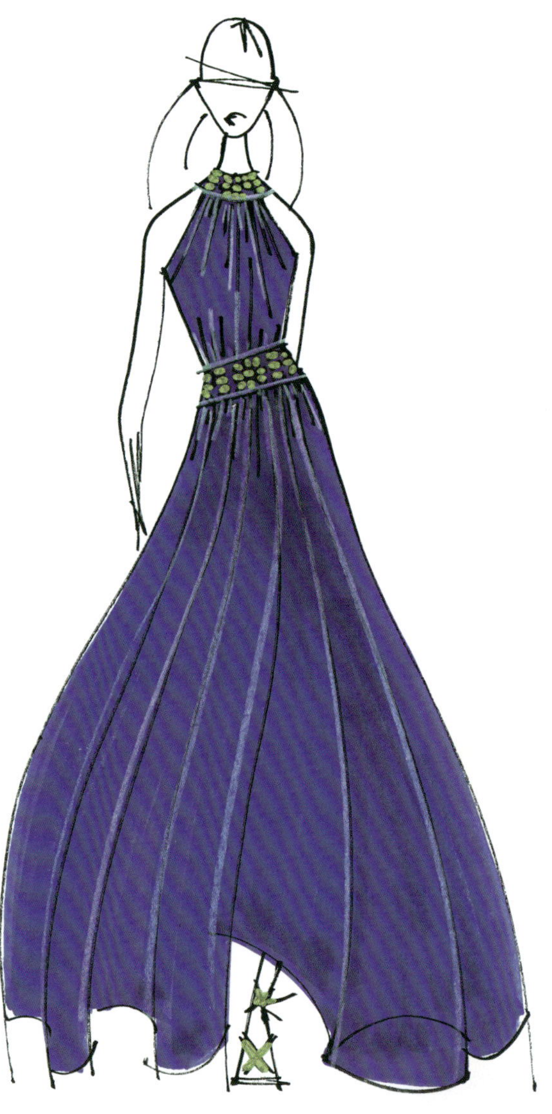

Chili Pepper
PANTONE 19-1557

Blue Iris
PANTONE 18-3943

2009

PANTONE 14-0848

Mimosa

Profound economic uncertainty sat side by side with historical political change as Barack Obama entered the White
House. The need for optimism was paramount. And no other
color expresses hope and reassurance more than the most
uplifting shade of yellow, Mimosa.

2010

PANTONE 15-5519

Turquoise

The serene qualities of blue had been in demand on and off
for a decade, but now for the first time they were decisively
wed to the invigorating aspects of green. By turns soothing,
languorous, escapist, and energizing, Turquoise restored a
sense of well-being.

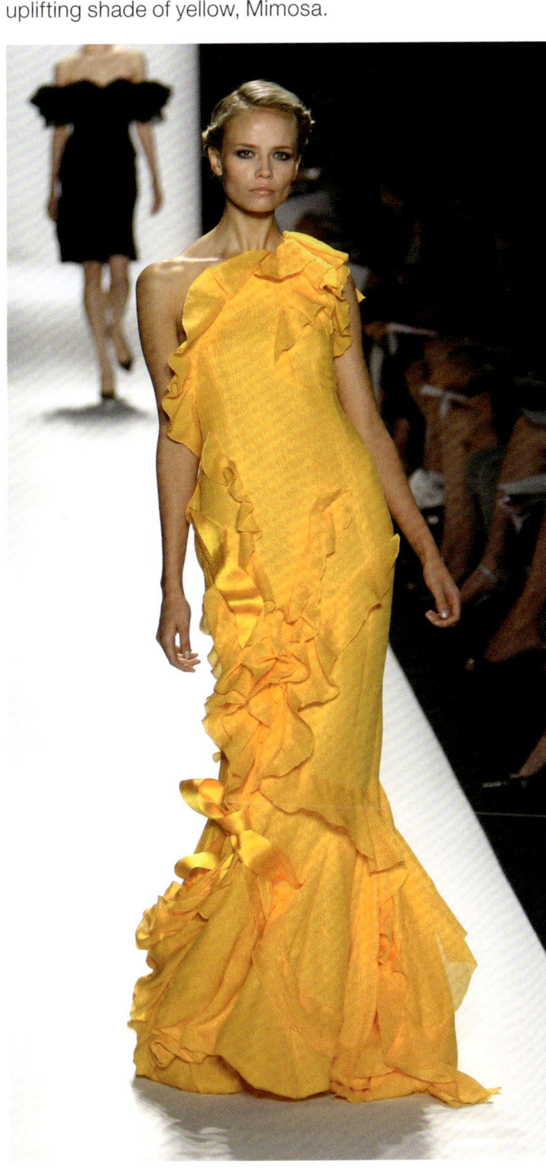

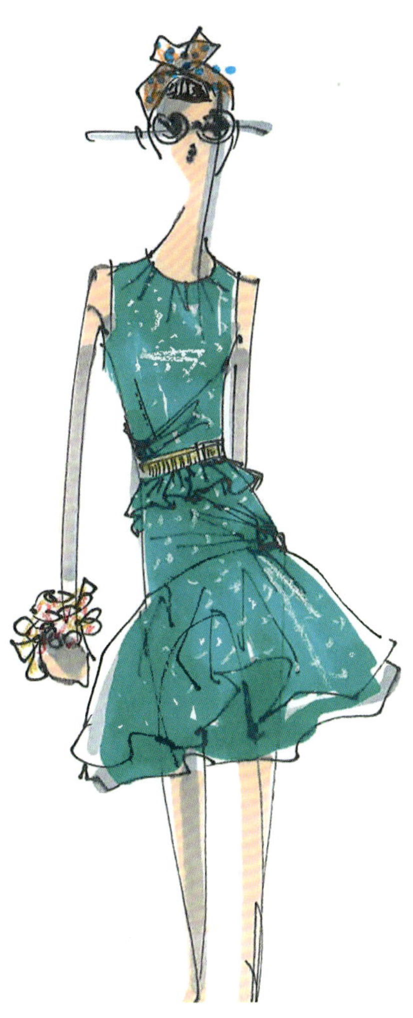

Mimosa
PANTONE 14-0848

Turquoise
PANTONE 15-5519

2011

PANTONE 18-2120

Honeysuckle

Honeysuckle, a dynamic reddish pink, evoked vibrancy and
vigor. Encouraging and uplifting, it was a shade to elevate the
psyche, instilling the confidence, courage, and spirit to meet
the sometimes exhausting challenges of modern life.

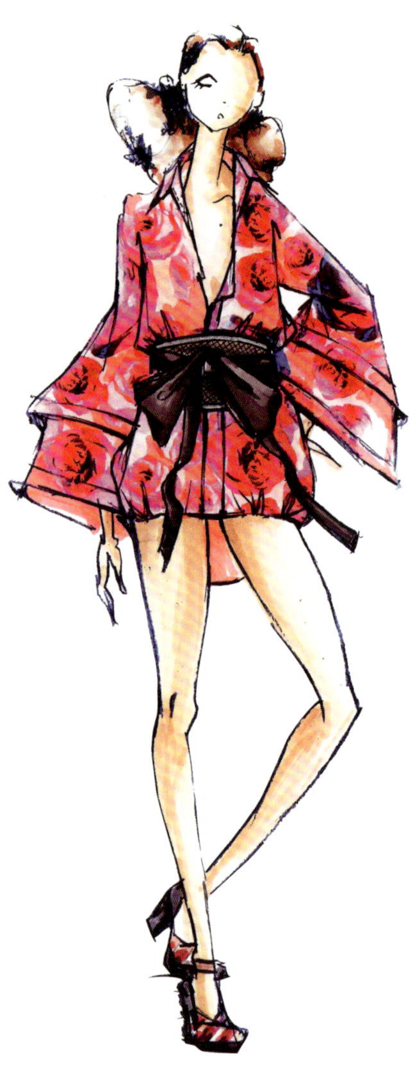

2012

PANTONE 17-1463

Tangerine Tango

It was no coincidence that in the second decade of the
century orange gained increased acceptance. As the times
became more spirited and ready to move forward, Tangerine
Tango, a dramatic, high-visibility hue emanating heat and
energy, proffered a recharging boost.

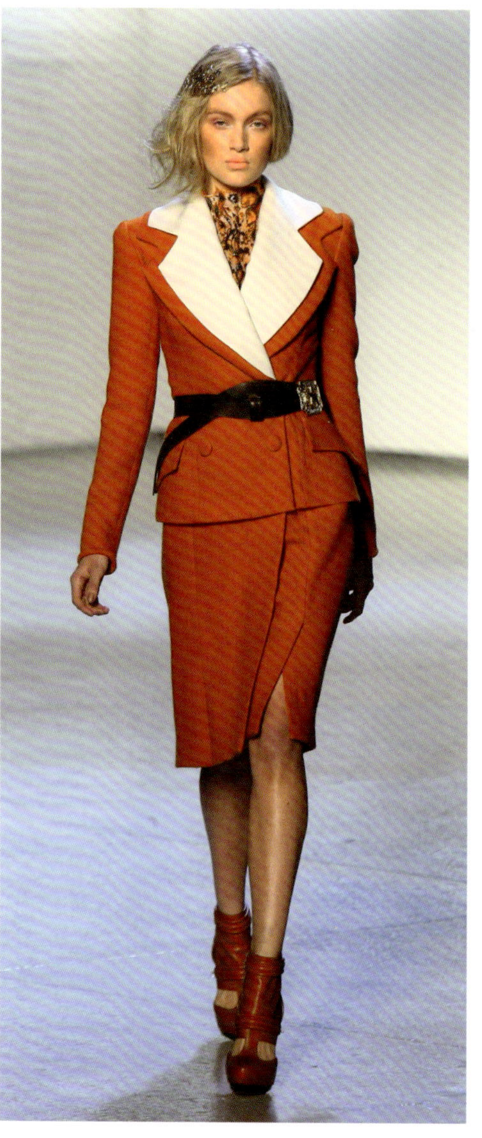

2013

PANTONE 17-5641

Emerald

Growth and renewal, healing and prosperity, unity and
clarity—2013 brought hope for regeneration. Sophisticated
and luxurious, the verdant green Emerald—the powerful
color of beauty and new life—enhanced a sense of well-
being by promoting insight, balance, and harmony.

2014

PANTONE 18-3224

Radiant Orchid

In 2014, the captivating warmth of Radiant Orchid—an
expressive, confident, and embracing purple—intrigued
the eye and sparked the imagination. Emanating joy, love,
and health, the beguiling charm of this rosy, glowing shade
encouraged innovation, originality, and creative thinking.

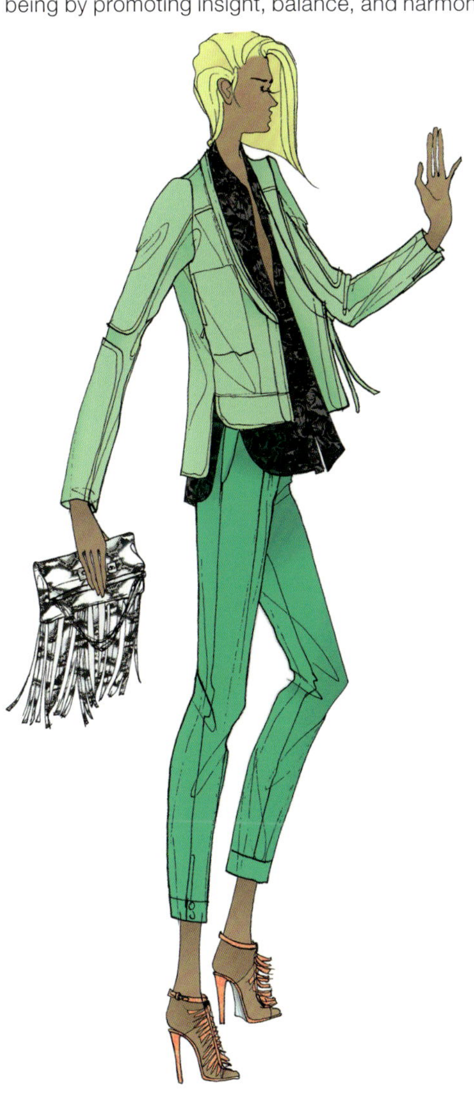

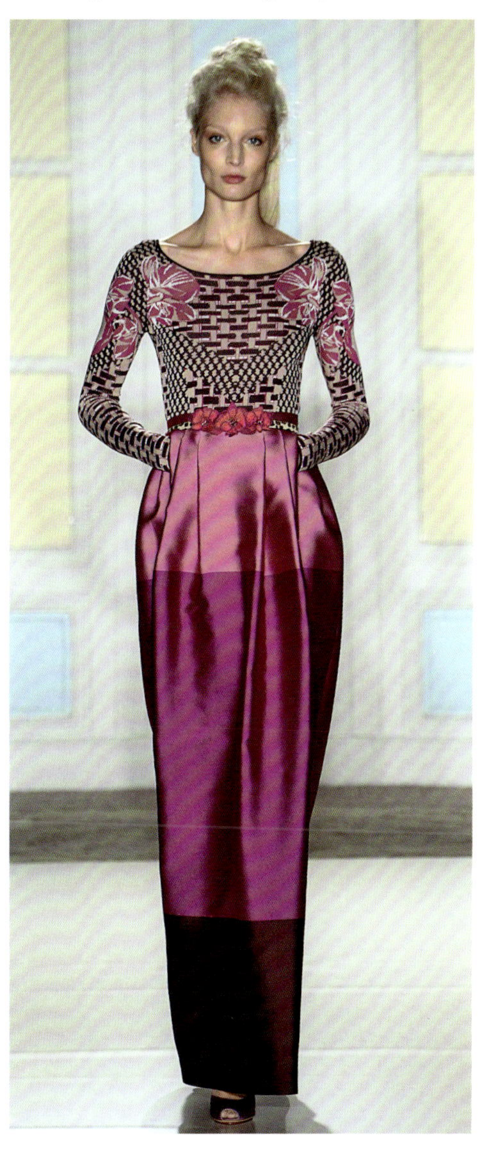

Emerald
PANTONE 17-5641

Radiant Orchid
PANTONE 18-3224

Endnotes

1 Elena Phipps, "Cochineal Red: The Art History of a Color," *The Metropolitan Museum of Art Bulletin*, Winter 2010: 5.

2 Colin McDowell, *Fashion Today* (London: Phaidon, 2000), 60.

3 Carmel Snow with Mary Louise Aswell, *The World of Carmel Snow* (New York: McGraw-Hill Book Company, 1962), 170.

4 Sam Irvin, *Kay Thompson: From Funny Face to Eloise* (New York: Simon & Schuster, 2010), 242.

5 *World of Carmel Snow*, 170.

6 *Kay Thompson*, 242.

7 Marvin Klapper and Mort Sheinman, *Fashion, Retailing and a Bygone Era: Inside Women's Wear Daily* (Washington, DC: Beard Books, 2005), 44.

8 Erika Stalder, *Fashion 101: A Crash Course in Clothing* (San Francisco: Zest Books, 2008), 25.

9 Ravi Mehta and Rui Juliet Zhu, "Blue or Red? Exploring the Effect of Color on Cognitive Task Performances," *Science 27*, vol. 323 no. 5918 (February 2009).

10 Grace Coddington, "Grace Notes: An Excerpt from Grace Coddington's Memoir," Vogue.com, October 18, 2012, http://www.vogue.com/magazine/article/grace-coddington-notes-excerpt-from-grace-a-memoir/#1.

11 "Zandra Rhodes: A Lifelong Love Affair with Textiles," University of Michigan School of Art & Design's Penny W. Stamps Speaker Series, Fall 2011, http://vimeo.com/34954653.

12 Krissi Murison, "I'm with the Band," *The Guardian*, March 20, 2008, http://www.theguardian.com/lifeandstyle/2008/mar/21/fashion.popandrock.

13 Richard Martin, "Edward H. Molyneux," *Fashion Designer Encyclopedia*, http://www.fashionencyclopedia.com/Ma-Mu/Molyneux-Edward-H.html.

14 Ernestine Carter, *Magic Names of Fashion* (Englewood Cliffs, NJ: Prentice-Hall, 1980), 73.

15 Tracey Lomrantz Lester, "Carolina Herrera Says Orange Is the New Red: What Do You Think?", *Glamour* blog, June 8, 2009, http://www.glamour.com/fashion/blogs/slaves-to-fashion/2009/06/carolina-herrera-says-orange-i.html.

16 Laura Jacobs, "From Hermès to Eternity," *Vanity Fair*, September 2007.

17 Bernadine Morris, "To Help Festival, Knits Are Danced Through Fashion Show," *The New York Times*, February 23, 1973.

18 Alexandra Kotur, *Carolina Herrera* (New York: Assouline, 2004), 144.

19 Corina Miller, "Carolina Herrera: Fashion Designer," *Latino Leaders* 8, no. 2 (April 2007).

20 Fabricio Forastelli, "Scattered Bodies, Unfashionable Flesh," *The Latin American Fashion Reader*, edited by Regina A. Root (Oxford, UK: Berg, 2005), 288.

21 Interview with Ida Johansson conducted February 14, 2013.

22 Diane Dakers, *Calvin Klein: Fashion Design Superstar*, New York: Crabtree Tree Publishing (2011): 25.

23 Akiko Fukai and Tamami Suoh, *Fashion: The Collection of the Kyoto Costume Institute: A History from the 18th to 20th Century* (New York: Taschen, 2002), 620.

24 Suzy Menkes, "McCartney Grows Up, Vuitton Is Charming, Elbaz for Lanvin Houses a Question of Identity," *The New York Times*, March 12, 2002.

25 "That Jantzen Girl Is Here Again!", Jantzen Knitting Mills advertisement (1941), illustrated by Alberto Vargas.

26 Jean Demachy and Francois Baudot, *Elle Style: The 1980s*, Paris: Filapacchi Publishing (2003): 12.

27 Lauren David Peden, "Dossier in Conversation with Shelly Steffee," *Dossier Journal*, May 14, 2010, http://dossierjournal.com/style/fashion/dossier-in-conversation-with-shelly-steffee/.

28 "Fashion Color Report Spring/Summer 2005," *Pantone* 22 (September 2004).

29 Daniela Morera, "Giorgio Armani," *Interview*. http://www.interviewmagazine.com/fashion/giorgio-armani/#_

30 Bernadine Morris, "Saint Laurent Draws Cheers and Tears," *The New York Times*, January 25, 1990.

31 Ibid.

32 Alicia Drake, *The Beautiful Fall: Fashion, Genius, and Glorious Excess in 1970s Paris*, New York: Black Bay Books, 2006: 211.

33 "Daily Hues for Fall 1998," *Pantone* 9, no. 5 (1998).

34 Kate Betts, "Fashion: Tahari on a Tear," *TIME*, October 29, 2006.

35 "Prada," *Voguepedia* blog, http://www.vogue.com/voguepedia/Prada.

36 Cathy Horyn, "Whirling and Twirling, Prada Shows Its Skirts," *The New York Times*, April 13, 2006.

37 Maxwell Gillingham-Ryan, "An Interview with Todd Oldham," *Apartment Therapy* blog, November 8, 2012, http://www.apartmenttherapy.com/next-thursday-nov-8th-todd-oldham-apartment-therapy-design-evenings-179754.

38 "7th on Sixth Fashion Color Report, Spring 2000," *Pantone* 12 (September 1999).

39 Robert Janjigian, "American Fresh," *Palm Beach Life* (December 2005), 74.

40 Meenal Mistry, "Max Mara's Secret Weapon." *Departures Magazine,* November/December 2011.

41 Ibid.

42 Blessing Maregere, *Who Said You Can't Be Young and Successful?* (Bloomington, IN: Xlibris, 2011), 98.

43 Charlotte Cowles, "Dynasty Costume Designer Nolan Miller is Dead," *New York Magazine* blog, http://nymag.com/thecut/2012/06/dynasty-costume-designer-nolan-miller-is-dead.html.

44 Sarah Mower, "Review: Alexander McQueen Fall 2012," *Vogue* blog, http://www.vogue.com/fashion-week/fall-2012-rtw/alexander-mcqueen/review/#.

45 Betty Wilson, "Schiaparelli Inspired by Wattle and Rabbits," *The Sydney Morning Herald*, July 1, 1937.

46 Elsa Schiaparelli, *Shocking Life* (London: V&A Publications, 2007), 89.

47 Diana Vreeland, *D.V.*, ed. George Plimpton and Christopher Hemphill (New York: Da Capo Press, 1997), 106.

48 "Marilyn Monroe: William Travilla Interviewed," original footage from A&E, http://www.youtube.com/watch?v=6DAHcwgQv5k.

49 Kate Finnigan, "Dressing Marilyn Monroe," *Telegraph UK*, October 9, 2011, http://fashion.telegraph.co.uk/news-features/TMG8811806/Dressing-Marilyn-Monroe-html.

50 Bernadine Morris, *Valentino* (New York: Universe/Vendome, 1996), 76.

51 Bill Blass, *Bare Blass* (New York: HarperCollins, 2003), 108.

52 "Biography: Valentino Garavani," Valentino Garavani Virtual Museum, http://www.valentino-garavani-archives.org/.

53 "Valentino," *NYTimes*.com, http://topics.nytimes.com/top/reference/timestopics/people/v/valentino/index.html.

54 Brenda Dionisi, "Elio Fiorucci," *The Florentine*, January 28, 2010, http://www.theflorentine.net/articles/article-view.asp?issuetocId=5297.

55 "Sun Goddess," Nelson Mandela Square at Sandton City, http://www.nelsonmandelasquare.co.za/libprop/content/en/nelson-mandela-square/nelson-mandela-square-store-search?oid=440&sn=Detail&pid=115.

56 "South African Fashion: Sun Goddess," YouTube video, September 2, 2007, http://www.youtube.com/watch?v=_5klFd1cjb0.

57 "About: Designer Profile: Yeohlee," YEOHLEE, yeohlee.com/about/, accessed November 21, 2012.

58 Jill Fairchild, "The House That Hannant Built," *Avenue Magazine*, January 2010.

59 Mark Badgley. *CFDA* blog. http://www.cfda.com/members#!mark-badgley.

60 "Fashion Color Report Fall 2004," *Pantone* 21 (February 2004).

61 Ibid.

62 Janet Ozzard, "Ralph Lauren," *Style.com* blog, http://www.style.com/fashionshows/review/F2004RTW-RLAUREN.

63 Elizabeth Hawes, *Fashion Is Spinach* (New York: Random House, 1938), 337.

64 Christian Esquerin, *Adrian: Silver Screen to Custom Label* (New York: The Monacelli Press, 2008), 20.

65 Janet Markarian, "Allard, Linda," *Fashion Designer Encyclopedia*, http://www.fashionencyclopedia.com/A-Az/Allard-Linda.html#ixzz2Qte1sFuv.

66 "Interview: Christopher Bailey," *Stylist UK* blog, http://www.stylist.co.uk/fashion/londonfashionweek/interview-christopher-bailey#imagerotator-1.

67 Deborah Arthurs, "Naughty but Nice! Christopher Bailey Gives Burberry a Kinky Makeover," *Daily Mail* (blog), February 18, 2013, http://www.dailymail.co.uk/femail/article-2280653/London-Fashion-Week-Christopher-Bailey-wows-Burberry-Christine-Keeler-inspired-Cara-Delevingne-rubber-skirt.html.

68 Ibid.

69 R. Couri Hay interviewing Michele Gerber Klein, "The Charles James Story," video, Anton Perich (New York City, 2008), https://www.youtube.com/watch?v=jxGHaR5QXp0.

70 Joan Kron, "Exhibition-ism: History as Fashion Power," *New York Magazine*, January 12, 1976.

71 Anne Hollander, *Feeding the Eyes: Essays* Berkeley: University of California Press, 2000 51.

72 "Amy Smilovic," *Huffington Post*, http://www.huffingtonpost .com/amy-smilovic/.

73 "Paris Couturiers Show New Style," *The New York Times*, July 27, 1926.

74 Valerie Steele, *Paris Fashion: A Cultural History* (Oxford, UK: Oxford University Press, 1988) 247.

75 "Paris Designs Winter Coats," *The New York Times*, September 19, 1926.

76 "A Genius's Guide to Cutting to the Curve," World Intellectual Property Organization site, http://www.wipo.int/ipadvantage/ en/details.jsp?id=2720.

77 Ibid.

78 Diana Lurie, "Close-Up: When Mollie Parnis Thinks a Dress Will Sell, It Goes," *LIFE*, June 17, 1966.

79 Ibid.

80 Andrew Bolton, *Anna Sui* (San Francisco: Chronicle Books, 2010), 189.

81 Robert Janjigian, "American Fresh," *Palm Beach Life* (December 2005).

82 Leatrice Eiseman, *Colors for Your Every Mood* (Washington, DC: Capital Press, 1998), 92.

83 "Augusta Bernard Is at the Forefront of Parisian Fashion," *L'Officiel de la Mode* 94 (1929): http://patrimoine. jalougallery.com/lofficiel-de-la-mode-numero_94-page_18- detailp-13-88-18.html#.

84 "Augustabernard," The Museum at FIT, http://fashionmuseum . fitnyc.edu/view/people/asitem/A/15.

85 Stephen Gaines, *Simply Halston* (New York: G. P. Putnam's Sons, 1991), 115.

86 Ibid., 125.

87 Jerry Bowles, "Will Halston Take Over the World?", *Esquire*, August 1975.

88 Stephen Gaines, *Simply Halston* (New York: G. P. Putnam's Sons, 1991), 138.

89 Rosamond Bernier, *Some of My Lives* (New York: Farrar, Straus, and Giroux, 2011), 76.

90 Chad Burton, "Lie Sang Bong," *1883 Magazine*, http:// www.1883magazine.com/features/features/lie-sang-bong.

91 Lie Sang Bong, "Biography: Lie Sang Bong," http://www .liesangbong.com/gb/index-eng.php?mains=4&subs=1.

92 Sarah Mower, "Bottega Veneta Gall 2012 RTW," Vogue.com, February 25, 2012, http://www.vogue.com/fashion-week/ fall-2012-rtw/bottega-veneta/review/#

93 "Paris Style Shows Confirm New Lines: Jean Patou Apparently Received Inspiration from His American Mannequins," *The New York Times*, February 6, 1925.

94 Maggy Rouff, *La Philosophie de l'Elegance* (Paris: Éditions Littéraires de France, 1942), 240.

95 Elinor Renfrew and Colin Renfrew, *Basics/Fashion Design 04: Developing a Collection* (Lausanne: AVA Publishing, 2009), 125.

96 Penny Martin, "Interview: Eley Kishimoto," SHOWstudio, http://showstudio.com/project/fashion_panopticon/ interview_eley_kishimoto.

97 Bernadine Morris, "A Blaze of Colors Marks Fall Fashion Shows, *The New York Times*, May 3, 1984.

98 Elisabeth Längle, *Pierre Cardin: Fifty Years of Fashion and Design* (New York: The Vendome Press, 2005), 13.

99 Elisabeta Tudor, "Mugler Menswear Fall Winter 2013 Paris," *NOWFashion*, January 16, 2013, http://nowfashion .com/2013-01-16-mugler-menswear-fall-winter-2013-paris- review-698.html.

100 "Fashion Color Report Fall 2006: Steadfast and Stunning," *Pantone 6* (February 3–10, 2006) http://www.pantone.com/ pages/Pantone/Pantone.aspx?pg=20018&ca=4.

101 Rocco Leo Gaglioti, "Cythia Steffe Interview," *Fashion News Live*, http://www.fashionnewslive.com/2012/06/27/cynthia- steffe-fall-collections-from-the-ny-olympus-fashion-week- 2006-at-fashion-news-live/.

102 "Fashion Color Report Fall 2006," *Pantone* 25 (2006).

103 Ibid.

104 Ibid.

105 Cathy Horyn, "Evolution on the Runway: Room to Grow," *The New York Times*, February 11, 2006.

106 Christian Dior, *The Little Dictionary of Fashion* (New York: Harry N. Abrams, 2007): 14.

107 "Muriel King: Artist of Fashion at The Museum at FIT," PRWeb, March 5, 2009, http://www.prweb.com/releases/2009/03/ prweb2210104.htm, accessed June 8, 2013.

108 Barbara Burn, ed., *The Metropolitan Museum of Art Catalog: Yves Saint Laurent* (New York: Clarkson Potter, 1983), 22.

109 Ibid.

110 Fiona McCarthy, "How Mrs. Overall Hacked It with the Country Set," *The Daily Mail UK*, November 28, 2009, http:// www.dailymail.co.uk/home/you/article-1228941/How-Mrs- Overall-hacked-country-set.html.

111 Christian Dior, *The Little Dictionary of Fashion* (New York: Abrams, 2007), 14.

112 Amy de la Haye, "Gilded Brocade Gowns and Impeccable Tailored Tweeds: Victor Stiebel (1907–1976), A Quint- essentially English Designer," *The Englishness of English Dress*, edited by Christopher Breward, Becky Conekin, and Caroline Cox (Oxford, UK: Berg, 2002), 147–160.

113 Eunice W. Johnson, "Behind the Seams," *Ebony*, February 2006.

114 Bibby Sowray, "Richard James's Sunnier Climates," *The Telegraph UK*, June 18, 2013, http://fashion.telegraph.co.uk/ news-features/TMG10121607/London-Collections-Men- springsummer-2014-live-blog.html

115 Claire McCardell, *What Shall I Wear?: The What, Where, When, and How Much of Fashion* (New York: Overlook/ Rookery, 2012), 28.

116 Janet Ozzard, "Michael Kors Spring 2005," *Style.com*, September 14, 2004, http://www.style.com/fashionshows/ review/S2005RTW-MKORS/.

117 "Fashion Color Report Spring 2005," *Pantone* 22 (September 2004).

118 Dr. Jessica R. Metcalfe, "Ralph Lauren and the American Dream," *Beyond Buckskin* blog, May 23, 2012, http://beyond buckskin.blogspot.com/2012/05/ralph-lauren-and-american- dream.html.

119 "About Luca Luca," Luca Luca site, http://www.lucaluca.com/ about/.

120 Mary Gregory, "In Memoriam: Ursula Sternberg-Hertz," *Chestnut Hill Local*, September 28, 2000, http://inliquid.org/ complete-artist-list/sternberg-ursula-hertz/.

121 "Fashion Color Report for Fall 2008," *Pantone* 29 (February 2008).

122 "Designer Dialogue: Sean Kearney," *Lord & Taylor* social media site, http://lordandtaylor.tumblr.com/post/ 17190433700/designer-dialogue-sean-kearney.

123 Robert L. Chesanow, "Nancy Berg," *IMDb*, http://www.imdb .com/name/nm0073855/bio.

124 Ibid.

125 "Hattie Carnegie Dies Here at 69," *The New York Times*, February 23, 1956.

126 Linda Watson, *20th Century Fashion* (Buffalo, NY: Firefly Books, 2004), 314.

127 Shelley DuBois, "Your Wardrobe Is Your Professional Armor," *Fortune*, April 29, 2013, http://management.fortune.cnn .com/2013/04/29/fashion-nanette-lepore/

128 Marcel Schlutt, "Walter Van Beirendonck Fall 2012–2013!" *Kaltblut Magazine*, March 6, 2012, http://kaltblut-magazine .com/walter-van-beirendonck-fall-2012-13/.

129 "Poiret: Orientalism," The Metropolitan Museum of Art, http:// www.metmuseum.org/en/exhibitions/listings/2007/poiret/ orientalism.

130 Cathy Treadaway, "Digital Imagination: The Impact of Digital Imaging on Printed Textiles," *Textile* 2, no. 3 (2004).

131 Beth Schepens, "Basso & Brooke Find Freedom in Fashion This Year," *The Wall Street Journal* blog, February 18, 2012, http://blogs.wsj.com/runway/2012/02/18/ basso-brooke-find-freedom-in-fashion-this-year/.

132 Pierre Galante, *Mademoiselle Chanel*, (Chicago: Henry Regnery, 1973), 94.

133 Ibid., 113.

134 Michael Specter, "High-Heel Heaven," *The New Yorker*, March 20, 2000.

135 Ibid.

136 Simone S. Oliver, "Tracy Reese Celebrates Five Years in the Meatpacking District," *The New York Times*, June 9, 2011.

137 Rocco Leo Gaglioti, "Tracy Reese Chats with Rocco Leo Gaglioti at Spring/Summer 2009," *Fashion News Live*, August 10, 2013, http://www.youtube.com/watch?v=4l076gCcli4.

138 "Brand," Alena Akhmadullina site, http://alenaakhmadullina.com/story.

139 Ibid.

140 "Designer Interview: Yigal Azrouël," *The Standard*, February 12, 2012, http://standardculture.com/posts/6076.

141 Victoria Dawson Hoff, "NYFW: According to Yigal Azroël Women Need Not Bare Skin to Look Sexy," *ELLE*, September 8, 2013, http://www.elle.com/news/fashion-style/nyfw-spring-2014-yigal-azrouel-runway-collection-interview.

142 "Random Questions For…Y & Kei," *The Fashion Informer*, July 25, 2007, http://thefashioninformer.typepad.com/informer/2007/07/random-questi-3.html

143 Stephen Schiff, "Lunch with Mr. Armani, Tea with Mr. Versace, Dinner with Mr. Valentino," *The New Yorker*, November 7, 1994: 196.

144 Lisa Armstrong, "Paris Haute Couture: Armani Privé Spring/Summer 2012," *The Telegraph UK*, January 24, 2012, http://fashion.telegraph.co.uk/article/TMG9036345/Paris-Haute-Couture-Armani-Prive-springsummer-2012.html.

145 Tim Blanks, "Armani Privé Spring 2012 Couture Collection," *Style.com*, January 23, 2012, http://www.style.com/fashionshows/review/S2012CTR-APRIVE.

146 "Giorgio Armani's Influence on Hollywood," *Behind the Label*, Reserve Channel, September 7, 2012, http://www.youtube.com/watch?v=LBrH_CAYwJQ&noredirect=1.

147 Amy M. Spindler, "The Lives They Lived: 01-07-01 Bonnie Cashin, b. 1915; Design For Living," *The New York Times*, January 7, 2001.

148 Carrie Donovan, "Celebrating the New Freedom in Fashion," *The New York Times*, March 5, 1978.

149 Bernadine Morris, "New Designers Add Perspective to Fall Fashions," *The New York Times*, July 14, 1977.

150 Murray Healy, "The Vuitton Set," *LOVE Magazine* 9 (Spring/Summer 2013).

151 Ibid.

152 Judith A. Bellafaire, *The Women's Army Corps: A Commemoration of World War II Service*, CMH Publication, 72–15, http://www.history.army.mil/brochures/WAC/WAC.HTM.

153 "Igor Chapurin," Nymphenburg, http://www.nymphenburg.com/en/artists-and-designers/fashion-designers/igor-chapurin/.

154 Rocco Leo Gaglioti, Tia Cibani interview Fall/Winter 2008 New York Fashion Week, *Fashion News Live*, http://www.youtube.com/watch?v=9IiAxVsNYec.

155 Jennifer Craik, *Uniforms Exposed: From Conformity to Transgression* (Oxford, UK: Berg, 2005), 213.

156 Ruth La Ferla, "Fashion's Military Invasion Rolls On," *The New York Times*, February 19, 2010.

157 "Akiko Ogawa," Virtual Japan, http://www.virtualjapan.com/wiki/Akiko_Ogawa.

158 Graham Payn with Barry Day, *My Life with Noël Coward* (Milwaukee: Applause Theatre & Cinema Books, 2000), 272–274.

159 Brenda Polan and Roger Tredre, *The Great Fashion Designers* (Oxford, UK: Berg, 2009), 125.

160 Linda Wells, "The Wedding: Formalities," *The New York Times*, January 28, 1990.

161 Personal correspondence with Yuki, May 14, 2013.

162 "Arden Shows Designs by de la Renta," *The New York Times*, September 19, 1963.

163 "Fashion Color Report Spring/Summer 2002," *Pantone* 16 (September 2001).

164 Ibid.

165 Ibid.

166 "Montgomery Ward: Business and History at Western," Western Libraries Ontario Canada, http://www.lib.uwo.ca/programs/generalbusiness/montgomerywardbusinessandhistoryatwestern.html.

167 Penny Martin, "Phoebe Philo Designs the Clothes Women Actually Want to Wear," *The Gentlewoman* 1 (Spring/Summer 2010).

168 Ibid.

169 "Céline," *Voguepedia* site. http://www.vogue.com/voguepedia/Celine.

170 Andrew Bolton and Harold Koda, *AngloMania: Tradition and Transgression in British Fashion* (New York: Metropolitan Museum of New York, 2007), 107.

171 "Fashion Color Report Fall 2006," *Pantone* 25 (February 2006).

172 "Evening Dress (Spring 1992)," Calvin Klein, *The Museum at FIT*, Object Number: 94.143.1.

173 Stephen Schiff, "Lunch with Mr. Armani, Tea with Mr. Versace, Dinner with Mr. Valentino," *The New Yorker*, November 7, 1994.

174 Ibid.

175 Ginette Spanier, "The Classic Tradition: Inside Couture," *Couture: An Illustrated History of the Great Paris Designers and Their Creations*, edited by Ruth Lynham (Garden City, NY: Doubleday, 1972), 11.

176 "Robert Lee Morris," Savor Silver site, http://www.savorsilver.com/designers/robert-lee-morris.html.

177 J. Anderson Black and Madge Garland, *A History of Fashion* (New York: William Morrow, 1980), 265.

178 Michael Gross, "Patterns," *The New York Times*, January 18, 1988.

179 Amy M. Spindler, "Three Major Designers Clothe the Naked City," *The New York Times*, April 12, 1997.

180 Woody Hochswender, "The Green Movement in the Fashion World," *The New York Times*, March 3, 1990.

181 Lou Stoppard, "In Fashion: Iris Van Herpen," SHOWstudio, April 5, 2013, http://showstudio.com/project/in_fashion/iris_van_herpen.

182 "Collections," Iris Van Herpen, http://www.irisvanherpen.com/about#collections.

183 Caroline Rennolds Milbank, *New York Fashion: The Evolution of American Style* (New York: Harry N. Abrams, 1989), 167.

184 Ira Niemark, *Crossing Fifth Avenue to Bergdorf Goodman* (New York: Specialist Press International, 2006), 13.

185 Bernadine Morris, "Norman Norell Stresses Full Skirts, High Waists," *The New York Times*, January 18, 1965.

186 Bernadine Morris, "A Talk with Norell," *The New York Times*, October 15, 1972.

187 Carrie Donovan, "Culottes are Wonderfully Practical, Women Who Bought Them Decide," *The New York Times*, September 26, 1960.

188 Marilyn Bender, "Norell Likes Capes, Black for Dresses and an Elongated Torso," *The New York Times*, July 17, 1963.

189 Christopher Nickens and George Zeno, *Marilyn in Fashion: The Enduring Influence of Marilyn Monroe* (Philadelphia: Running Press, 2012), 104.

190 Suzy Menkes, "Fashion's Poet of Black: Yamamoto," *The New York Times*, September 5, 2000.

191 This phrase is the title of Yuniya Kawamura's 2004 book, published by Berg.

192 Richard Martin and Harold Koda, *Orientalism: Visions of the East in Western Dress* (New York: The Metropolitan Museum of Art, 2000), 77.

193 Kennedy Fraser, "The Great Moment," *Scenes from the Fashion World* (New York: Alfred A. Knopf, 1987), 83.

194 Maisee Skidmore, "Who, What, Why: Pleats Please Anniversary," *AnOther Magazine* blog, August 1, 2012, http://www.anothermag.com/current/view/2093/Pleats_Please_Anniversary.

195 "Yohji Yamamoto," *Voguepedia*, http://www.vogue.com./voguepedia/Yohji_Yamamato.

196 Frances Corner in conversation with Yohji Yamamoto, University of the Arts London: London College of Fashion at the Victoria & Albert Museum, 2011, http://www.youtube.com/watch?v=SyCdbBiiKyE&feature=related.

197 Jennet Conant, "'The Monk' and 'The Nun'," *Newsweek*, February 2, 1987.

198 Eugene Rabkin, "An Interview with Ann Demeulemeester," *ABlogCuratedBy*, August 16, 2010, http://www.anothermag.com/reader/view/1858/An_interview_with_Ann_Demeulemeester_by_Eugene_Rabkin

199 Michael Gross, "Alaia Show at Palladium Mixes Fashion and Flash," *The New York Times*, September 6, 1985.

200 *Madame X (Madame Pierre Gautreau)*, John Singer Sargent, The Metropolitan Museum of Art, Gallery 771, http://www.metmuseum.org/Collections/search-the-collections/20012492.

201 *Vogue*, October 1, 1926.

202 Stephanie La Cava, "Chanel," *Voguepedia*, http://www.vogue.com/voguepedia/Chanel.

Alexander, Ron. "Here Come the Consultants." *The New York Times*, November 21, 1993.

Alexander McQueen website. "Sarah Burton." http://www.alexandermcqueen.com/alexandermcqueen/experience/about-sarah-burton,en_US,pg.html.

Anders, Gigi. "Pretty Woman." *Obit Magazine,* January 23, 2009.

Andrew Gn website. "Biography: Andrew Gn." http://www.andrewgn.com/#/int/en/about-andrew-gn/biography.

Ascher, Kate. "The Heights: Anatomy of a Skyscraper." Lecture at The Skyscraper Museum. December 1, 2011. http://www.skyscraper.org/programs/booktalks/kate_ascher/ascher.htm.

Arthurs, Deborah. "Audrey Hepburn's 'Lucky' Oscar Dress Set to Fetch £60,000 at Auction." *Daily Mail UK*, November 3, 2011.

BAK, "Bonwit Teller." *The Department Store Museum* (blog). http://departmentstoremuseum.blogspot.com/2010/06/bonwit-teller-new-york-city-new-york.html.

Bailey, Glenda. "In the Trenches: Christopher Bailey." *Harper's Bazaar*, November 17, 2011.

Barmash, Isadore. "The Decline of Bonwit Teller: Did Time Pass Retailer By?" *The New York Times*, April 14, 1990.

Barnett, Leisa. "Valentino: Spring/Summer 2008." *Vogue UK* (blog). January 23, 2008. http://www.vogue.co.uk/fashion/spring-summer-2008/couture/valentino.

Barneys website. "60 Years of Chloé: Spotlight on Clare Waight Keller." March 12, 2013. http://thewindow.barneys.com/60-years-of-chloe-spotlight-on-clare-waight-keller/

———. "About the Brand: Azzedine Alaïa." http://www.barneys.com/Azzedine-Alaia/AZZEDINE_ALAIA,default,pg.html.

Barnhart, Robert K., ed. *Chambers Dictionary of Etymology.* New York: Chambers, 1988.

Baschet, Francois and Bernard. "Sound Sculpture Robe." SHOWstudio website. http://showstudio.com/shop/product/sound_sculpture_robe.

Baskett, Mary. "Cincinnati Art Museum: Where Would You Wear That?" Interview, July 10, 2007. http://www.youtube.com/watch?v=7ec1E3ZHdSU.

Basso & Brooke website. "About: Basso & Brooke." http://www.bassoandbrooke.com/about/.

Beatric, Luca and Matteo Guarnaccia, eds. *Vivienne Westwood: Shoes.* Bologna: Damani, 2006.

Beevor, Anthony and Artemis Cooper. *Paris After the Liberation 1944–1949.* Rev. ed. New York: Penguin Books, 1994.

Bella Freud website. "Bella Freud Biography." http://www.bellafreud.co.uk/bio/.

Bender, Marilyn with Monsieur Marc. *Nouveau Is Better Than No Riche At All.* New York: G. P. Putnam's Sons, 1983.

Benjamin, Brittney. "An Interview with Issey Miyake." *The Harvard Advocate.* http://www.theharvardadvocate.com/content/interview-issey-miyake.

Benetton Group. "United Colors of Benetton Fall/Winter 2012 Collection Press Release." http://www.benettongroup.com/archive/press-release/united-colors-benetton-fallwinter-2012-collection.

Berger, Marilyn. "Mollie Parnis, Designer, Dies in Her '90s." *The New York Times*, July 19, 1992.

Bernier, Rosamond. "Fashion Week, 1947." *The Paris Review* (blog). http://www.theparisreview.org/blog/2011/09/12/fashion-week-1947/.

Beyfus, Drusilla. "The Heights of Fashion." *The Telegraph.* September 15, 2007.

Biography Channel, The. "Gianni Versace." http://www.biography.com/people/gianni-versace-9517836.

Birtwell, Celia with Dominic Lutyens. *Celia Birtwell.* New York: St. Martin's Griffin, 2011.

Blackman, Calley. *100 Years of Fashion Illustration.* London: Laurence King Publishing, 2007.

Blanchard, Tamsin. "The Sartorial Network: Opening Ceremony founders Carol Lim and Humberto Leon on their new role at Kenzo." *The Telegraph*, March 9, 2012.

Blaszczyk, Regina Lee. *The Color Revolution.* Cambridge: MIT Press, 2012.

Blue Alchemy: Stories of Indigo. DVD. Directed by Mary Lance. Corrales, NM: New Deal Films, Inc., 2011.

Blum, Dilys E. and H. Kristina Haugland. *Best Dressed: Fashion from the Birth of Couture to Today.* Philadelphia: Philadelphia Museum of Art, 1997.

Bourke, Joanna. "The Great Male Renunciation: Men's Dress Reform in Inter-War Britain." *Journal of Design History* 9, no. 1 (1996).

Bradley Bayou website. "Biography: Bradley Bayou." http://bradleybayou.com/biography/.

Breward, Christopher, Edwina Ehrman, and Caroline Evans. *The London Look: Fashion from Street to Catwalk.* New Haven: Yale University Press, 2004.

British Museum, The, website. "Mexican Turquoise Mosaics," http://www.britishmuseum.org/explore/highlights/article_index/a/mexican_turquoise_mosaics.aspx.

Bye, Elizabeth. *Fashion Design.* Oxford, UK: Berg, 2010.

Carneiro, Solange. "Reflecting Roots—Ida Johansson SS2012." *We Are Selecters* (blog), January 31, 2012. http://mag.weareselecters.com/2012/01/reflecting-roots-ida-johansson-ss-2012/.

Carrara, Gillion. "Mariano Fortuny." *The Berg Companion to Fashion*, edited by Valerie Steele, 351. Oxford, UK: Berg, 2010.

Carter, Michael. "J. C. Flügel." *The Berg Companion to Fashion*, edited by Valerie Steele, 341–343. Oxford, UK: Berg, 2010.

Carter-Morley, Jess. "A Subdued Swansong as McQueen Leaves Givenchy." *The Guardian*, March 31, 2001.

Caygill, Marjorie. "The Provenance of Three British Museum Turquoise Mosaics," *Mexicolore* (blog). http://www.mexicolore.co.uk/aztecs/moctezuma/provenance-of-three-british-museum-turquoise-mosaics.

Civilian (blog). "Basso & Brooke: A Decade of Digital Design." http://www.civilianglobal.com/gallery/basso-brooke-digital-print-archive-fashion/.

Clarke, Mary. "Isabel Toledo, 1997." *Index Magazine* website. http://www.indexmagazine.com/interviews/isabel_toledo.shtml.

Cochrane, Lauren. "Valentino: The Last Emperor, A Gold Mine of Snappy Lines." *The Guardian*, June 4, 2010.

Collins, Amy Fine. "All Eyes on Alaïa." *Vanity Fair*, August 22, 2012.

Corset and Underwear Review, The, 17 (April 1921).

Coughlan, Robert. "Designer for Americans." *LIFE*, October 17, 1949.

Council of Fashion Designers of America. "CFDA Fashion Awards 2004." http://cfda.com/cfda-fashion-awards.

———. "Jill Stuart." http://www.cfda.com/members #!jill-stuart.

Cribb, Tim. "Fallen." *OUT Magazine*, October 2003.

Cronin, Emily. "Fall 2013 Ready-To-Wear: Monique Lhuillier." *Style.com.* February 9, 2013. http://www.style.com/fashionshows/review/f2013rtw-monique.

Czerwinski, Michael for Design Museum. *Fifty Dresses That Changed the World.* New York: Conran Octopus Ltd, 2009.

Dabramo, Letizia Annamaria. "André Courrèges." *Vogue Italia* (blog). http://www.vogue.it/en/encyclo/designers/c/andre-courreges.

Daves, Jessica and Alexander Liberman, eds. *The World in Vogue.* New York: The Viking Press, 1963.

Davey, Monica. "2005: In a Word." *The New York Times*, December 25, 2005.

de Grazia, Victoria and Ellen Furlough, eds. *The Sex of Things: Gender and Consumption in Historical Perspective.* Berkeley: University of California Press, 1996.

Denza, Diana. "Rebecca Taylor on How to Flatter Your Figure + Her Fall Fashion Favorites." *Betty Confidential* (blog), October 14, 2012. http://www.bettyconfidential.com/ar/ld/a/rebecca-taylor-how-to-flatter-your-figure-her-fall-fashion-favorites-.html.

Design Singapore website. "President's Design Award 2007: Designer of the Year: Andrew Gn." http://www.designsingapore.org/pda_public/gallery.aspx?sid=81.

Desveaux, Delphine. *Fortuny: Fashion Memoir.* Paris: Assouline, 1998.

Diamonstein-Spielvogel, Barbaralee. "Bill Blass." Interview (1983). https://www.youtube.com/watch?v=pwaSxkK4bcc; http://library.duke.edu/digitalcollections/dsva/.

Diana Vreeland: The Eye Has to Travel. Film. Directed by Lisa Immordino Vreeland, Frédéric Tcheng, and Bent Jorgen-Perlmutt. Gloss Studio, 2011.

Donovan, Carrie. "Fashion: Couture Report; Paris: Long and Strong." *The New York Times*, February 23, 1992.

Douglas Hannant website. "About Douglas." http://www.douglashannant.com/about-douglas.

Downey, Lynn. *Levi Strauss and Co.* Charleston: Arcadia Publishing, 2007.

Druesedow, Jean L. "In Style: Celebrating Fifty Years of the Costume Institute." *The Metropolitan Museum of Art Bulletin* 45, no. 2 (Autumn 1987).

———. "Linda Allard for Ellen Tracy: Fashioning a Career." Broadbent Gallery, Kent State University Museum. http://www.kent.edu/museum/exhibits/exhibitdetail.cfm?customel_datapageid_2203427=2268712.

Dubrovnik (blog) "The Missoni Family." January 11, 2013. http://www.dubrovnikoldtown.com/2013/the-missoni-family/.

Duka, John. "Fashion; New Architects of Fashion." *The New York Times*, August 16, 1981.

Durrell, Jane. "Art: Wearable Art." *City Beat* (blog), July 4, 2007. http://www.citybeat.com/cincinnati/article-2871-art_wearable_art.html.

Edermariam, Aida. "Christopher Bailey: When Two Worlds Collide." *The Guardian*, February 12, 2010.

Egan, Jennifer. "James Is a Girl." *The New York Times*, February 4, 1996.

Eley Kishimoto website. "Curriculum Vitae." http://www.eleykishimoto.com/cv/.

Eliott, Osborn. "Fashion: The American Look." *TIME*, May 2, 1955.

Esquire (blog), "21 Moments that Made Ralph Lauren." November 7, 2007. http://www.esquire.com/style/laurenmoments1107.

Evans, Caroline. *Fashion at the Edge: Spectacle, Modernity, and Deathliness.* New Haven: Yale University Press, 2003.

Evans, Caroline and Susannah Frankel. *The House of Viktor & Rolf.* London: Merrell, 2008.

Farrell-Beck, Jane. "Girdle." *The Berg Companion to Fashion*, edited by Valerie Steele. Oxford, UK: Berg, 2010.

Fashion Channel. Videos. "Isaac Mizrahi: Autumn Winter 1997 1998 New York." http://www.youtube.com/watch?v=kdA5OnkhwMk; http://www.youtube.com/watch?v=XKJsFnRUcCA; http://www.youtube.com/watch?v=BX0CvtbYOHQ.

———. "Issey Miyake: Spring Summer Collection 1993." https://www.youtube.com/watch?v=VEUlKfiNaU0; https://www.youtube.com/watch?v=8YZHZXds1Tw&NR=1&feature=endscreen; https://www.youtube.com/watch?feature=endscreen&NR=1&v=BsRCVIYuKF0; https://www.youtube.com/watch?v=NqJhWIJKivw&feature=endscreen&NR=1; https://www.youtube.com/watch?NR=1&feature=endscreen&v=NvSBMaTQBIw.

———. "Thierry Mugler Spring Summer 1999 Paris Pret a Porter Woman (Part 5 of 5)." November 7, 2012. http://www.youtube.com/watch?v=GFCcRlqVEPY.

Fashion Foie Gras (blog). "The Missoni Olympic Love Story." August 6, 2012. http://www.fashionfoiegras.com/2012/08/Missoni-love-story-1948-olympics.html.

FIDM Museum and Gallery (blog). "Carolina Herrera." July 15, 2010. http://blog.fidmmuseum.org/museum/2010/07/carolina-herrera-evening-gowns.html.

———. "Mae West Objects on Display." April 5, 2012. http://blog.fidmmuseum.org/museum/mae-west/.

Fischer, David. "Eley Kishimoto for Werk Magazine 'No. 17.'" *Selectism* (blog). http://www.selectism.com/2010/06/15/eley-kishimoto-for-werk-magazine-no-17/.

Foley, Bridget. "Moment 50: Pouf Goes Lacroix!" *Women's Wear Daily*, November 1, 2010.

———. "Talking Shop with Isaac Mizrahi." *Women's Wear Daily*, November 4, 2009.

Forbes website. "Ralph Lauren." http://www.forbes.com/profile/ralph-lauren/.

Forrest Gump. DVD. Directed by Robert Zemeckis. Hollywood: Paramount Pictures, 1994.

Fraser, Paul. "Audrey Hepburn Oscar Dress Auctions for $131,292 at Kerry Taylor Sale." Paul Fraser Collectibles. December 1, 2011. http://www.paulfrasercollectibles.com/News/MEMORABILIA/2011-News-Archive/Audrey-Hepburn-Oscar-dress-auctions-for-$131,292-at-Kerry-Taylor-sale/9102.page.

Friedman, Vanessa. "Lunch with the FT: Christopher Bailey." *Financial Times* (blog). January 11, 2013. http://www.ft.com/cms/s/2/639fba8e-59a8-11e2-88a1-00144feab49a.html#axzz2QTqcvSjr.

Garnham, Emily. "Stunning Pictures: Twiggy Marks 60th with Iconic Show." *Daily Express*, July 8, 2009.

George, Christina. "Critics Scoffed but Women Bought: Coco Chanel's Comeback Fashions Reflect the Desires of the 1950s American Woman." *The Forum: Cal Poly's Journal of History* Vol. 3, Issue 1, Article 13. http://digitalcommons.calpoly.edu/cgi/viewcontent.cgi?article=1048&context=forum.

Goulet, Lucie. "Shock of Pink: How a Colour Shaped Schiaparelli's Vision." *WORN Fashion Journal.* July 12, 2010. http://luciegoulet.tumblr.com/post/801538357/worn-fashion-journal-shock-of-pink-how-a-colour.

Grazia UK (blog). "Eley Kishimoto." http://www.graziadaily.co.uk/fashion/people/eley-kishimoto.

Gross, Michael. "The Great State of Montana." *New York Magazine*, July 31, 1989.

Gucci website. "Frida Giannini: Creative Director of Gucci." http://www.gucci.com/us/worldofgucci/articles/creative-director.

Guillaume, Valérie. *Courrèges.* New York: Assouline, 2004.

Head to Toe Fashion (blog). "Maggy Rouff." http://headtotoefashionart.com/maggy-rouff-1896-1971-1/.

Holt, Emily. "Akris: Spring 2012 RTW." *Vogue* blog. http://www.vogue.com/collections/spring-2012-rtw/akris/review/#.

Hollander, Anne. *Feeding the Eye: Essays.* Berkeley: University of California Press, 2000.

———. *Sex and Suits: The Evolution of Modern Dress.* New York: Alfred A. Knopf, 1994.

Holstead, Carol E. "Vargas, Alberto." American National Biography Online. February 2000. http://www.anb.org/articles/17/17-01424.html.

Honan, William H. "H. R. Ball, 79, Ad Executive Credited with Smiley Face." *The New York Times*, April 14, 2001.

Horyn, Cathy. "Review/Fashion; Some Things New, Most Borrowed." *The New York Times*, September 11, 2001.

———. "Review/Fashion; Up and Out, Jil Sander Makes a Clean Sweep." *The New York Times*, February 25, 2000.

———. "So This is It: Valentino." *The New York Times*, January 23, 2008.

Huffington Post. "Brooke Shields on Her 1980 Calvin Klein Campaign: 'I'm Still Kind of Shocked.' June 26, 2010. http://www.huffingtonpost.com/2010/04/26/brooke-shields-on-her-198_n_551681.html.

Hulanicki, Barbara. *From A to BIBA: The Autobiography of Barbara Hulanicki.* London: V & A Publications, 1983.

IMDb. "Breakfast at Tiffany's." http://www.imdb.com/title/tt0054698/.

———. "Sex and the City (1998–2004)." http://www.imdb.com/title/tt0159206/.

J. Mendel Paris website. "Heritage." http://www.jmendel.com/house-of-mendel/heritage/.

J. Paul Getty Museum website. "Fernand Khnopff." http://www.getty.edu/art/gettyguide/artMakerDetails?maker=3613.

"Jacques Hits the Jackpot," *LIFE*, October 2, 1964: 70.

James, Darrell. "Bellas-Hess Catalog Retailer Used Sears Warehouse Longer than Sears Did." *The Examiner.* April 5, 2010. http://www.examiner.com/article/bellas-hess-catalog-retailer-used-sears-warehouse-longer-than-sears-did.

Johnston, Robert. "Leading Lights: Interview with Burbery Designer Christopher Bailey." *British GQ* (blog). March 5, 2013. http://www.gq-magazine.co.uk/style/articles/2013-03/05/christopher-bailey-burberry-designer-interview.

Jones, Dolly. "Paul Smith Women." *Vogue UK*, February 15, 2006.

———. "Roland Mouret." *Vogue UK*, October 1, 2010.

Jones, Terry and Susie Rushton. *Fashion Now 2.* Cologne: Taschen (2008).

Keane, Maribeth and Jessica Lewis. "How Miriam Haskell Costume Jewelry Bucked Trends and Won Over Hollywood." *Collectors Weekly*, September 23, 2009.

Kellog, Ann T., Amy T. Peterson, Stefani Bay, and Natalie Swindell. *In an Influential Fashion: An Encyclopedia of Nineteenth- and Twentieth-Century Fashion Designers and Retailers Who Transformed Dress.* Westport, CT: Greenwood Press, 2002.

Kent, Jacqueline C. *Business Builders in Fashion.* Minneapolis: The Oliver Press, 2003.

Kirkland, Sally. "Claire McCardell." *American Fashion*, edited by Sarah Tomerlin Lee. New York: Quadrangle, 1975.

Korom, Joseph J. *The American Skyscraper, 1850–1940: A Celebration of Height.* Wellesley: Branden Books, 2008.

Krick, Jessa. "Charles Frederick Worth (1825–1895) and The House of Worth." *Heilbrunn Timeline of Art History.* New York: The Metropolitan Museum of Art, 2004.

Kriemler, Albert. "Sensibility: The Fabric Is the Medium." *Akris: Fashion from St. Gallen*, edited by Christoph Doswald. Zurich: JRP Ringier, 2006.

Kyoto Costume Institute, The. "Jeans [Bottoms] (1971)." Levi's. Inventory Number: AC9758 99-1-5. http://www.kci.or.jp/archives/digital_archives/detail_189_e.html.

LaCava, Stephanie. "Chloé's Clare Waight Keller." *Interview* magazine. http://www.interviewmagazine.com/fashion/chloe-clare-waight-keller.

Lacroix, Christian. *On Fashion.* London: Thames & Hudson, 2008.

Lada, Diana. "Mollie Parnis." Jewish Women's Archive. http://jwa.org/encyclopedia/article/parnis-mollie.

Landmarks Preservation Commission. "American Surety Company Building." June 24, 1997. www.nyc.gov/html/lpc/downloads/pdf/.../amersurety.pdf.

Lane, Mary M. "Hubert de Givenchy Remembers Audrey Hepburn." *The Wall Street Journal*, September 4, 2012.

Langley, Susan. *Roaring 20s Fashion: Deco.* Atglen, PA: Schiffer Publishing Ltd., 2006.

Larocca, Amy. "Vera Wang's Second Honeymoon." *New York Magazine*, January 14, 2006.

Levy, Tobin. "Book Review: Bare Blass." *Look Online* (blog). http://www.lookonline.com/billblass.html.

Lhuiller, Monique. "Monique Lhuillier." http://moniquelhuillier.com/the-world-of-ml/life/monique-lhuillier/.

LIFE. "Riches for Wragge and also a Winnie." October 7, 1957.

L'Officiel 1000 Modéles 62, Hiver 2006–2007. http://patrimoine.jalougallery.com/lofficiel-1000-modeles-numero_62-avril-2006-detail-28-1561.html.

Loriot, Thierry-Maxime. *The Fashion World of Jean Paul Gaultier: From the Sidewalk to the Catwalk.* New York: Abrams, 2011.

Loschek, Ingrid. *When Clothes Become Fashion: Design and Innovation Systems.* Oxford, UK: Berg, 2009.

Louboutin, Christian and Eric Reinhardt. *Christian Louboutin.* New York: Rizzoli, 2011.

Love Fashion Money (blog). "Diane von Furstenberg's Very DVF Apartment," http://lovefashionmoney.com/2012/11/23/diane-von-furstenbergs-very-dvf-apartment/.

Lowry, Joe Dan and Joe P. Lowry. *Turquoise: The World Story of a Fascinating Gemstone.* Layton: Gibbs Smith, 2010.

"Robert Lutyens." *Lutyens Furniture & Lighting* website. http://www.lutyens-furniture.com/index.php?contentid=robert-lutyens

Mace, Christine. "The Hypersexualization of Fashion." MA thesis. Parsons The New School for Design, 2012.

Martin, Richard. *Charles James.* New York: Assouline, 2006.

Martineau, Pierre. "The Personality of a Retail Store." *Harvard Business Review* 36 (1958).

———. "Maurice Adelaar Dies At 83." *Palm Beach Daily News.* November 29, 1988.

Meder, Danielle. "The Masculine Renunciation." *Final Fashion* (blog). May 29, 2012. http://finalfashion.ca/the-masculine-renunciation/.

Medici: Godfathers of the Renaissance. DVD. Directed by Justin Hardy. Lion Television in association with PBS and Devillier Donegan Enterprises, 2004.

Melly, George. "Obituary: Leonor Fini." *The Independent*, July 25, 1996.

Mendes, Valerie. *Dressed in Black*. London: V&A Publications, 1999.

Mercedes Benz Fashion Week website. "Nicole Miller." http://www.mbfashionweek.com/designers/nicole_miller/.

Merceron, Dean L. *Lanvin*. New York: Rizzoli, 2007.

Metropolitan Museum of Art Costume Institute, The. "Boots (c. 1980), Fiorucci. Accession Number 1984.598.70a,b. All accessible through http://www.metmuseum.org/Collections/search-the-collections.

——. "Cocktail Dress (1934–1936)." Maggy Rouff. Accession Number C.I.59.37.2a,b.

——. "Corset (1920–1925)." Bienjay for Saks Fifth Avenue. Accession Number: 1981.518.10.

——. "Corset (1930–1935)." Facon for Saks Fifth Avenue. Accession Number: 2009.300.2834.

——. "It Is My Own Invention (Fall/Winter 1937)." Elizabeth Hawes. Accession Number: 2009.300.1010.

——. "Evening Coat (1927)." Gabrielle "Coco" Chanel. Accession Number: 1984.30.

——. "Evening Dress (1926)." House of Worth. Accession Number: C.I. 58.67.18.

——. "Evening Dress (1932)." Mariano Fortuny. Accession Number: 1996.497a,b.

——. "Evening Dress (1978)." Hanae Mori. Accession Number: 1996.130.5.

Milbank, Caroline Rennolds. *Couture: The Great Designers*. New York: Stewart, Tabori & Chang, 1985.

Miraval, Margaret. "Flea Market Fashions at Designer Prices." *The Christian Science Monitor*, September 22, 1983.

Miriam Haskell New York website. "History." https://www.miriamhaskell.com/content/history.

MoMu. "Walter Van Beirendonck: Dream the World Awake." September 14, 2011–February 19, 2012. http://www.provant.be/en/binaries/wvb%20expofolder%20en%20definitief_tcm10-148998.pdf.

Montgomery Ward. *Catalog 13* (Spring/Summer 1875). http://archive.org/details/catalogueno13spr00mont.

Montgomery Ward website. "About Us: Welcome to Montgomery Ward." http://www.wards.com/custserv/custserv.jsp?pageName=About_Us.

Moonan, Wendy. "Antiques: Decorating a Home Office for Louis XIV." *The New York Times*, October 9, 1998.

Moore, Jonathan. *Perry Ellis: A Biography*. New York: St. Martin's Press, 1988.

Morris, Bernadine. "An Italian Couple with Knack for Knits." *The New York Times*, November 24, 1971.

——. "Photos of Latest Fashion from Milan; In Milan, Short Skirts Inspire Inventive Spring Openings." *The New York Times*, October 6, 1987.

——. "Showings A Whirl of Color." *The New York Times*, November 20, 1972.

Moorisroe, Patricia. "The Punk God of Glamour." *New York Magazine*. http://nymag.com/nymetro/arts/features/n_10106/.

Morton, Camilla. "Zac Posen." *Vogue UK*, February 9, 2006.

Muira, Akira. "Hanae Mori, Yohji Yamamoto, Issey Miyake & Rei Kawakubo." *TIME*, November 3, 2006.

Murphy, Robert. "Obituary: French Artist Françoise-Xavier Lalanne." *Women's Wear Daily*, December 9, 2008.

Museum at FIT, The. "Cocktail Dress (1969)." Geoffrey Beene. Object Number: 2002.58.1. http://fashionmuseum.fitnyc.edu/.

——. "Evening Dress (1963)." Marc Bohan for Christian Dior. Object Number: 86.56.1. http://fashionmuseum.fitnyc.edu/.

Museum of Fine Arts Boston. "Wild Men and Moors." http://www.mfa.org/collections/object/tapestry-wild-men-and-moors-106003.

Nadelhoffer, Hans. *Cartier*. San Francisco: Chronicle Books, 2007.

New York Magazine. "Bette Franke." http://nymag.com/fashion/models/bfranke/bettefranke/.

——. "Rebecca Taylor." http://nymag.com/fashionshows/designers/bios/rebeccataylor/.

The New York Sun. "Zodiac Signs and Coinspots Inspire New Type Decoration." January 28, 1928.

The New York Times. "A. Montgomery Ward Dies." December 8, 1913.

——. "Evening Hours: Sweaters, Flowers and Man Ray's Art." September 16, 1990.

——. "Five New Colors in Paris Styles." January 27, 1927.

——. "Frocks Serve Many Uses." March 20, 1927.

Niven, Lisa. "Clare Waight Keller." *Vogue UK*. May 11, 2011. http://www.vogue.co.uk/spy/biographies/clare-waight-keller.

Nguyen, Long. "Azzedine Alaïa featuring Stephanie Semour." *Flaunt Magazine*, 2010. http://flaunt.com/features/109/azzedine-ala%C3%AF-featuring-stephanie-seymour.

Nowness website. "Valentino: The Museum." July 12, 2010. http://www.nowness.com/day/2010/7/12/791/valentino-the-museum.

O'Flynn, Kevin. "Max Mara Exhibit Bows in Moscow." *Women's Wear Daily*, October 11, 2011.

Okawa, Tomoko. "Licensing Practices at Maison Christian Dior." *Producing Fashion: Commerce, Culture, and Consumers*, edited by Regina Lee Blaszczyk. Philadelphia: University of Pennsylvania Press, 2008.

Oldham, Todd. *Without Boundaries*. New York: Universe Publishing, 1997.

Oliver, William. "Walter Van Beirendonck: The Joy of Six." *Dazed Digital*, 2011. http://www.dazeddigital.com/fashion/article/8203/1/walter-van-beirendonck-the-joy-of-six

Pantone. "Fashion Color Report Fall 2004." *Pantone* 21 (February 2004).

——. "Fashion Color Report Spring 1999." *Pantone* 10 (November 1998).

——. "Fashion Color Report Spring 2002." *Pantone* 16 (September 2001).

Past Perfect Vintage (blog). "Designer du Jour: Malcolm Starr." August 22, 2011. http://pastperfectvintage.blogspot.com/2011/08/designer-du-jour-malcolm-starr.html.

Patrick, Jon. "Burberry of London: Gabardine's Classic Check(ered) Past." The Selvedge Yard (blog). April 8, 2009. http://theselvedgeyard.wordpress.com/2009/04/08/burberry-of-london-check-ered-past/.

PBS website. "1930s High Society." http://www.pbs.org/opb/historydetectives/feature/1930s-high-society/.

Phelps, Nicole. "Fall 2013 Ready-To-Wear: Andrew Gn," Style.com. March 2, 2103, http://www.designsingapore.org/pda_public/gallery.aspx?sid=81.

Picturing America. "The Chrysler Building 1926–1930," Chapter 15-B. http://www.programminglibrarian.org/assets/files/pa/NEH-Teachers-Resource-Book.pdf.

Potvin, John. "From Gigolo to New Man: Armani, America, and the Textures of Narrative." *Fashion Theory* 15, no. 3 (2011).

Powell, Harriet Mays and Amy Larocca. "5×10." *New York Magazine*. http://nymag.com/fashion/features/16015/.

Randolph Duke website. "About Randolph Duke." http://www.randolphduke.net/ruke_introB.html.

Rasmussin, Cecilia. "Vargas' Pinups Inspired GIs, Became Icons of U.S. Culture." *The Los Angeles Times*, June 25, 2000.

Rebecca Taylor website. "About Rebecca Taylor." http://www.rebeccataylor.com/static-pages/rebecca/page/rebecca/.

Reference for Business. "Christian Dior, S.A." http://www.referenceforbusiness.com/history2/41/Christian-Dior-S-A.html#ixzz2C9gxPl00.

Riehecky, Janet. *Carolina Herrera: International Fashion Designer*. Chicago: Childrens Press, 1991.

RISD website. "About Pochoir." http://risd.libguides.com/pochoir.

Roberts, Mary Louise. "Samson and Delilah Revisited: The Politics of Women's Fashion in the 1920s France." *The American Historical Review* 98, no. 3 (June 1993).

Rodriguez, David. "Profile." http://www.davidrodriguez.net/profile.asp.

Roitfeld, Carine. *Vogue Paris Collections* 2, Fall–Winter 2007.

Ross, Josephine. *Society in Vogue: The International Set Between the Wars*. New York: The Vendome Press, 1992.

Rossimoda website. "History." http://www.rossimoda.com/en/history.aspx.

——. "Production." http://www.rossimoda.com/en/production.aspx.

Russell, Patrick B. "Philip Mangone." Faces of the Hindenburg. October 8, 2008. http://facesofthehindenburg.blogspot.com/2008/10/philip-mangone.html.

Saltmarsh, Matthew. "Dior Fires John Galliano After Bigotry Complaints." *The New York Times*, March 1, 2011.

Schiro, Anne-Marie. "Azzedine Alaïa: New Sophistication." *The New York Times*, April 7, 1985.

——. "For Ferre of Milan, An American Debut." *The New York Times*, August 31, 1979.

Shaw, Madelyn. "Rouff, Maggy." *Fashion Designer Encyclopedia*. http://www.fashionencyclopedia.com/Ro-Sm/Rouff-Maggy.html.

Sherman, Lauren. "End of the Line for Lacroix." *Forbes*, May 28, 2009.

SHOWstudio. "Francois and Bernard Baschet." http://showstudio.com/contributor/francois_and_bernard_baschet.

Silva, Horacio. "Suzy Menkes Remembers Yves Saint Laurent." *The New York Times T Magazine*, June 2, 2008.

Sischy, Ingrid. "The Outsider," *The New Yorker*, November 7, 1994.

Snead, Elizabeth. "The Chic Life and Tragic Death of a Revered Costume Designer." *Hollywood Reporter*, March 29, 2013.

Spindler, Amy M. "Review/Fashion; Luminous Design from Jil Sander." *The New York Times*, March 8, 1995.

Steele, Valerie. *Akris 1922–2012*. New York: Assouline, 2012.

———. *Fashion and Eroticism: Ideals of Feminine Beauty from the Victorian Era to the Jazz Age*. New York: Oxford University Press, 1985.

Sterlacci, Francesca and Joanne Arbuckle. *The A to Z of the Fashion Industry*. Lanham: Scarecrow Press, Inc., 2008.

Stiebel, Victor. *South African Childhood*. London: Andre Deutsch Limited, 1968.

StyleSequel (blog). "Missoni Biography: The Life and History of Missoni." http://www.stylesequel.com/designers/missoni/biography.

Sun Goddess website. "About Sun Goddess." http://www.sungoddess.co.za/index.php?option=com_content&view=article&id=109&Itemid=144.

Talley, André Leon. "ALT on Yigal Azrouël." *Vogue*, September 13, 2001.

Tanenbaum, Carole and Puzant Apkarian. *Fabulous Fakes: A Passion for Vintage Costume Jewelry*. New York: Artisan, 2006.

Teunissen, José. "Deconstructing Belgian and Dutch Fashion Dreams: From Global Trends to Local Crafts." *Fashion Theory* 15, no. 2 (2011).

Thomas, Pauline Weston. "Trends Within the Fashion Silhouette." Fall 2005/Winter 2006." *Fashion-Era*. http://www.fashion-era.com/Trends_2006/3_fashion_trends_2006_wardrobe_tips_autumn_05.htm.

Tiffany, John A. *Eleanor Lambert: Still Here*. New York: Pointed Leaf Press, 2011.

Time Out Paris. "Hervé Léger." London: Time Out Guides Ltd., 2001.

Tonello, Michael. *Bringing Home the Birkin*. New York: Harper, 2009.

Tu, Thuy Linh Nguyen. *The Beautiful Generation: Asian Americans and the Cultural Economy of Fashion*. Durham: Duke University Press, 2011.

Turquoise Museum website. "The USGS History of Turquoise." http://www.turquoise-museum.com/usgshistoryturquoise.htm.

Turquoise Trail website. "History of the Turquoise Trail," http://www.turquoisetrail.org/history.

United Nations, The, website. "2005: A Good Year for Peacekeeping Operations," http://www.un.org/en/peacekeeping/publications/yir/2005/introduction.htm.

United States Tariff Department. "Tariff Information Surveys on the Articles in Paragraph 102 of the Tariff Act of 1913 and Related Articles in Other Paragraphs." Washington, D.C.: Government Printing Office, 1921.

University of the Arts London: London College of Fashion website. "London College of Fashion: Victor Stiebel Archive." http://www.vads.ac.uk/collections/LCFVS.html.

Valley, Alvin. "Heritage." http://www.alvinvalley.com/heritage-1974–1995.

Van Dyk, Stephen H. and Carolyn Siegel. "Vibrant Visions: Pochoir Prints in the Cooper-Hewitt Nation Design Museum." Cooper-Hewitt Nation Design Museum Library. http://www.sil.si.edu/ondisplay/pochoir/intro.htm.

Velasco, Schuyler. "$203,150 Purse: Hermes Bag Sells for What?!" *The Christian Science Monitor*, December 9, 2011.

Victoria and Albert Museum, The, website. "Day Dress: Victor Stiebel." http://collections.vam.ac.uk/item/O15662/day-dress-victor-stiebel/.

———. "Evening Dress (late 1930s)." Eva Lutyens. http://collections.vam.ac.uk/item/O15659/evening-dress-lutyens-eva/.

———. "Pair of Boots (1965)." André Courrèges. Fashion, Room 40, Case CA14. http://collections.vam.ac.uk/item/O135020/pair-of-boots-andre-courreges/.

Victoria and Albert Museum, The (blog). "Introduction to 20th-Century Fashion." http://www.vam.ac.uk/content/articles/i/introduction-to-20th-century-fashion/.

Villa Foscarini Rossi website. "Introduction." http://www.villafoscarini.it/cultura-eng.php.

Vinken, Barbara. *Fashion Zeitgeist: Trends and Cycles in the Fashion System*. Oxford, UK: Berg, 2005.

Vogue UK (blog). "A Decade of Eley Kishimoto." June 6, 2003. http://www.vogue.co.uk/news/2003/06/06/a-decade-of-eley-kishimoto.

———. "Imitation of Christ: Spring/Summer 2002 Ready-to-Wear." September 9, 2001. http://www.vogue.co.uk/fashion/spring-summer-2002/ready-to-wear/imitation-of-christ.

Voguepedia (blog). "Behnaz Sarafpour." http://www.vogue.com/voguepedia/Behnaz_Sarafpour.

———. "Carolina Herrera." http://www.vogue.com/voguepedia/Carolina_Herrera.

———. "Gianfranco Ferré." http://www.vogue.com/voguepedia/Gianfranco_Ferre.

———. "Marco Zanini." http://www.vogue.com/voguepedia/Marco_Zanini.

———. "Pierre Balmain." http://www.vogue.com/voguepedia/Pierre_Balmain.

———. "Twiggy," http://www.vogue.com/voguepedia/Twiggy.

Voight, Rebecca. "Atlas Move Over; Skinny Is Now the Chic Silhouette." *The New York Times*, January 15, 2003.

———. "Sonia Rykiel." *Interview*. 2008. http://www.interviewmagazine.com/fashion/sonia-rykiel-40th-anniversary#.

Walden, Celia. "Christian Lacroix: 'I am too angry to cry.'" *Telegraph*, June 21, 2009.

Walford, Jonathan. *Shoes A–Z*. New York: Thames & Hudson, 2010.

Walter Van Beirendonck website. "Fact File." http://www.waltervanbeirendonck.com/HTML/home.html?/HTML/CV/cv.html&1.

Ward, G. Dudley. "Swimming Suit Makes Its Bow in National Advertising." *Printers' Ink* 115 (June 2, 1921).

WGBH Educational Foundation for Public Broadcasting Service. "Skyscraper: Chrysler Building. http://www.pbs.org/wgbh/buildingbig/wonder/structure/chrysler.html.

White Carousel, A (blog). "To Sequin or Not to Sequin: That is the Question." November 20, 2010. http://awhitecarousel.com/2010/to-sequin-or-not-to-sequin-that-is-the-question/.

———. "Valentino Red." November 15, 2010. http://awhitecarousel.com/2010/valentino-red/.

Widjaja, Diana and Daniel Surya. "Color Story, or How to Use Color to Convey Your Message to Customers." *The Jakarta Press*, December 15, 2012.

Wilson, Betty. "'Star Turns' from Eva Lutyens's Show: Scientist Who Designs Frocks." *The Sydney Morning Herald*. August 4, 1938.

Wilson, Eric. "The Lives of Fashion Designer Lars Nilsson." *The New York Times*, March 31, 2010.

———. "Princess Irene Galitzine Dies; Founder of a Fashion House." *The New York Times*, October 22, 2006.

———. "Who Are You Calling Girly?" *The New York Times*, October 17, 2012.

Yenicag, Julie Paulino. "Hermès Boxes as Accessories." *Belle Vivir*. April 19, 2011. http://bellevivir.blogspot.com/2011/04/hermes-boxes-as-accessories.html.

Yeohlee Teng website. "Chemistry: Fall 2004." http://yeohlee.com/collections/fall-2004/.

Photo Credits

Page 8
Thomas Iannaccone/Fairchild Photo Service

Page 9
Top: © United Colors of Benetton/Image Courtesy The Advertising Archives
Bottom Left: Victoria and Albert Museum, London/V&A Images
Bottom Right: PYMCA/UIG/Bridgeman Art Library

Page 10
Left: © firstVIEW
Right: Victoria and Albert Museum, London/V&A Images

Page 11
Left: © firstVIEW
Right: © firstVIEW

Page 12
Left: Mario Torrisi/AP Photo
Top Right: © firstVIEW
Bottom Right: Victoria and Albert Museum, London/V&A Images

Page 13
Pierre Mourgue/National Magazines/Mary Evans Picture Library

Page 14
Luciano Insua/Ida Johansson Atelier

Page 15
Top Left: Heritage Auctions/Splash/Newscom
Bottom Left: © firstVIEW
Top Right: © The Museum at FIT

Page 16
Left: Helen Dryden/Conde Nast
Right: © Neal Barr

Page 17
Left: © firstVIEW
Right: © The Museum at FIT

Page 18
Left: © The Museum at FIT
Right: Express Newspaper Group/AP Photo

Page 19
Left: © Shelly Steffee
Right: Jantzen® is a registered trademark of Jantzen Apparel, LLC. All rights reserved. This book was published without verification of facts or approval by Jantzen Apparel, LLC.

Page 20
© firstVIEW

Page 21
Top Left: Karl Prouse/Catwalking/Getty Images
Bottom Left: © firstVIEW
Right: © The Metropolitan Museum of Art/Image Courtesy The Art Resource, NY

Page 22
Top Left: Jean-Claude Sauer/Paris Match/Getty Images
Bottom Left: © Bailly Creations, SAS/Victoria and Albert Museum, London/V&A Images
Right: © firstVIEW

Page 23
© Bellas Hess & Co.

Page 24
Marco Fattorusso/EPA/Newscom

Page 25
Left: © Tracy Reese
Right: © Elie Tahari
Bottom: Old Baltimore Village

Page 26
Left: © The Museum at FIT
Right: © Douglas Hannant

Page 27
Left: © firstVIEW
Right: © firstVIEW

Page 28
Top Left: © R&K Originals/Image Courtesy MyVintageVogue.com
Bottom Left: Irene C. Wang
Right: Chris Nicholls/The Jenny Yoo Collection

Page 29
Gamma-Rapho/Getty Images

Page 30
Steven Meisel/Art + Commerce

Page 31
Top: © House of Travilla/Image Courtesy Yellow House Art Licensing
Bottom: Asha Munn Photography/Justine Bradley-Hill Millinery

Page 32 & 33
Left: Jacques Brinon/AP Photo
Top Right: Regeneration Vintage Clothing
Center Right: © The Museum at FIT
Bottom Right: Thierry Orban/Sygma/Corbis

Page 34
Top Left: National Magazines/Mary Evans Picture Library
Top Right: Ivan Baude/Sun Goddess
Bottom: BloomersAndFrocks.com

Page 35
© MGM/Photofest NYC

Page 36 & 37
Left: © Louis Vuitton/Image Courtesy The Advertising Archives
Top Right: © Badgely Mischka
Bottom Left: Jason Szenes/EPA/Newscom
Bottom Right: Don Emmert/AFP/Getty Images

Page 38
Top Left: © Shelly Steffee
Bottom Left: © Ellen Tracy/Sequential Brands Group
Right: © The Metropolitan Museum of Art/Image Courtesy The Art Resource, NY

Page 39
© The Museum at FIT

Page 40
Left: MAXPPP/Newscom
Right: © firstVIEW

Page 41
Left: © firstVIEW
Right: Andrew Kelly/Reuters

Page 42
Left: © The Metropolitan Museum of Art/Image Courtesy The Art Resource, NY
Right: © Tibi

Page 43
Left: Wang Qingqin/Xinhua Press/Corbis
Right: © The Metropolitan Museum of Art/Image Courtesy The Art Resource, NY

Page 44
Left: Mary Evans Picture Library
Right: © John Rawlings/Image Courtesy MyVintageVogue.com

Page 45
Left: © firstVIEW
Right: Peter Michael Dills/Getty Images

Page 46
Left: Petre Buzoianu/Keystone Press/ZumaPress/Newscom
Right: BackInStyle.com

Page 47
Left: © Adelaar/Image Courtesy MyVintageVogue.com
Right: © Douglas Hannant

Page 48
Top: © Jill Stuart
Bottom: Renet Bouet-Willaumez/Conde Nast/CN Collection

Page 49
Left: Daniele La Monaca/Reuters
Right: © The Metropolitan Museum of Art/Image Courtesy The Art Resource, NY

Page 50
Top Left: Collection of Steven Porterfield/Photo by John Dowling, from the book *Roaring 20's Fashions*, Deco by Susan Langley.
Bottom Left: © The McCall Pattern Company/Image Courtesy MyVintageVogue.com
Right: © firstVIEW

Page 51
© Lie Sang Bong

Page 52
Photo by John Dowling, from the book *Roaring 20's Fashion: Deco* by Susan Langley. Schiffer Publishing.

Page 53
Top Left: Bob Bortfeld/Vintages Los Gatos
Bottom Left: © Fendissime for Fendi/Rossimoda Venezia
Right: © firstVIEW

Page 54
Left: © firstVIEW
Right: Conde Nast Archives/Corbis

Page 55
Top: Victoria and Albert Museum, London/V&A Images
Bottom: AFP/Getty Images

Page 56
Left: © Charlotte Ronson
Right: © firstVIEW

Page 57
Left: © Alvin Valley
Right: © Y & Kei, SK Networks Co., Ltd.

Page 58
Top: © Levi Strauss & Co.
Bottom: © Calvin Klein/Image Courtesy The Advertising Archives

Page 59
Left: © firstVIEW
Right: © The Museum at FIT

Page 60
Top Left: © J. Peterman Company
Bottom Left: © The Museum at FIT
Right: Image Courtesy Fashion Institute of Technology | SUNY | Gladys Marcus Library Department of Special Collections

Page 61
Ben Weller/www.Moloh.com

Page 62
Raymond Meier/Trunk Archive

Page 63
Top Left: © Tracy Reese
Bottom Left: © firstVIEW
Right: Adrian Woodhouse Collection/Mary Evans Picture Library

Page 64
Left: © firstVIEW
Right: © Michael Kors

Page 65
Left: © firstVIEW
Right: Durango Silver Company

Page 66
Left: Victoria and Albert Museum, London/V&A Images
Right: © firstVIEW

Page 67
Left: © firstVIEW
Right: © Cynthia Steffe

Page 68
© Leeds Ltd./Image Courtesy MyVintageVogue.com

Page 69
Left: © firstVIEW
Top Right: © The Museum at FIT
Bottom Right: © Opening Ceremony

Page 70
Left: Karl Prouse/Catwalking/Getty Images
Right: John Rawlings/Conde Nast Archive/Corbis

Page 71
Left: © Talbott/Image Courtesy MyVintageVogue.com
Right: Fairchild Photo Service/Newscom

Page 72
Top Left: © Nanette Lepore
Bottom Left: © Vogue® Patterns/The McCall Pattern Company/
Courtesy Floradora Presents on Etsy
Right: Fairchild Photo Services/Conde Nast/Corbis

Page 73
© firstVIEW

Page 74
Left: © Blanc de Chine
Right: © firstVIEW

Page 75
Top: LePetitPoulailler.com
Bottom: Victoria and Albert Museum, London/V&A Images

Page 76
Left: © firstVIEW
Top Right: © Tracy Reese
Bottom Right: © Christie's Images/The Bridgeman Art Library

Page 77
© Manolo Blahnik

Page 78
Left: © Y & Kei/SK Networks Co., Ltd.
Right: Alfred/SIPA/Associated Press

Page 79
Left: © firstVIEW
Right: Fashion Wire Daily/Jones/Newscom

Page 80
© firstVIEW

Page 81
Top Left: The Metropolitan Museum of Art/Image Courtesy The
Art Resource, NY
Top Right: © David Rodriguez
Bottom: Mary Evans Picture Library

Page 82
Left: © Ports 1961
Right: Boston Public Library, Print Department

Page 83
Left: Anthea Simms/Camera Press/Redux
Right: Damien Meyer/AFP/Getty Images

Page 84
Farfetch.com

Page 85
Top: © Ewing Krainin. All Rights Reserved./Image Courtesy
Time Inc.
Bottom Left: © firstVIEW
Bottom Right: Franco Origlia/Getty Images

Page 86
Top Left: © firstVIEW
Top Right: Domenico Stinellis/AP Photo
Bottom: Evening Standard/Getty Images

Page 87
© Vera Wang/Image Courtesy David's Bridal

Page 88
Kerry Taylor Auctions/dpa/Corbis

Page 89
Top: © David Rodriguez
Bottom Left: Victoria and Albert Museum, London/
V&A Images
Bottom Right: © firstVIEW

Page 90
© Gap/Image Courtesy The Advertising Archives

Page 91
Top Left: © firstVIEW
Bottom Left: Philippe Wojazer/Reuters
Right: © Cynthia Steffe

Page 92 & 93
Top Left: © Midwest Catalog Brands/Montgomery Ward Catalog
Collection, American Heritage Center at the University of
Wyoming/Image Courtesy MyVintageVogue.com
Top Right: © Burberry/Image Courtesy The Advertising Archives
Bottom Left: PPS Worldwide/ZumaPress/Newscom
Bottom Right: Victoria and Albert Museum, London/
V&A Images

Page 94
Left: Fairchild Photo Service
Right: Stephen Lewis/Art and Commerce

Page 95
Left: © The Museum at FIT
Right: Roger Prigent/Conde Nast/CN Collection

Page 96
© firstVIEW

Page 97
Top: © Laura Poretzky for Abaete
Bottom Left: © firstVIEW
Bottom Right: © Giorgio Armani/Image Courtesy The Advertising
Archives

Page 98
Left: Conde Nast/CN Collection
Right: © firstVIEW

Page 99
Left: Archives Charmet/The Bridgeman Art Library
Right: © firstVIEW

Page 100
Top: © The Metropolitan Museum of Art/Image Courtesy The Art
Resource, NY
Bottom: © American Enka Company/Image Courtesy
MyVintageVogue.com

Page 101
Left: © firstVIEW
Right: Gareth Cattermole/Getty Images

Page 102
© firstVIEW

Page 103
Top Left: © firstVIEW
Bottom Left: © The Museum at FIT
Right: Horst P. Horst/Conde Nast/CN Collection

Page 104
Top Left: © firstVIEW
Bottom Left: Victoria and Albert Museum, London/
V&A Images
Right: © firstVIEW

Page 105
© The Museum at FIT

Page 106
Top Left: Peter Tahl/From the exhibition *Azzedine Alaia in the
Groninger Museum*, 12/07/08–03/08/1997, Image Courtesy The
Groninger Museum
Top Right: Edith Head/Christie's Images/The Bridgeman
Art Library
Bottom: © Donna Karan/Image Courtesy The Advertising
Archives

Page 107
© Man Ray Trust/Artists Rights Society (ARS), NY/ADAGP,
Paris 2013/Image Courtesy Christie's Images/The Bridgeman
Art Library

Page 108
© firstVIEW

Page 109
Left: © firstVIEW
Right: © firstVIEW

Page 110
Left: © firstVIEW
Right: © firstVIEW

Page 111
Left: © Alice Roi by Jason Cauchi
Right: Fairchild Photo Service

Page 112
Left: Alain Benainous/Gamma-Rapho/Getty Images
Right: © Reem Acra

Page 113
Left: Frazer Harrison/IMG/Getty Images
Right: © Peter Som

Page 114
Left: © Nanette Lepore
Right: Neilson Barnard/Getty Images

Page 115
Left: © Tracy Reese
Right: © firstVIEW

The authors wish to thank: Frank Burrafato, Yolanda Cazares, Julie Chen, Joyce Corrigan, Brian Cottle, Herb Eiseman, Gretchen Fenston, Stefan Freed, Bobbie Hawkes, Lisa Herbert, Tim Heyer, Brooke Johnson, Caitlin Kirkpatrick, Karen Lantelme, Bob Lynn, Christine L. Mace, Gena McGregor, Ellen Pinto, Lynne K. Ranieri, Leigh Saffold, Judy Theuerkauf, Gnyuki "Yuki" Torimaru, Elizabeth Vitiello, Shawn Waldron, and Bridget Watson Payne, as well as their supportive family and friends.

Library of Congress Cataloging-in-Publication data available.
ISBN: 978-1-4521-1535-1

Manufactured in China.

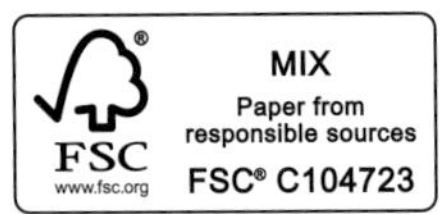

Designed by Brooke Johnson
Typesetting by DC Typography

10 9 8 7 6 5 4 3 2 1

Chronicle Books LLC
680 Second Street
San Francisco, CA 94107
www.chroniclebooks.com

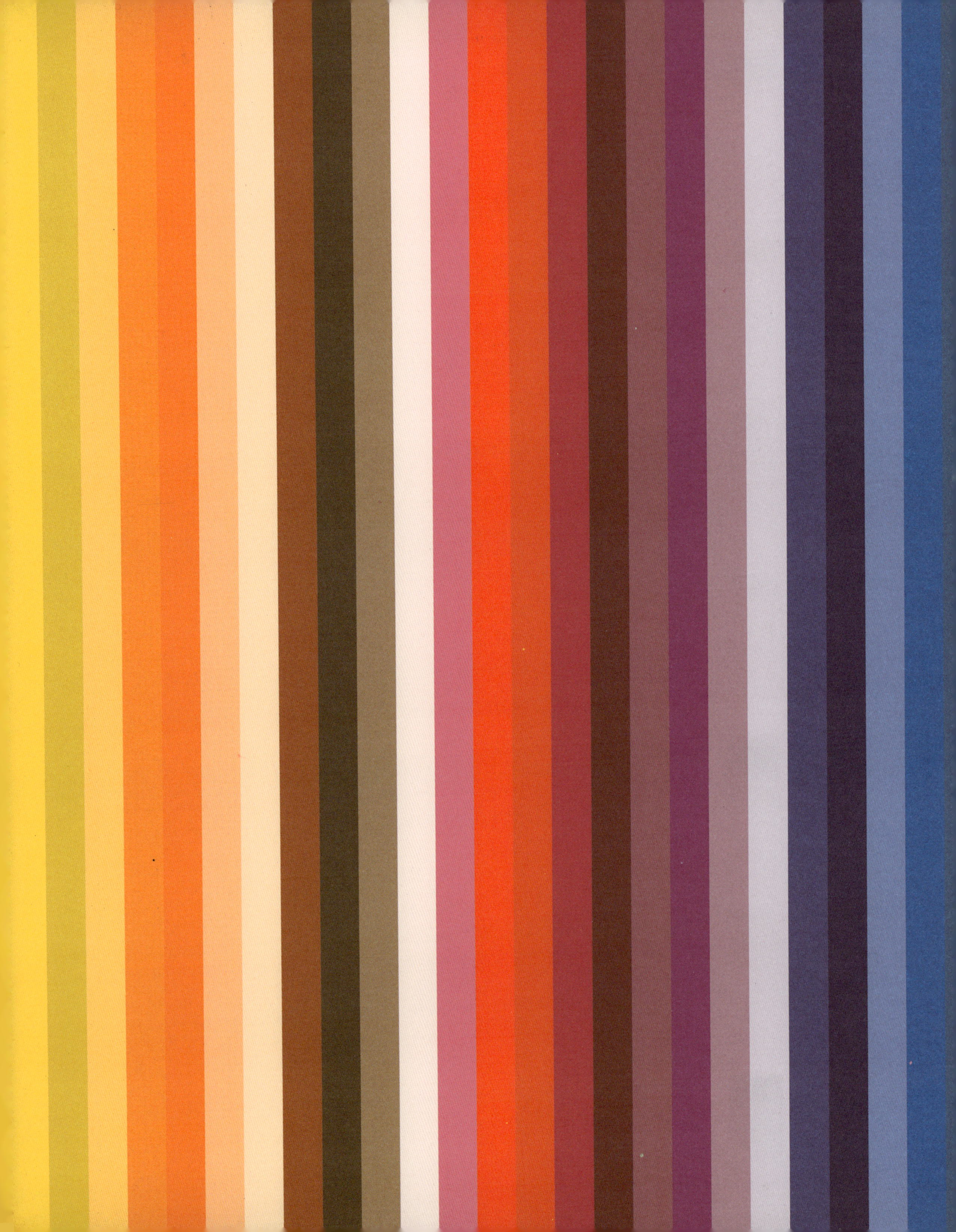